Latin America 1973

Latin America 1973

Edited by Lester A. Sobel

Contributing editors: Chris Hunt
Mary Elizabeth Clifford

Indexed by Grace M. Ferrara

FACTS ON FILE, INC. NEW YORK, N.Y.

Latin America 1973

Copyright, 1974, by Facts on File, Inc.

All rights reserved. No part of this book may be reproduced in any form without the permission of the publisher except for reasonably brief extracts used in reviews or scholarly works.

Published by Facts on File, Inc.,
119 West 57th Street, New York, N.Y. 10019.

Library of Congress Catalog Card Number 73-83047
ISBN 0-87196-251-9

9 8 7 6 5 4 3 2 1
PRINTED IN
THE UNITED STATES OF AMERICA

Contents

	Page
FOREWORD	1
REGIONAL DEVELOPMENTS	3
ARGENTINA	17
Pre-Election Developments	17
Peronists Win Elections	22
Campora Becomes President	31
Peron Returns	36
Campora Vacates Presidency	39
Peron Elected President	45
BOLIVIA	52
8 'Plots' Thwarted	52
BRAZIL	63
CHILE	79
Turmoil Precedes Coup	79
Congressional Elections	83
U.S. Probes ITT Actions	86
'Plots' & Strikes	93
Military Coup d'Etat, Allende Commits Suicide	110
Junta in Office	114
Defense of Coup & Junta	123

COLOMBIA 134
   Economic Improvements & Problems 134
   Guerrillas Active 137
   Political Developments 140
   Other Developments 144
CUBA 148
   Relations with Communist Countries 148
   The U.S. & Western Hemisphere 149
   Other Developments 153
DOMINICAN REPUBLIC 155
   Guerrilla Action Fails 155
   Politics & Violence 158
   Economic Developments 162
ECUADOR 163
   Oil Developments 163
   Other Events 164
HAITI 168
MEXICO 172
   Guerrilla Activity 172
   Student Unrest 173
   Politics & Government 175
   Foreign Relations & Trade 177
   Economic & Other Developments 180
NICARAGUA 182
PANAMA 186
PERU 190
PUERTO RICO 199
URUGUAY 204
   Government-Military Clash 204
   Military Precipitate Crisis,
      Constitutional Rule Suspended 211
VENEZUELA 222
   Latin American Relations 222
   Unrest, Terrorism 223
   Oil & the Economy 226
   AD Wins Elections 228

OTHER AREAS 232
   Bahamas. 232
   Belize. 233
   Costa Rica 233
   El Salvador. 235
   Guatemala 236
   Guyana 238
   Honduras 240
   Jamaica 241
   Montserrat 242
   Paraguay 243
   Surinam 245
   Trinidad & Tobago. 247
   U.S. Virgin Islands 247
   West Indies Associated States 248
INDEX. 251

Foreword

THIS IS THE SECOND volume of the FACTS ON FILE annual on Latin America. It records the history of Latin America and the Caribbean area during 1973.

The purpose of this series is to give researchers, students, educators, librarians and others a convenient, reliable, unbiased and inexpensive source of information on the many events that take place each year in this important part of the world. The 1973 volume, therefore, records the essential details of such events as Juan Perón's return to Argentina and to power, the overthrow and suicide of Chile's Salvador Allende and the dispute between the U.S. and Panama over the future of the Panama Canal and Canal Zone. But it also covers more than just the most important occurrences. It provides facts on economic developments, guerrilla operations, labor action, diplomatic relations, government corruption, political maneuverings, student activism, military affairs and the many other events that make up the history of Latin America and the Caribbean area during 1973.

The material of the book consists largely of the Latin American record compiled by FACTS ON FILE in its weekly reports on world events. Such changes as were made in producing this book were largely for the purpose of eliminating needless repetition, supplying necessary amplification or correcting error. Yet some useful repetition was provided deliberately: for example, when two countries are involved in a single event, the report, or at least part of it, is often carried in the chapter for each of the two countries; this means more complete coverage of each country in the place the reader is most likely to look, makes it less likely that these items will be overlooked and reduces some of the need to consult the index and other chapters to locate a specific fact.

Regional Developments

IAPA issues 1972 press report. The 1972 report of the Inter-American Press Association (IAPA) said that five Latin American countries had no press freedom, El Nacional of Caracas reported Jan. 2. The countries were Brazil, Cuba, Haiti, Panama and Paraguay.

The report noted that rapidly growing pressures from various sources were threatening freedom of the press in Chile, Guyana, Ecuador, Peru and Uruguay.

At the same time, it said, the press was facing increasing difficulties in performing its job in Argentina, Bolivia, Guatemala, Mexico and Nicaragua, whose governments it considered relatively liberal.

Germán Ornes, chairman of the IAPA's committee on press freedom, reported to the association's executive board Jan. 27 that antagonism between governments and the press was a symptom of a hemisphere-wide attempt to undermine the letter and spirit of basic human rights.

An Associated Press report on the flow of information, reported in El Nacional Jan. 7, stated that censorship was a growing problem to foreign journalists in Chile, Brazil, Argentina, Uruguay, Cuba, Haiti and St. Kitts.

U.N. Council agrees to meet in Panama. The United Nations Security Council formally agreed Jan. 26 to accept an invitation to meet in Panama City March 15-21. The meeting's agenda would cover not only the issue of U.S. control of the Panama Canal Zone but all the problems of Latin America.

The projected meeting was opposed by the U.S., Great Britain and Australia, but all three deferred to the other council members' desire to set the session. The three reportedly feared that the council's effectiveness in an emergency would be impaired if the body was away from U.N. headquarters in New York.

Following the council vote, Panamanian Ambassador Aquilino E. Boyd—who would preside over the Panama session expressed hope that the council would find "formulas to defuse the explosive situation caused by the colonialist-type enclave called the Panama Canal Zone, which bisects my country and stands in the way of its territorial, political, economic and social integration."

Boyd had asserted Jan. 16 that "Panama claims effective sovereignty and exclusive jurisdiction over the [Canal Zone] ... A power foreign to the territory of Panama occupies the area and the council is needed to eliminate [this] conflict." George Bush, U.S. ambassador to the U.N., had objected to bringing before the council issues under active bilateral negotiation, adding: "With due reference to the history of the area and the issues, we, of course, do not accept the [Panamanian] contention that the Canal Zone is an 'inner colonialist enclave.'"

The Panama meeting would have a staff of 150 persons in addition to the U.N. secretary general and his staff, and would cost an estimated $92,000. All Latin American nations were expected to be represented and to be invited to appear before the Security Council.

U.S. vetoes Security Council resolution. The U.S. cast its third veto in the United Nations Security Council March 21, against a moderate resolution on the current U.S.-Panamanian negotiations over control of the Panama Canal and Zone.

The vote came on the fifth and last day of a Council meeting on Latin American problems, held in Panama City at the request of the Panamanian government. The meeting was characterized by complaints by Latin American countries against the U.S. and particularly against what Panama called the U.S. "colonialist enclave" in the Canal Zone. Nine Latin nations were represented by their foreign ministers, and others by less important officials.

The vetoed resolution took notice of the expressed willingness of Panama and the U.S. to reach an agreement abrogating the 1903 isthmic treaty and setting a new, "just and equitable" pact that would "fulfill the legitimate aspirations of Panama and guarantee full respect for the effective sovereignty of Panama over all its territory." The resolution urged the two governments to continue "on a high level of friendship, respect and cooperation" their current talks for a swift resolution of the canal conflict, and said the Security Council would keep the matter under consideration.

Only the U.S. opposed the resolution. Of the other 14 Council members, 13 voted for it and Great Britain abstained.

The U.S. representative to the U.N., John Scali, said he regretted having to veto the resolution "because there is so much in it with which we agree." However, he reiterated the U.S. view that negotiations between the U.S. and Panama were bilateral and continuing. For the Security Council to pass a resolution on them constituted inappropriate "outside pressure," he said. Scali also criticized the resolution as being cast in "sweeping generalities when we know that the real difficulties lie in the application of those generalities."

The overwhelming rejection of the U.S. position by some Council members was not expected, the New York Times reported March 22. Great Britain, France and Australia earlier had appeared to back the U.S. position that the Council should not interfere in bilateral negotiations, but the latter two voted for the resolution. The French delegate said he could support the measure because it "did not go into details." The British representative, Sir Colin Crowe, called the final turn of events "a matter of profound regret."

The final vote followed the apparent failure of negotiations to avert a veto between Scali, Panama's military ruler, Gen. Omar Torrijos, and its foreign minister, Juan Antonio Tack.

Panama had maintained in speeches over the previous five days that the canal was a "natural resource" which it had the right to exploit, and the resolution had said in its preamble that "the free and advantageous exercise of the sovereignty of peoples and nations over their natural resources should be fomented through mutual respect among nations."

However, Scali asserted the canal was "not a work of nature, or ... a natural resource. The canal is a very complex enterprise, and the working out of a new regime for it cannot be accomplished by the wave of a hand or the quick stroke of a pen."

During the sessions, Scali had clashed repeatedly with the Panamanian delegate, Aquilino Boyd, who also presided over the Security Council in March. The two had argued over U.S. foreign aid programs, the U.S.-imposed isolation of Cuba, and alleged racial discrimination in the Canal Zone.

During a special session March 21 to mark the International Day for the Elimination of Discrimination, Boyd virulently attacked what he called the "odious discrimination maintained by the United States in the Canal Zone, not only in matters of skin color, but in salaries, education and housing." He cited figures showing the differences in salaries earned by Panamanians and U.S. citizens in the

Zone, and invited delegates to see for themselves the discrimination in housing.

In an angry reply, Scali demanded to know if Boyd was speaking as president of the Security Council, saying his remarks were "not befitting" for the president. Boyd, however, had spoken as the Panamanian delegate. His charges were supported by Kenya, the U.S.S.R. and India.

Boyd said March 22, after the U.S. veto, that Panama would carry its demand for control of the Canal Zone to the U.N. General Assembly.

In other action March 21, the Security Council passed a resolution condemning acts of "economic coercion" by multinational corporations and industrial powers against Latin American nations. The vote was 12–0, with the U.S., Great Britain and France abstaining.

Torrijos criticizes U.S.—At the opening session of the Security Council meeting March 15, Gen. Torrijos had severely criticized U.S. policies in Latin America and asked the "moral support" of the world for Panama's efforts to regain control of the Canal Zone.

Torrijos said it was "difficult to understand how a country which has characterized itself as not being colonialist can insist on maintaining a colony in the heart of our country."

Torrijos also criticized U.S. policy in Latin America, particularly U.S. opposition to the governments of Chile, Peru and Cuba. Noting the hostile U.S. reaction to the nationalization of copper in Chile and oil in Peru, in which the U.S. had economic interests, Torrijos asked: "Wasn't the copper Chilean? Wasn't the oil Peruvian? Or is it that [the U.S.] wants these natural resources to serve developed countries so they can exploit the soil and men of poor countries?"

Torrijos also denounced "a certain group of nations that are scandalized because peoples want to exploit their own natural resources, the riches of their seas, of their ports, of their land, of their soil, of their labor and of their geographical position for the benefit of their citizens and not against them."

Of U.S. policy toward Cuba, Torrijos said: "Each hour of isolation suffered by our brothers the people of Cuba, represents 60' minutes of hemispheric shame. The [U.S. and other Latin American nations'] blockades and pressures should be more embarrassing to those who impose them than to those who suffer them."

U.S. delegate Scali responded sharply to Torrijos after the speech. He said he took a "rather dim view" of the reference to Cuba since the blockade of the island was undertaken in accord with a nearly unanimous resolution by the Organization of American States. "For the sanctions to be lifted, Cuba has to stop trying to overthrow other Latin American governments," Scali said.

As for the Canal, Scali said: "The world knows the U.S. is ready to modernize the treaty arrangements with the Panamanians, but it takes two to negotiate. Problems with the Canal will be solved by very quiet and painstaking negotiations, and not by speeches before an international forum."

IDB sets Salto Grande power loan. The Inter-American Development Bank (IDB) had authorized an $80 million loan to help finance construction by Argentina and Uruguay of a 1,620,000 kilowatt hydroelectric power station at Salto Grande on the Uruguay River, it was reported Jan. 17.

The station would provide power for a 110,000 square mile market area in Uruguay and northeast Argentina with a population of 5.2 million. The total cost of its first stage was estimated at $432 million, of which the IDB loan would cover 18.5%, suppliers' credits 23.6%, and the Argentine and Uruguayan governments 57.9%.

The loan for the project, the largest ever granted by the IDB, was set in December 1972. The bank awarded a record $807 million in credits in 1972, of which $213 million went to Brazil, according to an IDB report Jan. 15.

Japanese financial mission on tour. A 35-member Japanese financial mission left Tokyo Jan. 24 on a tour of Mexico, Panama, Peru, Chile, Argentina, Brazil, Venezuela and Colombia. The group, composed of executives of Japan's major banks and corporations, would ascertain what role Japan could play in the development of the Latin nations' economies, according to El Nacional of Caracas Jan. 25.

U.S. drug report disclosed. Washington columnist Jack Anderson reported Feb. 4 that a secret General Accounting Office (GAO) study in his possession showed narcotics smuggling into the U.S. through Latin America remained extensive despite U.S. efforts to eliminate it.

The GAO report, Anderson said, "has been hidden under the secrecy stamp because the government would prefer to have the public believe the smuggling crackdown has been a success." The study, like other U.S. drug reports disclosed by Anderson, showed smuggling was widespread in most Latin American countries, due in part to the effectiveness of international measures against European smuggling routes.

The report also described new smuggling methods introduced by the "Latin American Connection," Anderson said. Bodies of Latin Americans who died in Europe had been filled with packets of heroin before being shipped home, and the heroin had been removed by smugglers in Latin America before the bodies were turned over to their families. Drugs with telltale smells, such as marijuana, had been hidden among fruit with pungent odors destined for U.S. Gulf ports, Anderson reported.

In South America, Anderson continued, cocaine—which had an ever increasing market in the U.S.—was carried across remote Andean borders by peasants working for wealthy smugglers. Small planes called Mau Maus sometimes carried narcotics "from one airfield to the next through Latin America on into Florida in a daring game of hopscotch," Anderson reported.

Among countries and areas singled out by the GAO report:

Argentina—"Argentina has become a significant transit point for hard narcotics destined for the U.S.," the report said. "Cocaine is moved in from Bolivia in the form of coca paste and then is refined into cocaine in Argentina. The Argentine government ... is acting against the traffickers [but] provincial police, whose jurisdiction is outside Buenos Aires, have virtually no narcotics capabilities."

Caribbean—"All types of narcotics flow from Europe into the Caribbean and are transshipped to the U.S.," according to the report. "Thousands of small craft cruise the Caribbean waters, which makes it almost impossible to monitor and prevent smuggling ... It is very difficult to control the transfer of drugs from ship to ship in many harbors." The Netherlands Antilles had become "a major hard drug transit point" and Jamaica was becoming one, the GAO reported.

Ecuador—Clandestine laboratories on the Ecuadorean coast were believed to be producing cocaine and heroin for the U.S. market, but control of the narcotics traffic was very difficult "because the national police and other governmental authorities are susceptible to bribes and because the police force is undermanned, ill-trained and ill-equipped," the GAO reported.

Panama—Panama was "the crossroads of major sea and air traffic routes [and] a major contraband and smuggling center," the report asserted. "Heroin and cocaine pass through Panama bound for the U.S. [from] Chile, Peru, Bolivia, Ecuador and Colombia ... Panamanian officials do not seem to fully comprehend the need to control drug production and traffic. The U.S. mission also reported there were some indications that Panamanian officials and security agents might have been involved in narcotics trafficking."

Paraguay—Paraguay was "a major transit area for the smuggling, storage and distribution of heroin from Europe," the GAO reported. Although the country's "concern about illicit international trafficking has increased recently because of unfavorable press reports," a Latin American narcotics control agency was "not confident that a crackdown on officials involved in drug trafficking would take place," the report said.

Venezuela—Venezuela had become an important transshipment point for U.S.-bound heroin and cocaine, the report stated. "Venezuela is serviced by numerous international airline flights; there is a significant volume of light-aircraft movement over the country; and its land and sea frontiers are clearly vulnerable."

The GAO said Latin American governments were paying increasing attention to the flow of narcotics through their countries to the U.S. because their own youths had begun taking the drugs, Anderson reported. Because "the use of narcotics, amphetamines and barbiturates in Latin America is increasing, particularly among the young people," there was a growing awareness among local governments that "narcotics addiction is a worldwide problem," the GAO concluded.

Telecommunications consortium. The London newsletter Latin America reported Feb. 9 that a Latin American telecommunications consortium would begin operation before the end of April.

In addition to Mexico, which proposed its formation, the consortium was to consist of state communications agencies of Brazil, Colombia, Costa Rica, Chile, Ecuador, El Salvador, Guatemala, Panama, Paraguay, Peru, Uruguay and Venezuela.

It was aimed, Latin America said, at displacing U.S. telecommunications concerns.

El Nacional of Caracas reported Feb. 14 that Argentina, Chile, Paraguay and Brazil were scheduled to integrate their telecommunication systems by the end of February.

Jet fleet planned. The Andean Development Corp. (CAF) was planning to buy a fleet of jumbo jets, which it would charter to Andean countries' airlines, the newsletter Latin America reported Feb. 9. According to CAF co-ordinator Edgar Camacho, this would enable the airlines to standardize their equipment and save them large capital expenditures.

The president of LAN-Chile, Teodoro Ruiz Diez, suggested, however, that the Andean countries pool their resources and set up a unified Andean airline capable of competing with other world airlines.

200-mile waters limit endorsed. The Inter-American Juridical Committee (IJC) of the Organization of American States, meeting in Rio de Janeiro Feb. 11, endorsed the decision by certain Latin American countries to extend their territorial waters to 200 miles offshore.

The IJC distinguished, however, between two zones: the first up to 12 miles offshore, and the second from that limit up to 200 miles. In the second zone the maritime state had exclusive rights to exploit, explore, investigate or conserve the natural resources in the sea and on or under the seabed, while other states had free navigation and overflying rights.

The delegates from Brazil, Colombia and Peru—among the strongest defenders of the 200-mile limit—opposed the division of territorial waters into two zones. The representatives of Argentina and Trinidad and Tobago abstained from the formal vote.

Peru & Ecuador seize U.S. boats—Peru seized 20 U.S.-owned tuna boats Jan. 10–20 for fishing within Peru's declared 200-mile offshore territorial limits. The boats were fined according to weight, forced to buy Peruvian fishing licenses and then released. The penalties were said to average $30,000 a boat, but one vessel, a California boat seized Jan. 20, reportedly paid $100,000 in fines and license fees.

A U.S. State Department spokesman said Jan. 19 that the U.S. had formally protested the seizures and put military sales to Peru under review. The U.S. recognized only a 12-mile territorial limit, and reimbursed boat owners who were fined for fishing within the 200-mile limit.

U.S. Rep. John M. Murphy (D, N.Y.) charged Jan. 18 that Peru had seized some of the tuna boats with destroyers and other ships leased from the U.S. Navy, and said he was introducing legislation in Congress directing the U.S. to take back ships used by foreign nations to seize other U.S. vessels. Ecuador used converted U.S. patrol boats to seize U.S. tuna vessels, Murphy charged.

Peruvian Fisheries Minister Javier Tantalean denied Jan. 20 that U.S.-leased ships were used to capture tuna boats. He said Murphy's proposed legislation reflected the thought of "a person who still believes in the 'big stick' policy." He added that 21 foreign vessels, including ones from Canada, the U.S., Ecuador, Japan and France, had voluntarily bought Peruvian fishing licenses in January.

Peru Jan. 25 seized two more U.S. tuna boats—its 21st and 22nd of 1973—and Ecuador confiscated three more Feb. 9–

10 for fishing within their declared 200-mile territorial waters. Ecuador released the 3 boats after levying fines and license fees totaling $224,000, according to the American Tunaboat Association (ATA) Feb. 17.

The ATA said Feb. 5 that a disabled U.S. tuna boat had been seized by an Ecuadorean gunboat while being towed to the Galapagos Islands for repairs. Ecuador said the boat had been seized at the islands Jan. 13 and forced to pay fines and fees totaling $78,800. Ecuadorean officials said repairs could not be made in the islands, which were Ecuadorean possessions.

Meanwhile, the Soviet Fisheries Minister, in Lima to discuss cooperation on technical questions, had asserted the Soviet Union would always respect Peru's territorial waters, the newsletter Latin America reported Feb. 2. The pledge was considered important because the U.S.S.R. had normally joined the U.S. in defending the 12-mile limit, according to the newsletter.

Argentine action—The enactment of an Argentine bill banning foreign trawlers from fishing within 200 miles of the Argentine coast was reported Feb. 16. The signing followed Argentina's decision Jan. 19 not to ratify a 1967 agreement with Brazil which allowed both countries' vessels to fish in each other's territorial waters up to six miles from the coast without paying duty. Argentina had arrested four Brazilian fishing boats Jan. 13 and another one Jan. 15 for alledgedly violating Argentine territorial waters.

1980 population projected. A United Nations study estimated that Latin America's population would reach 372 million in 1980, El Nacional of Caracas reported Feb. 20. The region's 1970 population totaled 279 million.

The projection, in a study by the Economic Commission for Latin America, was based on an examination of demographic trends between 1960 and 1970. During that period, the study found, the birth rate decreased from 40.1 per thousand to 38.2 and the death rate from 11.1 to 9.2 per thousand. Life expectancy rose from 57.6 to 61.2 years.

Cuba joins Latin Group talks at U.N. Cuba was invited to participate in a caucus of the Latin American delegations to the United Nations Feb. 26, the Washington Post reported March 2.

Latin American diplomats insisted the decision to allow Cuba to participate in a discussion of regional strategy for an upcoming meeting on a law-of-the sea conference was "unique." They emphasized that Cuba remained outside the official Latin American group at the U.N.

The Cuban delegation had been excluded from similar meetings since 1961.

ECLA meets in Quito. The U.N. Economic Commission for Latin America (ECLA), marking its 25th year of activity, held its 15th general assembly in Quito, Ecuador March 23-30. The meeting's major accomplishment was adoption March 30 of an ECLA report on international development strategy, which held structural change was the basis for social and economic development.

The report, called the Declaration of Quito, was approved 22-0. Only the U.S. abstained. France and Canada expressed reservations about some of the report's conclusions, but voted for it, as did all Latin American nations represented. Brazil cast a favorable vote despite the report's expressed reservations about the "Brazilian model" of development.

According to La Prensa of Buenos Aires March 30, the ECLA study maintained structural changes were necessary to any integrated process of development. It said development was furthered not by partial efforts in some sectors of an economy or social system, but by "simultaneous progress in all aspects." The report warned that "traditional structures, insofar as they create obstacles to change, impede social progress and economic development."

The study stressed the negative impact on developing countries of "the breakdown of the international monetary system," for which they were in no way responsible. It warned industralized nations that nothing could be gained from excluding developing countries, as in the past, from future talks on world monetary and trade problems.

The report also condemned economic pressure by industrialized nations and

REGIONAL DEVELOPMENTS

multinational corporations against countries changing their structures along lines recommended by the 1970 U.N. study on international development strategy. These nations deserved "international backing," the report asserted.

This assertion was among many singled out for criticism by the U.S. delegation. The U.S. said the report was valuable, but excessively emphasized the conflict of interests between industrialized and developing countries. The report charged that in 1970–72 industrial nations offered less financial assistance, and at more onerous terms, and criticized the U.S. for failure to deliver promised preferential treatment to Latin American exports. It went on to call for a moratorium on all debt service payments by developing nations to the U.S., a recommendation the U.S. specifically rejected March 29.

The conference was characterized by attacks on the U.S. and other industrial nations and calls for Latin American unity on world economic problems. The strongest attack on the U.S. was delivered March 27 by the chief Cuban delegate, Carlos Rafael Rodriguez, who charged the U.S. with direct responsibility for the underdevelopment of Latin nations.

Rodriguez also sharply criticized the Brazilian "model" of development as an example for other Latin nations to emulate. He noted that Brazil's impressive industralization "coincides with even more impressive evidence of unequal distribution of wealth," which was steadily worsening. Citing ECLA statistics, Rodriguez noted that 5% of the Brazilian population, "that is to say the privileged oligarchy and foreign investors," received 43% of the national income, while 20% of the population, "or dozens of millions of citizens, have to be content with distributing among themselves 3% of the national income."

IAPA meets in Jamaica. The Board of Directors of the Inter-American Press Association (IAPA) held its midyear meeting in Montego Bay, Jamaica April 2–6. A declaration issued April 6 warned that freedom of the press and information were essential to achieve a "more dignified, more just and more prosperous future" in the hemisphere.

The directors April 6 approved a number of resolutions, including one to broaden the activities of IAPA's Freedom of the Press Committee, renamed the Freedom of the Press and Information Committee. Among the resolutions:

Recent threats to press freedom in the U.S. were noted with "particular alarm."

Chilean President Salvador Allende was urged to cooperate with his country's National Press Association to assure economic stability for Chile's newspapers.

Jamaican Prime Minister Michael Manley was encouraged to use his influence to secure "freedom for Cuban political prisoners and particularly for journalists jailed for exercising their right and duty to inform and criticize."

Lack of press freedom was deplored in Haiti, Panama and Paraguay, and recent press restrictions in the Dominican Republic and Ecuador were noted. The Nicaraguan government was urged to lift the martial law and press restrictions imposed after the December 1972 Managua earthquakes, and Argentina was asked to remove restrictions on the importation of newsprint and the ban on news of guerrilla activities.

The Freedom of the Press Committee had delivered a report to the meeting April 5 which concluded "freedom of the press is being torn to pieces in the Americas." Many governments, the report said, "think the press is an instrument for their policies, rather than a servant of society." It said the press was under attack even in countries of traditional press freedom, notably the U.S. and Chile.

The report said there was no press freedom in Brazil, Cuba, Haiti, Panama and Paraguay, and an "unsatisfactory" situation in the Bahamas, Grenada, St. Kitts, Antigua, Guyana, Ecuador and Peru. The report attacked the Cuban government, charging "the regime of Premier Fidel Castro suppressed all vestiges of liberty, as well as respect for the dignity of human beings."

Prime Minister Manley addressed the meeting April 4, calling on the press in developed countries to foster a "critical conscience" in the public.

OAS holds General Assembly. The third regular session of the Organization of

American States (OAS) General Assembly was held in Washington, D.C. April 4-15. Delegates from the 23 member states approved a number of resolutions, including provisions for restructuring the OAS and recognition of a "plurality of ideologies" in the hemisphere.

The major resolution, passed April 13, approved creation of a committee of all the member states to begin a "critical study, analysis and evaluation of the philosophy, structure and functioning" of the inter-American system, and to propose the "restructuring and reforms" necessary to "respond to the new political, economic, social and cultural conditions of all member states, and to hemispheric and world circumstances."

Among the other resolutions adopted, reported April 15:

■ The General Assembly declared that "under the [OAS] Charter, plurality of ideologies is a presupposition of regional solidarity," implying the "duty of each state to respect the principles of nonintervention and self-determination of peoples." In an apparent rebuff to Cuba, however, the assembly reaffirmed its support for a 1972 OAS resolution condemning support by one nation for "subversive, terrorist or armed activities" against another.

■ The assembly urged adoption of "whatever measures may be necessary" to prevent multinational corporations from engaging in "acts of intervention in the internal or external affairs of the states." The U.S. abstained on this vote.

■ The U.S. was urged to exercise care in projected sales from its stockpiles of tin, tungsten, zinc, copper and lead to avoid harming the economic or social development of Latin America's ore producing nations. The U.S. and Honduras abstained.

■ A working group was established to find a compromise solution on the readmission of Cuba to the OAS. The group included Chile and Brazil, which represented extreme opposite viewpoints on the matter. A majority of delegates reportedly favored an end to Cuba's isolation, but backed away from an outright confrontation with the U.S., which objected to Havana's military links to Moscow and maintained that Cuba was still interfering in other countries' internal affairs.

The assembly session was characterized by criticism of U.S. domination of the OAS and calls for a complete restructuring of the organization. The criticism was begun April 5 by the Peruvian foreign minister, Gen. Miguel Angel de la Flor, who said OAS meetings had "turned into expressions of agreement with the policies of the big country to the north." He made several proposals for reorganizing the OAS, including moving its headquarters from Washington.

De la Flor also listed grievances expressed by many Latin nations against U.S. economic and trade policies, and declared: "Imperialism has been and still is present in America in both its old and new manifestations, from which we must defend ourselves and make a common front."

Similar speeches were made by the other representatives in the following days. The Panamanian foreign minister, Juan Antonio Tack, said April 9 that his country would "support without reserve any resolution which tends to radically change the structure of this organization, which is dying publicly and whose requiem is being sung in this debate."

The U.S. delegation reportedly remained aloof throughout the conference, stating a general policy of disengagement from hemispheric affairs and even hinting it might leave the OAS. Led by John H. Crimmins, acting assistant secretary of state for inter-American affairs, the delegation worked with moderate Latin nations to avoid open confrontations with other members.

President Nixon sent a message to the assembly April 5 which asserted "the days of paternalism have ended" and urged the OAS states to seek "a strong new relationship." Referring to past U.S. initiatives in Latin America, Nixon said: "The days of promising more than could ever be realized have also ended."

Secretary of State William P. Rogers addressed the assembly April 6, urging Latin nations to "concentrate" with the U.S. on "areas where our interests converge." He recognized the growing divergences over economic and political issues among hemispheric nations, and expressed support for a review of inter-American relations. In a move to ease some of the criticism of the U.S., Rogers announced the Nixon Administration's new trade bill would include generalized tariff preferences to developing countries.

A U.S. official said April 13 that Rogers would visit 11 Latin nations in May, including Chile and Peru, and that Nixon would visit Latin America later in 1973.

Rogers on tour. U.S. Secretary of State William P. Rogers visited eight countries in Latin America and the Caribbean May 12-28, conferring with government officials in an attempt to begin what he called "a new era of interest and cooperation" between the U.S. and other hemispheric nations.

Rogers visited Mexico, Nicaragua, Venezuela, Peru, Colombia, Brazil, Argentina and Jamaica. He delivered a major policy speech in Colombia, and attended the inauguration of Argentina's new Peronist government.

Rogers was accompanied by his undersecretary for economic affairs, William J. Casey; the new assistant secretary of state for inter-American affairs, Jack B. Kubisch; and the State Department's counsel, Richard F. Pedersen.

Rogers visited Mexico May 12-14. He conferred May 12 with Foreign Minister Emilio Rabasa, and the next day with President Luis Echeverria Alvarez. After the second meeting, Rogers said he had presented "a concrete and serious proposal" to end the long-standing dispute between the U.S. and Mexico over the high salinity of Colorado River water flowing into Mexico. He declined to give details of the plan, but press sources said the U.S. had agreed to spend $50 million–$60 million to improve the quality of the Colorado River water.

Rogers stopped briefly in Managua, Nicaragua May 14, pledging increased U.S. aid to help rebuild the city, which was ravaged by earthquakes in December 1972.

Rogers arrived in Caracas, Venezuela May 14, and conferred the next day with President Rafael Caldera and Foreign Minister Aristides Calvani, touching on petroleum matters and other economic issues. At a luncheon given by Calvani, Rogers said the U.S. was prepared to enter a long-term arrangement for capital and technology to develop the Orinoco heavy oil belt.

Students rioted in Caracas and other cities May 15-16 to protest Rogers' visit. A worker was killed in the capital on the second day of disturbances.

Rogers proceeded to Lima, Peru May 16, where he held an unscheduled meeting with President Juan Velasco Alvarado, who was recovering from a leg amputation.

He also conferred with Gen. Edgardo Mercado Jarrin, president of the council of ministers. Mercado said afterwards that Rogers had come to see "the new Latin American reality."

Rogers also paid an unexpected visit to the headquarters of the five-nation Andean Group, and praised it for its contribution to Latin American economic integration.

Rogers flew to Bogota, Colombia May 17. Security measures at the airport were tight to protect him from student protesters, who unsuccessfully tried to block his route into the capital. Thousands of other students began a 48-hour strike to protest the visit. In Medellin, student demonstrators burned as U.S. flag and an automobile.

Rogers met May 18 with President Misael Pastrana Borrero and delivered the major speech of his tour, asserting U.S. policy toward Latin America had shifted from paternalism to fraternalism. He welcomed the growing nationalism in Latin America, and reiterated the points of what he called the U.S.' "moderate policy of mature partnership," which he introduced at the April meeting of the Organization of American States in Washington.

Rogers also met May 18 with Foreign Minister Alfredo Vasquez Carrizosa, who assured him that Colombia planned more vigorous action against the international drug trade.

Rogers continued to Rio de Janeiro May 19. After a long weekend, he flew to Brasilia May 22, where he conferred with Foreign Minister Mario Gibson Barboza. He met the next day with President Emilio G. Medici, reportedly discussing the international petroleum situation and other issues. He told newsmen afterwards that the U.S. did not seek to promote Brazilian hegemony in Latin America, and that it sought to discourage an arms race among Latin nations.

Rogers arrived in Buenos Aires late May 23. He attended various ceremonies for foreign delegations May 24, and witnessed the inauguration of President Hector J. Campora the next day. He held what he called a "useful" discussion with Chilean President Salvador Allende later May 25.

Rogers met with Campora May 26, saying afterwards that they had "agreed to close and very active consultations to make sure that no misunderstandings develop between us." He added that he did not expect "any serious problems" to arise with the Peronist government.

Rogers left Buenos Aires May 26, flying to the Caribbean island of Curacao for a rest. He continued to Kingston, Jamaica, May 28, where he conferred with Prime Minister Michael Manley and other officials before returning to Washington.

Nixon plans trip—President Nixon said May 3 that he would visit Latin America "at least once" in 1973, and defended what he called the U.S.' policy of "mature partnership" and "low profile" in the hemisphere.

Dorticos on Rogers tour—Cuban President Osvaldo Dorticos said June 4 that U.S. Secretary of State Rogers' recent Latin American tour was "a major failure." Referring to Rogers' security problems during the Argentine presidential inauguration, Dorticos said: "He couldn't even attend the investiture, because the masses prevented it."

Rogers had said he was satisfied with the trip, and that "not one hostile act" had been directed against him in Latin America, the Miami Herald reported May 31. He said the U.S. could "cooperate fully" with "the growing feeling of nationalism" in the nations he visited, and was prepared to adjust to restrictions on capital flows imposed by hemispheric countries.

Dorticos said Cuba would not rejoin the Organization of American States, or participate in efforts to restructure it, as some nations had suggested. He said his country supported creation of an organization of Latin American states without U.S. participation.

U.S. jet fighter sales authorized. President Richard M. Nixon, in a break with previous U.S. policy, had authorized the sale of F-5E supersonic jet fighter planes to Chile, Argentina, Brazil, Colombia and Venezuela, it was announced June 5.

Secretary of State William P. Rogers made the disclosure while testifying before the House Foreign Affairs Committee. He said the U.S. "should no longer attempt to determine for the Latin Americans what their reasonable military needs should be."

The U.S. previously had tried to dissuade Latin governments from buying advanced military equipment, but had failed and consequently lost markets in military equipment to France and other countries, a Washington official said. He added that the Nixon Administration had decided sales of the jet aircraft would provide additional leverage in negotiating with Latin countries.

The sales would be financed by military credits, according to a State Department official. Under the Foreign Military Sales Act of 1968, such transactions in jet aircraft were barred unless the President decided they were "important to the security of the United States." Rogers said Nixon had "exercised the waiver authority granted him by Congress" in finding the five Latin nations eligible for F-5E purchases.

Rogers stressed that the finding of eligibility did not mean a sale was imminent, but only that negotiations were possible. Chile was reported June 11 to be studying purchase of 16 aircraft, but Colombia said June 8 that it had no plans to buy F-5E's. Brazil had announced purchase of 48 of the jet fighters May 30.

The F-5E jet was produced by the Northrop Corp. and cost about $1.6 million.

Peru urges end of arms race—Peruvian President Juan Velasco Alvarado urged other Latin American nations to abandon their arms race and "invest in development" instead. In a newspaper interview June 10, Velasco noted the large military purchases of neighboring countries and asked: "What are they arming for? Fireworks?"

Peru had announced the previous week its purchase of 40 aircraft, including French Mirage and British Canberra jets, for the air force and for domestic and international passenger flights, El Nacional of Caracas reported June 11.

CIAP criticizes U.S. The Inter-American Committee of the Alliance for Progress (CIAP) accused the U.S. June 5 of "frequently adopting negative attitudes" toward Latin American countries in which it had investments.

The committee's annual report on U.S. ties and investments in Latin America criticized what it called the U.S. policy of "cuts in aid, vetoes of multilateral loans, restrictive trade measures, and punitive announcements that do little to dissipate frustrations and nationalist sentiments." Frequently, such a policy "wiped out political advances made by firms that responded to national aspirations, and exposed ... the United States and North American companies," the report asserted.

CIAP urged the U.S. government to support developing nations and international organizations in their efforts to define "norms" for foreign investments, and then oblige U.S. companies to abide by those norms. It also asked the U.S. to eliminate the political aspect of investment by reducing the number of situations in which companies could appeal to the U.S. government to resolve their conflicts with developing nations.

The U.S. rejected the committee's criticism June 8. John Hennessy, assistant Treasury secretary for international affairs, said U.S. "preoccupation" was justified when U.S. property was seized without compensation. He said investors and the nations in which they invested—not the U.S. or international organizations—should determine any new norms for investment.

OAS restructuring studied. The Special Committee to Study the Inter-American System convened in Washington Sept. 4 to begin considering structural changes in the Organization of American States (OAS), which was under increasing attack in Latin America as obsolete and overly dominated by the U.S.

The committee, with representatives from all 23 OAS member states, was created under a resolution passed by the OAS General Assembly in April. It met first in Lima, Peru June 20–July 13, where it resolved to completely restructure the inter-American system and draft a new OAS Charter.

The Lima meeting resolved at least two important issues—it rejected the expulsion of the U.S. from the OAS, as proposed by Argentina, and confirmed the exclusion of Cuba from the committee's deliberations—but left open the controversy over whether the OAS should promote "participatory democracy" or accept the principle of "ideological pluralism," championed by Mexico and seemingly endorsed by the OAS Assembly in April.

Raul Quijano, an Argentine delegate, went before the committee Sept. 6 to denounce the 1947 Inter-American Treaty of Reciprocal Assistance, or Treaty of Rio, the hemispheric security pact used to justify, among other actions, the OAS sanctions against Cuba.

Quijano charged that "tortuous interpretations, omissions and abuses" of the treaty had turned it into an "instrument of imperialist intervention." He said Argentina would support proposals which "transform the treaty into a pact for maintenance of peace in the continent, controlling the imbalance of forces existing in America."

Quijano's remarks were rejected by a Nicaraguan representative, Guillermo Sevilla Sacasa, who called the Rio treaty "the pride of the inter-American system," and asserted: "Intervention is not always aggression."

The treaty was also defended by the chief U.S. delegate, Joseph John Jova, who said it had been used to temper a series of potentially explosive disputes in Central America, including, most recently, the 1969 war between El Salvador and Honduras.

Peru, whose suggestions at the Lima meeting had been considered the most radical, joined Argentina in attacking the Rio treaty, and proposed creation of a mechanism to guarantee the "economic security" of American states. Peruvian delegate Luis Alvarado said the mechanism should combat both direct "economic aggression" and less overt actions which might threaten the economic development of one or more states.

(Peru had suffered for more than four years from an aid and loan embargo imposed by the U.S. after the military government expropriated, without compensation, the U.S.-owned International Petroleum Corp. The embargo had recently ended.

U.S. policy criticized—U.S. Senator Lawton Chiles (D, Fla.) Aug. 31 had criticized what he called the lack of a recognizable U.S. policy toward Latin America, and urged Washington to focus more attention on the region.

Speaking on his return from a tour of four Latin nations, Chiles said Latins "now refer to what our government is doing in relation to Latin America" as "non-policy," "non-profile," or "benign neglect." "This just can't go on," he asserted.

Chiles said an increasing number of Latin governments appeared ready to disregard OAS sanctions against Cuba and unilaterally resume ties with the island's Communist government. He said such action had "some merit," and should be accepted by the U.S. as an expression of Latin American individuality.

Chiles dismissed the possibility of an early rapprochement between the U.S. and Cuba, asserting: "Right now Cuba doesn't want to resume ties with us. Cuba has an aggressive policy toward the United States. [Premier Fidel] Castro doesn't show any interest [in changing this policy] and I don't think we should take any initiative there."

U.S. asks 'new dialogue.' U.S. Secretary of State Henry A. Kissinger called on Latin American governments Oct. 5 to join the U.S. in shaping new hemispheric policies based on "common needs."

"We [in the U.S.] are serious about starting a new dialogue with our friends in the Americas," Kissinger declared in his first policy speech on Latin America, to a gathering in New York of foreign ministers and ambassadors from all Latin nations except Cuba.

"We ... will approach this dialogue with an open mind. We do not believe that any institution or any treaty arrangement is beyond examination," he said, in apparent reference to the Organization of American States (OAS), which was currently studying its own restructuring.

Kissinger conceded that U.S. relations with Latin America had been "characterized by alternating periods of what some of you have considered intervention with periods of neglect." However, he offered the Latin envoys "a friendship based on equality and on respect for mutual dignity."

"If the technically advanced nations can ever cooperate with the developing nations, then it must start here in the Western Hemisphere," Kissinger declared.

Kissinger offered no specific proposals, asserting that a new hemispheric policy made "no sense if it is a United States prescription, handed over to Latin Americans for your acceptance or rejection ... It should be a policy designed by all of Latin America for the Americas."

Kissinger asked Latin Americans for suggestions on how to proceed, specifically, whether the new policy should be worked out through committees, subcommittees, or individual contacts among nations.

He did not mention the current U.S. embargo of Cuba, which had come under increasing attack in Latin America. (Kissinger had said during Senate hearings on his confirmation as secretary of state that he wished to discuss U.S. policy toward Cuba with other Latin governments. However, he held out no prospects for an early change in this policy.)

Kissinger's remarks were praised by Leopoldo Benites of Ecuador, president of the United Nations General Assembly. Benites said the secretary's words were of "overriding significance," Latin America's response was "eminently positive," and the day marked "the start of a new chapter in hemispheric relations." His sentiments were echoed by Alfredo Vasquez Carrizosa, Colombia's foreign minister.

(In a related development, Kissinger had announced Aug. 23 that President

Nixon would not visit Latin America in 1973 as planned. He said the trip's indefinite postponement was due to the Watergate scandal and other internal U.S. matters.)

Energy organization established. Ministers of energy and hydrocarbons from 24 hemispheric nations, including Cuba, held their Third Advisory Meeting in Lima, Peru Oct. 29–Nov. 2 and gave final approval to creation of the Latin American Energy Organization (OLADE).

The organization, to be based in Quito, Ecuador, would work for integration, preservation, coordinated marketing, rational use and defense of all regional energy resources, including oil, coal, and hydroelectric and nuclear power. Some officials reportedly saw OLADE as a first step toward a continental system to control exploitation of these resources by foreign interests.

The ministers also heatedly debated a report by Venezuela on creation of a Latin American organization to finance regional energy development projects. No final decision on the organization was made.

Peru made strong appeals during the meeting for hemispheric solidarity in the defense of energy resources from unfair exploitation by developed countries. Peruvian Mines Minister Gen. Jorge Fernandez Maldonado said Oct. 29 that production and export of petroleum "should not expose developing countries to blackmail, threats or aggression from societies of uncontrollable and irrational energy macroconsumption."

Creation of OLADE seemingly gave new impetus to ARPEL, an existing organization of the state oil companies of eight Latin American nations, according to the Andean Times' Latin America Economic Report Nov. 23. At a meeting in Caracas, Venezuela after the Lima conference, ARPEL voted to form a Latin American oil and gas marketing organization. ARPEL previously had limited itself to making studies and providing a forum for its companies to discuss common problems.

IDB gets Japan loan. The Inter-American Development Bank (IDB) announced Nov. 8 it had received an $18.5 million loan for Latin American development projects from the Import and Export Bank of Japan. It was Japan's ninth loan to the IDB, bringing the credit total to $86.5 million.

Foreign ministers meet. Foreign ministers of 18 hemispheric nations and special representatives of six others met in Bogota, Colombia Nov. 14–16 and approved an agenda for future talks with U.S. Secretary of State Henry Kissinger to improve strained relations between Washington and Latin America and the Caribbean.

Kissinger, who had called Oct. 5 for a "new" hemispheric "dialogue", was invited to the conference but did not attend because of a previous commitment to visit the Middle East and Asia. He expressed approval of the Bogota meeting Nov. 16 and said he hoped to meet with hemispheric envoys at an "appropriate" time. The foreign ministers tentatively scheduled a meeting with Kissinger for Feb. 5, 1974 in Mexico.

The issues to be discussed with Kissinger included the need for cooperation in development, control of the activities of multinational corporations, Panama's claim to full sovereignty over the Panama Canal, U.S. economic reprisals against nationalist governments, more equitable hemispheric trade relations, transfer of technology from the U.S. to developing countries, a role for developing nations in world monetary talks, and a significant restructuring of the inter-American system.

The foreign ministers Nov. 16 signed a declaration, called the "Bogota Document", which called generally for changes in U.S. political and economic policies in the Western Hemisphere.

Cuba was not on the conference's agenda, having been relegated to further discussion within the Organization of American States (OAS), but the issue reportedly was debated and left the foreign ministers divided. Mexico and Peru reportedly urged a resolution of the question outside the OAS framework, while Colombia argued the opposite.

Although most foreign ministers praised the conference's achievements, there was also skepticism of its possible effectiveness. Observers said the absence of the foreign ministers of Brazil, Argentina, Bolivia and Paraguay made the meeting unrepresentative. Others pointed out that previous Latin American declarations on the same issues had been ignored by the U.S.

OAS Secretary General Galo Plaza charged Nov. 15 that the meeting was merely a "show". He later tried to deny making the assertion, but a Mexican journalist had recorded it and played it back for proof.

Argentina

Juan Domingo Perón, the ousted former dictator, returned to Argentina during 1973. Perón was quickly reelected president, and the enthusiastic electorate indorsed Perón's selection of his third wife as vice president. The election was the second held for a president in 1973. After the departing military regime had barred Perón from the year's first presidential election, Hector J. Campora, Perón's candidate, won the first election and became president. Then, following Perón's return, Campora vacated the presidency to clear the way for Perón's election.

Pre-Election Developments

Election slates set. Nine political parties and coalitions filed lists of candidates for the March 11 elections before the official deadline Jan. 2. In addition to the president and vice president of Argentina, voters would select 69 senators, 243 parliamentary deputies, 595 mayors and 6,250 municipal councilmen.

The presidential candidates and their running-mates:

Popular Alliance—Oscar Alende and Horacio Sueldo.
Federalist Popular Alliance—Francisco Manrique and José Rafael Martinez Raymonda.
Federal Republican Alliance—Brig. (ret.) Ezequiel Martinez and Leopoldo Bravo.
Popular Left Front—Jorge Abelardo Ramos and José Silvetti.
Justicialista Liberation Front—Hector Campora and Vicente Solano Lima.
Integration and Development Movement (Desarrollistas)—Arturo Frondizi and Americo Garcia.
New Force—Julio Chamizo and Raúl Ondarts.
Socialist Workers party—Juan Carlos Coral and Nora Sciapone.
Radical Civic Union—Ricardo Balbin and Eduardo Gamond.

Democratic Socialist ticket approved—The national electoral judge Jan. 24 approved the presidential ticket of the Democratic Socialist party, which reportedly had missed the official deadline for completion of registration forms.

The Democratic Socialist ticket was headed by Americo Ghioldi and Rene Balestra.

Lanusse sees continued military power—President Alejandro Lanusse had asserted the armed forces intended to retain an active role in the government which emerged from the March elections, it was reported Jan. 3.

In a message read over the state radio station, Lanusse admitted the new government would not be a "genuine democracy," but rather "transitional," because "no party is in a position to act alone and because we should relearn the uses of democracy." Lanusse criticized "some naive people" (implicitly Peronists) who "are trying to cut out the armed forces without accepting that their participation has no other purpose than to guarantee respect for the people's choice."

(The joint chiefs of staff decided Jan. 4 to maintain the existing state of siege in view of "the resurgence of subversive and terrorist actions." Lanusse had said in November 1972 that he would lift the siege by the end of that year if conditions permitted.)

Military chiefs back elections—The armed forces commanders issued a statement after a meeting Jan. 24, pledging to continue the electoral process, with participation of "all those who obey the laws at present in force"; to guarantee the full effectiveness of all republican institutions, insuring an authentic democracy; to guarantee the independence and fixed tenure of the judiciary; to prevent any indiscriminate amnesties for those charged with or convicted of crimes of subversion; and to share power with the future elected government through the designation by the armed forces themselves of military members of the Cabinet.

A virtually identical statement was signed by nearly all army generals in active service following ex-President Perón's remark that the military would not easily give up power, the newsletter Latin America reported Feb. 16. [See above] The navy issued a separate statement backing the elections but asserting it would not accept the victory of those who sought to restore "the vices of past times." The air force declared its determination to "transfer power to the majority" in "a clean process without proscriptions."

Charges brought against Perón. The government began legal proceedings against ex-President Juan Perón Jan. 17, charging recent statements he made in Madrid were "instigations" to violence.

The charge stemmed from a news conference by Perón in Madrid Dec. 31, 1972, in which the ex-president denounced the "outrageous gorillas of the military dictatorship who scourge [Argentina]," and asserted "if I were 50 years younger, it wouldn't be hard to understand if I went around planting bombs and taking justice into my own hands."

Television and radio officials had said Jan. 14 that the government had ordered them not to broadcast Perón's political opinions. The official prohibition referred to "comments made abroad about the [March] elections by persons not involved in the electoral process." Perón had refused his Justicialista party's presidential nomination in December 1972 after the government disqualified his candidacy.

Peron excluded, FREJULI sued. The regime Feb. 6 barred Peron from returning before May 25 and began legal action to dissolve Perón's political coalition, the Justicialista Liberation Front (FREJULI). The action followed, among other developments, disclosure of an opinion poll taken by military intelligence which indicated FREJULI would win 53%-55% of the vote in the first round of the general elections March 11.

Perón was barred until after the new elected government took power (May 25, according to current plans) because of "new evidence concerning [his] conduct and intentions." Perón had sharply criticized the Argentine regime in an interview in the Rome newspaper Il Messagero Feb. 5, saying President Alejandro Lanusse "wants to continue the dictatorship . . . The military men who boast of power will not give up the reins so easily. They are beasts."

Perón warned that the Argentine people "could be incited to violence" if the armed forces canceled the March elections. Of FREJULI presidential candidate Hector Campora, whom Perón designated after the military barred his own candidacy, he said: "[Campora] is very loyal. Because of his loyalty, he will make an excellent president." Perón said he had abandoned his own presidential ambitions, but added: "I am still the strategist, the leader. A leader who is more Argentine than Peronist."

The government's suit against FREJULI was based on one of the coalition's electoral slogans, "Campora to the government, Perón to power," which the public prosecutor alleged violated the principle of representation set forth in Article 22 of the Constitution. FREJULI was also accused of violating articles 22 and 50 of decree-law 19,102, which governed the reconstitution of political parties under the current regime. The articles provided for suppression of any

ARGENTINA

party which incited its followers to violence.

According to the London newsletter Latin America Feb. 9, the alleged incitement to violence related to the failure of Justicialista leadership to condemn acts of violence by urban guerrillas, whom they clearly respected; the chanting of pro-guerrilla slogans at FREJULI rallies; and the Peronist insistence on amnesty for political prisoners.

The suit against FREJULI was strongly opposed among civilians and within the government by Interior Minister Arturo Mor Roig, who threatened to resign if FREJULI were proscribed, and Gen. Alcides López Aufranc, chief of the general staff, Latin America reported Feb. 16. López Aufranc was reported Jan. 26 to be opposed to further military intervention in the electoral process, believing that only trouble had resulted from Lanusse's efforts to reach a workable contract with civilian politicians, and that if the military were to govern it should do so directly.

The government, meanwhile, reportedly controlled the information media to exclude Peronist propaganda as far as possible, prevented massive Peronist rallies and harassed Peronist leaders.

Peron, who continued to live in Madrid, visited Rumania Feb. 6–10 on invitation from the Rumanian Institute for Cultural Relations with Foreign Countries. He met Feb. 8 with President Nicolae Ceausescu, discussing Rumanian "relations with Argentina" and "problems of current international developments, action by peoples for peace, and national independence and well-being," according to the Rumanian press agency Agerpress.

Perón sees first-ballot victory. Ex-President Juan Perón predicted in an interview in the French newspaper Le Monde Feb. 26 that his Justicialista Liberation Front coalition (FREJULI) would win a majority of the votes in the first round of the general elections March 11, obviating the runoff balloting scheduled for March 25.

Perón noted, however, that "it is one thing to reach the government and another to take power. That is why I say, first the government, and a month later

power." The military regime was due to transfer power to an elected government May 25, but there were reports it would refuse to do so if the Peronists won the elections.

Perón's prediction was supported Feb. 25 by ex-President Arturo Frondizi, whose Integration and Development Movement was a member of FREJULI. Frondizi charged "para-official groups" were responsible for the incidents which frequently disrupted FREJULI meetings and rallies.

FREJULI presidential candidate Hector Campora Feb. 24 denounced the government for its "campaign of incitement and intimidation" against the coalition. His press secretary read a long list of government actions that Campora said "engendered violence." The actions included raids on regional Peronist headquarters and the homes of FREJULI candidates, false allegations against coalition leaders and candidates, and the arrest or detention of numerous Peronists, including 380 young FREJULI campaigners.

Brazilian encroachment charged. A FREJULI senatorial candidate, Marcelo Sanchez, accused Brazil Jan. 17 of seeking "to install itself in a fringe of Argentine Antarctic territory." The Argentine press had expressed alarm in December 1972 at a projected Brazilian scientific expedition to the Antarctic, where Argentina, Chile and Great Britain claimed national sovereignty.

Sanchez also criticized the government for its stand on the hydroelectric power station Brazil would build at Itaipu on the Parana river, which flowed into Argentina. He said FREJULI presidential candidate Hector Campora had promised that if elected, one of his first acts would be to renounce the October 1972 Argentine-Brazilian accord on the projected power station.

Fishing bill signed. President Lanusse's signature of a bill banning foreign trawlers from fishing within 200 miles of the Argentine coast was reported Feb. 16. The signing followed Argentina's decision Jan. 19 not to ratify a 1967 agreement with Brazil which allowed both countries' vessels to fish in each other's territorial waters up to six miles from the coast without paying duty. Argentina had arrested four Brazilian fishing boats Jan. 13 and another one Jan. 15 for alledgedly violating Argentine territorial waters.

Foreign debts exceed $6 billion. Argentina's total public and private sector foreign debts, including interest owed, had reached $6.22 billion at the end of 1972, according to an unofficial computation cited Feb. 14 in the U.S. weekly Noticias, a news digest published by the National Foreign Trade Council. More than one-third of the sum reportedly fell due in 1973. In other economic developments:

The government had canceled plans for the private steel firm Propulsora to build a plant, financed by the Italian group Finsider, with a capacity of 1.36 million tons a year, Latin America reported Jan. 5. The decision was seen as a victory for the state concern Somisa, which reportedly wanted to exclude the private sector from Argentina's steel expansion plans before a new government took over in May.

It was reported Jan. 2 that the cost of living in Buenos Aires had risen by 64.1% in 1972. The London newsletter Latin America reported Jan. 12 that the Argentine cost of living had risen by 80% during 1972.

Public Works Minister Pedro Gordillo said Jan. 4 that government expenditures in public works and services would increase by 60% in 1973.

Unpaid doctors in Cordoba public hospitals voted Jan. 13 to extend until Jan. 18 the strike they began Dec. 30, 1972. Cordoba municipal workers and employes ended a two-day strike Jan. 10 after being paid their December 1972 wages.

The government had admitted that the national treasury's cash deficit had risen by 83.1% in 1972, it was reported Jan. 31.

Imports reached $1.87 billion in 1972, up only .5% over 1971 but considerably higher than the government had expected, it was reported Feb. 14. The year's trade balance closed with a $24 million deficit.

The chamber of Argentine exporters had fixed a 1973 export target of $2.3 billion, a rise of $500 million over 1972, the London newsletter Latin America reported Feb. 2. The newsletter said Feb. 23 that the government had effectively devalued the Argentine peso for manufactured goods exporters by 9%, to help them combat the results of inflation.

Finance Minister Jorge Wehbe had announced that "rigid controls" would be established to prevent unjustified price increases in 1973, it was reported Jan. 31. The National Statistics and Census Institute reported Feb. 6 that consumer prices had risen by 4.6% in January.

The Labor Ministry had announced the minimum legal wage and minimum amount of severance pay would soon be increased, it was reported Feb. 14. Collective wage bargaining reportedly had neared an end with the signing of 473 agreements before the official deadline Feb. 5. The government said that most of the 140 agreements still pending had been held up for formal motives, and would be signed soon. Most of the agreements signed in January included increases of 30%–35%, but many subsequent ones went above 40%. The highest increase, 55%, was granted to metal workers. Negotiations for the agreements were marked by strikes in numerous industries.

Terrorism continues. A nightclub in Rosario was destroyed early Jan. 4 by a bomb explosion set off by six persons claiming to be members of the Revolutionary Armed Forces (FAR). The FAR, of Peronist orientation, had claimed credit for the assassination Dec. 28, 1972 of Rear Adm. Emilio Berisso.

A band of terrorists attacked a small Buenos Aires police installation Jan. 1, wounding two officers and stealing a number of weapons.

Bomb explosions in Tucuman Jan. 11 damaged the homes of an industrialist and a local leader of the General Labor Confederation. members of the People's Revolutionary Army briefly occupied a train in Rosario later the same day, distributing leaflets and painting slogans on the cars.

A Buenos Aires automobile dealer was released by kidnappers after being held for almost a week, it was reported Jan. 17. His family did not comment on reports that it had paid a ransom of $30,000–$50,000.

The young son of a television actress was kidnapped in a Buenos Aires suburb Jan. 18 and released Jan. 20 after his family paid a ransom equivalent to $310,000.

A Buenos Aires businessman was kidnapped Jan. 19 and freed Jan. 21 after his family paid a ransom equivalent to $70,000.

Terrorists in La Plata Feb. 16 set off bombs at the homes of a government official, a former governor of Buenos Aires province and a Peronist candidate for Congress. Similar explosions were reported in Santa Fe, Cordoba and Tucuman Jan. 26.

About 40 members of the left-wing People's Revolutionary Army (ERP) temporarily occupied a military installation in Cordoba Feb. 18, disarming 70 soldiers and officials and escaping with an army truck carrying arms and ammunition. Other ERP guerrillas simultaneously occupied a nearby police installation to prevent police from intercepting the commandeered truck, which the guerrillas later burned.

The president of a Buenos Aires soft drink bottling company was released by kidnappers Feb. 21 after being held for two weeks. A communique from his captors claimed a large ransom had been paid, but did not give the sum.

Police in La Plata announced Feb. 21 they had captured a seven-person FAR cell implicated in, among other crimes, the kidnappings of British businessman Ronald Grove and Italian industrialist Enrico Barella. The group was said to be led by Francisco Urondo, a journalist and poet.

Naum Kacowicz, a prominent Buenos Aires businessman, was kidnapped Feb. 16 and reported freed Feb. 21 after a record $1.5 million ransom was paid.

Fourteen detainees, including six accused of taking part in important kidnappings, escaped from a police installation in the Buenos Aires suburb of San Martin early Feb. 24.

Prison doctor seized, then freed—
Hugo Norberto D'Aquila, chief of psychiatric services at Buenos Aires' Villa Devoto prison, was kidnapped Jan. 11 by members of the Liberation Armed Forces (FAL) and released unharmed Jan. 13. The FAL said D'Aquila had been interrogated on conditions among political prisoners in Villa Devoto.

Members of the Third World Priests Movement had charged in a press conference in Buenos Aires Jan. 10 that Argentine political prisoners were subjected to "inhuman treatment." Rev. Osvaldo Catena, a movement official who had been jailed for nine months, said he and all other prisoners had been "underfed and deprived of medical care." He estimated there were 1,200 political prisoners in Argentina, and asserted the families of many had not been informed that they had been arrested.

*Sánchez assassins sentenced—*Three persons were sentenced to life imprisonment and two others to jail terms of nine and 11 years Feb. 9 for taking part in the April 1972 assassination of Gen. Juan Carlos Sánchez, commander of the army's 2nd Corps in Rosario. Among those sentenced to life terms was alleged FAR member Luis Alejandro Gaitini.

*Sallustro killers sentenced—*The special tribunal for subversive cases March 16 sentenced three persons to life imprisonment and seven others to jail terms of 1–12 years for complicity in the 1972 kidnap-murder of Fiat executive Oberdan Sallustro. Twenty-six members or suspected members of the People's Revolutionary Army (ERP), a Trotskyist guerrilla movement, had been arrested in April 1972 in connection with the case. A three-judge panel declared that two of the defendants had been tortured, the Miami Herald reported March 20.

Peronists assassinated. An aide to José Rucci, secretary general of the Peronist-dominated General Labor Confederation, was shot to death in Buenos Aires Feb. 14 by gunmen attempting to break up a FREJULI meeting. It was the fifth politically motivated slaying in four weeks.

Gunmen in the Buenos Aires suburb of Lanus Jan. 22 had killed Julian Moreno, a Metallurgical Workers Union official and FREJULI candidate for Lanus municipal intendant, and fatally wounded his chauffeur. The Revolutionary Armed Forces (FAR) accepted responsibility for the killings and for the earlier assassination of two other Peronists, Jose Alonso and Augusto Vandor. The FAR said its victims—members of the labor sector which, led by Rucci, had sought to cooperate with the government—were traitors to the Peronist movement.

Seven persons were wounded Feb. 18 when a gun battle broke out at a FREJULI meeting in Mar del Plata.

Policemen assassinated. Unidentified gunmen killed two policemen in separate attacks in the Buenos Aires suburbs of Lanus and San Justo Feb. 21 and 22. A third policeman and a civilian were wounded in the second attack.

In Cordoba, soldiers of the army's 3rd Corps continued extensive raids Feb. 23 in search of the People's Revolutionary Army (ERP) guerrillas who raided a local army installation Feb. 18. The raid, the most successful in the ERP's history, was said to have netted the guerrillas two anti-aircraft guns, 75 rifles, 60 pistols and machine pistols, two machine guns, and other equipment.

Many of the Cordoba raids were on the homes of FREJULI leaders, even though the ERP was Trotskyite and not Peronist. The chief of the general staff, Gen. Alcides Lopez Aufranc, was reported Feb. 23 to have warned that guerrillas had "infiltrated" political groups, particularly FREJULI. He alleged that two members of the Revolutionary Armed Forces (FAR), a Peronist guerrilla group, were Congressional candidates in Buenos Aires province.

Prisoners mutiny. About 100 inmates at Buenos Aires' Caseros prison revolted Feb. 19, setting fire to parts of the jail in a demand for better food and living conditions, more humane treatment and an end to the alleged practice of taking inmates' blood for sale outside the prison. Armed police put down the mutiny, reportedly wounding a number of prisoners. No official account of the incident was released.

A month earlier, political prisoners in the Patagonian army prison at Rawson, the Buenos Aires prison ship Granaderos and the capital's Villa Devoto jail had gained public sympathy with a three-week hunger strike, begun before Christmas of 1972. According to the newsletter Latin America Jan. 19, their complaints against solitary confinement, censorship of mail and obstacles to visits were supported by a federal court ruling that the conditions in which they were held were inhuman.

Report on U.S. envoy scored. The U.S. embassy in Buenos Aires issued a statement Feb. 24 denouncing as "wholly without foundation" a Washington Post report that Ambassador John Davis Lodge was considered in diplomatic circles as an ineffectual curiosity. The report also said he had alienated U.S. embassy staff members.

The report, by Post correspondent Lewis H. Diuguid, was published Feb. 18. The embassy said it "ordinarily would not dignify with comment" an article of such "obvious inaccuracy and malicious intent," but noted that two Argentine newspapers had carried accounts of the story, which "questioned, by implication, the loyalty and integrity of [embassy] personnel."

The article said Lodge, 69, was best known among diplomats in Buenos Aires for "his boisterous after-dinner songfests and an apparent lack of interest in political discussion." It said Lodge rarely conferred with Argentine officials.

Lodge, appointed in 1969 by President Nixon, had formerly served under the late President Dwight D. Eisenhower as ambassador to Spain.

Lanusse in Spain. President Lanusse visited Spain Feb. 24–27, conferring with Generalissimo Francisco Franco on bilateral and world affairs. A communique issued by the two leaders Feb. 27 pledged support for each other's national development programs and condemned internal and international "acts of violence and terrorism."

Peronists Win Elections

FREJULI sweeps elections. Ex-President Juan Perón's Justicialista Liberation Front (FREJULI) swept the first round of general elections March 11, virtually securing the presidency, a majority of provincial governorships and control of both houses of Congress.

ARGENTINA

The elections were the first relatively free ones since Perón won his second term in 1952, and the first of any kind since 1965. The armed forces had barred Peronists from full electoral participation since overthrowing Perón in 1955, and had barred Perón's presidential candidacy.

With most of the more than 12 million ballots counted March 13, Peron's hand-picked presidential candidate, Hector J. Campora, led with 49%, followed by Ricardo Balbin of the Radical party with 21.2%. Campora and his followers charged, however, that the military government had miscounted the ballots to keep him under the 50% plus one vote required for a first-ballot victory.

Despite Campora's failure to win a majority, President Alejandro Lanusse recognized Campora's victory in a nationwide television speech March 12, and Balbin reportedly said the same day that the Radicals would not oppose Campora in a second presidential vote.

Lanusse, whose willingness to turn over power to the Peronists had been in doubt, said March 12 that he and the armed forces together would see that "the popular mandate is carried out inexorably." He said his government would consult with Campora and his running mate, Vicente Solano Lima, to insure a smooth succession May 25.

Although a vote count on Congressional races was not available, FREJULI was assured control of both houses of the national legislature, El Nacional of Caracas reported March 15. FREJULI March 14 claimed 136 of the 243 seats in the Chamber of Deputies and an absolute majority in the 69-seat Senate. FREJULI was also credited with majorities in the provincial legislatures and most municipal governments, and at least seven provincial governorships.

The Buenos Aires newspaper La Opinion asserted March 13 that FREJULI's victory represented an overwhelming repudiation of the armed forces' interference in Argentine political life. The Washington Post noted the same day that the parties associated with the military regime had received less than 5% of the vote.

Perón struck a conciliatory note in messages from his exile home in Madrid March 12 and 13, urging unity among all parties and praising the armed forces for pledging to respect the election results. He said he would like to be present at Campora's inauguration May 25, but would not return to Argentina before then unless "things go wrong." The military regime had barred Peron from returning until after power was transferred to the elected government.

Perón had bitterly attacked the regime before the vote, warning his followers March 6 that "the military clique in power ... is trying to prostitute the elections as a means to thwart the people's will and prevent the victory of the majority." He charged "the groundwork has been laid for new juridical monstrosities," in apparent reference to a government suit to dissolve FREJULI, which was pending in the courts on election day. The suit was part of the government's general harassment of FREJULI, which included, during the last days of the campaign, crude attacks on the coalition on news programs broadcast over government-owned radio stations.

Campora too had attacked the government during the campaign, asserting he would accept no limitations from the armed forces on his administration's freedom, and praising the Peronist youth wing, which openly supported the Montoneros and other Peronist urban guerrilla groups. In response to military charges of Peronist links with revolutionaries, Campora had said: "the violence does not originate with us, it comes from above."

In an interview with the news agency LATIN March 10, Campora said his administration would institute "immediate and massive" wage increases and a series of "measures for economic reactivation" including nationalization of credit and foreign trade; cessation of imports that were or could be produced domestically; reactivation of "paralyzed" public works projects; promotion of industrial development throughout the country; new statutes to govern foreign investments, and reform of the agrarian and tax systems.

Campora also pledged full amnesty for political prisoners, and establishment of diplomatic relations with Cuba, North Korea and North Vietnam. Treaties signed "behind the backs of the people, such as the one in New York between Argentina and Brazil" (on the utilization of the Parana River system) would be repudiated, Campora asserted.

Campora victory declared official. The armed forces commanders March 30 declared Hector J. Campora president-elect of Argentina for a four-year term beginning May 25.

The announcement followed release of the official count for the March 11 elections, which gave 49.56% of the 11,920,925 votes cast to Campora and Vicente Solano Lima, his running-mate on the Justicialista Liberation Front (FREJULI) ticket. They were trailed by Ricardo Balbin and Eduardo Gamond of the Radical party, with 21.29%, Francisco Manrique and Rafael Martinez Raymonda of the Federalist Popular Alliance, with 14.9%, and Oscar Alende and Horacio Sueldo of the Revolutionary Popular Alliance, with 7.43%. The rest of the votes were divided among five other tickets.

The count left Campora short of the 50% plus one vote needed for a first-ballot victory, but the Radicals announced they would not participate in a presidential runoff election. Balbin reportedly had declined to run on grounds that a second round of voting would only further polarize Argentine politics. The Radicals said they would, however, participate in runoff elections for governorships and Senate seats. Runoffs in 13 provinces were scheduled for April 15.

The unusually slow vote count was attributed by the military government to a computer breakdown. Campora, however, had charged March 22 that the regime knew he had won over 50% of the vote and was "refusing to recognize its defeat." He warned there would be many military "maneuvers" and "provocations" to keep his Peronist coalition from power.

Campora also warned the military regime, which he refused to recognize as a legitimate government, against making any "decisions that compromise the elected government." The statement apparently referred to a number of recent military decrees, including a stipulation that the three branches of the armed forces be entitled to appoint their own commanders in chief.

Campora, Perón in Italy, Spain—Campora flew to Rome March 25 to meet with his political mentor, ex-President Juan Perón, and Italian and Roman Catholic Church officials. He accompanied Peron back to his home in Madrid March 31 and the two conferred with Generalissimo Francisco Franco before Campora returned to Argentina.

Campora said upon arrival in Buenos Aires April 1 that Perón would "continue to make contacts with European countries willing to collaborate with our government."

Perón had said March 23, on arriving in Italy from Spain, that he would not share power with Campora, but would remain "just a soldier in the ranks." He emphasized that he was "only the head of a political movement. The president-elect of the Argentine Republic is Dr. Campora." Of the FREJULI election slogan "Campora to the government, Peron to power," the ex-president said: "that is just a call devised by the boys. The government is in Campora's hands."

Perón had said in an interview with the Rio de Janeiro magazine Manchete March 21 that the armed forces would transfer power to Campora because "80%" of the officers supported FREJULI's victory. He asserted 20% of those officers were "intimately tied to the people," and the other 60% "are not with anybody, or, to put it better, are with the side that wins."

Campora met March 27 with Italian Premier Giulio Andreotti and later the same day with President Giovanni Leone. A brief communiqué issued after the Andreotti meeting reaffirmed Argentine-Italian friendship. Peron had made a brief "courtesy visit" to Andreotti shortly before Campora's arrival in Rome March 26.

Campora and his family were granted a private audience with Pope Paul VI at the Vatican March 29. The Vatican stressed that the conference did not touch on politics, but it was disclosed later that Campora had also met with two other Vatican officials, Msgr. Agostino Casaroli, the Vatican's "foreign minister," and Msgr. Giovanni Benelli, its deputy secretary of state. Peron was not allowed to accompany Campora at those meetings, having been excommunicated from the church in 1955 for persecuting Argentine bishops and priests.

ARGENTINA

Troops quell police revolt. Tanks and troops March 21 broke into the barricaded police headquarters in La Plata, capital of Buenos Aires province, to end an occupation by about 5,000 policemen demanding higher wages and better equipment.

At least four persons were killed in a brief gun battle after two tanks smashed the gates to the headquarters building. Rebel policemen with machine guns fired on troops from the roof of the building, and troops fought back with mortar bombs. The rebels were subsequently dislodged with tear gas, and 500 were detained for questioning.

The rebellion was connected with a series of actions by policemen in several provinces demanding better equipment and wage increases to at least $115 a month, the amount earned by federal policemen in Buenos Aires. The government had offered a 25% wage increase, considerably short of the policemen's demand.

Police strikes reportedly began in six provinces—Mendoza, San Juan, Tucuman, Santa Fe, Cordoba and Neuquen—soon after the March 11 elections. Policemen reportedly had wanted to strike at the beginning of March, but had waited in order not to jeopardize the elections, the first since 1965. The strikes eventually spread to Buenos Aires and Chubut provinces.

Policemen in Rosario (Santa Fe) reportedly occupied their headquarters March 13, remaining there until March 21, when the government called them to "civil defense service," placing them under military direction. The same measure was applied to striking policemen in the other provinces. Policemen had struck March 20 in Mendoza, Buenos Aires, Tucuman and Chubut, and the next day in those provinces plus Santa Fe and Neuquen. The strike in La Plata began March 20 and the occupation took place early March 21.

The armored attack on the La Plata police headquarters was ordered by Gen. Tomás Sánchez de Bustamante, who was suspected of seeking a major incident, according to the London newsletter Latin America March 30. Sánchez was said to have argued before the elections for proscription of the eventual winners, the Peronist Justicialista Liberation Front (FREJULI). The independent business daily El Cronista Comercial linked the La Plata attack with a plan by die-hard anti-Peronists to prevent the transfer of power to FREJULI, Latin America reported.

The government asserted March 22 that despite attempts by unidentified "political interests" to promote "anarchy and chaos," a civilian administration would take power May 25.

Wave of terrorism. More than 100,000 soldiers were reported mobilized April 12 to forestall possible guerrilla violence coinciding with the April 15 runoff elections. The move followed an increase in killings, bombings and kidnappings by terrorist groups in the wake of the first round of general elections March 11.

Most of the violence was attributed to the Trotskyist People's Revolutionary Army (ERP), which contended that election of a Peronist government would only delay an Argentine revolution. Some observers said ERP terrorism was designed to force the military to remain in power, while others speculated the guerrillas wanted important hostages to insure that President-elect Hector Campora kept his promise to release all political prisoners. The ERP was said to be again under the leadership of Roberto Santucho, who escaped from prison and fled to Chile and then Cuba in August 1972. He had reportedly returned to Argentina.

Peronist guerrillas were said to have halted most operations to insure that the armed forces transferred power to Campora May 25. However, the assassination of an army intelligence officer April 4 was laid to the Peronist Montonero group.

Campora said April 8 that the popular verdict in the March 11 elections rendered all terrorist activities "inadmissible." He had appealed earlier to guerrillas to "think and give us a sufficient truce so that we can prove whether or not we are on the path of liberation."

The military regime asserted April 4 that "nothing and no one will stop the process that climaxed with the March 11 election. The decision of the people will be respected at any price and the government will be delivered to the new authorities May 25."

Army colonel assassinated—Col. Hector A. Iribarren, chief of intelligence of the army's 3rd Corps headquartered in Cordoba, was shot to death by several gunmen April 4. President Alejandro Lanusse immediately met with the navy and air force commanders and ordered precautions against similar incidents. The assassination was later blamed by authorities on the Montoneros, according to the Miami Herald April 8.

Iribarren's murder followed the kidnapping April 1 of retired Rear Adm. Francisco A. Alemán, a former naval intelligence chief and merchant marine under-secretary. Alemán was taken from his Buenos Aires apartment by ERP guerrillas.

An ERP communique April 3 said Alemán was being held "as a prisoner of war" to further "the people's struggle for the liberation of all political and social prisoners." Alemán told his family he was well and being treated "correctly" in a letter printed by La Prensa of Buenos Aires April 9.

Alemán's abductors painted a number of ERP slogans in his apartment, including "Popular Justice for Trelew." The message referred to the August 1972 killing of 16 suspected guerrillas at the Trelew naval prison following the escape of Roberto Santucho and others. Santucho's wife was among those killed. A survivor of the incident, Maria Antonia Berger, charged March 1 that the killings were "cold and premeditated executions" by prison authorities.

The ERP April 14 gave the press another letter from retired Rear Adm. Francisco Alemán, who told his family he was in good health and being treated well. The ERP denied authorship of communiques sent to the press the day before saying Aleman had been "executed."

Other terrorist developments—A powerful bomb explosion killed one person and injured others March 30 in the Buenos Aires building housing the naval commander's offices. The blast was one of four that day in the capital and Rosario. One Rosario explosion, apparently directed against Peronist leader Ruben Contesti, killed Contesti's mother.

Separate attacks against five policemen and assaults on three police headquarters, all attributed to the ERP, were reported by the Miami Herald March 28. ERP guerrillas March 25 temporarily occupied an atomic plant under construction in Atucha, 62 miles north of Buenos Aires, painting slogans on walls and stealing weapons from plant guards.

Gerardo Scalmazzi, Rosario branch manager of the First National Bank of Boston, was kidnapped March 28 and freed April 4 after the bank paid a ransom estimated at $750,000-$1 million.

Pinuccia Cella de Callegari, wife of a Zarate industrialist, was kidnapped March 19 and released three days later after payment of a $250,000 ransom.

Angel Fabiani, son of a Buenos Aires businessman, was abducted April 2 and freed April 5 after payment of a "large ransom," according to press reports.

The technical operations manager of Kodak Argentina S.A., a subsidiary of the U.S.-based Eastman Kodak Co., was kidnapped in Buenos Aires April 2 and freed unharmed April 7 after Kodak paid a $1.5 million ransom. The executive, Anthony R. DaCruz, reportedly was the first U.S. businessman kidnapped in Argentina. His abductors were identified as members of the Liberation Armed Forces.

The New York Times reported April 3, before DaCruz' release, that about 50 business executives had been kidnapped in Argentina during the past two years, and almost $5 million in ransom money had been paid for their release.

A shootout April 4 between Cordoba police and two men attempting to kidnap jeweler Marcos Kogan resulted in the deaths of Kogan and the abductors, La Prensa reported April 5.

The daughter of one of the nation's most powerful army commanders, Gen. Manuel A. Pomar, was kidnapped by presumed urban guerrillas April 5, according to military sources.

Alberto Faena, a Buenos Aires textile executive, was kidnapped by Liberation Armed Forces guerrillas April 6 and freed April 10 after payment of a reported $500,000 ransom.

Francis V. Brimicombe, a British tobacco company executive kidnapped April 8, was freed unharmed April 13 after his company paid a reported $1.5 million ransom.

ARGENTINA

A number of ERP guerrillas attacked a small airfield outside Buenos Aires April 15 and destroyed two small aircraft, one belonging to the Argentine air force.

About 20 ERP "August 22" members took temporary control of the police station, post office and railway depot in the Buenos Aires suburban community of Ingeniero Maschwitz April 21. They set fire to the police station after taking arms, uniforms and documents from it. No casualties were reported.

The ERP April 26 seized Lt. Col. Jacobo Nasif, the third-ranking officer of the Cordoba frontier guard, which had been reorganized to combat guerrillas. Nasif's wife was told by an anonymous telephone caller that her husband would be questioned and then released unharmed.

Santiago Soldati, son of a Swiss businessman, was kidnapped in Buenos Aires April 29 and freed unharmed May 4. The newspaper Cronica reported the next day that his family had paid a $1.5 million ransom.

Miguel Minossian, a Buenos Aires businessman, was kidnapped April 26.

Youths shouting Peronist slogans temporarily seized two railway stations in suburban Buenos Aires April 25, cutting telephone cables and robbing commuters.

FREJULI sweeps runoff vote. President-elect Hector J. Campora's Justicialista Liberation Front (FREJULI) swept the second round of general elections April 15, taking nearly all the Senate seats and provincial governorships at stake.

More than seven million persons voted in the Federal District (Buenos Aires) and 14 provinces where candidates failed to win majorities in the first round of the elections March 11. FREJULI lost only the Senate seat in Buenos Aires and the governorships of Neuquen and Santiago del Estero, the latter two to Peronist dissidents.

A provisional count in the two rounds of elections gave FREJULI 20 of the 22 provincial governorships, 45 of the 69 Senate seats and 146 of the 243 seats in the Chamber of Deputies, La Prensa of Buenos Aires reported April 17. The major opposition group in the legislature would be the Radical Civic Union, which won 12 Senate and 51 Chamber seats.

Radical senatorial candidate Fernando de la Rua defeated FREJULI candidate Marcelo Sanchez Sorondo in the Buenos Aires race, giving the Radicals two of the three Senate seats from the Federal District. De la Rua reportedly was supported by anti-Peronist groups, the Communist party (which supported FREJULI in other runoff contests), and the Jewish community, which considered his opponent an anti-Semite. Sanchez Sorondo, of FREJULI's conservative nationalist sector, was only nominally backed by the coalition's left wing.

According to the Washington Post April 17, the defeat of FREJULI in the capital might be due to the recent wave of terrorism by left-wing guerrillas, which voters had come to associate with Peronism. Peronist guerrillas remained active despite a peace call by Campora. The most active terrorist group was the Trotskyist People's Revolutionary Army (ERP), which had informed Campora that it would continue to fight the armed forces and foreign corporations, the Post reported.

According to the London newsletter Latin America April 13, the continuation of Peronist terrorism was intended to ensure the release of political prisoners and institution of revolutionary changes by the new government, which could not easily disavow its guerrilla supporters.

ITT contract denounced. Public Works Minister Pedro Gordillo announced April 18 that he had asked the attorney general to begin annulment proceedings against two contracts signed by the state communications firm ENTel with a West German concern and a subsidiary of the U.S.-based International Telephone and Telegraph Corp. (ITT).

Gordillo and ENTel administrator Horacio Sidders told a press conference that the two companies, ITT's Standard Electric and an affiliate of Siemens AG, had overcharged the government $40 million under contracts for telephone equipment signed in 1969. The Standard contract totaled $135 million and the Siemens contract $65 million.

Sidders reportedly had denounced irregularities in the contracts in August 1972, but the government did not take action until a FREJULI senatorial candidate, Marcelo Sanchez Sorondo, publicized the charges in his campaign.

Trelew investigation vowed. A group of newly elected FREJULI legislators inspecting the army maximum security prison at Rawson, in southern Chubut Province, denounced the conditions in which political prisoners were kept and promised an investigation of the "massacre" of 16 prisoners at the nearby Trelew naval prison in August 1972.

The legislators said at a press conference April 20 that after the inauguration of the new government they would propose a law to free "all political, union and student prisoners."

Falklands talks resume. Argentine and British negotiators met in London April 27-28 to discuss the future of the Falkland (Malvinas) Islands, which were administered by Great Britain but claimed by Argentina. No communique was issued after the talks, the first in six months.

Great Britain April 27 reiterated its opposition to handing over administration of the islands to Argentina without prior approval by the Falklands' 2,000 inhabitants. The delegates later discussed ways of improving communications between the islands and the two countries.

In a related development reported May 4, the British ambassador in Madrid paid a courtesy visit to ex-President Juan Perón. The call was seen as a demonstration of British desire for a new relationship with the Peronist movement.

Emergency declared. The military government declared a state of emergency in the Federal District and the five most populous provinces April 30, after left-wing guerrillas assassinated the ex-chairman of the joint chiefs of staff, retired Rear Adm. Hermes Quijada.

The decree placed the armed forces in direct control of the capital and the provinces of Buenos Aires, Santa Fe, Cordoba, Mendoza and Tucuman. It said assailants of military or police personnel would be prosecuted in special military courts and sentenced to death, without the right of appeal. It also decreed the death penalty for persons making, selling or possessing unauthorized arms, ammunition or explosives.

Military commanders took control of the capital and provinces May 1, and subsequently decreed other severe measures.

Quijada had been shot to death by two men disguised as policemen as he rode to work in Buenos Aires. His chauffeur, who was injured in the incident, fatally wounded one of the assailants, later identified as a leader of the Trotskyite People's Revolutionary Army (ERP).

The ERP sent a communique to the press April 30 taking credit for the assassination. Quijada had chaired the joint chiefs of staff in August 1972, when 16 guerrillas were killed at the naval prison near Trelew, in Chubut Province. The ERP had vowed to avenge the killings, and had assassinated another naval officer linked with Trelew in December 1972.

President Alejandro Lanusse cabled President-elect Hector Campora soon after Quijada's murder, urging Campora to return from Madrid, where he was conferring with his political mentor, ex-President Juan Peron. Campora complied, returning to Buenos Aires May 2.

Campora met May 3 with Lanusse and the other armed forces commanders, navy Rear Adm. Carlos Coda and air force Brig. Carlos Alberto Rey. No details of the three-hour meeting were released, but Coda said afterwards that it had been "very positive." Campora later issued a statement saying his government would assume office as scheduled May 25 and the armed forces would subsequently remain "subordinate to the national authorities."

Campora's statement referred only indirectly to recent guerrilla actions, expressing "deep concern that national pacification be achieved" with the "normalization of the country" after he assumed the presidency. Campora previously had refused to condemn Argentina's five guerrilla groups, seeking the continued support of the Peronists among them and of the Peronist youth movement, which supported the guerrillas. However, he was reported May 4 to have assured the commanders he would not tolerate guerrilla attacks on the armed forces after May 25.

The assassinations of Quijada and of army Col. Hector Iribarren and the kidnapping of retired rear Adm. Francisco Aleman reportedly alarmed the armed forces and led the navy to press for the declaration of a state of emergency. Lanusse was booed and insulted by angry naval officers at a wake for Quijada May 1. Ex-President Arturo Frondizi, whose political movement joined the Peronist coalition for the March general elections, was pushed to the ground by naval officers when he attempted to attend the wake.

The navy was said to be the most hostile of the armed forces branches to the transfer of power to Peronists. (In a move to reduce this and other military opposition, Peronist officials April 29 announced the resignation of Rodolfo Galimberti, leader of the movement's youth wing. Galimberti had alarmed the military by announcing Peronist youths would form a "people's militia" to protect the new government.)

Congress meets. The two houses of Congress held their first joint constituent session May 3, distributing posts, forming working committees and setting legislative schedules. Members of the Peronist Justicialista Liberation Front (FREJULI) were elected to all the major posts.

FREJULI Sen. Alejandro Diaz Bialet was elected provisional Senate president, and two copartisans, Sens. José Antonio Allende and Americo Garcia, were chosen first and second vice presidents, respectively. Raul Lastiri of FREJULI was elected president of the Chamber of Deputies, and Salvador Busacca and Isidro Odena of the coalition were chosen first and second vice presidents.

The Radical Civic Union, with the largest representation in Congress after FREJULI, reportedly was bitter that the Peronists had denied it any major legislative post.

Emergency lifted. The government May 19 ended the state of emergency in effect since May 1 in most of Argentina. Martial law was lifted in the Federal District and the provinces of Buenos Aires, Cordoba and Santa Fe. It had been lifted earlier in Mendoza and Tucuman following a decrease in guerrilla violence.

President Alejandro Lanusse said after announcing the action May 18 that "no guerrilla is capable of stopping our progress toward national unity to transform our Argentina into a modern and free society." He asserted the armed forces were "genuinely proud" that the March elections took place and that civilian rule would be restored May 25 with the inauguration of President-elect Hector J. Campora and his Peronist government.

Campora had moved during the previous two weeks to reach a consensus with almost all important national groups, the New York Times reported May 17. His statements reportedly were intended to quiet fears of his government among military officers, business associations, wealthy farmers and ranchers, and Roman Catholic Church officials.

Campora said at a Buenos Aires press conference May 8 that "the government and the governed should abandon party and sectarian attitudes" after May 25 and "accept a real political and social truce."

The president-elect proposed a five-point "national reconstruction agreement" for all political and civilian groups. Its points included Argentine participation in Latin American integration programs; respect for the multi-party agreements reached before the March elections; a truce between labor unions and business management; a pledge of respect for the national Constitution; and military participation in national life strictly as provided in the Constitution.

Roman Catholic bishops said after meeting with Campora that there was a feeling of "real hope and enthusiastic community effort" toward the new government, it was reported May 17. Church relations with Peronists had been strained since Peronists burned a number of churches in the 1950s.

The Rural Society, representing the wealthiest cattle ranchers and wheat farmers, also issued a statement supporting Campora. The nation's largest business association supported Campora's recent statements and issued a joint call with the Peronist-dominated General Labor Confederation (CGT) for a moderate economic program providing wage increases and a temporary freeze on prices.

Terrorist developments. Dirk Kloosterman, secretary general of the powerful Mechanics Union, was killed by unidentified gunmen in La Plata May 22. He was identified with conservative Peronist labor leaders who had been under attack by left-wingers in and out of the Peronist movement.

In another shooting reported the same day, two Argentine executives employed by the Ford Motor Co.'s Buenos Aires subsidiary were wounded by unidentified gunmen as they left the company plant.

José Marinasky, a Buenos Aires businessman kidnapped May 14, was freed unharmed May 18. He said he did not know if his captors, who did not claim to be guerrillas, had been paid a ransom. He was an uncle of Mario Raul Klachko, sought in connection with the 1972 kidnap-murder of Fiat executive Oberdan Sallustro. Klachko's wife, Giomar Schmidt, who had been accused of killing Sallustro, had been acquitted of all charges, La Prensa of Buenos Aires reported May 16.

About 20 guerrillas attacked a police radio station near Buenos Aires May 20, leaving one officer dead and three wounded. Some of the attackers also were reported wounded.

Three business executives were reported kidnapped in separate incidents near the capital May 20.

A bomb explosion May 21 destroyed a police installation in Mar del Plata. A communique to a local newspaper attributed responsibility to the Peronist Armed Forces.

The Argentine president of the Coca-Cola Bottling Corp. in Cordoba was reported kidnaped by two men May 22.

Ford grants ERP demands. The Argentine affiliate of the Ford Motor Co. agreed May 23 to distribute $1 million worth of medical equipment, food and educational materials to prevent further attacks on its employes by guerrillas of the ERP's August 22 column.

Ford Argentina May 28 began payment of $400,000 to be shared equally by two hospitals in Buenos Aires and Catamarca. A company spokesman said construction of ambulances for use in various provinces had begun in Ford factories, and $200,000 had been allocated for dried milk to be distributed in shantytowns around the capital. A further $300,000 would be spent on supplies for needy schools in the Buenos Aires area.

The ERP had sent Ford and the press communiques May 22 claiming responsibility for a machinegun attack earlier that day on two Ford executives, and warning of further attacks if Ford did not provide $1 million in welfare donations. The notes said the Ford employes, Luis Giovanelli and Noemi Baruj de Da Rin, had been wounded when Giovanelli resisted a kidnap attempt.

Edgar R. Molina, Ford's vice president for Asian, Pacific and Latin American operations, said at the company's U.S. headquarters May 23 that Ford believed "we have no choice but to meet the demands." The company began negotiating with the guerrillas the same day on ways to distribute the money. A Ford spokesman in Argentina said the military government did not participate in the talks.

Economic developments. The cost of living rose by 8.6% in March, for a total increase of 22.2% since Jan. 1 and 76.5% since April 1, 1972, according to statistics from the National Statistics and Census Institute reported April 6.

The price of cattle on the hoof rose by 20% in February, helping reduce meat exports by the same amount and stimulating inflation, it was reported April 6. Beef prices had risen by 40% since Jan. 1.

Bus and subway fares rose by 25% and railway fares by 33% April 1, following a 20% rise in the price of gasoline March 28. In announcing the rises March 27, the government criticized President-elect Campora for not initiating consultations "on this delicate matter."

The Canadian government and an Italian engineering firm were awarded a $220 million contract to build Argentina's first nuclear power plant, it was reported March 21. A Canadian government firm, Atomic Energy of Canada Ltd., would receive about $100 million to design and supply the nuclear reactor, while Italy's Societa Italimpianti per Azioni would get about $120 million to design and build the plant. The two firms outbid two U.S. concerns and a West German firm.

Italy's Fiat Motor Co. denied rumors that by investing heavily in a new plant in Brazil, it planned to decrease its investments in Argentina, it was reported March 30. A company spokesman said Fiat expected to double its export earnings in Argentina in 1973, and to proceed with plans to invest $90 million in the country over the next few years.

Airline strike—Aerolineas Argentinas, the state airline, was paralyzed May 15–19 when terminal workers and flight attendants struck for higher wages.

In earlier strikes:

Primary and secondary school teachers across the country struck April 17–18 and 25–26 for higher wages and benefits and other demands.

Railway service was paralyzed April 10 as workers struck to protest administrative reforms, promotions and other measures decreed by the military administrators of the state railway firm. The Railway Workers Union said such measures should be left to civilians who would administer the railways after May 25.

Mrs. Perón in China. Isabel Martinez de Perón, wife of ex-President Juan Perón, arrived in Peking May 9 to prepare for Perón's projected visit to China. She was honored May 13 at a reception given by Premier Chou En-lai, and flew to Shanghai May 17 for a brief visit before returning to her home in Madrid.

Campora Becomes President

Campora inaugurated. Hector Jose Campora assumed the presidency of Argentina May 25, ending seven years of military rule and returning Peronists to power after 17 years of political proscription.

Hundreds of thousands of citizens marched in the streets of Buenos Aires, hailing ex-President Juan Perón and heaping abuse on the outgoing regime of Gen. Alejandro Lanusse. About 20 persons were reported injured in clashes between demonstrators and security forces after youths stoned the cars of several military officials on their way to the inaugural ceremony.

Vicente Solano Lima was inaugurated as vice president and eight Cabinet officials were sworn in. Civilian provincial and municipal authorities also took office.

In a three-hour inaugural speech before Congress, Campora outlined a nationalist and moderately leftist program for his four years in office, calling for a revitalization of the nation's economy, for public health, welfare and education projects, for economic benefits for workers and for relations with "all countries in the world."

He defended the record of Perón's government (1946–55) and promised to restore full rights to the ex-president, including his old rank of army general. Campora also pledged to revive the Eva Peron Foundation—the charity organization run by Perón's second wife, the late Eva Duarte—and turn it over to the ex-president's current wife, Isabel Martinez.

(Peron did not attend the inaugural ceremonies, remaining at his home in Madrid in order not to "distract attention" from Campora.)

Campora denounced the military officers who ousted Perón in 1955 and those who ruled Argentina directly or indirectly since then. He charged post-Peronist governments had sold out to foreign banks and multinational corporations, allowing Argentina to fall from 15th to 26th in the ranking of nations by wealth. In an apparent reference to the nation's guerrilla groups, Campora praised Argentine youth for "fighting [government] violence with violence."

Campora also pledged to support an amnesty bill introduced in Congress calling for release of political prisoners. He announced an executive pardon for all political prisoners later in the day, and signed the amnesty bill May 27.

Campora said he would send to Congress legislation to nationalize the banking system and establish state control over the meat and cereal trades. He asserted a reorganization of the country's financial system was necessary to turn the banks into "true public services, so the national savings can be managed by the state and allocated to the areas and sectors of highest priority."

The new president said his government would seek close relations with all nations, moving closest to "the countries of the Third World and particularly those of Latin America." He praised the six-nation Andean Group, offering it "intimate ties with Argentina," and stressed the need to revitalize the stagnant Latin American Free Trade Association.

Finally, Campora reminded the armed forces that he was now their commander in chief, and that their role, as strictly defined by the Constitution, was to "defend sovereignty" and assure "the fulfillment of the people's will."

Campora announced a major shake-up in the armed forces later in the day, naming new commanders in all three branches. The new leaders were Gen. Jorge Raul Carcagno of the army, Vice Adm. Carlos Alvarez of the navy, and Brig. Hector Luis Fautario of the air force. Carcagno pledged May 29 to support the new government as long as it abided by the Constitution.

(In promoting Carcagno, the army's youngest divisional commander, Campora forced the resignation of older generals who had helped oust Peron and had dominated the government in recent years. Observers noted that Argentine officers usually lost their influence in the armed forces soon after retirement.)

Following his inaugural address, Campora flew by helicopter to the presidential palace, where he received the baton of office from Lanusse. Dozens of foreign delegations attended the ceremony, and two presidents, Salvador Allende of Chile and Osvaldo Dorticos of Cuba, stood behind Campora throughout. U.S. Secretary of State William P. Rogers, who attended the inaugural ceremony in Congress, was kept from attending the investiture by his security men, who felt the motorcade ride to the palace might be dangerous.

After his investiture, Campora swore in eight members of his Cabinet, most considered to be moderate Peronists. The key Interior Ministry went to Esteban Righi, a professor of law and nephew of Campora. Juan C. Puig, another law professor, was named foreign minister and Jose Gelbard, founder and leader of the General Economic Confederation, which represented small and medium businessmen, was named finance minister.

The other ministers were union leader Ricardo Otero (labor), Jorge Taiana (education), Jose Lopez Rega (welfare), Antonio J. Benitez (justice), and Angel Robledo (defense). Ministers were yet to be named for the portfolios of agriculture and livestock, industry and commerce, and works and public services, all of which were temporarily managed by Gelbard.

Lanusse, whose retirement from the armed forces and public life was effective with Campora's investiture, had made his farewell address on nationwide radio and television May 24. He wished the new government success, and expressed "eternal gratitude to the men and women of my country in the name of a government which they did not elect but which gave them the possibility of electing."

Lanusse was insulted by spectators as he left the presidential palace after the investiture. Inside, he had been praised by Campora and Allende for restoring civilian rule in Argentina.

Political prisoners freed—Campora declared an immediate amnesty for political prisoners late May 25, after some 50,000 Peronists threatened to break down the gates of Buenos Aires' Villa Devoto prison, and prisoners belonging to the People's Revolutionary Army (ERP) occupied prison offices.

Prisoners began leaving the jail soon after the decree was announced, but the demonstration continued, resulting in clashes in which two persons were killed and about 65 arrested. Most of those arrested were detained only briefly.

At least 375 prisoners from different jails were released early May 26, and some counts put the total at more than 500. Those released included guerrillas jailed in connection with the killings of Fiat executive Oberdan Sallustro, ex-President Pedro Aramburu, and army Gen. Juan Carlos Sánchez.

An amnesty bill for political prisoners was passed by Congress May 27 and signed by Campora the same day. The president also signed legislation dissolving the military regime's special "anti-subversive" courts and repealing the ban on the Argentine Communist party.

(About 60 political prisoners were reported freed after the military regime lifted the state of siege May 23. The measure, in effect since June 30, 1969, had allowed the chief executive to order arrests without formal charges and to close information media.)

The ERP issued a statement May 27 asserting that despite the amnesty for political prisoners, it would continue to attack businesses and the armed forces. It also criticized Campora and some of his key conservative labor union supporters, charging they "did not vacillate in openly supporting the military dictatorship" before May 25 and now sought a "national unity between the army oppressors and the oppressed, between exploitative businessmen and the exploited workers, between the oligarchs who own the fields and the ranches and the dispossessed peons."

Nasif, Aleman freed. The Trotskyite People's Revolutionary Army (ERP) released its major hostages, Lt. Col. Jacobo Nasif and retired Rear Adm. Francisco Alemán.

Nasif, a regional police commander in Cordoba, was freed June 5 after 40 days in captivity. An ERP communiqué said he had been released only after the guerrillas determined that recently pardoned political prisoners were in good health.

Alemán, held 68 days, was freed June 7 after he admitted wrongdoing by the navy in the August 1972 killing of 16 imprisoned revolutionaries at the naval air base prison near Trelew, Chubut Province. Alemán said in a statement released by the ERP, that the killings "were a sad affair," and that the version presented by his captors indicated the navy's role in them was "ignominious." He also asserted the recently supplanted military government was a dictatorship that tortured political prisoners.

Earlier, the ERP had freed an Argentine business executive in exchange for a ransom equivalent to $1 million. The executive, Aaron Beilinson, was released June 3 after 10 days' captivity. He read a statement to a press conference in which the ERP pledged to use the ransom money to "help finance the revolutionary struggle."

Release of the hostages came amid a mounting political campaign by conservative and moderate Peronists against the guerrillas. Ex-President Juan Perón condemned guerrilla "provocations" in a statement published May 31. President Hector Campora met June 14 with 20 recently pardoned guerrilla leaders, and told them he wanted peace in Argentina by June 20, when Perón was scheduled to return from Spain.

The Peronist youth movement also attacked the ERP, with one group vowing to kill 10 guerrillas "for every Peronist that falls."

The ERP, for its part, vowed to fight on against "all injustice and postponements, against the exploitation of the worker, against all suffering by the people," until capitalism was "definitely eliminated" and "workers' power" established. In a statement May 29, the guerrillas attacked the government's attempts to reach a "national accord," and called on "progressive and revolutionary Peronist and non-Peronist" groups to join them in attacking "imperialist firms and the army oppressors."

The ERP and the major Peronist guerrilla groups—the Montoneros and the Revolutionary Armed Forces—held clandestine conferences with selected newsmen June 8. The Peronists issued a statement afterwards vowing a continued battle against "the military imperialist clique" but also pledging to destroy any guerrilla group that opposed the Campora government.

Newsmen reportedly met four ERP leaders, including Roberto Santucho.

Santucho said that "the causes of social exploitation and the political-economic dependency of the country have not disappeared or even been touched by the new government," but asserted the ERP would not attack the government or the police "if they do not repress the people."

The ERP leaders reportedly denied their organization had kidnapped a British businessman, Charles Agnew Lockwood, held since June 6 for a reported $2 million ransom. They also denied responsibility for the blackmail threats against Ford Argentina and subsidiaries of the U.S. firms Otis Elevator Co. and General Motors.

(According to the London newsletter Latin America June 8, the ERP was suffering from internal problems. There was an open split between the ERP majority and the August 22 column, with the latter reportedly supporting the government and criticizing continued guerrilla activities as rigid and sectarian.)

Otis' Argentine subsidiary flew 13 foreign executives and their families to Brazil May 31, after receiving a telephone call from a professed ERP member who threatened to kill an Otis executive unless the company granted its workers 100% wage increases and distributed $500,000 in food, medical supplies and clothing to hospitals and slum residents. Otis refused to meet the demands, and expressed doubt the caller actually belonged to the ERP.

General Motors Argentina received a call June 1 threatening ERP reprisals unless it rehired 1,000 employees dismissed over the past two years. The company refused to comply.

Peronist clashes. Moderate and left-wing Peronist factions clashed throughout Argentina in early June, occupying government offices, hospitals and radio stations in an attempt to prevent each other from assuming positions of power.

The most serious clash reportedly occurred June 7 in Buenos Aires, where Peronist youths and sympathetic employes seized a Culture Ministry building to prevent the new undersecretary, Ignacio Anzoategui, a former rightist, from taking office.

The day before, a right-wing Peronist group called the National Liberating Alliance had occupied the National Commission for Scientific and Technical Investigations and said it would "prevent by any means" the appointment to the commission of left-wing Peronists.

In Cordoba, Mendoza and Mar del Plata, Peronists of various tendencies occupied government radio stations, in some cases changing the stations' names and modifying their programs, it was reported June 8.

In Buenos Aires, Peronist youths seized the building of Radio Municipal, which broadcast classical music and cultural programs, and said the station would end its "sophisticated" programming and devote itself "to the service of popular culture."

Cuba recognized. Campora met May 28 with Cuban President Dorticos, and announced afterwards that Argentina and Cuba had established diplomatic relations. Dorticos hailed the resumption of ties between the two nations as "a gesture of sovereignty and independence."

Campora had met May 27 with Chilean President Allende, who, like Dorticos, had repeatedly been hailed in large street demonstrations by leftists and Peronists. Allende gave a farewell speech the same day on behalf of foreign diplomats who attended Campora's inaugural, supporting Latin American unity on the basis of nationalism, "ideological pluralism" and a desire for independence from U.S. policies.

North Korean, East German ties. The government established diplomatic relations with North Korea June 1 and East Germany June 26.

University takeover. The government took control of the 19 national universities May 30, appointing to each an official "intervenor," or special trustee who would have ultimate power in all administrative and ideological questions.

The action, ordered to put the schools "at the service of the people," followed growing disorders on the campuses because of financial problems, political strikes by students, and disputes between teachers and administrators. Several universities and large sections of the University of Buenos Aires recently had been seized by employes and students demanding that the government take them over.

In announcing the takeover, Education Minister Jorge Taiana said there would be reforms of "the objectives, content and teaching methods with participation of all university groups." He gave no details of the reforms.

Taiana asserted the "crisis that Argentine universities are undergoing reflects the economic and political dependence the country is suffering in the cultural sphere," in apparent reference to complaints by nationalist and left-wing students against what they called foreign, often U.S. methodological and statistical approaches to sociological and political subjects.

Students also complained of the lack of "relevance" in their courses. Medical students protested they had no opportunity to see live patients, and architectural students said they were offered no practical projects.

The intervenor of the University of the South in Bahia Blanca, Victor Benamo, had been jailed twice for political activities, it was reported June 1. The anti-Peronist Review of the River Plate charged "his qualifications are a series of entries and exits from most of the prisons of the country since 1958, most recently because of presumed links with the guerrillas," it was reported June 22. The new dean of law and social science at the University of Buenos Aires, Mario Kestelboim, had defended captured guerrillas, it was reported June 22.

Peronist students reportedly had been split between factions favoring a government takeover and others supporting the tradition of university autonomy. However, the takeover drew no strong protests from students, unlike the military takeover of the universities in 1966.

Labor-management pact. President Hector Campora June 8 announced an agreement between Peronist labor and management groups designed to revive the economy and give wage earners a greater share of the national income.

The two-year pact was negotiated in close collaboration with the government, and was expected to be the basis for the government's economic policies, including determination of wage levels for all Argentine workers. The Peronist-dominated Congress was expected to approve the pact's recommendations.

The agreement was worked out by the General Labor Confederation (CGT), the largest labor federation, and the General Economic Confederation (CGE), a Peronist management group representing small and medium enterprises. The CGE was not as representative of business interests as the CGT was of labor, but was expected to be the main voice for private enterprise in dealing with Campora's government.

The pact imposed austerity on both labor and management, providing for moderate wage and pension increases as well as a price freeze and some price rollbacks where justified. [See below] Like other government economic plans in recent years, it sought to arrest inflation by holding wage increases below the rise in the cost of living.

Salaries were raised across the board by about $20 monthly, and the minimum monthly wage was increased to $100. Family allowances were raised by 40%, and pensions by 28%. A labor-management price and wage commission was proposed, and a more equitable tax system was promised.

The plan also outlined government objectives in housing, education, employment, and small and medium industry. It recommended that the rates of state utilities be increased to reduce the huge losses at which they operated. It also pledged nationalization of the cattle and grain export trades—the country's major sources of foreign revenue—and regulation of foreign investments.

Campora hailed the pact before Congress as providing the basis for "the national reconstruction" promised by his government. He charged the outgoing military government had left the economy in a shambles.

The president promised that within four years, the wage earners' share of the national income would return to the levels achieved under ex-President Juan Peron. According to Peronist statistics, wage earners received 50% of the national income in 1955, the last year of Peron's rule, while they currently received only 36%.

If these statistics were true (they were disputed), the percentage was likely to fall still further during the two-year period of the pact, the Washington Post reported June 10. The pact recommended only a 20% wage hike, following a 37% hike for the first half of 1972 under the outgoing government, while inflation was reported running at 75%–80% annually.

Campora defended the pact's economic conservatism, asserting it conformed to what he called Peronist socialism. "It is not a Utopian socialism," he said. "It rejects dogmatic international socialism and asserts that the essence of its doctrine is genuinely national, popular and Christian."

CGT President José Rucci said the salary increases were less important than "the fact that we have returned to a policy destined to increase salaries."

The plan was denounced as "a complete fraud" by Agustin Tosco, head of the Cordoba light and power union and one of the country's major left-wing labor leaders. "Workers are being offered less than even the military government would have given them," Tosco charged.

Prices frozen—The government June 9 froze consumer prices and imposed price ceilings on 20 basic food items, including milk, bread and butter. It also intervened in six major private markets in Buenos Aires, and said it would continue the beef rationing in effect in the nation's restaurants.

Cattle and beef price ceilings had been imposed June 1. Ranchers had initially withheld cattle from the market, but yielded when government agents threatened compulsory purchase.

The National Meat Board announced June 16 that the government would set beef export quotas.

Banks to return to local control—The government June 15 advised the foreign owners of seven Argentine banks that Congress would pass a law expropriating their stock in the banks.

Alfredo Gómez Morales, president of the Central Bank, said the owners would be compensated. He asserted President Campora would not incorporate the banks into the state banking system, but would allow them to continue operating privately.

The banks had all come under foreign control since 1966. Their owners included U.S., Spanish and West German interests.

Foreign investment curbs proposed—The government June 12 proposed laws that would curb foreign involvement in the economy by limiting investments and restricting bank deposits.

Peron Returns

Shootouts greet Perón's return. At least 20 persons were killed and 300 wounded near Ezeiza international airport June 20, when rival Peronist groups exchanged gunfire in a crowd of nearly two million people awaiting the arrival of ex-President Juan Perón.

Perón, who returned from exile in Spain accompanied by President Hector Campora, was forced to land at the Moron military air base and to cancel a scheduled address to the crowd. He was taken directly to his home in the Buenos Aires suburb of Vicente Lopez.

Machinegun and handgun fire broke out shortly before Peron's plane landed, and continued sporadically into the evening. Several reporters said the initial fire came from snipers in woods near the stage from which Perón was to speak. Neither troops nor police were near the scene, since security had been entrusted to armed members of the Peronist youth wing.

According to the Washington Post June 22, much of the fire was exchanged between rival factions of Peronist youths, who had been bitterly divided over which would direct security operations. The groups, one "socialist" and the other "nationalist," began by shouting slogans at each other and then resorted to gunfire, the Post reported.

According to another report, the shooting erupted when young left-wing Peronists tried to mount the stage to place guerrilla banners in full view of the crowd. They were blocked by conservative trade unionists, who had played a key role in organizing Perón's homecoming. A trade unionist reportedly fired a warning shot into the air, and then volleys were unleashed from both sides.

Snipers and gunmen reportedly stalked each other and terrorized thousands of bystanders for more than an hour, and indiscriminate shooting continued even after ambulances began removing the dead and wounded, according to the report.

Government sources reported June 22 that moderate Peronists, including many congressmen, were demanding the resignation of Interior Minister Esteban Righi, who entrusted security to the Peronist youths. Righi was involved in a serious dispute with the federal police, having accused it of collaborating with the outgoing military government and ordered numerous changes in police procedures. He had also abolished the police intelligence squad and ordered its records destroyed.

The left-wing Peronist Youth (JP) June 22 accused right-wing Peronists and U.S. Central Intelligence Agency infiltrators of provoking the Ezeiza shootouts. It alleged that retired Lt. Col. Jorge Osinde, who organized the homecoming, had directed an "ambush" by "three hundred armed mercenaries" to keep Peron from speaking.

The JP asserted Osinde's men opened fire when one of its columns tried to join the crowd near the stage. It also charged unnamed persons had tried to remove wounded JP members from hospitals, and had tortured others at Ezeiza's international hotel.

Another group, the Peronist Working Youth, also blamed Osinde and other homecoming organizers for the bloodshed. "The committee organizing [the celebration] had been taken over by those who, having been traitors for a long time, had opposed Perón's order designating Campora as the [Peronist] presidential candidate," the group charged.

Perón urges unity—Perón deplored the shootouts and called for national unity in a radio and television speech June 21.

"We have a revolution to carry out, but for it to work it must be a peaceful reconstruction that does not cost the life of a single Argentine," Perón asserted. "We cannot continue destroying, faced with a destiny full of pitfalls and dangers." The nation was living through a "post-civil war" period, Perón asserted.

"Each Argentine, whatever he thinks and feels, has the inalienable right to live in peace and security," Perón continued. "Whoever violates that principle, ... no matter what side he is on, will be a common enemy that we must fight without pause."

Peron also made overtures to the military, stating: "If in the armed forces, each citizen, from soldier to general, is prepared to die in the defense of national sovereignty and the established constitutional order, sooner or later he will join the people, which will await him with open arms as one awaits a brother returning to the united home of the Argentines."

Perón's speech was greeted favorably in the next few days by moderate and conservative Peronists and even formerly diehard anti-Peronists, it was reported June 26.

Francisco Manrique, a center-right presidential candidate in the March elections, said the speech was "a good starting point, serene and realistic." Ex-President Roberto Levingston, who headed the military regime in 1970-71, reportedly welcomed Peron's call for national unity.

Ricardo Balbin, who ran second behind Campora in the elections, June 22 applauded Perón's emphasis on consolidating the peace and assuring legal and constitutional order, which he said had been the main goals of his (Balbin's) campaign. Perón and Balbin met for an hour in Congress June 24.

Campora, who sat silently behind Perón throughout his speech, said June 23 that the speech would be "a constant fountain of inspiration for the task of the government of the people."

There had been numerous reports of strained relations between Campora and Perón during Campora's visit to Spain June 15-19. Peron had not attended the elaborate receptions held for Campora by the Spanish government, and had forced Campora to come to his residence each time they met. Perón's aides said he was "indisposed" due to a digestive ailment, but most sources reported Perón's motives were political.

Some reports suggested Perón was angry with Campora for being unable to restore civil peace in Argentina after his investiture.

In a tough radio and television address June 25, Campora assailed divisive elements within Peronism and "ideological groups outside the law," warning that his government would "exercise its authority to assure orderly change." He called for an end to all guerrilla activity, and issued new instructions to police to clamp down on possession of firearms and explosives.

ERP scores government—The People's Revolutionary Army (ERP) charged at a news conference June 27 that the government was responsible for the Ezeiza killings and that Campora was defrauding the people who elected him.

Roberto Santucho, the guerrilla group's leader, told 22 selected newsmen that fascist gangs organized by "the Social Welfare Ministry under the immediate supervision of the torturer Osinde" had carried out the "unexpected and ferocious attack against revolutionary Peronists" near the airport. He claimed at least 25 persons were killed.

Santucho denounced Campora's June 25 speech as "provocation." He said the president's orders, "added to the economic and political plans of the government, signify a betrayal of the popular will, of the mandate received." He said the government should be modeled after Cuba's socialism, but stressed that Cuba had given the ERP only moral support.

Santucho denied the ERP was Trotskyite, as was commonly assumed. He asserted: "The ERP is Socialist, with a broad program attracting comrades of distinct tendencies—Marxists, Peronists, Catholics, but no Trotskyites."

The guerrilla leader noted that two factions had split off from the ERP but were still using that name. One of them, the ERP-August 22, appeared to have seceded because of the majority faction's intransigence regarding Peronism. Santucho said that group was very small.

Santucho asserted the ERP had been incorrectly held responsible for several recent kidnappings and extortions. He admitted his group had carried out kidnappings since Campora's investiture, but would not say which of four cases involving foreigners were ERP operations. He also acknowledged recent ERP invasions of factories.

Three foreign executives had been kidnapped recently, and a fourth, British financier Charles Lockwood, continued to be held for a reported ransom demand of $2 million.

John Thompson, president of the Argentine affiliate of the Firestone Tire & Rubber Co., was kidnapped June 18 in what appeared to be a guerrilla operation. Ten armed men intercepted his car after it left the Firestone plant in a Buenos Aires suburb. A $1 million ransom demand was reported by newspapers June 21.

Hans K. Gebhardt, a West German technical manager of a women's apparel manufacturer, was seized by armed men June 19. Mario Baratella, an Italian banker, was reported kidnapped June 25 and held for a reported $2 million ransom.

Six persons were kidnapped in Cordoba June 26, less than 24 hours after Campora's speech.

In a related development June 25, Ford executive Luis Giovanelli died of wounds sustained in a kidnap attempt May 22.

Congressman slain—Ernesto Armesto, a Peronist congressman, was killed by an unidentified gunman June 25.

Rightists accused in Ezeiza killings—A special government commission investigating the Ezeiza shootouts received overwhelming evidence that the violence was initiated by right-wing Peronists, it was reported June 29.

Leonardo Favio, a movie actor and director who witnessed the bloodshed, said at a press conference June 24 that the shooting was begun by thugs hired by leaders of the General Labor Confederation (CGT) and by retired Lt. Col. Jorge Osinde, who organized Peron's homecoming rally. Favio added that he had seen prisoners taken by the thugs beaten and tortured at the airport's international hotel.

Favio's testimony—reversing his previous contention that the left-wing Peronist Youth (JP) began the violence—corroborated reports by the JP, Argentine journalists and some congressmen.

The investigating commission, appointed by President Campora, included Vice President Solano Lima, Foreign Minister Puig, and Education Minister Jorge Taiana.

U.S. executive freed. U.S. businessman John Thompson was freed by guerrilla kidnappers July 5.

The People's Revolutionary Army (ERP) confirmed July 10 that it had held Thompson since June 18, and that Thompson's firm, Firestone Tire & Rubber Co., had paid a record $3 million "revolutionary tax" for his release. Firestone declined comment on this and other ransom reports.

At least six new kidnappings were reported in different parts of the country June 27–July 4, and other abductees were ransomed. Hans Gebhardt, a businessman kidnapped June 19, was ransomed for $80,000 July 2. Mario Baratella, an Italian banker seized June 25, was reported ransomed July 5. Raúl Bornancini, assistant manager of First National City Bank of New York in Cordoba, was abducted July 2 and reported released July 13.

The government took a number of steps to end the kidnapping wave, including establishment of a special kidnapping unit in the federal police July 2. All permits to carry arms were revoked July 3 by Interior Minister Esteban Righi, who charged violence was being promoted by "sectors of the privileged oligarchy obedient to imperialist designs."

Two ERP members were arrested in Cordoba June 30, and another was seized July 7. The arrests were the first of guerrillas since the amnesty of political prisoners May 25.

Campora Vacates Presidency

Campora resigns. President Hector Campora and Vice President Vicente Solano Lima resigned July 13 to enable Juan Perón to regain the presidency through new elections.

Raúl Lastiri, Chamber of Deputies president and a conservative Peronist, was sworn in as interim president. He was required by the Constitution to call new elections within 30 days.

The Cabinet also resigned, but Lastiri retained all but two ministers, both identified with the left wing of the Peronist movement. Interior Minister Esteban Righi was replaced by Benito Llambi and Foreign Minister Juan Carlos Puig by Alberto Vignes. Both new ministers were considered conservatives.

In a nationally broadcast speech explaining his resignation, Campora said: "I have always had very clear in my consciousness the conviction that my election was for no other reason than to restore to Gen. Perón the mandate that was taken from him unjustly" in a military coup in 1955.

In an emotional broadcast later July 13, Perón hinted he would run for the presidency, asserting: "If God gives me health ... I will spend the last efforts of my life fulfilling my mission." He vowed to fight for all Argentines and to respect the Constitution "to the letter."

Perón praised Campora's seven-week term of office for its "excellent execution," but said Campora had promised him before the March elections to resign "so that the people could truthfully and genuinely elect the candidate they wanted."

The sudden resignations caused widespread confusion. Some Peronist politicians ascribed the developments to Campora's alleged inability to carry out Perón's policies and to forge a stable government. One close aide to Peron, Hector Villalon, called the administration "anarchic and nepotistic."

Other Peronist spokesmen cited Campora's apparent inability to deal with the broad splits within the Peronist movement, which encompassed rightwing, left-wing and moderate political tendencies.

Since his return from Spain June 20, Perón reportedly had ignored his movement's internal conflicts and concentrated on building bridges with his traditional enemies—the armed forces and opposition parties.

The army commander, Gen. Jorge Carcagno, issued an order to all army commands July 14 to respect the transfer of power, "as long as it takes place within the limits of the national Constitution." Perón, restored to his old rank of army lieutenant general June 12, had met with Carcagno and the navy and air force commanders during the previous week.

A spokesman for the Radical Civic Union, the main opposition party, said July 15 that the party would support Perón in the elections. There was a reported understanding that Radical leader Ricardo Balbin, who ran second to Campora in March, would be Peron's vice presidential candidate.

The principal opposition to Perón's scheme came from left-wing Peronists, who feared the new government would be more conservative than Campora's. A communique from left-wing Peronist groups July 16 warned that a "handful of traitors within the Peronist movement," including Lastiri and Social Welfare Minister José Lopez Rega, sought to take advantage of Campora's resignation to provoke "bloody aggression against the working class."

The groups called for a leftist government program including "socialization of the means of production, popular participation in all government decisions, and a rupture with and attack on imperialism and its agents, thus solidifying [Argentina] with the peoples of the Third World."

Fearing that the removal of Righi and Puig was a prelude to a widespread purge, students and teachers briefly occupied the University of Buenos Aires July 15 in support of the left-wing administrators appointed by Campora. University rector Rodolfo Puiggros asserted they acted "to defend the university."

Socialist and Communist youths had joined left-wing Peronists in occupying the university's law, philosophy and medical faculties July 13 to protest what some of them called "this right-wing coup."

Cordoba labor strife. More than 10,000 automobile mechanics and light and power workers struck in Cordoba July 17 to protest increased attacks by right-wing Peronists on left-wing labor union leaders.

Armed rightists had briefly seized the headquarters of the automobile mechanics' union and the local CGT office late July 16. They also attacked the headquarters of the light and power union, reportedly blowing open the front door with a bomb and firing on the building with machine guns, rifles and hand guns. Union leaders inside returned the fire, fighting off the rightists until police arrived. No injuries were reported.

Agustin Tosco, the light and power union leader and Argentina's most important left-wing unionist, charged July 17 that the rightist gunmen were "paid assassins" of national CGT leader José Rucci, a conservative Peronist.

Rucci had declared all CGT regional offices "vacant" July 1 in an attempt to purge left-wing regional leaders. Cordoba, where Marxists and left-wing Peronists had gained control of the city government and many unions, was considered the major target of the action.

Elections set; Perón, wife nominated. The provisional government July 20 scheduled presidential elections for Sept. 23 and the transfer of power to a new chief executive Oct. 12. The Justicialista party, the largest in the nation, Aug. 4 unanimously voted its presidential and vice presidential nominations, respectively, to Juan Perón and his wife, Isabel Martinez.

Perón said Aug. 5 that he would decide whether to accept the nomination "after consulting with the doctors" about his health. He said his wife would make her decision independently.

Many political observers in all parties assumed Mrs. Perón's nomination was "symbolic," and she would step down in favor of Radical party leader Ricardo Balbin, favored by the armed forces and, according to most reports, by Peron himself. However, Mrs. Perón and Balbin denied such a change would occur.

The government asserted "everyone" would be able to vote, including Communists, and no presidential candidates would be barred. The only person to challenge Perón thus far was former Social Welfare Minister Francisco Manrique, who ran third in the March presidential elections. He announced his candidacy Aug. 3.

Manrique called the resignations of President Hector Campora and Vice President Vicente Solano Lima a "degrading spectacle" staged by "those who wish to inherit [Perón's] power or his myth."

Perón had been under pressure from the left-wing Peronist Youth (JP) to name Campora as his running mate, to assure radical representation in his increasingly conservative circle of advisers. Social Welfare Minister José López Rega, called a "counterrevolutionary" by left-wing Peronists, was the major backer of Mrs. Perón for the vice presidential nomination.

Perón had avoided the JP since returning to Argentina in June, but met with four of its representatives July 21, after 30,000 youths demonstrated in front of his private residence. The JP reaffirmed its support for Perón after the meeting, but rejected his suggestion that López Rega act as a liaison between them.

Perón's subsequent actions appeared to confirm reports that he was dissociating himself from his left-wing followers. He excluded radicals from the new executive committee of the Superior Council of the Justicialista Movement, appointed July

ARGENTINA

29, and condemned young "hotheads" in a speech the next day.

The new Justicialista committee effectively replaced party Secretary General Juan Abal Medina, considered close to the JP. It consisted of Jose Rucci, representing party unionists; Humberto Martiarena, politicians; Silvana Roth, women; and Julio Yessi, youth. The JP professed not to know Yessi, a member of López Rega's personal staff. The Superior Council as a whole represented the least combative sectors of Peronism, according to the London newsletter Latin America Aug. 3.

Perón's speech July 30, to the General Labor Confederation (CGT) leadership, attacked "hotheads" in his party who "think that things move too slowly and that nothing is being accomplished because people are not killed." Perón also criticized right-wing Peronists, calling for a middle course "between these two pernicious extremes," but press sources noted he was joined on the platform by conservative labor and political leaders who had been denounced by the JP.

The JP had urged July 17 that provisional President Raúl Lastiri call elections for the earliest possible date, fearing the longer he was in office the more solidly right-wing Peronists would become entrenched in power. Lastiri was considered conservative and loyal to Perón.

Lastiri warned in a televised speech July 31 that his government would be inflexible with groups which "seek through violence to prevent or twist the unequivocal popular will." He said special groups would be created in the federal and provincial police forces to coordinate anti-guerrilla activities, and steps would be taken to prevent publication of guerrilla statements in newspapers.

Newspapers recently had printed communiques attacking Lastiri's government from the Montoneros and the Revolutionary Armed Forces, two Peronist guerrilla groups, and from the Marxist People's Revolutionary Army (ERP), the nation's strongest guerrilla organization.

Meanwhile, conflicts between conservative and radical Peronists continued in Buenos Aires, Cordoba, Mendoza and Tucuman, where the provincial governors either actively supported or did not oppose the advance of radical Peronists, according to the newsletter Latin America July 27. In Buenos Aires, Deputy Gov. Victor Calabro, a supporter of CGT leader Rucci, had actively sought the removal of Gov. Oscar Bidegain, who had appointed JP members to key provincial posts. Peron reportedly mediated between the two sides.

In Cordoba, 13 unions formed the Cordoba Combative Labor Movement July 31 to emphasize their independence from the conservative national CGT leadership. One person had been killed and three wounded in the Cordoba city of San Francisco July 30, in disturbances growing out of a strike by the regional CGT to protest the failure of workers at an occupied noodle plant to receive recent wages and bonuses.

Meanwhile, Perón, the only person considered capable of uniting the disparate Peronist movement, was the subject of wildly varying rumors of failing health. Reports described him as suffering from influenza, pneumonia, a mild heart attack or cancer of the prostate. However, Latin America commented July 27 that a sick man could not have kept the busy political schedule Perón had maintained since returning to Argentina.

Perón, wife to run for office. Ex-President Juan Perón and his wife, Isabel Martinez, Aug. 11 accepted the presidential and vice presidential nominations of Perón's Justicialista movement.

Ricardo Balbin, leader of the opposition Radical Civic Union (UCR), accepted the Radical presidential nomination the same day. His running mate would be Sen. Fernando de la Rua. Balbin ran a distant second in the March presidential vote, and lost to Peron the last time he ran against him—in the 1951 presidential elections.

A third candidate, Francisco Manrique, Aug. 12 accepted the presidential nomination of the Federalist Popular Alliance, a coalition of seven small provincial parties. His running mate would be Rafael Martinez Raymonda, with whom he ran third in the March elections.

Peron said he had postponed his acceptance for "medical reasons," but leading politicians suggested he had wanted to test reaction among Peronists, the armed forces and the opposition to the nomination of his wife. The left-wing Peronist Youth had continued to oppose Mrs.

Perón's candidacy, favoring ex-President Hector Campora instead, but no other groups had raised strong objections.

Hopes for a Perón-Balbin coalition ticket, favored by the two candidates and the armed forces, apparently were ended by strong opposition within the UCR. Two important Radical leaders, Raúl Alfonsin and ex-President Arturo Illia, and the party's important Cordoba branch had been reported opposed to a coalition July 27.

Perón officially accepted the Justicialista presidential nomination at that party's convention Aug. 18, pledging to run "an austere and responsible administration that will end 18 years of improvisation and waste." His wife, Isabel, the Justicialista vice presidential nominee, repeated that she would not step down in favor of another candidate.

The Socialist Workers party became the fourth and last group to offer a presidential ticket by the official deadline Aug. 25. Its presidential nominee was Juan Carlos Coral, who lost in the March presidential election. His running mate was Francisco Jose Paez.

Agustin Tosco, the Cordoba left-wing labor leader, had declined the Socialist Workers presidential nomination Aug. 16, in apparent response to appeals from the Cordoba labor movement and left-wing Peronists.

Communists back Perón. The Argentine Communist party, recently restored to legal status, voted Aug. 23 to support ex-President Perón in the September presidential election. Party sources stressed their support for Peron's goals of "national liberation" and an independent foreign policy.

Expulsion of U.S. diplomat asked. The Chamber of Deputies unanimously recommended Aug. 1 that President Lastiri expel Max V. Krebs, U.S. charge d'affaires, for interfering in internal Argentine affairs by expressing misgivings about certain economic bills before Congress.

The Senate also condemned Krebs Aug. 3, but did not ask his expulsion. A Senate resolution said it was up to Lastiri to "see if the time has not come to declare [Krebs] persona non grata."

The newspaper Cronica had published July 31 leaked memoranda from Krebs to the Finance Ministry warning that certain draft legislation would have "an unjust effect on the legitimate interests of foreign investors" in Argentina. The legislation, approved by the Chamber Aug. 2, would renationalize a number of banks purchased by foreign interests since 1966; limit foreign investment in a number of areas including exploitation of natural resources; limit access by foreign firms to local and international credit; and limit to 12.5% the profits sent abroad by foreign companies.

Cronica also quoted Finance Minister José Gelbard as characterizing the memoranda as "veiled threats" and "improper intrusion in the internal affairs of our country."

Cronica's report touched off an immediate controversy, with legislators and the Peronist General Labor Confederation calling for Krebs' expulsion. Ex-President Juan Perón took a detached attitude, however, asserting Aug. 2: "It is of no importance to me. [Krebs] is a disrespectful character who directed himself disrespectfully to the government, and it was logical that the government had to silence him."

The U.S. State Department expressed its regret over the affair Aug. 2.

Political sources quoted by the New York Times Aug. 3 said Krebs had written the memoranda in late July at the request of Lastiri, to whom he had verbally expressed his reservations over the draft legislation. Lastiri gave the documents to Gelbard, who returned them to Krebs with the protest quoted by Cronica. Krebs apologized for his action to Foreign Minister Alberto Vignes, who summoned him July 26, and the incident appeared ended. However, the government subsequently leaked the documents.

The Krebs controversy contrasted with the current good relations between Buenos Aires and Washington. The New York Times had quoted top U.S. State Department officials July 29 as saying they had come to view Peron, an old enemy, as the best hope for stability and economic progress in Argentina.

Among other foreign developments:

■ The government told Brazil it was renouncing the agreement reached by the

ARGENTINA

two countries in New York in September 1972 over use of Parana River waters, it was reported July 13. Argentina objected that the text of the pact "permits and stimulates differences of opinion."

■ Provisional President Raúl Lastiri and his Cabinet visited the Argentine air base on Seymour Island in the Antarctic Aug. 10, to emphasize Argentine claims to sovereignty over a wedge the size of Alaska in the area, stretching to the South Pole. Great Britain and Chile claimed much of the same territory.

■ Talks between Argentina and Great Britain over the Falkland Islands had broken down again after Carlos Ortiz de Rosas, Argentina's ambassador to the U.S., accused Britain of "virtually paralyzing" negotiations, it was reported Aug. 24. Argentina charged Britain sought to confine the talks to air and sea communications with the mainland and to avoid serious discussion of a transfer of sovereignty over the islands from Britain to Argentina.

Foreign news agencies restricted. A government decree Aug. 20 forbade foreign news agencies to supply Argentine newspapers with domestic news, and directed the nation's mass media to devote 50% of their news coverage to Argentina.

The measure, dated Aug. 16 and effective upon publication in the government's official bulletin, meant that only the government press agency, Telam, would be able to provide Argentine news to the dozens of small and medium-sized newspapers that could not afford their own correspondents outside their immediate locales.

The foreign news agencies affected by the decree were the Associated Press (AP) and United Press International (UPI). Based in the U.S., both used mainly Argentine correspondents for domestic news. They and other foreign agencies would still be allowed to provide international news to Argentine publications.

The decree also required news publications and radio and television broadcasts to give priority first to news of Argentina, then news of Latin America, and finally news of the rest of the world. However, it did not say how these priorities should be carried out, or how the government planned to enforce the 50% requirement on domestic news.

The presidential press secretary said the decree was issued because the government "must preserve the fidelity and consistency of news and information, controlling their veracity and adjudicating responsibility to those who diffuse them."

The Argentine Association of Newspaper Publishers warned Aug. 22 that the decree could have "grave consequences" and requested an "urgent" meeting with provisional President Raul Lastiri.

Cuba credits granted. The government Aug. 24 granted Cuba $200 million in credits to purchase trucks, tractors, agricultural machinery and other items manufactured in Argentina.

The credits had been announced Aug. 6 by Finance Minister José Gelbard, who had said Argentina would follow an independent international economic policy, trading with all countries of the world. "Our popular government does not and will not admit pressure from anyone, either from inside or outside, from the left or from the right," he had asserted. "We will have a policy for Argentina."

Ex-President Juan Perón had devoted most of his energies recently to developing an independent foreign policy, the London newsletter Latin America reported Aug. 17. Peron was reported moving Argentina closer not only to Cuba, but to Peru (with its "third position" between capitalism and communism) and the Arab nations.

Gen. Jorge Carcagno, the army commander, recently had visited Lima, where he had conferred with his Peruvian counterpart, Gen. Edgardo Mercado Jarrin, in what he later called highly productive talks. Perón recently had conferred with Ibrahim Ibjad, director of Libya's information services, who subsequently praised Perón's leadership of the Third World.

Clashes mark Trelew anniversary. Some 2,000 youths battled riot police in downtown Buenos Aires late Aug. 22, after a rally to commemorate the first anniversary of the killing of 16 guerrillas at the Trelew naval air base prison.

The rally, with an initial attendance of about 8,000, was ending when some youths hurled fire bombs and fired guns. Police moved in, and in the ensuing battle 12 persons were injured and 98 arrested.

The demonstrators, violating a government ban on street rallies, also protested the government's failure to reopen an investigation of the Trelew killings. In another part of the capital, some 50,000 Peronist youths gathered in a stadium to mark the anniversary, but also pledged their support for the government.

The Peronist rally demonstrated the continued allegiance to ex-President Peron of the left-wing Peronist Youth (JP), claiming 200,000 members, despite Peron's repeated criticism of the JP and his approval of the creation of several right-wing Peronist youth groups. Members of the JP and three Peronist guerrilla groups said at the rally that they supported Perón in the Sept. 23 elections despite his selection of his wife as his running mate. Mrs. Perón was close to Social Welfare Minister José López Rega, the subject of numerous obscene chants at the rally.

Lockwood ransomed. British financier Charles A. Lockwood was ransomed July 29 as the wave of kidnappings and extortion continued.

Lockwood was released in good health in Buenos Aires after being held for 53 days. He conceded press reports of $2 million ransom were "pretty close." He added that he did not know to which organization his abductors belonged. The Trotskyist People's Revolutionary Army (ERP) had alternately claimed and denied responsibility.

At least 10 major kidnappings were reported in the press July 21–Aug. 7, four of them in Cordoba. Provincial Gov. Ricardo Obregon met Aug. 9 with local business representatives to discuss means of preventing further abductions and extortion. Business sources in Cordoba reported Aug. 12 that some 100 executives had moved away recently to avoid becoming victims.

The Interior Ministry claimed to have "cleared up" 27 kidnapping and extortion cases, identifying 83 suspects, and to have recovered $4.5 million in ransom money since Provisional President Lastiri ordered a crackdown on abductions July 31, it was reported Aug. 10. More than 100 kidnappings had been reported since the beginning of 1973.

The ERP, which continued its severe criticism of the government, kidnapped an ex-policeman in Rosario July 18 and released him unharmed July 23 after questioning him about "torture and repression of the people" under the recently supplanted military government, and specifically about the kidnapping and murder of a young Peronist activist, attributed by the guerrillas to police officers.

The ERP was held responsible for the machinegun slaying Aug. 5 of the Tucuman police chief, Hugo Tamagnini, accused by the guerrillas of torturing political prisoners. Before dying, Tamagnini reportedly identified one of his slayers as ERP member Carlos Santillan. An ERP communique later claimed responsibility for the murder, according to press reports.

The U.S.-based Coca-Cola Export Corp. began removing its executives and their families to Uruguay and Brazil Aug. 11, after professed ERP guerrillas demanded that the firm pay $1 million to specified charities or face attacks on its executives.

ERP outlawed, Rucci killed. The ERP was outlawed by provisional President Raúl Lastiri Sept. 24. CGT Secretary General Jose Rucci was assassinated less than 24 hours later.

Rucci, his driver and a bodyguard were cut down by unidentified gunmen as Rucci left the house of a relative in western Buenos Aires. The government blamed the ERP for the attack, but there was also speculation it might be the work of left-wing Peronists, who had bitterly opposed Rucci's conservative union leadership.

The CGT began a 30-hour general strike to protest the murder at 6 p.m. Sept. 25, virtually paralyzing the country. Lastiri appeared on television afterward to warn that the government would meet "violence with violence, whether from the right or left." Labor unions, professional organizations and political groups across the country denounced Rucci's killing Sept. 26.

A left-wing Peronist, Enrique Grimberg of the JP, was murdered Sept. 26, causing fear of open warfare between conservative and radical Peronists. Thousands of workers at Rucci's funeral the same day clamored for "vengeance" against "Yankees and Marxists."

Marcelino Mancilla, leader of the Mar del Plata CGT and an orthodox Peronist, had been murdered Aug. 27, apparently by guerrillas of the FAR. Members of the JP at Mancilla's funeral the next day led chants against Peronist guerrillas, and floral offerings were refused from left-wing Peronist officials such as Buenos Aires Province Gov. Oscar Bidegain.

A group of professed ERP guerrillas had seized a military supply center in Buenos Aires early Sept. 6 and held it under police and army siege for five hours, killing one officer before surrendering. Police said 11 guerrillas had been arrested at the scene and others detained elsewhere. Lastiri called an "urgent" Cabinet meeting the same day to consider the attack, and the government later pledged to throw "the full weight of the law" against guerrilla groups.

Professed members of the ERP's breakaway August 22 column Sept. 9 kidnapped a director of the Buenos Aires newspaper Clarin and held him until Sept. 11, after Clarin published documents by the guerrillas urging support for the Peron-Peron ticket in the Sept. 23 elections and sharply criticizing Lastiri and Social Welfare Minister López Rega. An unidentified armed group threw firebombs and shot into Clarin's offices later Sept. 11. Several newspaper employes and attackers were reported injured.

Headquarters of the Socialist Workers party in Mar del Plata were damaged Sept. 30 by a bomb explosion.

Other terrorism—Spokesmen for two U.S.-based airlines, Pan American World Airways and Braniff International, said Oct. 1 the companies had been threatened with reprisals unless they each paid extortionists, identified by police as ERP members, the equivalent of $1 million. The companies, which claimed to have received numerous such threats recently, said they had adopted stricter security measures.

David Heywood, an executive of Nobleza Tabacos, a subsidiary of the British-American Tobacco Co., was kidnapped Sept. 21 and freed by police Oct. 20. Police said they arrested four of the abductors, all "common criminals," and recovered more than $280,000 in ransom money.

Bomb explosions in Cordoba Oct. 9 caused considerable damage to the offices of two U.S.-based companies, Firestone Tire & Rubber Co. and Coca-Cola Co., and a West German concern, Mercedes-Benz.

Peron Elected President

Perón, wife elected. Ex-President Juan Perón and his third wife, Maria Estela (Isabel) Martinez, were elected president and vice president of Argentina Sept. 23.

The Peróns, running on the Justicialista Liberation Front ticket, crushed their nearest rivals, Ricardo Balbin and Fernando de la Rua of the Radical Civic Union. Final results reported Sept. 25 gave the Peróns 61.8% of the more than 12 million votes cast, to 24.3% for Balbin and de la Rua. The two remaining tickets —Francisco Manrique-Rafael Martinez Raymonda of the Federalist Popular Alliance, and Juan Carlos Coral-Francisco José Paez of the Socialist Workers party—trailed.

Hundreds of thousands of Peronists celebrated their victory in the streets of Buenos Aires after the voting Sept. 23 and again Sept. 24. An official Peronist statement called the election result "a national definition: to win liberation from all foreign interests and to construct, according to the Peronist motto, a nation that is socially just, economically free and politically sovereign."

Perón, just short of his 78th birthday, had campaigned little, sending his wife on provincial campaign tours. He admitted Sept. 14 that he suffered from a "pericardiac problem " and had been advised by his doctor to "spend three months without excitement."

Perón vowed in a radio and television address Sept. 21 that if elected, he would seek the help of "qualified [persons] of all significant political parties" to govern. He pledged to use "emergency" measures to combat any violence that might persist after the election.

Perón attributed recent political and criminal violence in Argentina partly to "a political and economic disturbance" in which he saw "the foreign influence of imperialism, which has never stopped working against freely elected governments." He asserted "the revolution we long to carry out will be for Argentines."

An estimated 300,000 Peronists had held a rally to support Perón in Buenos Aires Aug. 31, during a 14-hour strike called by the Peronist-dominated General Labor Confederation (CGT), the nation's largest labor group. The largest single contingent at the rally was a 25,000-member group organized by the left-wing Peronist Youth (JP), which had repeatedly criticized the CGT leadership as too conservative.

Perón had improved his relations with the JP and other left-wing Peronists during the campaign. He met Sept. 8 with leaders of the JP, the Peronist Working Youth, the Peronist University Youth, and two Peronist guerrilla groups, the Montoneros and the Revolutionary Armed Forces (FAR). Most of the youth leaders called the meeting "very positive," and reaffirmed their support for the ex-president. Peron had also sent one of his most conservative aides, Social Welfare Minister Jose Lopez Rega, on a tour of foreign nations to placate left-wing Peronists.

Military & middle-class aid sought— Peron had made a number of moves before the inauguration to secure support for his government from the armed forces and middle classes and to avoid the combined opposition that toppled the left-wing Chilean government of the late President Salvador Allende.

He pledged Oct. 4, before the General Economic Confederation, a management organization, that the new government would not alter Argentina's general economic orientation. He met Oct. 6 with the three armed forces commanders, provisional President Lastiri and the defense and economy ministers. And in an unprecedented move, the Peróns were escorted to Congress for the inaugural Oct. 12 by the military commanders.

In another apparent bid for middle class and military support, Perón Sept. 29 issued strict instructions to Justicialistas to eliminate "Marxism and Marxists" from the movement and from provincial governments it controlled. He ordered all groups in the movement to officially declare themselves against Marxism, and demanded the expulsion of any group refusing to participate in the "war" against the philosophy.

The orders appeared to threaten the left-wing Peronist Youth, but the London newsletter Latin America noted Oct. 12 that Perón was less opposed to socialism than to the rifts within his movement, caused in part by antagonism between Marxists and non-Marxists, and to the Marxist idea of class struggle, which opposed Perón's call for a "class alliance" to solve Argentina's social and economic problems.

(The ambiguities of Perón's position, Latin America reported, were illustrated in his support for Buenos Aires University Rector Rodolfo Puiggros, a Marxist intellectual. Puiggros had been forced to resign Oct. 1 by Education Minister Jorge Taiana, who attempted to replace him with a conservative, Alberto Banfi. Students, fearing Perón had ordered the change as part of a purge of leftists, occupied the university and prevented Banfi from taking office. Perón subsequently expressed his continued confidence in Puiggros, and Taiana admitted the decision to replace the rector had been provisional President Lastiri's. Finally, a political ally of Puiggros, Ernesto Villanueva, was appointed rector, Latin America reported.)

In still another move to insure government control over the military, Perón had secured issuance of a decree by Lastiri modifying the structure of the armed forces, Latin America reported Oct. 12. The autonomous high command of each of the three services was abolished and replaced by a general staff within the Defense Ministry.

Perón, wife inaugurated. Juan Domingo Perón and his wife, Maria Estela (Isabel) Martinez, were inaugurated president and vice president of Argentina Oct. 12, more than 18 years after Perón was overthrown by the armed forces and sent into exile.

Perón, wearing his army general's uniform for the first time since his ouster, took the oath for his third term of office in the main hall of Congress in Buenos Aires, before some 500 legislators and guests including three ex-presidents. His wife became the first woman vice president in Latin American history.

The administration of the oaths was preceded by an address by the interim Senate president, José Antonio Allende, who called the Peróns' overwhelming victory in the Sept. 23 elections "testimony of the vocation of the Argentine people" for peace, "national reconstruction, restoration of the institutions, [and] establishment of a modern democracy with an organic sense and a [true] social accent."

Following the inaugural ceremony, the Peróns were taken under extreme security measures to the presidential palace, where interim President Raúl Lastiri gave Perón the baton and sash of office and Perón swore in his Cabinet, the same eight officials who served in Lastiri's three-month government.

Perón then briefly addressed a crowd of some 100,000 cheering persons from the palace balcony. He vowed to serve the Argentine people "to the last breath," and asked them to help by "maintaining peace, unity and solidarity, each fulfilling the mission he will receive to [further] the greatness of the fatherland and the happiness of the people."

In a special appeal to Argentine youth, Perón expressed his "deep affection" for young people and urged them to "work and train themselves, for [they] will be the authors of the destiny we dream of." Perón's Justicialista movement had long been split between its largely leftist youth wing and older party conservatives.

Finally, Perón pledged to keep in close contact with the people and to follow "the old Peronist custom" of appearing on the same balcony each May 1 "to ask the people if they are satisfied with the government's performance."

Inaugural celebrations took place without incident, partly because of the severe security measures and partly because of an agreement by the feuding Peronist factions to overlook their differences for the day. The only trouble occurred when unknown persons spiked orangeade being sold outside the palace with a nausea-inducing chemical, causing scores in the crowd to fall ill.

Executive units created. President Peron issued a decree Oct. 17 establishing two new executive units, the Technical Secretariat and the General Secretariat, to assist him in his presidential duties and coordinate government activities, respectively. The second and more important unit was turned over to ex-Vice President Vicente Solano Lima.

Solano Lima would be assisted by four subordinate secretaries for politics, military affairs, trade unions and youth. His task, according to the London newsletter Latin America Oct. 26, was to hold together Perón's complex civilian movement and insure the loyalty of the armed forces.

The political secretary had a wide mandate to "assist the president ... in everything related to internal political activity ..., promoting concord and unity in pursuit of the essential goal of reconstruction and national liberation." The trade union and youth secretaries would attempt to restructure the unions and prevent further conflict between the radical youth and conservative labor wings of Perón's movement.

Finance Minister José Gelbard, recently named economy minister, would work within this new political framework, but would retain great freedom in directing economic policy, Latin America reported. His first tasks reportedly were with the development of basic industry, planning power supplies, and dispersal of the population.

Peronist leader assassinated. Constantino Razzetti, a Peronist leader in Rosario, was shot to death Oct. 14, presumably by right-wing Peronists.

Razzetti, a biochemist and vice president of the Rosario municipal bank, reportedly had been close to ex-President Hector Campora and leaders of the left-wing Peronist Youth (JP). He was killed soon after delivering a speech at a Peronist luncheon severely criticizing the conservative Peronist labor bureaucracy.

The leader of that bureaucracy, José Rucci, had been assassinated three weeks earlier, possibly by left-wing Peronists. The government initially had blamed the outlawed People's Revolutionary Army (ERP) for the killing. The guerrilla group, denying responsibility Sept. 27, issued a communique that asserted: "ERP policy is not to execute union bureaucrats, because they are not the monopolies or the army oppressors."

(Buenos Aires television station Channel 9 had been closed by authorities Sept. 28–29 and the newspaper El Mundo had been closed Sept. 28–Oct. 1 for reporting the ERP communique.)

Another conservative Peronist, Julian Julio, leader of a bus drivers' union in Mar del Plata, had been killed by unidentified gunmen Oct. 9.

In another apparently political murder, José Domingo Colombo, political and union news editor of the San Nicolas (Buenos Aires Province) newspaper El Norte, was shot to death by gunmen who invaded the paper's offices Oct. 3. El Norte's director said fliers distributed in the city a few days earlier quoted the JP as charging the newspaper employed "Communists and Trotskyists."

There was other political violence Oct. 4–22, including several attacks on radical Peronists. Jorge Lellis, a JP leader in Rosario, narrowly escaped assassination Oct. 4 when gunmen in a passing vehicle fired on him. In Cordoba the same day, two construction union members were reported wounded when gunmen fired on local headquarters of the General Labor Confederation, dominated by left-wing Peronists.

In Buenos Aires, offices of the JP magazine Militancia were severely damaged by a bomb explosion Oct. 9. JP headquarters in Formosa were fired on Oct 17, with no injuries reported. And in Mendoza, a bomb explosion Oct. 22 nearly destroyed the offices of provincial Gov. Alberto Martinez Baca, who had been criticized by conservative Peronists for not ridding his administration of radical Peronists.

Despite these developments, the JP was attempting to cooperate with President Peron, and the union bureaucracy was taking a conciliatory line toward the leftists, the London newsletter Latin America reported Oct. 19. The most active JP sections reportedly had been working with the armed forces in a program to repair flood damage in Buenos Aires Province, a pilot project which might be repeated in all parts of the country.

However, at least one blow to the JP by Peronist leaders was reported Oct. 19. The Superior Council of the Justicialista Movement, dominated by conservatives, ruled that only duly authorized organizations could operate as branches of the movement. The decision reportedly was aimed at the hundreds of political halls opened by various left-wing Peronist groups, particularly the JP.

Leftist Peronists killed. Three more leftwing Peronists were assassinated as conservative Peronists, aided by their own terrorist groups, continued to try to purge the Justicialista movement of "Marxist infiltrators."

Pablo M. Fredes, a leftist leader of the Transport Workers Union, was taken from his Buenos Aires home Oct. 30 and shot to death by unidentified gunmen. Bus drivers struck briefly the next day to protest the assassination.

Antonio J. Deleroni, a leftist lawyer, and his wife, Nelida Arana de Deleroni, were killed in Buenos Aires Nov. 27 by a gunman later identified as a member of a right-wing Peronist youth group and former bodyguard for the Social Welfare Ministry. Lawyers' groups in the capital protested the killing Nov. 29.

Ruben Fortuny, a radical former police chief of Salta Province, was shot to death Nov. 29 by a former police officer whom he reportedly had fired for torturing political prisoners during the supplanted military government.

A member of the left-wing Peronist Youth (JP) was stripped and beaten by right-wing Peronists Nov. 2, and a leftist member of the Transport Workers Union was kidnapped and tortured Nov. 21. Following the first incident, leaders of the JP obtained an audience with Interior Minister Benito Llambi and Federal Police Chief Miguel Antonio Iniguez to protest the right-wing campaign against Peronist leftists, which included not only murders and torture but almost daily bombings of leftist offices.

The National Council of Peronist Youth, representing the JP, the Peronist Working Youth (JTP) and the Peronist University Youth, issued a statement Oct. 25 denouncing rightist bands which "kill, kidnap and ambush Peronists." It blamed right-wing violence on Peronists who "betrayed Peronism, doubted the return of the general and exchanged views with [ex-President Alejandro] Lanusse."

The rightist campaign had been denounced Oct. 17 by the Argentine Communist party, which had supported President Peron in the September elections. It charged the Peronist right sought to separate Peron from his popular base, and demanded an end to repressive legislation and police action. (A bomb exploded outside a Communist office in Buenos Aires Nov. 21.)

Roberto Quieto, a leader of the Montoneros, a Peronist guerrilla group, protested the rightist campaign Nov. 2 at a meeting with ex-Vice President Vicente Solano Lima, who remained close to Peron despite resigning his office in July. The Montoneros issued a statement Nov. 6 pledging to fight "corrupt leaders and their bands of hired assassins."

As Quieto met with Solano Lima, some 20,000 JTP members rallied in a Buenos Aires stadium to protest the campaign and a projected labor union law which they and other leftists charged would benefit the conservative union leadership. The law would further centralize labor leadership and extend from two to four years the term of office for union officials.

The combative Cordoba Light and Power Union, led by the leftist Agustin Tosco, was disaffiliated by the Argentine Federation of Light and Power Workers Nov. 8 for allegedly trying to separate the federation from the national organized labor movement.

In a related development, Sen. Hipolito Solari Yrigoyen, a member of the Radical party, was wounded Nov. 1 when a bomb exploded in his automobile. Solari had represented combative labor unions and political prisoners accused of guerrilla activities.

In another development Nov. 7, army Col. Florencio Crespo was kidnapped in La Plata. The Cuban news agency Prensa Latina reported the ERP took credit for the abduction and accused Crespo of "collaborating with the U.S." and contributing to Argentine repression. Crespo reportedly had recently returned from an antiguerrilla training course in the U.S.

Campora named Mexico envoy. Ex-President Hector Campora, whose resignation in July enabled Perón to regain the presidency, was named ambassador to Mexico Nov. 9. He arrived in Mexico Dec. 2.

Campora had been under attack from conservative Peronists, who demanded his expulsion from the Justicialista movement for supporting radical Peronists during his brief rule. However, Perón publicly reaffirmed his confidence in Campora before naming him ambassador.

U.S. executive murdered. John A. Swint, general manager of a Cordoba subsidiary of Ford Motor Argentina, was assassinated Nov. 22. The Peronist Armed Forces (FAP), one of several terrorist groups supporting President Juan Perón, later took credit.

Swint and two bodyguards were killed in an ambush in suburban Cordoba by about 15 gunmen. A third bodyguard was seriously wounded. Eyewitnesses said there was no attempt to kidnap the U.S. executive.

The FAP claimed credit for the assassination in a communique to newspapers Nov. 28, and warned Ford headquarters in Buenos Aires that day that it planned to "knock off" other foreign executives and their families "one by one," and to blow up the main Ford plant in suburban Buenos Aires. Ford reportedly moved some 25 U.S. executives and their families out of the country Nov. 28–29.

The government promised the alarmed foreign community Nov. 30 that it would take all necessary measures to protect the lives of foreigners, and Interior Minister Benito Llambi offered armed government bodyguards to foreign executives Dec. 3.

Ford announced Dec. 6 that it would bring back the executives it evacuated after the Swint assassination. The announcement followed a meeting Dec. 4 between Ford executives and President Peron, who promised protection for Ford personnel and installations.

Border patrol troops armed with machine guns and automatic rifles began guarding Ford's plant in suburban Buenos Aires Dec. 5.

Meanwhile, kidnappings of foreign executives continued. David B. Wilkie Jr., president of Amoco Argentina, a subsidiary of Standard Oil Co. of Indiana, was kidnapped in suburban Buenos Aires

Oct. 23 and ransomed by his company Nov. 11. The company said the payment was "well below" the $1 million reportedly demanded by the kidnappers.

Nyborg Andersen, regional manager of the Bank of London and South America, a subsidiary of Lloyds Bank of London, was kidnapped in Buenos Aires Nov. 17. The abductors reportedly belonged to the Marxist People's Revolutionary Army (ERP) and demanded $1.2 million ransom.

Swissair said Nov. 29 that its Latin American director Kurt Schmid, abducted in Buenos Aires Oct. 22, was freed Nov. 28 and immediately left the country. The airline refused to say whether it had paid a ransom.

Victor Samuelson, manager of the Esso Argentina oil refinery at Campana, north of Buenos Aires, was kidnapped Dec. 6. He was the fourth U.S. businessman abducted in Argentina in 1973.

An ERP communique Dec. 8 said Samuelson would be "submitted to trial" on unspecified charges. A subsequent message Dec. 11 demanded a $10 million ransom. Reuters reported Dec. 12 that Esso, an affiliate of Exxon Corp., had agreed to pay the ransom.

The $10 million was demanded in food, clothing and construction materials to be distributed in poor neighborhoods across Argentina "as a partial reimbursement to the Argentine people for the copious riches extracted from our country by [Esso] in long years of imperialist exploitation."

Yves Boisset, factory director of the Peugeot auto plant outside Buenos Aires, was kidnapped Dec. 28. An American businessman, Charles Hayes, was also abducted in December.

The U.S.-owned Cities Service Oil Co. Dec. 13 evacuated three executives and their dependents from Argentina to prevent their possible kidnapping or assassination. The U.S.-based IBM World Trade Corp., Chrysler Corp. and St. Joseph's Mining Co. were reported Dec. 15 to have removed their executives from Argentina.

Two Rosario policemen were wounded Dec. 7 when they were ambushed by ERP members. The guerrillas were not captured.

Peronist attacks continue. Violence among Peronists continued Dec. 13 as bomb and gunfire attacks were reported against two Justicialista party offices in Buenos Aires, headquarters of the left-wing Peronist Youth (JP) in Santa Fe, and the homes of two leaders of the Metallurgical Workers Union in Cordoba.

The Santa Fe attack was perpetrated by the self-styled "Jose Ignacio Rucci" commandos, a right-wing Peronist group named in honor of the assassinated leader of the General Labor Confederation.

The Communist party, which previously had denounced the campaign to purge leftists from the Justicialista movement, charged Dec. 12 that recent violence in Argentina was part of a plan to precipitate "a coup d'état like Chile's." (A Communist office in Buenos Aires was bombed Dec. 15, but no injuries were reported.)

Army, navy chiefs quit. The commanders of the army and navy resigned following disputes with the government over promotions within their services. Observers linked the disputes to attempts by President Juan Perón to eliminate opponents of his Justicialista movement from the high military commands.

The Defense Ministry announced Dec. 18 that army commander Lt. Gen. Jorge Carcagno had resigned and been replaced by Gen. Leandro Anaya. Carcagno's resignation was attributed to the refusal by the Senate Dec. 13 to approve the promotion to brigadier general of four of 13 colonels suggested by the army commander.

The Senate had said it would withhold confirmation of the four until it received "new information" on them. Sources quoted by the news agency LATIN said three of the colonels—Juan Carlos Duret, Julio Cesar Etchegoyen and Juan Carlos Colombo—previously had been hostile to Peronism, and the fourth, Juan Jaime Cesio, chief of the army staff's political division, was close to left-wing Peronist youth groups. A fifth colonel, Eduardo Matta, reportedly had been dropped from Carcagno's list following government opposition to his promotion.

The four colonels subsequently had asked to be retired, leading Carcagno to consider submitting his own resignation, it was reported Dec. 17.

The navy commander, Adm. Carlos Alvarez, had resigned Dec. 6 and been replaced by Rear Adm. Emilio Massera. Alvarez reportedly had sought to have Massera, a fleet commander, sent to Washington, D.C. as a representative to the Inter-American Defense Board, despite opposition from Peron, Defense Minister Angel Robledo and high navy officers.

Massera's promotion reportedly forced the resignations of one vice admiral and seven rear admirals, effecting a thorough change in the navy leadership. The navy previously had been considered the armed service most hostile to Peron.

The Buenos Aires newspaper La Nacion asserted Dec. 16 that the disputes between the government and the military commanders involved "nothing less" than an effort by the government to insure its survival should Peron die or become incapacitated. Observers had said before that the armed forces might take power to prevent the succession of Vice President Maria Estela Martinez de Perón, who was considered inexperienced politically.

The magazine El Descamisado, organ of the leftist Peronist youth wing, had said in its last issue, reported Dec. 12, that the government was maneuvering to "eliminate... the sectors that could plot against the institutional process. More clearly, the sectors that could carry out a coup."

Economic plan set. President Juan Perón Dec. 21 announced a three-year plan designed to double the nation's economic growth rate and increase by a third the income of each family.

The scheme, called the Triennial Plan for Reconstruction and National Liberation, called for investment of $10 million in public works and housing projects and an expansion of exports from the current $2 billion to $5.8 billion by 1977. It would raise the gross national product by a record 7.8%, compared with the current growth rate of 4%.

The plan included construction of three hydroelectric plants at a cost of $2.5 billion, and an annual increase of 8.8% in electric power consumption. The plan also called for a sharp expansion in steel, petrochemical, oil, natural gas and coal production.

Perón told a nationwide radio and television audience that the plan was aimed at bringing Argentina to an "economic take-off" point and "recovering economic independence by demolishing foreign financial, technological and commercial control" over the economy.

Press sources noted that since coming to power in May, Peronist economists led by Economy Minister José Gelbard had succeeded in virtually halting inflation and in reducing unemployment from 6.6% to 4.5% of the work force.

IDB loan—Gelbard had announced Dec. 17 that the Inter-American Development Bank would grant Argentina loans totaling $665 million in 1974, to be used in small and medium industry, agriculture and rural development, capital goods exports, and urban infrastructure plans.

In other economic developments:

China and Argentina signed an agreement Dec. 14 under which China would buy three million tons of Argentine wheat and maize over the next three years. It was the first grain agreement between the two countries since 1966.

The Italian-owned Fiat-Concord Co. of Argentina signed a pact to export $100 million worth of vehicles to Cuba, it was reported Dec. 30. The U.S.-owned General Motors Corp. had agreed earlier in December to sell 1,500 tractors to Cuba as part of an Argentine credit package to Cuba.

Marine disaster. Two Argentine ships collided Oct. 28 in the narrow Punta Indio channel; 24 persons were missing and believed drowned.

Bolivia

8 'Plots' Thwarted

The government of President Hugo Banzer Suarez claimed to have thwarted at least eight revolutionary plots during 1973. Banzer announced in June that Bolivia would have elections in mid-1974 and return to constitutional rule. But toward the end of 1973 Banzer held that the country was not yet ready for such a change, and he postponed the elections for an additional 14 months.

First plot of 1973 smashed. The government claimed Jan. 11 to have discovered a new subversive plot and arrested its principal leaders. The alleged conspiracy, the latest of a series reported by the regime since it seized power in August 1971, was supposedly directed by two left-wing groups—the National Liberation Army (ELN) and the Revolutionary Left Movement—and aimed at infiltrating the armed forces.

According to Interior Minister Mario Adett Zamora, the plot was discovered in documents found in raids on "guerrilla hideouts" in La Paz. The documents allegedly revealed that a leftist agent named "Vicente" was "operating in military circles" in an attempt to "break the ironlike unity of the armed forces." Adett said "Vicente" still had not been identified, but "the principal ringleaders of the conspiracy are under arrest."

Adett's announcement followed a series of arrests in La Paz and Cochabamba. About 60 persons reportedly were arrested in Cochabamba Jan. 10, including a number of teachers accused of belonging to the Communist party and of having met secretly to "prepare actions to disrupt the public peace and ... the security of the government."

In a related development, the chief of staff of the Second Army, based at Oruro, Col. Humberto Cayoja Riart, was relieved of his command and appointed military attache in Washington only hours after flatly denying there were any guerrillas in his area, the London newsletter Latin America reported Jan. 19. His denial conflicted with repeated statements by Adett about guerrilla activity between Oruro and La Paz.

Ex-nun deported—Mary Elizabeth Harding, a U.S. citizen and former nun arrested Dec. 5, 1972 for alleged guerrilla activities, was released from jail Jan. 13 and deported Jan. 15.

Interior Minister Adett said Jan. 13 that Ms. Harding had confessed belonging to the ELN and had supplied the government with information which "proved valuable for learning the plans of the extreme left and the guerrillas with respect to Bolivia." Ms. Harding refused on arrival in the U.S. to comment on the charges or on her treatment in prison.

Friends reported she had complained of being beaten with a hard rubber mallet during her first 72 hours in jail, but Adett denied the allegation. The U.S. State Department said she had not requested deportation or counsel during her captivity, the New York Times reported Jan. 11.

Ms. Harding had arrived in Bolivia in 1959 as a member of the Roman Catholic Maryknoll order, first teaching in the tropical northeast and then doing parish work in La Paz. She had left the order in 1970, reportedly telling a friend she had become involved in political work and "did not want the Maryknoll order compromised." Between then and her arrest, she worked in a plastics factory and later as a teacher in a U.S. cultural center.

The ex-nun said in an interview in the Washington Post May 6 that between Dec. 5, when she was arrested, and Dec. 9, when she signed a confession to participating in subversive activities, she was "kept in a little closet" without food and was stripped and beaten with a piece of wood. She said that contact with Bolivia's harsh conditions had gradually made her a sympathizer, then a member of the leftist guerrilla group.

Juan José Loria, a Bolivian embassy official in Washington, said U.S. diplomats had visited Harding during her imprisonment and reported she was in good condition. She criticized the diplomats for these reports and for urging her to give Bolivian authorities all the information they sought.

Newspapers burned—Leaders in Santa Cruz of the ruling Nationalist Popular Front coalition had burned copies of the La Paz Catholic newspaper Presencia, which had carried a column criticizing the coalition's two civilian parties as inefficient, El Nacional of Caracas reported Jan. 6.

The burning of the papers was condemned by virtually the entire Bolivian press but treated lightly by Interior Minister Adett, who dismissed it as only a protest by the coalition at "having been attacked."

Priests protest government violence—More than 100 Catholic priests condemned the "institutionalized violence that has ruled Bolivia for at least three decades." In a statement published by Presencia Jan. 20, the priests said they had remained silent "out of fear and cowardice" before the "events that have shaken the country," but asserted that "to continue in silence would imply approval of those who usurp the Christian name to avenge, hate and oppress."

The document detailed violations of human rights throughout Bolivia's political history, citing assassinations and executions, physical and moral torture, rape of female prisoners, arbitrary arrests, suppression of the right of habeas corpus, and attacks on freedom of expression and the right to labor organization. It cited the following causes of "the most acute tensions today:" suppression of the autonomy of the judiciary and the universities, "persecution of citizens for their ideas," harassment and imprisonment of priests working for reforms, foreign interference in Bolivian affairs, and poverty, "aggravated by the monetary devaluation measures."

The priests asserted the current government had "inherited a situation of violence and servility to foreign powers," which it was obligated to break.

(A Spanish priest, José Barnadas, had been arrested on suspicion of being connected with "subversive" activities, the newsletter Latin America reported Jan. 5.)

Opposition pact reported. The centrist Christian Democratic party and the Nationalist Revolutionary Left Movement (MNRI) of ex-President Hernan Siles Zuazo had formed an opposition coalition, the newsletter Latin America reported Jan. 5. The alliance reportedly would give the proscribed MNRI a legal footing in the country.

Jet fighters ordered. The air force announced Jan. 18 that it had ordered a squadron of 12 T-33 jet fighters to be built in the U.S. and modified in Canada. The jets, costing $385,000 each, reportedly would be in operation by the end of January.

Steel firm established. The government had created a new, autonomous steel corporation, Empresa Siderurgica Boliviana S.A. (SIDERSA), to exploit the Mutun and other iron deposits in place of COMIBOL, the state mining concern, the London newsletter Latin America reported Jan. 26. COMIBOL henceforth would be limited to non-ferrous minerals. SIDERSA's equity initially would be owned 30% by COMIBOL, 20% each by the state oil concern and the armed forces' development corporation, and 10% each by three other state agencies. Shares would also be eventually sold to the public.

SIDERSA was authorized to set up joint ventures to exploit Mutun, and COMIBOL's negotiations to this effect were canceled. Gen. Rogelio Miranda, general manager of COMIBOL, denied speculation Feb. 3 that Brazilian capital would be sought for the joint ventures. Miranda said: "The iron is Bolivian, and there has been no thought of allowing any country participation in its extraction."

According to Latin America Feb. 2, Bolivia had few visible resources with which to exploit the Mutun deposits. The Mines Ministry reportedly had complained it was starved of funds by the central government.

Brazilian participation at Mutun would be justified in political rather than economic terms, since Brazil had abundant iron ore reserves, Latin America commented. Such participation would most worry Brazil's main rival, Argentina, which needed Bolivian iron for its steel industry. Gen. Miranda travelled to Buenos Aires Feb. 3, and later signed a contract to supply Argentina with iron ore.

The threat of Brazilian expansion into Bolivia was being widely discussed following publication by the Foreign Ministry of details of a revision of the frontier with Brazil, by which Bolivia lost a small strip of territory in the department of Santa Cruz (where Mutun also was located), Latin America reported Jan. 26. The Rio de Janeiro newspaper Jornal do Brasil simultaneously had been publishing reports on Brazilian colonization on the Bolivian bank of the Abuna River, which formed the northern limit of the department of Pando. The newspaper said: "in fact, the land is ours, but by law it belongs to them—the Bolivians." The opposition Christian Democrats reportedly had seized on the issue, charging Bolivia had never exercised effective sovereignty over its areas bordering on Brazil, and calling on the government to take remedial action.

Economic developments. The International Monetary Fund announced Jan. 17 that it had approved a stand-by arrangement under which Bolivia could purchase foreign exchange up to the equivalent of 27.3 million special drawing rights over the next 12 months.

Approval by the Inter-American Development Bank of a $10 million loan to help improve Bolivia's highway network was reported Jan. 10.

Bolivia's tin output in January-June 1972 totaled 10,351 tons, up from 9,380 tons in the same period of 1971, it was reported Jan. 17.

Ground had been broken on a $5 million plant to process antimony at Vinto, about 150 miles south of La Paz, it was reported Jan. 17. The plant, with a projected capacity of 5,000 tons annually, was financed by Czechoslovakia.

Bolivia had signed a contract with the Soviet firm Mashinoexport for a feasibility study for a $30 million zinc refinery with an annual capacity of 50-60 million tons, it was reported Jan. 5.

Two foreign firms, Petrochemie of France and Rosenlew of Switzerland, planned to invest about $15 million in constructing a plant to obtain specialized alcohols from pressed sugar cane for sale in the Andean region, it was reported Feb. 16.

Miners at the Siglo Veinte and Catavi tin installations declared a 48-hour strike March 1 to demand a 66.7% wage readjustment to compensate for the October 1972 peso devaluation.

The Bolivian regime was reported March 9 to have reached a controversial settlement with textile workers, granting them a "14th month's" pay, equivalent to an 8% wage hike.

FSB ousts Valverde. Health Minister Carlos Valverde had been dismissed as secretary general of the Bolivian Socialist Falange (FSB), one of the two civilian parties in the ruling Nationalist Popular Front coalition (FNP), according to reports Feb. 23. The reports were denied by Valverde but confirmed by the La Paz newspaper El Diario March 1.

Valverde's dismissal followed another eruption of his long-standing rivalry with the FSB chief, Foreign Minister Mario Gutierrez, the newsletter Latin America reported March 9. Valverde had recently sought to obtain joint control of the FSB with Gutierrez, openly challenging the party's "vertical" structure, and had disagreed with Gutierrez over the place of the Revolutionary Nationalist Movement (MNR), the other civilian party, in the FNP.

Valverde, a leader of a Santa Cruz guerrilla group during the last MNR government, wanted the MNR removed from the FNP, while Gutierrez saw advantages to using the MNR to counter military pressures to return Bolivia to outright military rule, Latin America reported. Both Valverde and Gutierrez reacted to growing secessionist pressures in Santa Cruz, the center of FSB support, with Valverde almost openly supporting secession and Gutierrez advocating a federal constitution to replace Bolivia's unitary structure, according to Latin America.

Valverde had called for withdrawal of the MNR from the government following MNR leader Victor Paz Estenssoro's assertion that his party had not supported the October 1972 devaluation. Paz was reported Feb. 12 to have said the government should not have yielded to International Monetary Fund pressure for a devaluation and should take "constructive" measures to resolve the social and economic problems generated by the measure.

The MNR and FSB pledged to continue to work together Feb. 19, and held their first joint meeting in the Chamber of Deputies in La Paz Feb. 28. Paz Estenssoro and Gutierrez met Feb. 27 with President Hugo Banzer Suarez, declaring afterwards that the conference had served to "consolidate" the FNP.

Banzer, meanwhile, faced threats to his rule from within the armed forces, Latin America reported March 9. Plotters against the president reportedly included Interior Minister Mario Adett Zamora, Gen. Rogelio Miranda, head of the state mining firm, and armed forces commander Joaquin Zenteno Anaya. Junior officers represented by Maj. Gary Prado reportedly were pressing Banzer to make the MNR the army's major partner in government instead of the FSB.

Adett Zamora recently had embarrassed the government by ordering the arrest of an Associated Press correspondent Feb. 3 for alleged subversive activities and then rescinding the order Feb. 7. Other erratic government actions ascribed to Adett Zamora included the recent release of 20 political prisoners following rejection of their lawyer's requests for habeas corpus, and the publication of an official statement praising a condemnation of government violence by 100 priests and nuns.

2 plots thwarted, Selich killed. The government claimed to have broken up two new subversive plots in April and May. An alleged leader of the second conspiracy, ex-Col. Andres Selich, was beaten to death by security officials.

Selich was reported arrested May 14 along with seven army colonels said to have conspired against President Hugo Banzer Suarez. Other military officers and prominent politicians also were reported detained. The government said later May 14 that Selich had been killed when he fell down a flight of stairs in an Interior Ministry building while "attempting to escape." However, the new interior minister, Alfredo Arce Carpio, admitted May 18 that Selich actually had been beaten to death by interrogators.

Arce's admission caused a furor in the right-wing Bolivian Socialist Falange (FSB), one of the two civilian political parties in the government. The party, in which Selich had many friends, demanded the minister's resignation. Troops occupied downtown La Paz May 19. Arce resigned May 21 and was replaced by Col. Walter Castro Avedano.

Arce had been named interior minister April 23 in a Cabinet shift that followed the government's alleged discovery of the first subversive plot.

The government said May 16 that four of Selich's co-conspirators had escaped from custody earlier in the day in the southern town of Tarija, near the Argentine border. Officials said the plotters, members of "the extreme right," had sought to seize power May 25, while Banzer was in Argentina for its presidential inauguration. They also allegedly planned to "execute a series of violent acts to drench the country in blood."

Selich, a leader of the 1971 military coup which brought Banzer to power, had lived in Argentina since May 1972, when he was dismissed as Bolivia's ambassador to Paraguay and accused of plotting against the president. He was said to have returned to Bolivia recently and to have met with civilians and army officers opposed to the Banzer regime.

Selich's murder coincided with the killing in La Paz of two members of the National Liberation Army (ELN), a leftwing guerrilla group. Authorities said Oswaldo Ucasqui, an Argentine citizen, and Monica Ertl, the alleged killer of a Bolivian consul in West Germany in 1971, were killed in a shootout with police May 13. A third guerrilla reportedly escaped.

Cabinet revised—Banzer had shuffled his Cabinet April 23 after allegedly discovering a subversive plot linked with the army and political interests.

The new interior minister, Alfredo Arce, said April 24 that 20 alleged plotters were being expelled to Paraguay. The Information Ministry added the next day that several other persons arrested in connection with the plot, including two newspaper editors, would be freed as a gesture of good will. Most of those expelled to Paraguay reportedly were linked with the Revolutionary Nationalist Movement (MNR)—the other civilian party in the government—and a dissident army group said to support the principles of the late President Rene Barrientos Ortuno.

The new Cabinet gave the army five portfolios—one more than before—with five each for the MNR and FSB and two for independent civilians. Nine ministers were reappointed, two shifted posts, and six new ministers were named. The Ministry of State was temporarily left unoccupied.

The new Cabinet:

Foreign affairs—Mario Gutierrez (FSB); defense—Gen. Jaime F. Mendieta; interior—Alfredo Arce Carpio (Independent); education—Jaime Tapia Alipaz (FSB); communications and transport—Ambrosio Garcia Ribera (FSB); mines—Raul Lema Patino (MNR); hydrocarbons—Roberto Capriles (Independent); industry and commerce—Lt. Col. Juan Pereda Asbun; finance—Luis Bedregal (MNR); planning—Julio Prado Salmon (MNR); rural affairs—Col. Ramon Azero Sanzetenea; agriculture—Lt. Col. Alberto Natus Busch; presidential secretary—Maj. Jaime Escobari Guerra; housing—German Azcarraga Jimenez (FSB); public health—Luis Leigue (FSB); labor—Guillermo Fortun Suarez (MNR); information and sports—Jaime Caballero Tamayo (MNR).

Observers cited by La Prensa of Buenos Aires April 25 noted that Banzer had dismissed one major MNR dissident and one from the FSB. Carlos Valverde, dismissed as public health minister, had feuded with FSB leader Mario Gutierrez, and Ciro Humboldt, fired as labor minister, had opposed leader Victor Paz Estenssoro in the MNR. The London newsletter Latin America noted May 4 that Col. Jose Gil Reyes, a leader of the army's Barrientista bloc, had been dismissed as agriculture minister. Latin America also noted Banzer had fired Interior Minister Mario Adett Zamora, who was corrupt and reportedly had plotted against him. Adett was appointed ambassador to Brazil April 25.

Banzer said April 24 that the new Cabinet was designed to "consolidate the economic development of Bolivia." Changes were announced the same day in important posts and in the Ministries of Information, Labor, Industry and Commerce, Agriculture, and Rural Affairs.

Armed forces chief fired. President Hugo Banzer Suarez assumed temporary control of the armed forces May 28 after dismissing their commander, Gen. Joaquin Zenteno Anaya. Zenteno had criticized the civilian parties in the government and reportedly urged Banzer's replacement by a military junta.

Banzer made other high-level changes in the armed forces to counter what appeared to be the most serious challenge to his rule since he seized power in 1971. The crisis resulted from the murder of ex-Col. Andres Selich, a former interior minister accused of plotting with right-wing elements against the president.

Army Commander Gen. Eladio Sanchez was replaced by Gen. Carlos Alcoreza Melgarejo and named to the new post of armed forces chief of staff. Col. Raul Alvarez Penaranda replaced Alcoreza as army chief of staff, and Gen.

BOLIVIA

Cesar Ruiz Velarde replaced the director of the national intelligence service.

Alvarez Penaranda's promotion suggested a group of younger officers had succeeded in placing limitations on Banzer's power, the London newsletter Latin America reported June 8.

Earlier, Banzer had named army officers to head the Interior Ministry and the national police, to mitigate the anger of the armed forces over Selich's murder. Col. Raul Tejerina was named police chief May 21, replacing police Col. Pablo Caballero. Caballero insisted Banzer had not known the true circumstances of Selich's death until the dismissed interior minister, Alfredo Arce, admitted he had been murdered.

Gen. Zenteno had said in a press conference May 19 that the armed forces were "very disgusted" with Selich's murder, and would demand the heaviest penalties for the culprits. He charged the incident had "compromised the operation" of Banzer's government.

Zenteno made another public statement May 24, criticizing as "inoperative" the two civilian parties in the government, the Revolutionary Nationalist Movement (MNR) and the Bolivian Socialist Falange (FSB). Banzer held emergency meetings with other armed forces leaders and his Cabinet later in the day. Defense Minister Gen. Jaime F. Mendieta announced afterwards that Banzer and the two parties had the "full support" of the armed forces.

Zenteno had sought Banzer's resignation and replacement by a military junta, Latin America reported June 8. Reports of Zenteno's forced resignation began to circulate May 25, and were confirmed by his replacement May 28.

The government claimed more than three persons had been involved in Selich's murder, and an official investigation was under way, the Miami Herald reported June 7. Three security officials had confessed beating the ex-colonel to death, asserting they had only wanted information from him.

Meanwhile, six FSB members implicated in Selich's aborted plot were reported May 20 to have been given preventive asylum in Salta, Argentina.

Oil discovered. President Banzer announced April 11 that oil had been discovered in the southern province of Gran Chaco. He said initial production at each well drilled there was expected to be 600 barrels daily. In other economic developments:

The government had asked the Inter-American Development Bank (IDB) for credits totaling $200 million for a three-year development program, mainly in the oil and mining industries, it was reported May 4. Bolivia's relations with the IDB were said to have improved under the Banzer regime, which had received $42 million from the bank in 1972.

A delegation from the state mining concern COMIBOL had reached agreement with Soviet officials in Moscow for an increase in the cost of constructing a tin refinery in Potosi, it was reported May 4. The Soviets reportedly offered more credit for the project, which would cost more than $2 billion.

Bolivia had denounced as "an unfriendly act" a Chilean decision to raise by 120% the port charges for Bolivian goods, it was reported May 2. Bolivia had threatened to divert its mineral exports to Peruvian ports after Bolivian and Chilean negotiators failed to reach a new goods traffic agreement.

Mines Minister Raul Lema Patino proposed April 12 that Latin American nations unite in opposing the U.S. plan to sell part of its stockpile of metals. Lema said the sale would cause "grave damage to the Bolivian economy."

The government April 27 announced formation of a joint Bolivian-Brazilian technical commission to study construction of a gas pipeline in which the two countries would invest a total of $100 million.

Mexico would invest some $26 million to build two cement factories in Bolivia with an annual capacity of 800,000 tons, it was reported April 13. The financing would come largely from the U.S.

The government May 2 granted a national holidays wage bonus to workers in factories and commerce to compensate for the October 1972 peso devaluation.

Bank strike. Employes of banks and insurance agencies struck across Bolivia April 24. A major strike demand was satisfied the same day when the managing director of the Bolivian Agrarian Bank,

Luis Mayser, resigned. A commission from the Finance and Labor Ministries was formed to resolve the conflict.

Tin crisis. The economy was seriously threatened by a crisis in the major tin smelting firm—the British concern William Harvey—and the sale by the U.S. of its tin stockpiles, El Nacional of Caracas reported June 10.

William Harvey, which smelted about 35 per cent of Bolivia's tin, was reported close to bankruptcy. The gravity of the situation had prompted a trip to London by Gen. Rogelio Miranda, head of the state mining concern COMIBOL, and Mines Minister Raul Lema Patino. Bolivia was ill-equipped to absorb William Harvey's smelting load, since national smelters at present could process less than a quarter of the total tin production.

The U.S. stockpiles sale, which began June 7, reportedly threatened to lower international tin prices. COMIBOL sources said a price drop of only 1c would cause the firm losses of $400,000. The stockpiles sale was criticized as "economic aggression" against Bolivia by a federation representing 25,000 mine workers June 7.

Torres in Argentina. Ex-President Juan Jose Torres, overthrown by Banzer in 1971, had met in Buenos Aires with Argentine President Hector Campora shortly before Campora's inauguration, Latin America reported June 8. Torres and other opponents of Banzer in exile reportedly had been encouraged by Campora's political mentor, ex-President Juan Peron.

While in Buenos Aires, Torres had called for formation of a National Left Alliance to combat the Banzer regime. Torres reportedly had adopted a more revolutionary ideology, and had the backing of the organization of young Bolivian army officers in exile.

Church group denounces government. The Bolivian Justice and Peace Commission, a Roman Catholic Church group, issued a report condemning the Banzer regime for systematically violating "the sacred rights of families, democratic institutions and individuals," and seeking to eliminate "every gesture implying freedom."

The document, as translated and published in the June 21 issue of Latinamerica Press, of Lima, Peru, charged Bolivian government repression was "not only harsh and indiscriminate, but permanent . . . Night after night houses are searched without benefit of the necessary signed authorization of a judge. The arrests based on mere suspicion or verbal accusations, the threats and the long periods during which those who are arrested are held incommunicado, have become almost daily affairs."

There were about 300 political prisoners in Bolivia, some 30 of them women, according to the report. In addition, the government reportedly had exiled 350 political prisoners, and some 5,000 others had left the country to escape political persecution.

In the past 20 months, the document charged, "more than 2,000 people have passed through Bolivian prisons for political reasons. The majority of them, after long questioning and much suffering, have been banished from the country . . . It is estimated that approximately 20 have died in prison due to torture and bad treatment." Several women testified that they had been raped in prison, and one man told of having a forced vasectomy, according to the report.

Prison conditions were bad, with small, cold, humid cells, and prisoners frequently became ill "due to the lack of adequate sanitary and hygienic facilities," the report charged.

The commission said it had been unable to carry out a full investigation of its subject because "political prisoners are not held in regular prisons but in so-called security houses. The location of these houses is known only after some macabre event takes place there and the public learns about it."

In a related development June 13, more than 100 mothers, wives and daughters of political prisoners demonstrated before the Interior Ministry in La Paz, offering themselves as "voluntary detainees and hostages" to secure legal trials for their relatives.

'74 elections planned. President Hugo Banzer Suarez, in a surprise announcement June 22, said the nation would return to constitutional rule through elections planned for 1974.

In a nationwide radio and television address, Banzer said concrete measures to implement this decision would be announced in the next few months. In the meantime he would appoint a commission to study electoral reforms to "channel aspirations for popular participation appropriate to this time."

The statement was hailed by ex-President Victor Paz Estenssoro, leader of the Revolutionary Nationalist Movement (MNR), which with the right-wing Bolivian Socialist Falange (FSB) formed the ruling Nationalist Popular Front (FPN). Paz Estenssoro said the MNR would decide at a meeting in the near future whether to run its own presidential candidate.

Banzer did not say whether he would be a candidate for the presidency, but the Cochabamba branch of the FPN said it would nominate him to as a "guarantee of the continuity" of the "process" begun with Banzer's military coup in August 1971. Foreign Minister and FSB leader Mario Gutierrez said July 5, after meeting with Banzer, Paz Estenssoro and Interior Minister Walter Castro, that the nation "yearned" for the president's candidacy.

A spokesman for the Left Revolutionary Nationalist Movement (MNRI) said Aug. 1 that ex-President Hernan Siles Zuazo would be the party's presidential candidate. Siles, a former MNR official, ruled Bolivia in 1956–60.

The Christian Democratic party June 27 proposed a "minimal political action plan" to unify all groups on the left. Its provisions included defense of natural resources, a substantial rise in the living standards of the poor, establishment of "participatory democracy," respect for constitutional liberties, and social mobilization led by a labor union movement serving "national and social interests."

Press sources described the planning of elections as a skillful move by Banzer to relieve political tensions, heightened by a recent aborted military coup, the murder of ex-Col. Andres Selich, conflicts between the MNR and FSB, and the internal split in the FSB.

Valverde plot charged. The government claimed Aug. 18 it had crushed a planned uprising against Banzer by right-wing dissidents of the FSB, led by ex-Health Minister Carlos Valverde.

Interior Minister Castro said the rebellion was to have taken place during a planned visit by Banzer to Santa Cruz, where secessionist feelings were strong. He linked the plot to Bolivian exiles in Chile and Peru, and asserted it had been infiltrated by extremists of both the right and the left. Castro added that the plotters had sought support from young army officers, but the officers had refused.

Valverde, a guerrilla leader during the last MNR government, was reported Aug. 18 to have dug in at a farm outside Santa Cruz with some 190 armed followers. Troops were sent from La Paz to the area, and the subversives reportedly fled the next day. Valverde was reported in Paraguay Aug. 21.

Anti-government exiles meeting in Caracas, Venezuela said Aug. 19 that the rebellion was of no importance, resulting as it did from internal rifts in the government, United Press International reported.

Valverde had announced June 21 that he was assuming the FSB leadership, in view of recent repudiations of party chief Gutierrez by several FSB regional organizations, including those of La Paz, Oruro and Tarija.

The La Paz organization had published a statement June 18 denouncing Gutierrez for "his incapacity to lead the party, for having ended his mandate, for being divisionist, and for continued abuses of authority which threaten the survival of the party."

Valverde's and the regional organizations' actions were condemned June 22 by FPN Secretary General Jaime Ponce Caballero, the FSB representative to the coalition, who asserted Gutierrez was the party's only leader. Ponce described Valverde's action as "hysterical" and motivated by "appetite for power."

Gutierrez, who had declined June 7 to stand for re-election to the FSB presidency, was nonetheless re-elected by acclamation at the party's convention in La Paz Aug. 11.

Officers ousted in Valverde 'plot'—The armed forces chief of staff, Gen. Eladio Sanchez, announced Aug. 22 that five military officers had been dismissed in Santa Cruz and three arrested in Cochabamba in connection with the alleged coup attempt by exiled FSB leader Carlos Valverde.

The officers dismissed were the commander of the army's 8th Division, Col. Armando Alvarez; the commander of its Manchego regiment, Col. Mario Serrate; the military aviation college commander, Col. Hugo Munoz; the departmental chief of intelligence, Frigate Capt. Juan Carlos Dorado; and the department's presidential coordinator, Capt. Ruddy Landivar.

The officers under arrest and facing courts martial were Maj. Humberto Campos and Capt. Rolando Saravia, former aides-de-camp of President Banzer, and a third man whose name Sanchez could not remember. All were arrested Aug. 19.

Valverde, whose flight to Paraguay was confirmed in Asuncion Aug. 27, denied conspiring against Banzer. In a letter printed in the Cochabamba newspaper Los Tiempos Aug. 29, he called the coup allegations "a pantomime mounted to seize the people who follow me," and accused the government of seeking "to take me out of circulation and perhaps assassinate me."

Valverde noted that a statement by Minister of State Waldo Cerruto Aug. 19 contradicted Interior Minister Castro's assertion the previous day that Valverde and 190 followers had dug in at the La Perseverancia cotton hacienda outside Santa Cruz. Cerruto said Valverde had at most 40 men with him, and authorities did not know if they had stopped at La Perseverancia.

Valverde's denial was supported by his wife, his father, the La Perseverancia manager, and a Santa Cruz women's civic group which had offered to mediate but was unable to find any alleged conspirators either at La Perseverancia or neighboring farms.

Cabinet revised. President Hugo Banzer Suarez revised his Cabinet Sept. 10 in an apparent attempt to control squabbling within the ruling Nationalist Popular Front coalition (FPN) before the projected 1974 general elections.

Banzer unexpectedly asked all ministers to resign Sept. 7 to give him "freedom of action to conduct the cleanest elections in Bolivian history." The request followed new flare-ups of the rivalry between the FPN's two civilian parties, the Revolutionary Nationalist Movement (MNR) and the Bolivian Socialist Falange (FSB).

The latest conflict concerned the MNR's apparent determination to run its own slate of congressional candidates in the elections, rather than join in a single FPN slate, as the FSB proposed. Both parties appeared ready to support Banzer's presidential candidacy.

The FSB leader, Foreign Minister Mario Gutierrez, proposed Aug. 30 that Banzer appoint military officers to head the Finance and Labor Ministries, controlled then and after the Cabinet shuffle by the MNR. He reportedly made it clear he did not want the MNR controlling economic and social institutions immediately before the elections. The proposal drew an angry reply from MNR leader Victor Paz Estenssoro, who asserted his party could win "without any ministries," provided the armed forces dismantled the "Berlin wall" they had erected against political activity among mine workers and peasants.

An aide to Gutierrez, Gustavo Stumpff, Sept. 7 rejected the MNR's contention that it had the largest following in Bolivia. Stumpff asserted: "When we made the nationalist revolution, ... quantitative calculations showed 100 Falangist combatants for each from the MNR, and it was the success of that revolution, commanded by Gen. Banzer and our chief Mario Gutierrez, which brought the MNR into the government."

Banzer appointed four new Cabinet ministers, all from the MNR, and kept the old Cabinet's balance of six military ministers, five MNR, five FSB and two independents.

The Cabinet:

Interior—Col. Walter Castro Avedano; foreign affairs—Mario Gutierrez (FSB); finance—Armando Pinel (MNR); information—Ramiro Arzabe (MNR); health—Luis Leigue Suarez (FSB); mining—Javier Bedregal (MNR); education—Jaime Tapia Alipaz (FSB); labor—

Angel Jemio Ergueta (MNR); transport & communications—Ambrosio Garcia (FSB); industry & commerce—Col. Juan Pereda Asbun; housing—Germán Azcarraga (FSB); planning—Julio Prado Salmon (MNR); defense—Gen. Jaime Mendieta; agriculture—Col. Alberto Natusch Busch; rural affairs—Col. Ramón Azero; energy & hydrocarbons—Roberto Capriles (independent); state—Waldo Cerruto (independent); presidential secretary—Maj. Mario Escobar.

In addition to the MNR-FSB split, Banzer faced some military opposition to the participation of the two parties in the government. Officers organized in the Staff of Young Officers had issued two documents calling for an outright military takeover, on grounds the MNR and FSB were anachronistic and corrupt, the London newsletter Latin America reported Sept. 14. The first document was published in La Paz and Cochabamba, but the second was banned by the government.

Further opposition came from Bolivia's 50,000 miners, whose delegates held a meeting in La Paz to announce reconstitution of the Bolivian Labor Federation (COB), banned since Banzer's military coup in 1971. Miners' delegates described the government as fascist, and said its economic policies favored multinational companies and encouraged the invasion of Brazilian firms financed by the U.S., Latin America reported Sept. 14. The delegates said they would fight for nationalization of the U.S.-based W.R. Grace mines.

Newspaper, radio strike. Privately owned newspapers and radio stations throughout the country struck Aug. 6–8 to protest alleged police brutality in a raid Aug. 4 on the independent newspaper Nueva Jornada. The Labor Ministry declared the strike illegal, but no action against the strikers was reported.

The raid on Nueva Jornada, ordered by a La Paz court, was to retrieve government-owned machinery used by the newspaper.

IDB oil loan. The Inter-American Development Bank Sept. 21 approved a $46.5 million loan to the state oil firm YPFB to increase its refining capacity from 21,000 barrels a day to 41,500 barrels a day by 1978.

'Leftist plot' crushed. The government announced late Sept. 23 that it had crushed an alleged left-wing plot against President Banzer and that 89 political and labor union leaders had been arrested in La Paz, Cochabamba, Santa Cruz and Oruro.

Interior Minister Walter Castro said the alleged conspiracy, by exiled Bolivians and radicals from Cuba, Chile, Argentina and other countries, was "a desperate action by the extreme left to try and regain ground on the continent" following the overthrow of the late Chilean President Salvador Allende Gossens.

Castro claimed the conspirators included ex-Presidents Hernan Siles Zuazo—to have been installed as president after Banzer's ouster—and Juan Jose Torres, as well as labor leader Juan Lechin Oquendo and ex-guerrilla leader Oswaldo "Chato" Peredo, all currently in exile. Siles denied particiation in the alleged plot Sept. 27, asserting in a letter to the Bolivian press that he had spent the previous two weeks in Santiago, Chile, helping exiled Bolivians there in the aftermath of the Chilean military coup.

Officials said Salustio Choque, a conspirator and former member of the Bolivian guerrilla group led by the late Ernesto "Che" Guevara, had been arrested Sept. 22, and arms were found in his house.

Thousands of bank and insurance clerks went on strike Sept. 24 to protest the arrest of their union leader, Mario Paz Soldan, and other labor leaders in connection with the alleged conspiracy. They were joined Sept. 25 by at least 25,000 factory workers in La Paz and Cochabamba. The bank employes returned to work Sept. 26, after the government threatened them with dismissal, but a number of their leaders began a hunger strike to last until Paz Soldan's release. Activities in La Paz were reported back to normal Sept. 27, but there were staggered stoppages that day in five other cities to demand the release of all labor leaders jailed Sept. 23.

Strike leaders denied any plotting against Banzer, asserting "the people and the workers do not believe in any conspiratorial plan," according to reports Sept. 26. They accused the government of trying to "decapitate Bolivia's organized labor movement."

Castro held a second press conference Sept. 26 to give more details of the alleged plot. He said the government had obtained from a Communist party member, at a "high" cost, a 13-page "operating plan" that included projected subversion in La Paz and other cities, simultaneous invasions from Chile and Argentina, and flying in of arms to Santa Cruz and Beni departments in planes with Cuban registrations.

Castro asserted the plotters, including members of Argentina's outlawed People's Revolutionary Army, had founded the Nationalist Left Liberation Alliance, with headquarters in Santiago and in Salta, Argentina. He said they planned to make Siles interim president of Bolivia and then to remove him and institute socialism in the country.

2 more plots foiled. Interior Minister Walter Castro claimed Oct. 31 that the government had thwarted two subversive plots and arrested their leaders.

One plot, described by Castro as "rightist," was allegedly led by ex-army Maj. Elias Belmonte, a member of the National Action Movement. The other, ascribed no ideological orientation, was supposedly led by three moderate politicians—Julio Prado Salmon, an MNR member dismissed as planning minister Oct. 5; Anibal Michel, an MNR executive board member; and Benjamin Miguel, leader of the Christian Democratic party.

The four alleged plotters reportedly were arrested Oct. 30. Prado Salmon was reported released Nov. 3, and Miguel Nov. 4. Belmonte and Michel were expelled to Paraguay, according to the Interior Ministry Nov. 4.

Prado Salmon had openly criticized the government's economic policies since his dismissal from the Cabinet, and Miguel reportedly had embarrassed the government with articles on the economic situation in the Catholic newspaper Presencia.

In a related development Nov. 4, Defense Minister Mendieta announced that the army intelligence chief, Gen. Cesar Ruiz Velarde, had been forced into retirement. It was reported Nov. 9 that Ruiz had been placed under virtual house arrest in a remote township in Beni department.

Miners re-elect Lechin. The 15th national congress of the Bolivian Mine Workers Federation ended early Nov. 20 with the re-election of Juan Lechin Oquendo as the federation's executive secretary, Victor Lopez Arias as secretary general, and Simon Reyes as secretary for relations.

The three leaders had been in exile since the 1971 military coup that ousted President Juan Jose Torres and installed President Banzer.

'74 elections postponed. President Hugo Banzer Suarez announced Dec. 20 that the general elections scheduled for June 1974 would be postponed until August 1975 because Bolivia was not yet ready for a return to constitutional rule.

The postponement was demanded by Defense Minister Jaime Mendieta and the armed forces commanders Dec. 4.

Banzer had announced Nov. 26 that he would not seek the presidency in the 1974 vote, as previously expected. This action too was reportedly demanded by the military, who were described as dissatisfied with the widespread corruption and economic mismanagement in Banzer's government, and the participation in it of two feuding civilian political parties, the Revolutionary Nationalist Movement (MNR) and the Bolivian Socialist Falange (FSB).

Banzer also shuffled his Cabinet Nov. 26, appointing five new ministers including two MNR dissidents opposed to party leader Victor Paz Estenssoro. The two were Raul Lema Patino, named mines minister, and Alfredo Franco, labor minister.

The MNR lost the Finance Ministry to an independent, Jaime Quiroga, whom it reportedly considered a representative of private enterprise. The FSB lost the Foreign Ministry as party leader Mario Gutierrez was replaced by Brig. Gen. Alberto Guzman. Gutierrez recently had called the FSB-MNR coalition "inoperative."

Paz Estenssoro announced Nov. 27 that the MNR was leaving the government "to take its distance" from it and presumably to build a separate popular base for the 1974 elections. However, the move only split the party as most MNR members chose to remain in their posts.

Brazil

Guerrilla group reported smashed. Authorities announced Jan. 10 that security forces had virtually "dismantled" the Popular Revolutionary Vanguard, an urban guerrilla movement once considered the best-organized in Brazil.

Security sources said six alleged Vanguard terrorists, including two foreign women, had been killed in shootouts in Paulista, eight miles north of Recife. The Vanguard movement, they said, had been preparing for a national congress at Paulista, where a guerrilla training center reportedly had been set up.

The Vanguard was said to have kidnapped several foreign diplomats in Brazil, including West German Ambassador Ehrenfried von Holleben in 1970. Von Holleben was freed in return for the release of 40 political prisoners, including one person killed at Paulista. The movement had been considered moribund after the killing in 1971 of its last important leader, Capt. Carlos Lamarca.

In the Amazon jungle, meanwhile, a Marxist-Leninist guerrilla group claimed it was gaining popular support despite extensive government anti-guerrilla operations. A pamphlet issued Jan. 1 in Rio de Janeiro charged the government had installed 3,000 soldiers in the Maraba area, 280 miles south of Belem, bringing in "helicopters, planes, tanks, motor launches, amphibian cars. They decreed immense zones of the forest as free fire zones. They bombed several places with napalm . . . Everywhere they spread terror, searching the population, confiscating simple hunting guns, torturing and even assassinating any persons suspected of sympathy [with the guerrillas]."

During the previous months travelers to the Maraba area had complained of being summarily arrested and interrogated by military authorities at roadblocks and during raids on homes they visited.

Communists killed. Authorities announced Jan. 17 that six members of the outlawed Revolutionary Brazilian Communist party, an offshoot of the pro-Moscow Communist party, had been killed in gun battles with police in two Rio de Janeiro suburbs.

In a related development, a Sao Paulo restaurant owner was reported killed Feb. 23 by gunmen claiming he had betrayed three urban guerrillas killed by police in 1972.

Opposition leader slain. Rubens Bernardo, a federal deputy and former vice governor of Guanabara state, was murdered in his Rio de Janeiro home Feb. 7 by unknown assailants. He was a founder of the local Continental Radio and Television and a leader of the Brazilian Democratic Movement, the token opposition in the legislature.

'Death squad' cases ignored. Only two of the hundreds of crimes blamed on Rio de Janeiro state "death squads" had been brought to court during the past two years, the newspaper O Estado de Sao Paulo reported Jan. 4. The Rio attorney general had appointed 18 prosecutors in 1972 to investigate 1,050 unsolved crimes—most of them blamed on the death squads—but they had filed no reports on the cases. Twelve of the prosecutors had been promoted to judgeships, the newspaper said. The death squads were assumed to comprise frustrated policemen who arrogated to themselves the right to kill those they considered dangerous criminals. But O Estado de Sao Paulo asserted that policemen belonging to death squads also directed the Brazilian narcotics traffic.

A former policeman arrested on counterfeiting charges had admitted once belonging to a death squad, the Miami Herald reported March 25. The man, Mariel Mariscott de Matos, testified in court that his squad was "nothing but a team of honest lawmen interested in protecting society by getting rid of irredeemable criminals."

Yellow fever epidemic. An outbreak of yellow fever in the central state of Goias had killed 38 persons, but health authorities claimed it had been brought under control, El Nacional of Caracas reported Jan. 6. The epidemic had caused alarm in the Federal District, which bordered on Goias.

Price control chief fired. Gen. Glauco de Carvalho, head of the food price control board, was removed from office without explanation Jan. 3. He had recently freed meat prices from controls, bringing an overnight 30% rise and widespread protests. The government had vowed to limit inflation to 12% in 1973, following a flood of price increases toward the end of 1972.

Economic developments. Brazil's economy grew by 9% in 1972 for the second consecutive year, while industrial production increased by 15%, according to the president of the national association of investment banks, cited in the newsletter Latin America Jan. 19. Export earnings exceeded $3.8 billion, led by coffee with $1.06 billion and followed closely by manufactured goods. Imports reached about $4.2 billion, but the huge inflow of foreign capital gave an overall payments surplus of $2.25 billion.

The cost of living in Guanabara state, which included Rio de Janeiro, rose 14% in 1972, compared with 19.1% in 1971, it was reported Jan. 19.

The state telecommunications company for the southern region had obtained a $35 million loan from the First National City Bank of New York to expand its network in 1973-75, according to a report Jan. 5.

Volkswagen's Brazilian factory would begin exporting vehicles to Nigeria in 1973 through the government trading company Brasafro, which had already set up an African distribution network based in Lagos, it was reported Jan. 5.

The Brazilian auto industry, growing at more than 20% annually since 1967, was currently ninth among world producers, the Miami Herald reported Jan. 15. Fiat and Alfa-Romeo were reported Feb. 23 to have signed an agreement for joint expansion of their production of commercial vehicles, excluding automobiles and tractors. Fiat, meanwhile, planned to produce 150,000 low priced cars annually in central Brazil in what was seen as another sign of the firm's gradual shift of emphasis from Argentina to Brazil.

General Motors planned to move a plant for constructing heavy trucks from Ireland to Brazil, Latin America reported March 2.

The Italian auto firm Fiat had signed an agreement with Minas Gerais state for construction of a $230 million plant with a capacity of 190,000 cars, it was reported March 19. Financing would be arranged jointly by Fiat, Minas Gerais and various foreign investors.

Firestone Tire & Rubber Co. had announced plans for a "multimillion dollar" expansion of its Brazilian subsidiary to meet expanding demand, the Miami Herald reported Feb. 7.

Three Washington-based lending agencies—the World Bank Group, the

U.S. Export-Import Bank (Eximbank) and the Inter-American Development Bank (IDB)—provided Brazil with more than $1 billion in loans and credits in 1972, it was reported Jan. 28. The World Bank led with $490 million, followed by Eximbank with $450 million and the IDB with more than $200 million.

A $63 million World Bank loan to the steel firm Usinas de Minas Gerais (USIMINAS), to expand its production, was reported March 16. The bank also provided $87 million for highway paving in the interior of Brazil. USIMINAS was reported April 18 to have ordered a steel mill worth $22.9 million from Ferrostahl AG of West Germany.

A consortium of U.S. banks led by Wells Fargo had arranged a $120 million loan to complete work on the Rio de Janeiro underground railway, Latin America reported March 2. A $10 million loan to Espirito Santo state by an international bank syndicate headed by Bank of America was reported by the Miami Herald March 2.

The European Brazilian Bank (Eurobraz) had completed arrangements for a 10-year loan of $40 million to help finance the BR-101 highway linking Santos and Salvador through Rio, Campos and Vitoria, it was reported April 13.

Braspetro, the international subsidiary of the state oil firm Petrobras, had signed a $10 million exploration agreement with the Egyptian General Petroleum Corp., Latin America reported Jan. 26. The pact provided for Braspetro to prospect in a 12,500 square kilometer area east of the Nile valley, with a right to 50% of the profits on oil finds. The favorable terms were ascribed in part to a recent attempt by Brazil to mediate in the Middle East conflict.

Petrobras, which made a $1.8 billion profit in 1972, would step up prospecting in Acre, on the Peruvian frontier; increase its range and volume of lubricants with a view to replacing all imports; and bring offshore wells in the northeast into production in 1973, it was reported Jan. 12.

Retired Gen. Ernesto Geisel, president of the state oil monopoly Petrobras, said in his annual report to stockholders March 23 that the company's profits had risen by 42.9% in 1972. He added, however, that expenditures for oil imports had risen and warned that the rise in world oil prices would make Petrobras vulnerable to foreign suppliers.

The Italian industrialist Adalberto S. di Campobianco planned to invest a further $70 million in projects in the states of Guanabara and Rio de Janeiro, Latin America reported Feb. 9. The plans included food industry projects, a special paper mill and a shipyard.

Shares of six largely state-owned companies currently accounted for more than half the total volume of trading on the Rio stock exchange, compared with about 35% at the beginning of 1972, it was reported Feb. 23.

The government announced it was taking over the group of companies headed by Francisco Pignatari, which it said was heavily in debt to the National Economic Development Bank and other agencies, Latin America reported Jan. 26. The state would pay nearly 300 million cruzeiros in compensation. Officials claimed the group's financial disorganization was clear evidence of its inability to handle the large Caraiba copper mining project, which the state would henceforth control along with a wide range of Pignatari metallurgical and mining enterprises.

Mitsubishi Corp., the Japanese conglomerate, planned to invest $1.2 billion in Brazil over the next five years, it was reported Feb. 14. The president of the Japanese chamber of trade and industry in Brazil was reported Feb. 23 to have forecast a doubling of total Japanese investment in Brazil to $8 billion over the next few years.

The Sanwa Bank of Japan had signed a letter of intent setting out terms under which it would obtain a 10% stake in the capital of Bradesco, the second largest privately owned bank in Brazil, Latin America reported Feb. 16.

The Bank of Brazil would join with U.S., Japanese, French, West German and Greek interests in financing the construction of merchant ships in Greece and Brazil, Latin America reported March 2.

Indian protectors to leave Amazon. Orlando and Claudio Villas Boas, famous for their work with the National Indian Foundation (FUNAI), announced Feb. 7

they would leave the Amazon jungle after 30 years of studying and attempting to protect its primitive Indian tribes.

The brothers said their decision was based on a conviction that "every time we contact a tribe we are contributing to the destruction of the purest things it possesses." They charged that FUNAI's attempts to "pacify" Indians as white settlers developed the Amazon only corrupted Indian culture. "Brazil has no Indian policy that can simultaneously pacify the Indian and isolate him from contact with whites," they said. "We have not been able to prevent the [physical] degeneration of the Indian race and the growth of corruption."

The Villas Boas' announcement came only one day after they had made what was believed to be the outside world's first contact with the Kranhacarore Indians, whose civilization they considered threatened by the construction of a road between Cuiaba and Santarem. The brothers' mission to contact the tribe had begun in January 1972 at the request of the government.

Elsewhere in the Amazon, Indians in the northernmost state of Roraima Feb. 1 attacked a government settlement, killing three FUNAI workers. The attack reportedly was to avenge insults to Indian women by local road workers.

Study denounces ranchers, firms—A study on the Brazilian Amazon published in Great Britain's Geographical Magazine said that "as in the American Old West, the rancher and the farmer, not to mention the modern multinational mining company, consider the Indians a bother at best and a danger at worst," El Nacional of Caracas reported Jan. 17.

The study, by Edwin Brooks of the University of Liverpool, said there was well-documented proof of atrocities by white ranchers in the Amazon, such as the fatal shooting and even crucifixion of Xavante Indians. However, it denied charges that the Brazilian government, which collaborated in the study, had sanctioned genocide. The Indian, it said, would be eliminated not "as a human being," but "as an Indian . . . He will remain alive, but in the last rank of racial mixture."

Publication censored. The new weekly Opiniao would be subjected to federal censorship prior to publication, the magazine said in its Jan. 1 issue. Opiniao had reported in December 1972 that Brazil's foreign debt for that year would reach $10 billion, considerably more than the government had estimated.

Federal police had held up 16 of 24 pages of Opinao for "examination," approving the other eight with substantial cuts, it was reported May 2. The action prevented the magazine from publishing on time for the second time in three weeks.

Opiniao's news editor, Antonio Carlos Ferreira, said he did not understand the action because "most of the pages had international news, without any hot stuff."

Brazilian President Emilio Medici June 24 reaffirmed the government's right to censor publications without consulting the courts, overruling a federal appeals court decision in favor of Opiniao.

The court had ruled Opiniao should be allowed to publish without first being checked by federal police. Medici reportedly overruled the decision on the basis of 1970 decrees allowing the president to declare a state of siege and order censorship of "correspondence, the press, telecommunications and other publications."

The Constitution imposed by the military stated that "publication of books and periodicals does not depend on permission by the authorities." However, the interior minister had added an interpretive decree which permitted prior censorship in the interest of "morality and good custom."

Among other censorship developments:

■ The publisher of the newspaper O Estado de Sao Paulo had been summoned to testify before a military court investigating a torture report published in the paper, the Miami Herald reported Jan. 12. O Estado had reported Dec. 12, 1972 that a man in Brasilia had been "forcibly taken from his home" by security officers who subjected him to "physical offenses, including electric shocks."

■ The government had banned the sale of erotic engravings by Pablo Picasso, which had been unavailable in bookstores for three years, the New York Times reported Jan. 10. The Rio de Janeiro newspaper Jornal do Brasil published an extensive report Jan. 8 on censorship of art exhibitions, theater, films, magazines and television.

Federal police officers seized from newsstands all copies of the new monthly magazine Argumento, a liberal political and literary review, because it had not been submitted to the required prior examination by government censors, it was reported Oct. 26.

Military corruption charges filed. The armed forces' prosecutor general had formally accused 11 high-ranking army officers before the Supreme Military Court of taking bribes and kickbacks on military purchases, the Miami Herald reported Feb. 22. Similar charges involving 63 army and 45 air force officers and millions of dollars in graft had been filed earlier in lower army and air force courts, the Herald said.

The prosecutor charged the 11 officers had conspired with seven private businessmen to take rake-offs of 1%-5% on military purchase contracts over several years, according to the Herald. Supply officers across Brazil were said to run "kitties" of unregistered funds donated by civilian suppliers.

The air force commander had ordered an investigation of corruption charges against nine highranking officers, the Herald reported Feb. 28. The officers were accused of taking kickbacks of up to 15% on supply contracts totaling hundreds of thousands of dollars.

The corruption charges followed extensive secret military investigations which reportedly shook the army high command and angered President Medici.

The charges against them were denied April 24 by two of the army officers accused, Gen. Henrique Faria Braga and Col. Orlando Gomes Christo. The army prosecutor in Brasilia charged they and other officers in charge of supplies operated "little boxes" of graft money on army bases across Brazil. "They organized a structure that functioned like the Mafia," the prosecutor said. "But they took the canteen to the well so many times it broke."

A military prosecutor April 25 accused 26 more officers of taking bribes and kickbacks on military purchases. Military sources said the graft totaled millions of dollars.

The regime banned all mention of the case in the press, radio and television.

President Medici dismissed six accused colonels July 17, six more in August and an additional six Nov. 9. (Medici Aug. 3 signed a decree dismissing 43 police officers for corruption.)

Argentine fishing dispute. Argentina's enactment of a ban on foreign trawlers from fishing within 200 miles of the Argentine coast was reported Feb. 16. The signing followed Argentina's decision Jan. 19 not to ratify a 1967 agreement with Brazil which allowed both countries' vessels to fish in each other's territorial waters up to six miles from the coast without paying duty. Argentina had arrested four Brazilian fishing boats Jan. 13 and another one Jan. 15 for allegedly violating Argentine territorial waters.

Antarctic encroachment charged—An Argentine senatorial candidate, Marcelo Sanchez, accused Brazil Jan. 17 of seeking "to install itself in a fringe of Argentine Antarctic territory." The Argentine press had expressed alarm in December 1972 at a projected Brazilian scientific expedition to the Antarctic, where Argentina, Chile and Great Britain claimed national sovereignty.

Sanchez also criticized his government for its stand on the hydroelectric power station Brazil would build at Itaipu on the Parana river, which flowed into Argentina. He said FREJULI presidential candidate Hector Campora had promised that if elected, one of his first acts would be to renounce the October 1972 Argentine-Brazilian accord on the projected power station.

U.S. drug pact signed. The U.S. and Brazil had signed an agreement to stop the shipping of illicit narcotics from Brazil to the U.S., it was reported March 1. Under the pact, Brazilian customs officials would be trained in the latest narcotics detection methods.

In related developments:

A former Brazilian honorary consul in the U.S. was on trial in Rio de Janeiro on charges of using his diplomatic privileges to enter Texas with more than 60 pounds of pure heroin and selling the heroin to a Mafia leader in New York, the Miami Herald reported Jan. 19.

Eight Brazilian soldiers, including a colonel, and two policemen had been sentenced to a total of 473 years in jail for torturing and killing four young soldiers arrested on suspicion of drug trafficking, the Herald reported Jan. 30.

Pollution curbs enacted. The government had begun a three-year, $9 million project to protect the Paraiba River valley, between Sao Paulo and Rio de Janeiro, from industrial pollution, the New York Times reported March 11.

The program, the government's first major offensive against pollution, followed two years of alarming reports on the country's diminishing resources—contamination of the waterways, poisoning of the beaches, devastation of the Amazon forests, and the dangers of air polluted by filth and noise, the Times reported.

Arrests, killings reported. An estimated 700-800 students, professionals and journalists had been arrested in March and April on suspicion of subversive activities, and some had been tortured in prison, the Miami Herald reported April 25. Five alleged subversives had been shot to death by police and soldiers in late March, the London newsletter Latin America reported April 6.

The armed forces claimed only to have charged 109 persons with subversion, the Herald reported April 26. Officials said several of those arrested belonged to a terrorist group called the National Armed Resistance. Most, however, were said to be orthodox Communists, the Herald reported.

According to the Herald April 25, nearly 300 persons had been arrested in Rio de Janeiro alone. Some had been released, but the arrests were continuing. Many released detainees reported they had been tortured.

Amnesty International, a London-based group working for the release of political prisoners, asked April 26 for an impartial investigation of the recent deaths of some 25 alleged subversives in police custody. The group said Brazilian political prisoners had been "run down" or shot by friends trying to free them "with such surprising frequency that we believe an impartial investigation is essential."

Among those "run down" was Alexandre Vanucchi Leme, a Sao Paulo student whose death March 17 caused a major controversy. Police claimed that Leme, whom they called a terrorist, was killed by a truck as he tried to escape. However, their version was disputed by students and others who noted that other prisoners' deaths had been described nearly identically. Leme was buried immediately, and requests by his parents for an exhumation were denied, leading to speculation his body showed signs of torture.

The bishop of Sorocaba, Jose Melhado Campos, charged at a memorial mass for Leme March 30 that police had tortured and killed the student. "It is not for me to deny the accusations of terrorism and robbery which the police made against the youth," Campos said. "But it is obvious that . . . the police ruthlessly eliminated one who, in a legal trial, could defend himself and, if it were the case, admit his acts and pay for them."

The service, attended by about 3,000 students, was presided over by the archbishop of Sao Paulo, Cardinal Paulo Evaristo Arns.

The government imposed complete censorship on any reference to the mass. A Sao Paulo television station was punished for reporting it and the left-wing weekly Opiniao printed a report on the mass and an interview with Arns, who said the people of Sao Paulo were living in a "situation of emergency in relation to wages, health and public security."

Opiniao was subsequently ordered to submit all material to federal censors 48 hours before going to press, which reportedly made publication impossible. The weekly refused to comply, and its next issue was confiscated. Opiniao's publisher and two top editors were arrested and held briefly April 15.

According to the newsletter Latin America April 20, the mass for Leme revealed a new and aggressive militancy in the Catholic Church. This reportedly was confirmed by the appointment by Pope Paul VI of Aloisio Lorscheider to be archbishop of Fortaleza, in northeastern Brazil. Lorscheider was said to be a "reformer" like two other northeast prelates, archbishops Helder Camara of Recife and Avelar Brandao of Salvador.

The conclusions of the biennial assembly of the National Council of Bishops, made public March 15, vowed that the church would defend human rights and inform public opinion of violations of those rights. The bishops denounced government repression; discrimination against peasants, workers, blacks, women, and the political opposition; and the oppression of Indians, who were "in the process of being exterminated."

'Terrorists' sentenced. Seven persons had been sentenced to 12 years in jail by a military court in Fortaleza after being convicted of "terrorist activities," it was reported April 20.

Hydroelectric project set. Brazil and Paraguay signed a partnership agreement April 26 to build what was expected to be the world's largest hydroelectric project, at Itaipu on the Parana River between the two countries.

The pact was signed in Brasilia by Foreign Minister Mario Gibson Barboza and his Paraguayan counterpart, Raul Sapena Pastor. President Emilio G. Medici and Paraguayan President Alfredo Stroessner attended the ceremony.

Argentina, which had opposed the project for two years, recalled its ambassador from Brasilia to protest the agreement. Argentine officials had demanded prior assurance that projects such as Itaipu would not harm navigation downstream in Argentina, or jeopardize other Parana hydroelectric schemes planned at Yacyreta-Apipe and Corpus between Argentina and Paraguay.

The Itaipu project, with a planned capacity of 10 million kilowatts, reportedly would cost $2 billion. It was planned by the International Engineering Co. of the U.S. and Electroconsult SpA of Italy.

A dam 720 feet high and 4,600 feet long would create a 515-square-mile reservoir, half to cover Brazilian territory and half Paraguayan territory.

Brazil and Paraguay agreed to set up a joint company to build and run the project, and to divide the power production equally. Paraguay was expected to have a surplus, which it would sell to Brazil for use in the developing industrial areas of Sao Paulo and other states. Brazil's power consumption had been growing by 10%-12% annually.

Before the agreement was signed, Brazil and Argentina had made efforts to resolve their conflict, agreeing to exchange advice and information about their hydroelectric projects and plans. However, Argentina had subsequently protested the way in which Brazil warned that it was temporarily restricting the flow of Parana waters to fill the reservoir of another big hydroelectric project, at Ilha Solteira in Sao Paulo state.

Other power developments—The World Bank April 12 approved a $20 million loan to Servicos de Electricidade to help finance expansion of electric power subtransmission and distribution facilities in Rio de Janeiro, Sao Paulo and surrounding areas. The project, costing the equivalent of $382.6 million, would help meet rising demand and provide service for more than 700,000 new residential customers.

Centrais Electricas de Sao Paulo S.A., the utility supplying electricity for Sao Paulo state, had been granted private joint financing totaling $248 million from French, British, Japanese and other banks for construction of the Gua Vermelha power station and extension of the Ilha Solteira station, both part of the Urusupunga electric complex in northeastern Sao Paulo, it was announced March 22.

Economic developments. The government devalued the cruzeiro April 24, setting the buying rate at 6.06 to the U.S. dollar and the selling rate at 6.1. The currency had been revalued by 3% Feb. 14 to offset the dollar devaluation, and had been devalued eight times in relation to the dollar in 1972.

Planning Minister Joao Paulo dos Reis Veloso said Brazil's external debts stood at $11 billion, it was reported March 16. He asserted the debts were a stimulus to the economy, which should continue its current rates of growth until the end of the 1970s, by which time the nation's per capita income should have reached $900–$1,000 per year.

The Hilton Hotels Corp. April 13 reached agreement with a Brazilian construction company, Sisal, for construction of 30–50 hotels in Brazil. Brazilian authorities, who offered the companies tax incentives, said investment would total $120 million.

A consortium of nine West German companies would invest some $350 million in the meat packing industry in Sao Paulo, Goias and Mato Grosso states, it was reported March 23.

U.S. multimillionaire Daniel K. Ludwig had announced plans to invest about $180 million in a ship repair yard near Recife, it was reported March 16.

Brazil raised coffee export prices by 3¢ a pound March 16 in anticipation of increases in world coffee prices. Brazil was the world's largest coffee producer, and the U.S. was its biggest customer.

The cellulose and paper concern Suzano would invest about $60 million to expand its cellulose production with hopes of making Brazil self-sufficient in the product and an exporter, it was reported April 27.

President Medici decreed an 18.6% increase in the minimum wage, it was reported May 4.

Poland and Brazil had signed a $130 million agreement providing for the delivery of 4 million tons of Polish coal in exchange for 5.5 million tons of Brazilian iron ore, it was reported May 4.

Mercedes Benz would invest $10 million in a new iron foundry in Sao Paulo state, to help meet growing demand for buses and trucks, it was reported June 1.

The textile concern Bangu would join Dutch interests in an expansion program to include the importation to Rio de Janeiro of an automated factory, creating 2,000 new jobs, it was reported June 1. Four-fifths of the production would be marketed abroad by the Japanese consortium C. Itoh.

The government had lifted the requirement imposed in 1972 that 25% of all foreign loans be deposited in the Central Bank, it was reported June 22.

Brazilian exports for January–March totaled nearly $1 billion, 37% higher than in the same period of 1972. Imports grew by 30% during the first quarter of the year.

Coffee export prices were raised by 1–4¢ a pound June 20. The 1973 coffee harvest was estimated at only 16 million bags, the lowest in 10 years, while the total demand for export and domestic consumption was 26–27 million bags. Brazil recently had been buying coffee from other countries.

Economic inequality stressed. A recent report by the United Nations Economic Commission for Latin America (ECLA) showed Brazil's current economic boom was not affecting the vast majority of the population, the London newsletter Latin America reported March 9.

According to ECLA, as much as 80% of the wage-earning population had an annual income below the average for the country as a whole. Half the working population received only 15% of the national income, and had an average per capita income equivalent to only $252. In contrast, the middle classes, forming 15% of the population, received 22% of the national income with an annual per capita average of $1,230, while the upper 5% took 40% of the national income with an annual per capita average of $6,720.

The figures did not include the high proportion of unemployed, according to Latin America.

The plight of the worker in the Amazon area was particularly bad, Latin America reported. The Brazilian press had recently carried reports of "slave labor" conditions on vast development projects in the region, notably the 200,000 acre forestry and farming estate of U.S. multimillionaire Daniel K. Ludwig.

Workers reportedly were lured to the Amazon with promises of relatively high wages, which were then effectively reduced by "lodging" charges and high prices at company stores. As a result, the workers fell heavily in debt to their employers and were thus forced to renew their contracts to pay off the debts.

President Emilio G. Medici reportedly expressed indignation at working conditions at Ludwig's estate after visiting it Feb. 22. Newspapers reported workers on the estate received no medical attention and inferior yet expensive food, and could not return to their homes because their low pay was as much as four months in arrears.

President Medici had announced three new draft laws to improve the lives of the poorest sectors of the population, it was reported April 27. They included improvements in conditions for rural workers and for the poor in large cities, and stimulation of "a progressive redistribution of wealth and an increase in incomes."

The government had announced plans to build two million low-cost houses over the next decade at an expense of about $5 billion, it was reported April 8. The project would be financed by the National Housing Bank, the government's principal home finance association. The growth of cities and accompanying social problems had become a major national issue.

Peasants attack estate—Some 150 armed peasants attacked a Mato Grosso estate July 8, killing four workers, and then looted stores in the neighboring town of Porto de Lacerda, the French newspaper Le Monde reported Aug. 10.

The estate belonged to a landowner whom the peasants accused of stealing the land they cultivated. Such attacks by peasants against landowners had occurred previously in Mato Grosso, Le Monde reported.

Agriculture minister quits. Agriculture Minister Luis F. Cirne Lima resigned May 9 over disagreements with the government's economic policy. He was replaced by Jose de Moura Cavalcanti, director of the National Colonization and Agrarian Reform Institute.

In a public letter of resignation, kept out of the press by censors, Cirne Lima charged the government's policies, "without achieving the stability desired by the urban consumer, have favored the industrial sector and export businesses—increasingly foreign-owned—giving to fewer and fewer Brazilians the benefits of the nation's prosperity."

The protection Brazil accorded "to capital," Cirne Lima said, was incompatible with social justice. "As you have repeated," he told President Medici, "economic growth is not an end in itself, but an instrument of social justice. It is your concern and that of all Brazilians to join development and the fight against hunger, misery, poverty and disease."

Cirne Lima charged that the government, in its concern with efficiency and productivity, was slighting "the agricultural producer, the small and medium industrialist and the small and medium businessman," while favoring multinational corporations. He said multinationals were "indispensable, but ought to be subordinated to the collective interest."

Cirne Lima also attacked the government's anti-inflation measures, charging they favored urban interests.

The ex-minister also complained about the government's emphasis on beef exports at the expense of the domestic market, and its refusal to raise farm prices. As a result of the latter policy, farmers had reduced production of wheat by some 30%, and were reported doing the same with milk, maize and other products, according to the newsletter Latin America May 18.

Bishops score government. The National Council of Bishops (CNBB), holding its biennial general assembly in Rio de Janeiro, published a resolution Feb. 16 condemning the military regime's "policy of repression" and "the disregard for human rights in the country," the French newspaper Le Monde reported Feb. 18.

Two bishops at the conference announced the Roman Catholic Church would disseminate knowledge of human rights by publishing low-priced pamphlets, according to a report Feb. 23. One of the bishops, Geraldo Fernandes, later attacked the current press censorship as "one of the worst calamities to befall the country."

The assembly was also concerned with the need to bring more laymen into ecclesiastical activities to compensate for the increasing scarcity of priests. Recent surveys showed a decrease in the number of priests, stagnation in the number of baptisms and weddings and a drop in confirmations, accompanied by an expansion of Pentecostal churches and African voodoo cults, according to the New York Times Feb. 8.

Camara aide kidnapped—Archbishop Helder Camara, a frequent government critic, had asked authorities to investigate the kidnapping of one of his aides in Recife, it was reported Jan. 26. He said the aide, Joao Francisco de Souza, had been abducted by four men with submachine guns. Another of Camara's aides had been kidnapped in May 1969 and later found dead.

Church criticizes government. A serious denunciation of the government and its economic policies was issued May 6 by 10 Roman Catholic bishops and three archbishops in the impoverished northeast. It was immediately banned by authorities.

The 30-page document, titled "Hear the Cries of My People," charged "economic institutions in Brazil are devoted only to oppression and injustice. Small minorities in our country, accomplices of international capitalism, are interested in preserving a situation created in their favor."

"Malnutrition, infant mortality, prostitution, illiteracy, unemployment, cultural and political discrimination, growing imbalance between rich and poor, and many other consequences characterize the institutional violations in Brazil," the prelates stated.

"The need for repression to guarantee the functioning and security of an associated capitalist system shows itself ever more imperious, revealing itself inexorable in closing legislative constitutional institutions and rural and urban workers' unions, depleting student leadership, imposing censorship and measures of persecution of workers, peasants and intellectuals, harassing priests and militant clergy, and assuming the most varied forms of imprisonment, torture, mutilation and assassination."

In the northeast, the prelates asserted:
■ Per capita income was barely half the average for the rest of Brazil, and 23% of the labor force was unemployed or underemployed.
■ Hunger and malnutrition were assuming "epidemic" proportions.
■ The infant mortality rate was 180 per 1,000 births; 47% of all deaths occurred before the age of five; and life expectancy was only 50 years for women and 47 for men. "As one can see, life in the northeast is short as well as severe," the document said.

The document asserted that the church could no longer remain "inert, waiting passively for the hour of change." It warned that "the suppressed masses of workers, peasants and numerous underemployed have taken note of what is going on and are progressively assuming a new liberating conscience."

Another church document attacking Brazil's so-called "economic miracle" was drafted in May by Archbishop Fernando Gomes dos Santos of the central city of Goiania, and six bishops from the surrounding region. It was banned in the local press, but was reported in El Nacional of Caracas June 21.

The document, titled "Marginalization of a People," charged that despite Brazil's growing wealth, millions of farmers were getting progressively poorer.

Government policies favored expansion of large agrarian concerns and estates, reducing the amount of land and work available to peasants, the bishops asserted. "According to this system, those with large properties obtain loans and financing. Peasants who have little or nothing obtain few or no loans," they charged.

More than half of Brazil's peasants earned less than $16 monthly, even though the federal minimum wage in the most backward rural areas was $35 per month, the document noted. Peasants demanding better wages, housing, medical treatment, or the right to unionize, were treated as criminals and Communists, the bishops charged.

The document deplored the recent sentencing to 10 years in prison of Rev. Francois Jentel, a French priest who organized small farmers against a government development project in Mato Grosso state. The military court sentence, the most severe against a priest in recent years, was reported May 29. It was condemned by Cardinal Avelar Brandao, archbishop of Bahia and a signatory of "Hear the Cries of My People," according to a report June 8.

In another development June 7, a military court acquitted 32 priests accused of violating the national security law in a document, published in Belo Horizonte in

1968, commenting on the killing of a student and on Brazil's political situation. The prosecutor requested the acquittal because of lack of evidence.

Priests score repression, torture. U.S. columnist Jack Anderson reported June 17 that documents prepared by Roman Catholic priests in Brazil accused the government of committing "unimagined violence" against dissidents and of torturing political prisoners.

The documents, by the priest-led Committee for Solidarity with the Political Prisoners of Brazil, were presented to the national bishops' conference in February and later smuggled to the U.S., Anderson reported. They accused the military regime of "murdering students who marched in the streets and workers who organized strikes for higher wages and the return of their rights."

Some prisoners, the priests charged, were tortured and quickly killed. Others were held for "several years without any trial," and still others were given "incredibly long sentences to justify the long time ... already [spent] in jail awaiting trial," the priests asserted.

A prison-by-prison account charged that:

■ Brutality against prisoners in Brasilia continued despite a hunger strike by inmates protesting "tortures and abuses, especially [of] a woman who was in late pregnancy."

■ In Recife, an imprisoned peasant organizer "was murdered simply because his sentence was about to end and he would soon have to be freed."

■ At Tiradentes prison in Sao Paulo, a "death squad" was allowed to take out some prisoners and murder them.

■ At the state penitentiary of Sao Paulo, jailed students were threatened with "rampant homosexuality," political prisoners suffered from poor health and food, and there were "thousands of rats in every part of the prison."

Anderson reported that the Nixon Administration had failed to make a single public protest against Brazilian repression and torture. He noted that the U.S. currently was giving Brazil $58 million in military aid and helped train its top police officers.

A second Anderson report June 30, based on the same documents, detailed specific cases of torture, naming victims and military officers who allegedly tortured them. The priests cited 28 deaths from torture and 15 others possibly caused by torture, Anderson reported.

(In Brazil, the National Council of Bishops charged June 22 that policemen and soldiers in Recife had raided church offices June 5 and 16 and had seized previously published documents supporting a Socialist economy and accusing the government of torturing political prisoners.)

Church condemns government. Roman Catholic Church officials severely criticized the government in July and August for harassing, imprisoning and beating priests who they said were seeking to improve the lives of impoverished Brazilian peasants.

The archbishop of Sao Paulo, Cardinal Paulo Evaristo Arns, denounced a military court in Campo Grande, Mato Grosso state, for upholding a 10-year prison sentence against Rev. Francois Jentel, a French priest accused of inciting peasants to fight landowners and resist eviction from lands they cultivated but did not own, it was reported July 10.

Arns declared it was "shocking to see confined in prison men who are only engaged in good works." Jentel, he asserted, "heroically defends the rights of small landholders. He is a man who has always worked on behalf of the poorest, creating cooperatives and schools in the abandoned interior, and who personally does not own anything except the clothes he wears."

The president, vice president and secretary general of the National Council of Bishops also defended Jentel and said the military court's decision "must be revised."

The bishop of the remote Mato Grosso town of Sao Felix do Araguaia, Rev. Pedro Casaldaliga, was increasingly harassed by state security forces in July for praising Jentel and defending poor settlers against the invasion of large development companies, according to several reports.

Casaldaliga charged in a letter to Cardinal Arns that he and four priests were held in his residence by armed police July 6-8; that police ransacked his residence and a neighboring nuns' residence July 7, forcing him to open his files; and that the four priests were taken away by police July 8 and "beaten brutally." Eight of Casaldaliga's lay workers were also reported arrested. The government announced an official investigation of the bishop's charges July 13.

Twenty bishops expressed their support for Casaldaliga and outrage at the police actions by holding a mass at Casaldaliga's residence Aug. 19.

The church Aug. 28 denounced press censorship of its reports of disappearances, arrests and seizure of church documents by security officials. Pope Paul VI, in an audience with Brazil's new ambassador to the Vatican, Antonio Borges Leal Castello Branco, urged the Brazilian government Aug. 28 to respect human rights and insure economic justice.

Brazil's best-known reformist priest, Archbishop Helder Camara of Olinda and Recife, asserted he thought police were secretly holding two of his lay workers who had been missing for three weeks, it was reported Aug. 18.

In an address to the Pernambuco state legislature in Recife May 31, Camara had reaffirmed his determination to continue to speak out. He had said: "We would not be worthy of Christ if we remained silent before the institutionalized injustices that maintain two-thirds of the population of our nation in conditions unworthy of human beings, and on the other hand if we would not use our voice on behalf of those who are barbarously tortured and not infrequently killed by a number of para-legal methods that sadly bring back to memory the hideous days of Stalin and Hitler."

In another church development, reported Sept. 28, Cardinal Avelar Brandao protested the decision by the governor of Pernambuco to cancel the planned award to him of the state's medal of merit. Brandao, archbishop of Bahia and a signer of "I Hear the Cries of My People," called the governor's action "a gesture of public hostility."

Camara aides disappear. Archbishop Helder Camara of Olinda and Recife said six of his closest aides had disappeared recently without a trace and another three had been picked up and abused by secret police in further attempts by the government to silence his outspoken criticism of its social and economic policies, Reuters reported Nov. 10.

The aides had worked with Camara in "Operation Hope," a rural campaign to show the poor in the Northeast how to help themselves. Camara asserted the government's "aim" in abducting his associates was "to force me to give up. But I will not, as much as it pains me to see all my friends being picked up one by one."

Camara reportedly was subjected to telephone taps and raids on his office in Recife, and was forced to spend much of his time personally accompanying his helpers across the city to prevent their arrest or harassment.

The archbishop's statements were barred from publication in the press under national censorship laws, and persons who sought his advice reportedly were questioned by the police. Camara communicated his views principally in his weekly sermons and in hand-printed pamphlets, but even these carried risks—a choir boy had been arrested recently and another youth distributing pamphlets at the church door had vanished.

'Death squad' murders. Police "death squads" were held responsible for the murders of five men whose bodies were found in various parts of Rio de Janeiro state June 2-4.

Each of the victims had been shot once in the head, and bore a tag describing the petty crimes for which he had allegedly been executed. The tags were signed with the initials of the death squad.

The killings brought to 12 the number attributed to death squads since March. There had been at least 1,300 such murders in the past 15 years, the Times of London reported June 14.

A former Sao Paulo police investigator, Geraldo Georgino das Neves, was sentenced to 31 years in jail for the squad executions of two petty criminals, one of whom reportedly had failed to pay a weekly protection fee for his drug-peddling trade, it was reported May 31.

A Sao Paulo jury had acquitted four death squad suspects of charges of murdering a criminal suspect in 1969, according to a report June 9. It was reportedly the first acquittal in such a case.

Fleury arrested—Sao Paulo police inspector Sergio Fleury, organizer of the city's political police and a leader of antiguerrilla operations, was arrested Oct. 23 for alleged corruption and participation in the "death squad" murder of a drug trafficker in 1969.

Fleury was considered chief of the Sao Paulo death squad and a brutal torturer of political prisoners, according to the French newspaper Le Monde Oct. 27. It was the 11th time he was accused of homicide, having previously escaped conviction because witnesses disappeared or retracted their charges, according to the newsletter Latin America Nov. 2.

Geisel to succeed Medici. President Emilio G. Medici announced June 18 that he would be succeeded by retired Gen. Ernesto Geisel, president of the state oil monopoly Petrobras and brother of the current army minister.

The selection, made by Brazil's top military leaders, would be ratified January 15, 1974 by an electoral college consisting of 66 senators, 310 deputies and 126 state assemblymen, most of them members of the government's ARENA party. Geisel's four-year term would begin March 15, 1974.

Medici praised Geisel's "austerity, imagination and efficiency," and asserted he had "absolute confidence" his successor would not allow "any deviation" from the "economic, social and political philosophy of the revolutionary order."

Geisel, 64, had headed Petrobras for four years, during which it grew by nearly 50% and expanded exploration activities to other Latin American countries, the Middle East and Madagascar. He reportedly had resisted all attempts by foreign capital to enter the oil and petrochemical industries.

Geisel also had served on the National Security Council and on the Supreme Military Court, where he was known as a stern judge in cases involving alleged subversion.

Geisel's selection reportedly followed tension within the armed forces between his supporters and backers of a second presidential term for Medici. There also were officers who talked of "a return by the military to the duties they are intended to carry out," believing 10 years of military rule were enough and responding to opposition charges that the regime had turned Brazil into "a paradise for multinational companies," the London newsletter Latin America reported June 15.

The government recently had increased press censorship to eliminate all reports on the presidential succession. The major targets were the influential Sao Paulo newspapers O Estado and Jornal da Tarde, and the Rio de Janeiro weekly Opiniao.

The president announced June 25 that retired army Gen. Adalberto Pereira dos Santos, 68, president of the Supreme Military Court, would be Brazil's next vice president.

Like Geisel and Medici, Pereira dos Santos was a former four-star army general from the southernmost state, Rio Grande do Sul. He played a key role in the 1964 overthrow of Brazil's last democratic administration, that of ex-President Joao Goulart, and was considered a hardliner on communism and civil liberties.

Geisel, meanwhile, maintained silence. Numerous sources reported he disagreed on many issues with President Emilio G. Medici, and might damage the government's image of unity—and hurt his own presidential prospects—by speaking out. Medici had opposed Geisel's nomination, acceding to it largely because of the influence of the candidate's brother, army minister Gen. Orlando Geisel, according to the London newsletter Latin America July 6.

Geisel recently had resigned from the presidency of Petrobras, the state oil concern, and had been succeeded by Adm. Floriano Peixoto Faria Lima, it was reported July 27.

In another political development reported Aug. 30, the government declared a "national security zone" in the city of Anapolis, southwest of Brasilia, and removed for 10 years the political rights of the mayor, Jose Batista, an MDB member. The government said it was acting under Institutional Act No. 5, the 1968 decree that gave the president virtually dictatorial powers.

Opposition names candidates. The Brazilian Democratic Movement (MDB), the only officially tolerated opposition party, selected presidential and vice presidential candidates to run in the January 1974 indirect elections, it was reported Sept. 10.

The presidential nominee was Ulysses Guimaraes, a Sao Paulo international law professor and leader of the MDB. His running mate was Barbosa Lima Sobrinho, a Rio de Janeiro economist.

Guimaraes said the MDB would participate in the elections "knowing they are a great farce organized by the government." Many party members had opposed participation, but others had supported it to enable the MDB to air its views.

The MDB leadership, in a declaration before Congress reported Sept. 1, charged the government ruled by means of illegal arrests, violence and censorship, and degraded Brazil in the eyes of the world. Lima Sobrinho asserted Sept. 6 that the nation's current economic boom was paid for by the average housewife, who "suffered terribly" from the high cost of living.

(A private poll commissioned by the ruling ARENA party showed the public preferred the MDB to ARENA by 45.8% to 32.5%, the news agency LATIN reported Sept. 10.)

'Great power' policy seen. The Rio de Janeiro weekly Manchete, which generally reflected government thinking, predicted April 28 that Brazil would adopt a "great power" policy to protect its trade, development programs, 200-mile offshore territorial limits, and hydroelectric projects.

Referring to recent purchases of French Mirage jets, Manchete said: "No one should be surprised if, after these, in an almost inevitable progression over the next 10 years, come Phantoms, F-111's, sophisticated tanks, amphibious vehicles, Polarises, aircraft carriers and atomic submarines, satellites, rockets and the atomic bomb itself."

Brazilian military power would act not as an "aggressive factor" but as a "dissuasive force," Manchete said. The bomb, it continued, was "perhaps a sort of military necessity for Brazil," since nations were treated as world powers only when they had a "respectable 'strike force'."

Medici in Portugal. President Medici visited Portugal May 14–19, conferring with President Americo Thomaz and other government officials.

A joint communique issued at the end of the visit surprisingly contained no reference to Africa, where Brazil sought closer trade relations with Portuguese colonies, the newsletter Latin America noted May 25. According to one report, Portugal was dissatisfied with Brazil's reluctance to openly support its African policies.

China sugar deal. A Sugar and Alcohol Institute official disclosed that the government had signed a contract to sell China another 240,000 metric tons of sugar, in the third sugar transaction with China in 12 months, it was reported June 6.

Brazil anticipated a profit of some $2 billion in extra sugar sales over the next five years, due to poor crops in the Soviet Union and Cuba in 1972 and 1973, the official asserted. The Soviet Union had bought 257,550 tons of Brazilian sugar in January–March, and 325,000 tons in 1972, it was reported May 4.

Gibson Barboza visits Andean countries. Foreign Minister Mario Gibson Barboza visited Colombia and Venezuela June 18–23 and Bolivia, Ecuador and Peru July 8–15 during a series of trips to five Andean Group nations to promote Brazilian trade and economic cooperation.

Gibson Barboza was in Bogota June 18–20. He conferred each day with Foreign Minister Alfredo Vasquez Carrizosa. Brazil and Colombia agreed as a result of the visit to jointly exploit Colombian coal reserves, it was reported June 29.

The foreign minister flew June 20 to Caracas. He conferred June 22 with President Rafael Caldera and Mines Minister Hugo Perez La Salvia, expressing to them Brazil's interest in buying more Venezuelan oil and petrochemical products.

He stopped in La Paz July 8–11, Quito July 11–13, and Lima July 13–15.

BRAZIL

Among results of Gibson Barboza's visits were a deal to develop Bolivia's steel industry and buy its natural gas; an agreement for Petrobras to help with Ecuadorean oil exploration; and a lengthy joint declaration with Peru.

Peru's left-wing military government and Brazil's rightist regime agreed to unite in defense of their declared 200-mile offshore territorial limits, and to press jointly for a greater share in world cargo traffic for the merchant marines of developing countries. Brazil also joined Peru in voicing concern over "the protectionist policies of certain industrialized nations"—presumably, the U.S.—in an apparent expression of independence from Washington.

Gibson Barboza visited Andean Group headquarters in Lima and said Brazil wished to create "concrete machinery for cooperation, to be defined and negotiated as soon as possible." He held an unscheduled meeting with the Chilean delegate to the group, but no details of the talk were released. Chile was the only Andean Group country not on Gibson Barboza's tour.

(A mission of army, navy and air force officers visited Senegal, the Ivory Coast, Ghana, Nigeria and Kenya in a follow-up to Gibson Barboza's 1972 African tour, Latin America reported June 29.)

East German ties set. Brazil and East Germany established diplomatic relations Oct. 23. Notes of recognition were exchanged in Brasilia between Foreign Minister Mario Gibson Barboza and Dieter Kulitzka, chief of the Latin American Affairs Division of the East German Foreign Ministry.

Record budget proposed. The government sent to Congress Aug. 31 a record $9.5 billion budget for 1974.

The largest share of the budget—$1.3 billion, or nearly 14%—would go to the three armed forces for unspecified expenditures, presumably including purchase of more foreign-made jet fighters, submarines and missiles. Some 5% of the budget was allocated to the Education Ministry, and only 1% to the Health Ministry.

Need for U.S. aid questioned—A report to the U.S. Congress Aug. 2 by its auditing agency, the General Accounting Office (GAO), said Brazil might have reached the point in its economic development where it no longer needed U.S. aid.

The report, dedicated originally to U.S. aid to Brazilian education, went beyond its topic to note that Brazil's gross national product had grown at an annual rate of 9.9% since 1968, that its foreign exchange reserves had reached record totals, and that the country had been receiving "substantial economic assistance from other sources," including $900 million in 1972 from the World Bank, the Inter-American Development Bank and the U.S. Export-Import Bank.

The report also noted that Brazil itself had extended loans to smaller Latin American countries and had pledged $2 million to the special fund of the African Development Bank.

The GAO conceded U.S. assistance to Brazil was being reduced, from about $50 million in fiscal 1973 to $17 million planned for fiscal 1974. However, it urged Congress to consider requiring the State Department and the Agency for International Development "to precisely identify, in objectively measurable terms, the point at which an assistance recipient no longer requires concessional U.S. assistance."

As for U.S. education aid to Brazil, the GAO said it had not been used effectively to increase educational opportunities for the poor, but had gone directly or indirectly to private schools, which the great majority of Brazilians could not afford to attend.

The report noted that only 53% of Brazil's primary school age population attended classes, and only 20% of these completed the fourth grade in four years. Only 27.5% of high school age Brazilians were in school, and in the universities, which enjoyed substantial government subsidies, only 4% attended.

Other economic developments—Brazil signed an agreement Aug. 1 to receive four World Bank development loans totaling $210 million. The largest were a $125 million credit to help build the Itumbiara hydroelectric project, and a $54 million loan for agriculture and livestock development, principally in meat processing.

The Inter-American Development Bank approved a $54.2 million loan to Brazil Sept. 13 and a $40 million credit Oct. 4. The first would help build the second stage of the electrical transmission system to connect the Ilha Solteira hydroelectric plant with the city of Sao Paulo. The second would help finance broad-scale development in the petrochemical and chemical industries.

Figures released by the Planning Ministry Sept. 17 indicated the volume of foreign investment in Brazil had increased from $1.6 billion in 1967 to $3..4 billion in 1973. Foreign investment in the country had increased by 5.5% annually during the period, the ministry said.

The government was reported Sept. 3 to have taken further steps to reduce the inflationary effects of foreign credits and financing in the economy. The National Monetary Council ordered 40% of foreign credits to Brazilian private borrowers deposited in an official bank, and the Finance Ministry said it would try to reduce the nation's foreign exchange reserves, which had reached a record $6.4 billion.

The cruzeiro was devalued for the third time in 1973, according to a report Sept. 20. Its buying rate was set at 6.12 per U.S. dollar, and its selling rate at 6.16.

The Japanese government said it would grant financial support to a private Brazilian forestry development project to be undertaken jointly by Japanese and Brazilian firms, it was reported Nov. 7. The project, to cost an estimated $1 billion, involved planting eucalyptus trees in a one million acre area in Espirito Santo state and constructing a pulp plant in Minas Gerais state.

Japan's Mitsui & Co. said it and two other Japanese firms—Nippon Steel Corp. and C. Itoh & Co.—would join Brazilian interests in building an integrated steel mill in Minas, it was reported Aug. 27. The three firms would own 16.7% of the $450 million venture.

West Germany's Deutsche-Sudamerikanische Bank, of Frankfurt, announced it would invest $45 million in Guanabara state's 1974 iron and steel works expansion program, it was reported Nov. 2.

The government said it would restrict steel exports, according to a report Nov. 9, and asked producers not to take on any new export commitments in 1974, because of difficulties in supplying the huge domestic demand. Government plans to import 1.7 million tons of steel in 1974 were reported Aug. 24. The state oil firm Petrobras and the ship-building industry reportedly would increase steel consumption by 70%, car manufacturers by 50%, and the electronics industry by 30%.

Brazil signed an agreement to sell Japan 2.5 million tons of soybeans in 1974 for a total of $1 billion, it was reported Aug. 18. The sale would push soybeans ahead of coffee as the nation's principal export earner. Farmers reportedly were substituting soybeans for the traditional coffee, wheat, corn and other crops to take advantage of the soybean prices on the international market.

Despite the growing substitution of soybeans, wheat production had picked up, with a 1973 harvest estimated at 1.5 million tons, it was reported Nov. 2.

The National Monetary Council approved a joint proposal by the Finance and Agriculture Ministries to cut meat exports to 80,000 tons in 1974-76 to avert a domestic shortage, it was reported Nov. 4. Meat exports in 1972 had totaled 110,000 tons. The government had decreed measures Oct. 21 to facilitate meat imports, and the Agriculture Ministry, according to a report Aug. 3, had announced $338 million would be invested in the cattle industry in 1974-75.

A three-year nonpreferential trade agreement was signed by Brazil and the European Economic Community Dec. 19 granting each other most-favored-nation treatment and nondiscrimination in future trade liberalization. EEC tariffs on imports of Brazil's soluble coffee and cocoa butter would generally be halved.

Chile

Turmoil Precedes Coup

Salvador Allende Gossens, Chile's Marxist president, was overthrown by a military coup d'etat Sept. 11. Rather than surrender, Allende committed suicide.

The coup was preceded by months of economic disruption, strikes and political violence.

Food limitations ordered. Finance Minister Fernando Flores announced Jan. 10 food distribution rules to combat speculation, inflation and the growing black market. The measure was one of several drastic moves that would put Chile on what the government called a "war economy."

Flores said a quota on about 30 essential foods—including oils, sugar, rice, meat and coffee—would be established for each family, and enforced by the Price and Supply Boards (JAPs), which were dominated by members of the ruling Popular Unity parties. The JAPs were authorized to determine the local needs for essential foods, supervise supplies and denounce merchants and speculators who subverted the plan.

Flores also announced elimination of trusteeships in state enterprises, establishment of the National Distribution Secretariat, elimination of direct sales to the public in factories, elimination of payment in products to industrial laborers, and state control of distribution and sales of agricultural and livestock products.

The measures were immediately denounced by Sen. Osvaldo Olguin, acting president of the opposition Christian Democratic party, as "so absurd as to give the impression the government wants a war with the public." Olguin said the system would only aggravate the food shortage, causing "desperation among the Chilean people." The other opposition parties protested Jan. 11, calling the government's economic policies "dictatorial."

The government, which had asserted Chile's economic difficulties were caused by the "imperialist blockade" and "internal aggression" by the opposition, rejected the opposition charges Jan. 11. The three military officers in the Cabinet declared the same day that they agreed with President Salvador Allende Gossens on the need to apply "urgent measures and the full weight of the law" to eliminate hoarding, speculation and the black market.

A government report recommending rationing, published in the left-wing weekly Chile Hoy, was cited in the London newsletter Latin America Jan. 5. It said the total food supply had increased by 27% in 1971–72—twice as much as it had in the previous five years—but that for a variety of reasons supplies in shops and markets had declined. The reasons included a lack of development in the transport system and warehousing arrangements; an uncontrolled increase in demand, caused by the extra spending power of the lower classes, the undiminished spending power of the upper and middle classes, an increase in employment and the results of many government social schemes; and the growth of the black market, which allegedly had halved the number of goods available through the official distribution network.

The government Jan. 12 took control of all wheat sales in what it called a "profound political and social move" to strengthen food rationing. Producers would be required to sell wheat to the state, which would then distribute the grain to mills and bakeries.

More than 8,000 workers at the Chuquicamata copper mine struck Jan. 16-17 to protest "serious food shortages" in the area and the food limitations. A government spokesman called the walkout "unjustified and unpatriotic," claiming it would cost Chile $2 million a day and was aimed at embarrassing the government before the March parliamentary elections.

'Rationing' label disputed—The government denied Jan. 11 that its new food distribution measures constituted "rationing," as the opposition charged and most newspapers reported. Debate over the implications of the measures continued for several days, with the government maintaining the measures would only assure "equitable" distribution of essential articles to Chilean families.

(According to the London newsletter Latin America Jan. 19, the measures constituted a form of wholesale rationing, although they left retailing to local shopkeepers. They did not include the ration books and strong bureaucratic control normally involved in rationing, and offered as many loopholes for abuse as the former system of distribution, which had led to artificial shortages and the large black market. Furthermore, the opposition in Congress had refused to grant the government power to make black market activities "economic crimes," the newsletter noted.)

The government also denied an opposition charge that with the measures, President Allende had taken Chile "to the edge of a dictatorship." Allende asserted Jan. 15 that the charge, made a few days earlier by the opposition newspaper El Mercurio, was "a lie," and that Chile would never have "a dictatorship of any kind, least of all, of course, a fascist one."

Allende admitted in a speech Jan. 20 that he had made many mistakes since taking power in 1970, including failing to disclose the extent of the huge foreign debt he inherited and to begin renegotiations immediately; failing to formulate a long-term policy for livestock; and failing to dissolve Congress and call a plebiscite soon after he was elected, to try to obtain the Congressional majority he lacked.

Allende also criticized working class supporters of his Popular Unity coalition (UP), as well as government officials, for "featherbedding inefficiency" and a lack of "revolutionary spirit." He was said to be disturbed by special privileges enjoyed by industrial workers—such as the large amounts of free cloth given annually to textile workers—and angry that copper workers, the elite of Chile's working class, should have struck earlier in the week for economic reasons.

(Millas, suspended as finance minister by the Chamber of Deputies late in 1972, was censured and dismissed from that office by the Senate Jan. 10. But he remained in the Cabinet as economy minister, and Fernando Flores, with whom he switched posts following his suspension, remained finance minister. Millas was the third Cabinet official impeached in 12 months.)

Armed forces control distribution. President Salvador Allende Jan. 22 placed the armed forces in charge of distribution of essential articles, naming air force Gen. Alberto Bachelet to head the new National Distribution Secretariat and three other military men to assist him. Creation of the secretariat was announced Jan. 10 as part of the government's food quota plan.

Economy Minister Orlando Millas said Jan. 23 that the appointments were "temporary" and that the officers would leave the secretariat "once the problems of supply and the black market are solved."

The appointments reportedly deflated increasingly bitter opposition criticism of the quota system. Critics of the scheme were said to feel confident the appointments would guarantee impartiality under the new food distribution measures. The right-wing National party asserted Jan. 23 that the appointments would prove to be "positive" if they "prevented all Marxist functionaries from interfering in the supplying of the population."

Copper shipment attached. A district court in Hamburg, West Germany Jan. 8 ordered a shipment of 3,000 tons of Chilean copper ore handed to a court-appointed officer pending settlement of a lawsuit brought against Chile by Kennecott Copper Corp. in connection with the nationalization of the U.S. firm's Chilean mining interests in 1971.

The shipment, reportedly valued at $3.5 million, had been provisionally unloaded by its purchaser, the North German Refinery. Kennecott claimed it owned the copper and the Chilean mine that produced it.

Attachment of the copper was criticized Jan. 9 by the Chilean government, which accused Kennecott of renewing its "moves to block the normal commercialization of Chilean copper." Kennecott had sought attachment of Chilean copper shipments in other European countries in 1972.

Chile's ambassador to Bonn, Federico Klein, noted Jan. 12 that West Germany was his country's most important copper customer, with annual imports of 520,000 tons of ore out of a total production of 700,000 tons. "It is clear that both countries are interested in an undisturbed transaction of the copper business," he said.

Klein announced Jan. 15 that Chile and the world's three other major copper exporting countries—Peru, Zambia and Zaire—had agreed not to replace copper on the world market where Chilean copper was seized as a result of legal action begun by Kennecott. He denied, however, reports that Chile would stop all copper exports or ban sales to West Germany if it lost its case in the Hamburg court. He said such moves were reserved only for extreme circumstances, and were not currently being considered.

Attachment lifted—The Hamburg court Jan. 22 released the disputed copper ore, and the ore was then handed over to the North German Refinery, which had purchased it from the Chilean state copper company, CODELCO.

The court ruled that Kennecott did not own the disputed copper, since the mine that produced it had been nationalized by Chile. It agreed with Kennecott that nationalization without compensation constituted "an important discrimination," but said it could not rule on the legality of the seizure of Kennecott's copper properties because they were all located in Chile. Kennecott, the court added, had failed to prove the existence of any "fundamental violation of law and order in Germany."

The court ordered Kennecott to pay the costs of the case, which Chilean President Allende estimated Jan. 25 at $50,000.

A Kennecott spokesman in New York disclosed Jan. 22 that the firm had filed another suit in Germany Jan. 16, seeking to hold the North German Refinery liable for the value of the disputed copper if it were processed and sold to consumers.

Chile denied a French report that it had made a $5 million "good-will payment" to Kennecott, the Miami Herald reported Jan. 20.

CODELCO disclosed that only two of the five copper mines nationalized by Chile had registered production increases in 1972, the Herald reported Jan. 27. Output had risen at the El Teniente mine, formerly owned by Kennecott, and the Andina mine, formerly owned by Cerro Corp., but had fallen at the Chuquicamata, Exotica and El Salvador mines, formerly owned by Anaconda Co.

Anaconda attachments let stand—The U.S. Supreme Court May 29 declined to review a preliminary court order attaching the New York City property of two Chilean state companies—the copper firm, CODELCO, and the development corporation, CORFO.

The attachment, ordered by a U.S. district court in 1972, had been obtained by Anaconda Co., which claimed Chile had stopped payment on promissory notes issued in 1969 for purchase of Anaconda's major Chilean properties, including the Chuquicamata mine. CORFO and CODELCO had sought the high court review on grounds they were part of the Chilean Republic and entitled to sovereign immunity from such court orders.

Kennecott Copper Corp., which once owned El Teniente, saw little hope for an amicable settlement of its long conflict with Chile. Kennecott President Frank Milliken told the company's stockholders May 1 that he saw "nothing going on that would lead me to believe there could be a rapprochement with the Allende government, and I do not know what kind of government might succeed him."

Soviet contract signed—CODELCO had signed an agreement to purchase machinery, equipment and spare parts from the Soviet Union, it was reported May 25.

Other economic developments—The cost of living had risen by 163.4% in 1972, according to government statistics reported by the Miami Herald Jan. 13.

Workers for bus companies providing service from Santiago to other provinces struck Jan. 6-9 to protest the refusal of Alberto Fernandez to resign as intervenor of the Via Sur Co. Fernandez had been replaced by the government following charges that he had led the firm to bankruptcy and illegally fired some 100 workers belonging to opposition parties, but he had declined to abandon his post. His replacement said Jan. 9 that the fired workers would be reinstated.

The government was developing a computer-controlled system to manage the entire economy, the newsletter Latin America reported Jan. 12.

Foreign relations. Chile announced Jan. 9 it was establishing diplomatic relations with the Cambodian government in exile of Prince Norodom Sihanouk. The prince would send a representative to open an embassy in Santiago.

China had granted Chile credits worth $62 million to purchase food, medicines, machinery and equipment from China, the newsletter Latin America reported Jan. 5.

Finland, Bulgaria and Rumania reportedly had offered credits totaling $40 million for expansion of the copper refinery and by-products at Ventanas, while East Germany had offered a loan of $15 million.

Chile and China had signed a maritime accord under which the state-owned Interoceanic Line of Chile and the Oriental Ocean Line of China would carry passengers and cargo between the two nations, it was reported Jan. 28.

Chile and Argentina signed an agreement Jan. 17 under which Argentina gave Chile credits worth $100 million to purchase food, automobile spare parts and capital goods. It was the largest loan ever made to Chile by Argentina.

Delegations from Chile and its 11 "Paris Club" creditors met in Paris Jan. 25-26 for further talks on repayment of Chile's foreign debt.

Visiting Chilean Education Minister Jorge Tapia announced in Lima that Peru and Chile had agreed to a large-scale exchange of teachers, the Miami Herald reported Jan. 18. Tapia said the exchange would help Chileans learn "the reforms implanted by Peru's revolutionary law."

A letter bomb addressed to the honorary Israeli consul in Santiago exploded Jan. 24 while being dismantled, blinding a police bomb expert and blowing off both his hands. Police said the device was mailed from Athens.

A group of terrorists in Guatemala City reportedly opened fire on the Chilean embassy there Jan. 25, damaging the ambassador's car but causing no injuries. The embassy had suffered two similar attacks in October 1972, when it was located in another part of the city.

Del Canto suspended. A Santiago court Jan. 27 fined and temporarily suspended Government Secretary General Hernan del Canto in a ruling on a suit filed by the Chilean Broadcasters Association. The suit cited Del Canto's closure in October 1972 of several stations which resisted the government's illegal takeover of radio broadcasting during the nationwide protest strikes.

Public works minister replaced. Rear Adm. Ismael Huerta, installed as public works minister shortly before the strikes ended, resigned Jan. 31. He was replaced by another naval officer, Rear Adm. Daniel Arellano.

Neruda to leave Paris post. President Allende announced Feb. 5 that Pablo Neruda, the poet and Nobel Prize winner, would resign as ambassador to France for health reasons. Neruda was 68.

Pre-election violence. Authorities were concerned about the increasing amount of campaign violence among supporters of the two political federations, La Prensa of Buenos Aires reported Jan. 21. Dozens of persons had been injured in street fights, some sustaining bullet wounds, and several political offices had been damaged by Molotov cocktail explosions. Interior Minister Carlos Prats made an appeal for electoral peace Jan. 18.

Prats announced Jan. 21 that the government was investigating a recent incident in Concepcion in which Arturo Frei Bolivar, running for re-election to the Chamber of Deputies, was allegedly stoned and fired at. Frei, a nephew of ex-President Eduardo Frei Montalva, charged his assailants were supporters of the government.

State ownership measure splits up. The ruling Popular Unity (UP) coalition suffered a split Jan. 26 when Allende's Socialist party publicly rejected a government bill which provided, among other measures, for the return to private owners of several dozen enterprises that had come under state control through interventions or requisitions.

The party said it had not been consulted on the bill before it was sent to Congress, and asserted it was opposed to the return of any state-controlled firm to the private sector. The party ordered one of its members, Economy Undersecretary Armando Arancibia, to resign from the government in protest. Arancibia's resignation was reported in Allende's hands Jan. 28, but the president took no immediate action on it.

The disputed bill was said to be the work of Economy Minister Orlando Millas, a member of the Communist party, with which the Socialists were at odds on a number of issues. The parties had criticized each other sharply in their respective newspapers, and there was fear within the UP that their feud would harm the coalition in the upcoming elections, in which it faced a relatively united opposition federation, according to La Prensa of Buenos Aires Jan. 29.

The Revolutionary Left Movement (MIR) issued a communique Jan. 26 supporting the Socialists and calling the Communists "revisionists" and "reformists." The MIR supported the re-election of Santiago Sen. Carlos Altamirano, the Socialist secretary general, who, because of electoral circumstances, would effectively be running against Communist Sen. Volodia Teitelboim, also of Santiago.

Congressional Elections

CODE wins vote; UP shows strength. The opposition Democratic Confederation (CODE) retained its Congressional majority in the March 4 elections, but President Salvador Allende's Popular Unity coalition (UP) showed surprising strength, gaining seats in both the Senate and the Chamber of Deputies.

Official results reported March 7 gave CODE 54.7% of the vote and the UP 43.4%. However, the UP gained six seats in the Chamber of Deputies, cutting CODE's majority there to 87-63, and two in the Senate, cutting CODE's margin to 30-20. All 150 Chamber seats and half of the 50 Senate seats were at stake in the elections.

CODE consisted of the National, Christian Democratic, Radical Left, Radical Democratic and National Democratic parties. The UP was composed of the Socialist, Communist, Radical, Independent Action and Christian Left parties and the United Popular Action Movement. The Popular Socialist Union, though not a member of the UP, usually was counted with it.

Votes were cast by 3.66 million of the 4.51 million eligible voters, an estimated 20% of whom were newly enfranchised

18-21-year-olds and illiterates. The voting was peaceful throughout the country.

Among Chile's four major parties—the Christian Democrats, Nationals, Communists and Socialists—Allende's Socialists made the greatest gains, picking up 14 Chamber and three Senate seats. The Communists gained three Chamber and three Senate seats, and the Nationals one Chamber and three Senate seats. The Christian Democrats, the country's largest party, made the poorest showing, gaining three Chamber seats but losing a Senate seat.

Both sides claimed victory late March 4 as the unusually long vote count began. Ex-President Eduardo Frei, elected to a Santiago Senate seat on the Christian Democratic ticket, called the vote a "clear" mandate for a change in government policies. Allende, on the other hand, claimed it was unprecedented in recent Chilean history for a government to surpass its winning presidential vote in subsequent parliamentary elections. Allende was elected with 36% of the vote in 1970.

(Frei received the highest vote among Santiago Senatorial candidates. He was followed by Communist Sen. Volodia Teitelboim and Socialist Sen. Carlos Altamirano, who were re-elected to their seats.)

The government won an important psychological victory in denying CODE the overwhelming public mandate it expected, according to the New York Times March 6. Opposition leaders had predicted a two-thirds majority for CODE, which would have enabled it to veto government legislation and even impeach Allende.

Throughout the often bitter campaign, CODE had characterized the elections as a "morally binding" plebiscite on government policies. The government, on the other hand, had minimized the importance of the vote, often calling it a routine democratic exercise, and predicting only that the UP would improve on its 1970 vote margin.

A high military source had told the Times Feb. 22 that the armed forces high command would not consider a simple majority victory by the opposition as "an expression by the country against the government" or its Marxist programs.

The source asserted the ranking military officials felt the opposition did not "represent a durable or consolidated force."

Numerous sources had noted that CODE's major parties, the center-left Christian Democrats and the right-wing Nationals, were united mainly in their opposition to the UP, and would oppose each other under normal circumstances. During Frei's presidential term, the Nationals had strongly opposed the government. However, observers also noted that one wing of the Christian Democrats was moving to the right.

Allende had issued a campaign platform Feb. 5 which pledged creation of "a new state" to guarantee workers and all Chilean people "the exercise of economic power and political power." The document proposed, among other measures, establishment of a unicameral "people's assembly" to replace the existing bicameral legislature, a new constitution, and simultaneous election of the president and Congress.

In releasing the platform, Allende had warned that if the Chilean right continued what he called its policy of obstruction and provocation, the "Chilean revolution would be forced to abandon the democratic road and embrace physical violence as an instrument." The warning followed attacks on a Christian Democratic senator and a National senatorial candidate for which the UP considered itself unjustly blamed. Attacks against two other opposition candidates caused Interior Minister Carlos Prats to meet Feb. 19 with leaders of all parties, who subsequently took measures to reduce campaign violence.

Six persons were reported killed during the campaign, considered normal for important Chilean elections.

Military officials leave Cabinet. President Salvador Allende March 27 accepted the resignations of the three military officers in his Cabinet, naming civilians to replace them.

The move was part of a general Cabinet shuffle following the resignation of all ministers March 23, to allow Allende to form a new government in the wake of the

March 4 Congressional elections. Nine ministers were reappointed to their posts, one was shifted to another post, and five new ministers were appointed. The new Cabinet represented all component parties in Allende's Popular Unity coalition (UP), but was said to be more moderate than its predecessor.

Allende said the three officers—army Gen. Carlos Prats, navy Rear Adm. Daniel Arellano and air force Gen. Claudio Sepulveda—would "return to their normal activities" because they had accomplished their appointed tasks: to resolve the crisis brought on by the October 1972 nationwide strikes and to guarantee the March 4 elections. Allende said, however, that the armed forces would continue to play an important role in government efforts to alleviate the existing economic crisis—in food distribution, transportation, port activities and certain industries.

Prats, Sepulveda and Rear Adm. Ismael Huerta had joined the Cabinet in November 1972 to help end the "bosses' strike" against the government and the resulting crisis. Prats was named interior minister, Sepulveda mines minister and Huerta public works minister. Huerta resigned in January in an apparent disagreement with the administration and was replaced by Arellano.

It was not immediately clear why the three officers left the Cabinet. Some reports said Allende had wanted to retain them in office, but they had made demands he was unwilling to accept. Others noted, however, that the president was under strong pressure in the UP, particularly from his Socialist party, to return to an all-civilian Cabinet.

Prats' crucial Interior Ministry post, second in power to the presidency, was assumed by Gerardo Espinoza Carrillo, 42. Espinoza was one of four Socialists in the new Cabinet, all counted in the moderate wing of the party, with which Allende generally sided. Allende reappointed two moderate Socialists, Foreign Minister Clodomiro Almeyda and Defense Minister Jose Toha, and replaced two members of the party's radical wing, Agriculture Minister Rolando Calderon and Government Secretary General Hernan del Canto.

The rest of the new Cabinet consisted of three Communists, three Radicals, two independents and one member each of the Independent Popular Action (API), Christian Left and MAPU (formerly United Popular Action Movement) parties. Observers reportedly were surprised that the smaller parties, which contributed little to the UP's March 4 vote, received eight Cabinet posts.

The new ministers and their parties:

Interior—Gerardo Espinoza Carrillo (Socialist); public works—Humberto Martones (Radical); agriculture—Pedro Hidalgo Ramirez (Socialist); land and colonization—Roberto Cuellar Bernal (API); mines—Sergio Bitar Chacra (Christian Left); government secretary general—Anibal Palma (Radical); foreign affairs—Clodomiro Almeyda (Socialist); economy—Fernando Flores Labra (MAPU); finance—Orlando Millas (Communist); education—Jorge Tapia (Radical); justice—Sergio Insunza (Communist); labor—Luis Figueroa (Communist); health—Arturo Jiron (independent); housing—Luis Matte (independent); defense—Jose Toha (Socialist).

In a speech shortly before swearing in his new Cabinet, Allende said Chile faced "difficult hours" in which it would have to overcome "serious economic difficulties," including a high inflation rate, speculation, hoarding and the black market. He called on "democratic sectors in the opposition" to "understand that flexibility is necessary to accept the changes that this country needs and demands." He also urged the UP parties to make clear within their ranks that "beyond us—the actors in this process—millions of human beings look with respect and admiration on our country's process of transformation."

Referring to conflicts within the UP, Allende said the new Cabinet would have to "concern itself with strengthening the unity and cohesion of the popular movement, recognizing and overcoming the errors we have committed."

New foreign minister. President Salvador Allende announced May 3 that Orlando Letelier would replace Foreign Minister Clodomiro Almeyda, who would resign to devote himself fully to Socialist party affairs. Letelier, currently Chile's ambassador to the U.S., was also a Socialist.

Crisis in MAPU. The tiny MAPU party expelled 15 members of its radical wing March 7, accusing them of "divisive activities" and of having contact with "ultra-leftist sectors that do not belong to the Popular Unity." Those expelled included the party's undersecretary for government, Eduardo Aquevedo.

The expulsions followed the disclosure shortly before the March 4 elections of an "internal" MAPU document criticizing a number of government actions, including the appointment of military officers to the Cabinet. The document, published by the conservative newspaper El Mercurio and exploited by opposition Congressional candidates, reportedly irritated President Allende. Allende was said to have told MAPU leaders that unless they provided a satisfactory explanation for the document, he would demand the resignation of every MAPU member in high government office. The expulsions reportedly were the party's response to that threat.

The 15 expelled MAPU members were said to be close to the extremist Revolutionary Left Movement (MIR), to have doubts about the participation of the armed forces in the government, and to oppose strongly the Communist strategy of consolidation within the UP and reconciliation with the major opposition party, the Christian Democrats.

U.S. talks held, 'impasse' reported. The U.S. and Chile held a second round of negotiations on financial and political problems March 22–23. A terse communique issued after the talks said "both parties expressed their respective points of view in an atmosphere of mutual respect, but no specific decisions or accords were reached." The left-wing magazine Chile Hoy reported March 31 that there was "a cruder truth: total impasse."

According to Chile Hoy, the U.S. negotiators "adopted from the very beginning a hostile, stubborn attitude which became threatening in the end." The London newsletter Latin America reported April 6 that the U.S. was more intransigent than it had been at the first round of talks in December 1972, demanding this time that Chile pay $700 million in compensation for nationalized U.S. assets before renegotiating its $1.7 billion U.S. debt.

A different report on the talks, published by the Washington Post April 1, said Chile had broken off negotiations in response to testimony before a U.S. Senate subcommittee on intervention in Chilean politics by the International Telephone and Telegraph Corp. (ITT). The testimony, which coincided with the U.S.-Chilean talks, reportedly convinced President Salvador Allende the U.S. had conspired with ITT to prevent his election in 1970.

Allende denied the Post report April 7, but denounced the U.S. April 10 for "collusion" with ITT's plans against his government. However, Chilean officials cautioned the attack should not be interpreted as a sign of "paralysis" of the U.S.-Chilean negotiations, and pointed out that Foreign Minister Clodomiro Almeyda, in Washington for an Organization of American States meeting, had met April 9 with John M. Hennessy, U.S. assistant secretary of the Treasury for international affairs, and John H. Crimmins, head of the U.S. negotiating team.

U.S. Probes ITT Actions

ITT's anti-Allende plans. A special U.S. Senate Foreign Relations Committee subcommittee on multinational corporations began a two-year investigation into the effects of those firms on the U.S. economy and conduct of foreign policy. Opening testimony was given by officials of International Telephone & Telegraph Corp. (ITT).

John A. McCone, former director of the Central Intelligency Agency (CIA) and a consultant to the agency since his retirement in 1965, told the subcommittee March 21 that he had met with Henry A. Kissinger, President Nixon's national security adviser, and Richard Helms, then director of the CIA and a "close friend," in mid-1970 to offer the U.S. government $1 million in financial aid from ITT. The money would be used to block the runoff election of Salvador Allende Gossens as president of Chile.

Allende, a Socialist, was elected Sept. 4, 1970 by a small plurality. He headed a left-wing coalition dominated by the Chilean Communist party. Allende took office in October 1970 after a joint session of Congress elected him president.

A year after his election, Allende expropriated the ITT-controlled telephone company in Chile. ITT filed a $92 million claim with the U.S. government's Overseas Private Investment Corp. (OPIC), which insured U.S. firms against foreign takeovers; any "provocation or instigation" by a client company, however, unless requested by the U.S. government, could invalidate such an insurance claim.

McCone made the $1 million offer in his capacity as a director of ITT. The money had been authorized by ITT President and Chairman Harold S. Geneen. McCone denied that the money was intended for "surreptitious" purposes or would be used to create "economic chaos."

"What he [Geneen] had in mind was not chaos but what could be done constructively. The money was to be channeled to people who support the principles and programs the U.S. stands for against the programs of the Allende-Marxists," McCone testified.

The money would be used in Chile, McCone said, for programs such as housing projects and technical agricultural assistance.

"International communism has said time and again that its objective is the destruction of the free world, economically, politically, militarily.... That was what Mr. Geneen was thinking of," according to McCone.

Members of the subcommittee expressed incredulity at McCone's testimony. Sen. Clifford P. Case (R, N.J.) noted that the U.S. had already given Chile more than $1 billion in economic aid over the past 10 years and that Allende had been elected anyway.

"How can a man of Mr. Geneen's intelligence possibly think that $1 million for these kinds of purposes in six weeks could make any difference?" Case asked.

The ITT plan proposed to Kissinger and Helms was termed the "Alessandri Formula." It called for financial support to be given to a coalition of the conservative National party, headed by Jorge Alessandri Rodriguez, and the Christian Democratic party, led by Radomiro Tomic. It was planned that they would oppose Allende in the expected runoff election and that Allesandri would be elected. He would then resign and call for new elections, permitting former President Eduardo Frei Montalva to challenge Allende in the subsequent two-man race.

"A number of people were trying to explore alternatives about what might be done. The Chilean military was discussing the Alessandri Plan. Mr. [William V.] Broe [director of clandestine operations in Latin America for the CIA] had a shopping list and the staff of the CIA had a shopping list," McCone told the subcommittee.

The plan was abandoned when Alessandri withdrew from the runoff race because of his lack of support in the Chilean Congress, where the final decision would be made.

McCone testified that Helms had told him "the matter was considered by an interdepartmental committee of senior representatives of the Defense and State Departments as well as the CIA, and the decision was reached that nothing should be done."

Although the ITT plan was rejected, McCone said that at his request, Helms put Geneen in contact with Broe. This corresponded with testimony given the previous day.

William R. Merriam, vice president of ITT and former director of its Washington office, had testified March 20 that ITT President Geneen had arranged to establish a working relationship between the corporation and the CIA in order to prevent the election of Allende as president of Chile, and, failing that, to bring about the "economic collapse" of Chile.

Merriam said his association with the CIA's Broe began at a Washington meeting held July 16, 1970 which was arranged and attended by Geneen. Geneen instructed him to "stay in touch" with Broe, Merriam testified, and subsequent phone conversations and meetings with the CIA agent occurred "many times."

Merriam told the subcommittee that Broe was impressed with the quality of information gathered by ITT operatives in Latin America. When shown a Sept. 17, 1970 cable from ITT officials Bob Berrellez and Hal Hendrix, Broe "approved" the recommendation, Merriam declared.

The cable urged ITT "and other U.S. firms in Chile" to head off Allende's election by contributing advertising funds to a conservative Chilean newspaper in financial difficulties. The report also recommended that ITT "bring what pressure we can" on the U.S. Information Agency to circulate the Chilean newspaper's editorial in Latin America and Europe. (In testimony given March 21, Hendrix claimed the plan was never carried out because its intent was too obvious.)

According to an ITT memo dated late September 1970, when the Chilean election results were still in doubt, ITT Senior Vice President Edward Gerrity told Geneen that Broe had suggested the company "apply economic pressures" to influence the voting.

Broe "indicated that certain steps were being taken, but that he was looking for additional help aimed at inducing economic collapse," Gerrity told Geneen, "Realistically I don't see how we can induce others involved to follow the plan suggested," Gerrity concluded.

As part of this plan, Merriam said the CIA made "repeated calls to firms such as General Motors, Ford Motor Co. and banks in California and New York." All refused to cease or reduce operations in Chile, according to ITT documents submitted to the subcommittee.

Other CIA recommendations called for cessation of U.S. aid to Chile, under the guise of a policy review, and government intervention with the World Bank group and the International Monetary Fund to halt their loans to Chile.

Merriam testified that ITT, at the instigation of the Anaconda Copper Co., organized an "Ad Hoc Committee on Chile" which met in his office in February 1971. "The thrust of the meeting was toward the application of pressure on the [U.S.] government wherever possible to make it clear that a Chilean takeover wouldn't be tolerated without serious repercussions following," according to Ronald Raddatz, a representative of the BankAmerica Corp., who was present. Others represented were Anaconda, Kennecott Copper Corp., W. R. Grace & Co., Pfizer Inc. and Ralston Purina Co.

No conclusions were reached, according to Merriam and he discounted the significance of the meeting itself. "We were just kicking around some ideas. We have these ad hoc committees all the time in Washington."

After the expropriation of the ITT Company in September 1971, Merriam wrote White House assistant Peter Peterson that there were "numerous justifiable leverages" the government could exert to protect American property in Chile.

The 18 suggestions included fostering "discontent" in the Chilean military, cutting off bank loans, restricting Chilean travel and slowing trade between the U.S. and Chile. "Everything should be done quietly but effectively to see that Allende doesn't get through the crucial next six months," the memo concluded.

Merriam justified the corporation's actions saying, "If Allende was faced with economic collapse, he might be more congenial toward paying us off."

In other testimony and documents submitted to the subcommittee, Merriam indicated that he made at least 25 visits to the State Department and had conferred for a "year" with officials in Kissinger's office.

According to another ITT memorandum submitted to the committee March 21, President Nixon had given the U.S. ambassador to Chile, Edward M. Korry, a "green light" in September 1970 to do everything possible short of military intervention to prevent the victory of Allende.

Helms had testified privately before the subcommittee March 5 prior to leaving to assume the post of ambassador to Iran. Broe was also questioned by the committee in secret session, the Washington Post reported March 22.

McCone and Geneen were interrogated March 16 in a private subcommittee meeting.

Geneen admits ITT offer. Harold S. Geneen, chairman of ITT, admitted to the subcommittee April 2 that he had twice offered money to the U.S. government to prevent Allende's 1970 election.

Geneen's admission regarding the first offer of funds was cautious. Having "no recollection to the contrary," Geneen told the subcommittee he would accept the testimony of William V. Broe, director of covert CIA operations in Latin America, that the money was offered at a July 1970 meeting and was intended to finance a CIA effort to stop Allende.

Geneen justified the gesture as an "emotional reaction" resulting from his conversations with Broe in which the CIA representative said the U.S. planned no efforts to circumvent the Chilean election of Allende, who was running on a Socialist-Communist platform.

According to Geneen, this policy of nonintervention represented the reversal of a 14-year U.S. "policy to maintain a democratic government in Chile." Geneen said he had been particularly disturbed by the talks with Broe because ITT had invested in Chile as part of the U.S. government's economic assistance policy to develop the country. In contrast to its past encouragement, the Nixon Administration appeared unwilling to aid ITT when the company anticipated the expropriation of its Chilean properties.

The matter "died right there," Geneen claimed, although he admitted making a second offer to the government in September 1970 when Allende had won his first election test and required ratification by the Chilean Congress in an October vote.

Geneen was unable to clarify contradictory testimony given earlier regarding the use of the slush fund. He claimed that the "amount mentioned of up to seven figures was intended to show a serious intent and to gain serious attention from the government" to finance "some socially constructive joint private industry and government projects" to induce Allende to make adequate compensation for ITT properties in Chile.

The hearings recessed following Geneen's appearance, but earlier testimony elicited further information regarding the extent of ITT's involvement in Chile's internal affairs.

ITT memo cites efforts—An ITT memorandum submitted to the subcommittee March 22 revealed that ITT had attempted to obtain compensation for the firm's telephone company in Chile, expropriated in September 1971 by President Allende, at the expense of other U.S.-owned companies also slated for nationalization.

The memo detailed a mutual assistance pact in which ITT would be compensated for loss of property and Allende would benefit politically by demonstrating his willingness to conclude a "fair deal" with the U.S. firm.

According to the memo, ITT hoped to persuade Allende that favorable world opinion would then allow him to confiscate the copper companies owned by Kennecott Corp. and Anaconda Copper Co. under the pretext that the seizures involved crucial natural resources and were distinct from the deal concluded with ITT.

The Chile plan failed when the Allende government broke off negotiations after columnist Jack Anderson made public ITT documents revealing ITT's intervention in the 1970 presidential elections in Chile aimed at the defeat of Allende.

According to the ITT memo, the company claimed success for its arrangement in 1968 when it had "handled the situation in Peru" on the "same basis." A petroleum subsidiary of the Exxon Corp. had been confiscated without compensation while ITT had received payment for the takeover of its telephone company.

ITT Senior Vice President Edward J. Gerrity gave testimony March 22 which contradicted the public statements of ITT director John A. McCone. McCone had said he had offered U.S. officials $1 million to finance an anti-Allende coalition.

Gerrity said he was "baffled" by McCone's disclosures. "The first I heard about it [the covert purpose of the fund] was here yesterday." Gerrity said ITT had intended that the money be used to finance "constructive" humanitarian programs in Chile.

Gerrity claimed that Jack D. Neal, ITT's director of international relations, had conveyed the offer of social assistance to the National Security Council and the State Department during September 1970.

In testimony March 20, Neal had said he "didn't elaborate" on the purpose of the money in his talks with government officials.

Arturo Matte Larrain, a prominent conservative Chilean politician, corroborated McCone's testimony March 23. Matte said he had rejected an offer by Robert Berrellez, an ITT official, to help anti-Allende forces block the final presidential vote in October 1970.

Matte, campaign manager for Jorge Alessandri, who was opposing Allende in the runoff race, said Berrellez "offered assistance but money was not mentioned. We turned him down."

Broe testified before a closed session of the subcommittee March 27. Portions of the transcript were made public March 28 after the CIA had reviewed it.

Broe described Geneen's offer made at a July 16, 1970 meeting in Washington to provide a "substantial fund" for the support of Alessandri's candidacy. The money was rejected, Broe testified, because the CIA refused to "serve as a funding channel."

"I also told him that the United States government was not supporting any candidate in the Chilean election," Broe said. He added that Geneen never suggested at that time that the money be used for social assistance programs.

According to Broe, Geneen told him that ITT and other American companies had raised money to influence the 1964 Chilean election of Eduardo Frei but that CIA Director John A. McCone had refused the offer.

After the Sept. 4, 1970 election in Chile when Allende won a small plurality of the vote, the CIA altered its policy of neutrality and met with ITT officials to devise anti-Allende plans, Broe testified.

During the same period in 1970, ITT held a board of directors meeting Sept. 8-9 when Geneen asked McCone to repeat the offer of financial assistance to the government with the new aim of funding an anti-Allende coalition before the second presidential vote. This plan, detailed by McCone at the hearings March 21, was termed the "Alessandri Formula."

Broe admitted devising a series of secondary proposals in September 1970 for Gerrity which would create economic chaos in Chile, also with the aim of preventing Allende's presidential victory.

Broe claimed he had acted with the full knowledge of CIA Director Richard Helms and that Geneen had initiated the company's first contact with the CIA in 1970.

Broe met with Geneen Sept. 29, 1970 to discuss plans for accelerating Chile's economic deterioration in order to "influence a number of Christian Democratic [party] congressmen who were planning to vote for Allende." Among the proposals Broe presented were delays in bank credits and delivery of spare part shipments, and withdrawal of technical assistance.

Broe also confirmed the testimony of another top ITT official, William M. Merriam, who had said Broe gave his approval Sept. 29, 1970 to a plan supporting an anti-Allende newspaper and "propagandists."

Other portions of the Broe testimony were released March 29 relating to the September 1970 conversations with Gerrity. Broe insisted that the CIA plan for the disruption of the Chilean economy had been approved by superiors in the intelligence gathering agency.

Charles A. Meyer, former assistant secretary of state for inter-American affairs and currently with Sears, Roebuck & Co., told the subcommittee March 29 that he saw no inconsistency between Broe's disclosures and his own testimony that the Nixon Administration had steadfastly maintained a policy of nonintervention in Chile.

Former Commerce Secretary Peter Peterson, then presidential adviser on international economic affairs, confirmed March 29 that he had met with Geneen Dec. 14, 1971 to discuss ITT's 18-point "action plan" to cripple the Chilean economy. Gen. Alexander Haig, presidential security adviser Henry Kissinger's principal adviser, was also present at the meeting. Peterson said the ITT proposal was never seriously considered by the Administration.

Edward Korry, U.S. ambassador to Chile from 1967 to 1971, testified March 27. He revealed that the CIA had commissioned polls to determine the outcome of the 1970 election and voiced his disagreement with the survey results. According to the CIA, Allende would win 40% of the vote. (He actually received 36%.) Korry said he had doubted the validity of the polls because they were based on a 1960 census.

Korry declined to answer other questions related to intervention in Chilean politics by the U.S. government or U.S. businesses. However, he did state that an ITT document claiming that President Nixon had given him a "green light" to oppose Allende was "erroneous."

As ambassador, Korry said he had tried to minimize intervention by his staff and by all Americans in Chile in the presidential election. Contacts with the Chilean military were specifically avoided, Korry said.

OPIC rejects ITT claim. The Overseas Private Investment Corp. (OPIC) April 9 denied International Telephone & Telegraph Corp.'s (ITT) insurance claim for $92.5 million sought as indemnity for its Chilean subsidiary seized in 1971 by the government of President Salvador Allende.

OPIC, a quasi-governmental agency which insured investments of U.S. companies from political risks abroad, based its rejection on ITT's "noncompliance with contractual obligations." It charged the firm with failing to "disclose material information to OPIC. In addition, ITT increased OPIC's risk of loss by failing to preserve administrative remedies as required by the contracts, and by failing to protect OPIC's interests as a potential successor to ITT's rights."

John W. Guilfoyle, ITT vice president and group executive for Latin America, announced that ITT would seek "immediate" arbitration of the decision. He said the company had paid nearly $6 million in premiums to OPIC.

Because further action was pending on the case, OPIC spokesmen refused to detail their reasons for denying the ITT claim; however, contractual grounds for default would include ITT's failure to pursue negotiations with Chile on compensation and evidence of "provocation or instigation by the investor [ITT]" causing expropriation of the property, unless undertaken at the "specific request" of the U.S. government. Dismissal of the OPIC claim did not invalidate ITT's right under international law to compensation from Chile, OPIC officials noted.

According to OPIC, 18 insurance claims had been filed in the past 2½ years by U.S. investors in Chile. Five claims were settled with payments of more than $80 million; the Chilean government and U.S. business interests, with the aid of OPIC guarantees, had agreed on settlements in two cases involving $26 million; OPIC was processing nine claims and had rejected a $154 million case brought by Anaconda Co.

Allende bars compensation for ITT. President Allende asserted April 10 that Chile would pay no compensation to ITT because of the revelations which emerged from the Senate subcommittee hearings.

"No one can dream that we are going to pay even half a cent to this multinational company which was on the verge of plunging Chile into civil war," Allende declared. He added that he "now could say North American officials and agencies of the U.S. tried to thwart the will of the Chilean people."

In making his address before a meeting of the World Labor Union Assembly, attended by 1,500 representatives from 70 countries, Allende extended his remarks on "imperialist" corporations to include Anaconda, Kennecott Copper Corp. and Cerro Corp., whose properties also had been seized.

Chilean Foreign Minister Clodomiro Almeyda declared April 9 in Washington that other ITT assets in Chile—two Sheraton hotels and a telephone equipment manufacturing company—"are in a very precarious position" because public opinion, outraged by disclosures made during the hearings, could force the government to make further expropriations.

'64 anti-Allende U.S. aid reported. The U.S. contributed considerable money and manpower to help elect Eduardo Frei president of Chile in 1964, the Washington Post reported April 6. Frei's Christian Democratic party disputed the report April 11.

The report, by Post staff writer Laurence Stern, said "knowledgeable officials" in Washington asserted the U.S. had dispatched up to $20 million and 100 agents of the Central Intelligence Agency (CIA) and State Department to help Frei defeat the current president, Salvador Allende.

"U.S. government intervention in Chile in 1964 was blatant and almost obscene," an intelligence officer told the Post. "We were shipping people off right and left, mainly State Department but also CIA with all sorts of covers," the officer asserted.

The Post said Cord Meyer Jr., whom it called a "Cold War liberal," directed the

CIA's covert programs to neutralize Communist influence in important opinion-molding sectors such as trade unions, farmer and peasant organizations, student activist groups and communications media before the elections.

One conduit for CIA money, the International Development Foundation, was employed in the 1964 campaign to subsidize Chilean peasant organizations, according to a former official responsible for monitoring assistance to Chile from the State Department's Agency for International Development (AID), the Post reported.

Covert financing reportedly was also arranged for a newspaper friendly to the interests of the Christian Democrats. "The layout was magnificent. The photographs were superb. It was a Madison Avenue product far above the standards of Chilean publications," another State Department veteran of the campaign recalled.

Among State Department personnel, another source told the Post, "individual officers . . . would look for opportunities. And where it was a question of passing money, forming a newspaper or community development program, the operational people would do the work. AID found itself suddenly overstaffed, looking around for peasant groups or projects for slum dwellers. Once you established a policy of building support among peasant groups, government workers and trade unions, the strategies fell into place."

A former U.S. ambassador to Chile privately estimated the covert program on Frei's behalf had cost about $20 million, the Post reported. In contrast, the figure that emerged in U.S. Senate hearings as the amount ITT was willing to spend to defeat Allende in 1970 was $1 million. AID funds alone were substantially increased for 1964, the Post reported.

The number of "special agents" dispatched to Chile at various stages of the campaign was estimated by one official at about 100.

The Post story was given extensive coverage in Chile by the official Communist newspaper El Siglo, which charged the story proved Frei guilty of treason, it was reported April 14.

Christian Democratic denial—The Christian Democratic party president, Renan Fuentealba, denied at a press conference April 11 that the U.S. had contributed $20 million to Frei's 1964 campaign. He also called for an investigation of the Post's charges and asked the Post to examine the financing of campaigns by Chile's Marxist parties.

Fuentealba asserted that Christian Democratic races in Chile were "fundamentally" funded by the monthly dues of some 70,000 paying party members. Party sources acknowledged some income from abroad, such as Chileans living outside the country and from companies doing business in Chile.

(It was also generally accepted that foreign counterparts of the party, as well as the Radical and Communist parties, contributed money, the Post reported April 14. German correspondents had tried to prove that the West German Christian Democratic party was a prime funder of its Chilean counterpart but had failed to do so, the Post reported.)

The party's vice president, Felipe Amunategui, noted that the $20 million figure included money given to Chile "under U.S. aid . . . approved by the Chilean Parliament with Allende voting in favor," the Post reported. This raised the question of when development assistance crossed the line into political bribery, the Post said.

Other sources disputed the original Post article's two specific cases of covert financing of Frei's campaign. Politicians from both left- and right-wing parties had been unable to find the "Madison Avenue" style newspaper which allegedly had supported Frei in the campaign and later disappeared. Extensive research in the Congressional archives, which filed every newspaper published, produced none fitting the description, the Post reported April 14.

The International Development Foundation, which allegedly had channeled CIA money to peasant organizations, had begun to operate in Chile only a month before the 1964 elections and had had impact on the country only after Frei's inauguration, the Post reported April 14.

Prats in U.S. Gen. Carlos Prats Gonzalez, army commander and former interior minister, visited Washington, D.C. May 3-6 as the guest of Gen. Creighton W. Abrams, U.S. Army chief of staff. Prats conferred with other U.S. military officials including Adm. Thomas H. Moorer, chairman of the joint chiefs of staff, and discussed Chile's need for U.S. military equipment, mostly logistical.

Prats said May 6 that Chile had not ruled out buying arms from the Soviet Union, emphasizing the nation did not want to "depend on any one line of supply." He was scheduled to visit Great Britain, the U.S.S.R. and other countries before returning to Chile.

'Plots' & Strikes

'Extremist' plan charged. Santiago riot police were placed on alert late April 10 against what the government called a plan by the extreme right and left to block roads and occupy factories.

Earlier in the day, members of the extremist Revolutionary Left Movement (MIR) had led residents of Constitucion, on the coast south of Santiago, in blocking the roads and railway into the town to demand government solutions to local housing and food problems. No serious incidents were reported.

Government Secretary General Anibal Palma charged extremists planned the Santiago occupations to disrupt food distribution, create a climate of agitation and embarrass the government, which they would then criticize for lack of authority. The plan had been originated by the extreme right, which had duped the MIR into cooperating, Palma asserted.

Palma said the government was once again "calling for the maintenance of order. Occupations and violent acts are not the way to solve problems."

President Salvador Allende had warned April 3 that MIR activists were planning assaults on private and state food distributors, and that strong measures would be taken against such actions. MIR militants surrounded the warehouse of the private distributor CENADI the next day but were dispersed after a battle with police. Thirty persons were reported arrested and 10 injured.

Santiago merchants April 5 praised the government's action against the MIR. The MIR denounced it as "police repression", and asserted occupations of factories and food distributors were not provocations but attempts by the people "to defend themselves against inflation and the shortage of essential articles." The MIR urged formation of "commando groups in each factory, farm, village and school" to combat government repression.

Works Ministry occupied—MIR militants occupied the Public Works Ministry April 23 and held it most of the day to demand a voice in the ministry's affairs and increased benefits for laborers working part-time on emergency repairs. They abandoned the building only after a personal appeal from Allende. No arrests were reported.

Christian Democratic challenge—The Christian Democratic party May 15 issued a statement pledging to use "all its power" to stop what it called the government's "totalitarian escalation."

The statement, approved at the party's national meeting ending May 13, accused the government of "seeking the totality of power, which means Communist tyranny disguised as the dictatorship of the proletariat."

The party approved a new executive board and president May 13. The president was Sen. Patricio Aylwin, who replaced Sen. Renan Fuentealba, not a candidate for re-election. Aylwin said the new board represented "categorical opposition to the government." Fuentealba warned the government that if it persisted in its policies it would be unable to "resist the current of popular discontent."

Education reforms postponed. The government announced April 13 that it would not decree its projected education reforms in 1973. It acted following expressions of doubt about the measures by the armed forces commanders and protests by high school students, the political opposition and the Roman Catholic Church.

Education Minister Jorge Tapia said the reforms would be sent to Congress, as demanded by the opposition and the student federations it dominated. However, he denied opposition charges that the measures were designed to impose a "Marxist consciousness" on students and constituted a "death-blow to freedom of education."

According to a government education official, Ivan Nunez, the reforms would establish the National Unified School (ENU), whose general purpose would be to replace the current "scientific-humanist" curriculum with a "polytechnic and general" one. Nunez said March 21 that ENU would effect "the changing of education from a socialist perspective."

The primary and intermediate education levels would be eliminated in favor of a straight 12-year program, Nunez said. The new program would be divided into three study areas: "common" courses similar to those currently offered; work courses to introduce students to industries, the agrarian reform and public services; and independent study consisting of courses selected by the students from the "common" program.

Msgr. Emilio Tagle, archbishop of Valparaiso Province, said March 21 that the Church opposed the ENU plan, fearing it could "give control of education to a partisan ideology." Other church officials protested the education reforms, as did opposition political parties. Students from the opposition-dominated Secondary School Students Federation in Santiago protested the measures April 13 in a demonstration broken up by police.

Tapia acknowledged at a press conference April 13 that high military officials had also expressed reservations about the projected reforms. He said he had talked for more than two hours with the armed forces commanders and about 150 officers, who had questioned him closely about the reforms.

Press scored on military. The government April 18 accused the opposition press of trying to "break the discipline of the armed forces" and discredit their commander, Gen. Carlos Prats Gonzalez.

The opposition newspaper La Segunda had alleged Prats had taken a political stance in favor of the government, telling a meeting of 800 officers that he supported the process of change instituted by President Allende. Other opposition papers had alleged that several senior officers, including Rear Adm. Ismael Huerta, had been prematurely retired because of their opposition to the government's projected educational reforms.

Defense Minister Jose Toha April 18 condemned the "repeated dissemination of false or alarmist" news about the armed forces, and asserted "the government has the obligation, which it will discharge effectively, of defending the prestige, discipline and unity of military institutions."

2 provincial intendants suspended. The Chamber of Deputies' approval of a motion by the Christian Democratic party to impeach Jaime Faivovich, the intendant of Santiago Province, was reported April 12.

Faivovich, a member of President Allende's Socialist party, was suspended pending Senate action on the impeachment measure. He was accused of excessive leniency toward extreme leftist elements and responsibility for an incident in which two young Christian Democrats were killed.

The Chamber vote was 65-0, with no government deputies in attendance. A government official charged Faivovich was prevented by the opposition from appearing in the Chamber to refute the charges.

The Chamber then suspended the intendant of Valparaiso Province, Carlos Gonzalez Marquez, June 5 on charges of ordering arbitrary arrests of members of the extreme right-wing Fatherland and Liberty party. The motion, introduced by the Christian Democrats, was approved 76-0 after all pro-government deputies walked out, according to the Cuban press agency Prensa Latina.

Impeachment procedures had also been introduced in the Chamber against the intendants of Talca and Nuble, Francisco Reyes and Luis Quesada respectively, it was reported June 15.

Rightist 'plot.' Some 40 to 50 members of the right-wing Fatherland and Liberty party were arrested May 11 in several cities in connection with an alleged plot against the government. Most were released after questioning. Interior Undersecretary Daniel Vergara said May 13 that the arrests were ordered for violation of the internal security and press laws. He said arms and ammunition held by detainees had been confiscated in Concepcion, Osorno and Chillan.

The alleged plot was reported in the left-wing press after two Fatherland and Liberty leaders, Walter Robert Thieme and Miguel Juan Sessa, were detained in Mendoza, Argentina, where they had flown in a private plane. The two requested political asylum and were granted it May 9. Chile asked Argentina to hold them pending a request for extradition.

Thieme had been reported dead Feb. 23 after his plane seemingly disappeared into the Pacific Ocean.

La Prensa of Buenos Aires reported May 9 that Thieme and Sessa had admitted to Argentine officials that they had plotted against Allende. They reportedly produced documents and plans for action against the government to begin May 15.

Thieme said at a Buenos Aires press conference May 12 that if "the price of liberation [in Chile] is civil war, we will have to pay it." He did not specify the role of the armed forces in such a conflict, but said he was convinced the military "know very well the responsibility that falls to them and will fall to them in the future when the people and all Chile react" against the government.

Outgoing Foreign Minister Clodomiro Almeyda said May 13 that Thieme's declarations exemplified "the subversive aims of the fascist sectors in Fatherland and Liberty, in sectors of the National party and even the leadership of the Christian Democrats."

(The president of Fatherland and Liberty's Valparaiso organization, Claudio Fadda Cori, had been arrested June 4 on charges of possessing various arms, Prensa Latina reported. Interior Minister Gerardo Espinoza had warned May 17 that police would arrest any party members carrying weapons. He accused Fatherland and Liberty of planning "armed violence" against the government.)

Defense Minister Jose Toha had denied before a Senate committee May 10 that his ministry had any evidence of "the possibility of armed aggression coming from a neighboring country" and asserted the press reports of a plot against the government were "alarmist."

Toha also denied a charge by Sen. Pedro Ibanez of the National party that Chile had agreed to turn over to the Soviet Union the southern port of Colcura, which was being constructed with Soviet technical assistance under a bilateral agreement signed in 1967.

Private buses halted. Private collective transport was paralyzed throughout Chile beginning May 22 as owners demanded higher fares and a solution to the shortage of spare parts. The government requisitioned all buses and microbuses not in operation, and placed an army general in charge of them. A settlement involving a 166% fare increase reportedly was reached with the owners May 24, but it was rejected by the drivers.

The Communist party, the second most important in the ruling Popular Unity coalition, called on Chilean workers May 31 to postpone their economic demands to help contain inflation. The cost of living reportedly rose by 34.4% in January–April.

Emergency declared in copper strike. The government May 10 declared a state of emergency in O'Higgins Province, where a strike at the El Teniente copper mine had entered its fourth week. The measure placed the province under military control.

The emergency declared earlier in Santiago Province was lifted May 17 by President Salvador Allende, who said the disorders there had ceased.

Interior Undersecretary Daniel Vergara May 10 said the O'Higgins emergency was imposed because the copper strike, though "partial," was having "such an impact on the national economy that its maintenance and prolongation mean ... a public calamity." Workers at Chuquicamata, the nation's other crucial mine, struck to support El Teniente May 11–12.

El Teniente's strikers claimed they had been cheated of a 41% pay raise, agreed to in 1972 but later deducted from a 100% raise granted by the government to all wage-earners to offset inflation. The government, which blamed "fascist" forces for the strike, reportedly offered a compromise bonus amounting to six weeks' pay, but this was rejected by the strikers. About half the miners at Chuquicamata began striking June 1 to support El Teniente.

According to the French newspaper Le Monde May 15, the most committed strikers at El Teniente were not the 8,000 workers, some of whom had returned to their jobs, but some 5,000 mine officials and administrators demanding a 41% wage supplement retroactive to October 1972. The copper strike threatened to spread to other sectors, having already stimulated transport strikes in Valparaiso and Concepcion, Le Monde reported.

About 120 striking miners and a policeman were injured May 9 in clashes in the town of Rancagua in O'Higgins Province, the Times of London reported May 12.

The opposition Christian Democratic party May 25 filed impeachment charges in Congress against two Cabinet officials—Labor Minister Luis Figueroa and Mines Minister Sergio Bitar—for allegedly precipitating the copper strike.

Copper exports halted—The government was forced to suspend foreign copper shipments June 5 as a strike at the El Teniente mine entered its 48th day and a solidarity strike at the Chuquicamata mine entered its fifth day.

The shipments, suspended at least until the end of June, were destined mainly for Great Britain and West Germany.

O'Higgins Province, in which El Teniente was located, continued under military rule following several eruptions of violence in the provincial capital, Rancagua, in which one person was killed and numerous others injured.

The worst violence occurred late June 1 and early June 2, after the funeral of a miner shot to death by a military patrol May 30. Strikers erected flaming barricades across at least 20 intersections, fired guns and hurled dynamite, reportedly blowing up the offices of several progovernment parties. Police and troops fought back with tear gas and water cannons. Two policemen were reported injured, and 86 persons were arrested.

The miner had been shot when he refused an order to halt and "imperiled" the lives of several soldiers on patrol, according to authorities. The government closed the right-wing radio station Radio Agricultura late May 30 for broadcasting "false and alarmist" reports of the killing. The closure order covered six days, but it was lifted by an appeals court officer June 3.

Students and striking miners had erected flaming barricades in Rancagua May 25, clashing with police and attacking a number of businesses which refused to strike in solidarity with El Teniente.

Clodomiro Almeyda, acting as vice president while President Salvador Allende attended Argentina's presidential inauguration, warned May 25 that striking miners would be fired if the conflict continued much longer. (Sixty-five strikers were reported dismissed June 5 in the first punitive action in the stoppage.)

Palma arrested—Government Secretary General Anibal Palma was ordered arrested by an appeals court judge June 5 on charges of "prevarication" and "disrespect" in connection with the closing of a right-wing radio station. Palma was later released on bail.

The station, Radio Agricultura, had been ordered closed by Palma for allegedly broadcasting false and alarmist reports on disturbances in Rancagua related to the copper strike. Radio Agricultura appealed the decision before an appeals court, and a court-appointed magistrate, Hernan Cereceda, lifted the closure order. Palma appealed that action before the supreme court. The court rebuked the minister for "disrespect," and assigned Cereceda to make a new investigation. Cereceda then accused Palma of "prevarication" in addition to "disrespect," and ordered him arrested.

The political commission of the governing Popular Unity coalition (UP) said June 6 it would begin impeachment procedures against the entire Supreme Court, which it denounced as having "lost all legitimacy and moral authority by becoming another bastion of reaction." The court, the UP charged, was guilty of a "new abuse of power, which once again tweaks the nose of the law."

Labor & mines ministers impeached—The Chamber of Deputies June 6 suspended

Labor Minister Luis Figueroa and Mines Minister Sergio Bitar for allegedly failing to comply with a law which would have raised the salaries of El Teniente's miners, and thus precipitating the current copper strike.

The motion, introduced by the Christian Democrats and backed by the right-wing National party, was approved 74–0 after all pro-government deputies walked out of the chamber.

Before the vote, a melee broke out among at least 60 government and opposition legislators. The fight was started by Communist Deputy Alejandro Rojas and Christian Democratic Deputy Carlos Dupre, who attacked each other during a heated argument.

About 20,000 workers had demonstrated in support of Bitar and Figueroa in Santiago June 5. The rally was organized by CUT.

Figueroa and Bitar were censured and dismissed by the Senate June 20. They were the fourth and fifth Cabinet officials impeached under President Salvador Allende.

The Senate motions were approved 26–0, with pro-government legislators boycotting both the debate and the vote. Allende made no immediate move to replace the two ministers.

Copper strike crisis deepens. Thousands of professionals, teachers and students in the five major provinces went on strike June 20 to support the 63-day stoppage at the El Teniente copper mine and to protest the government's economic policies.

Physicians, nurses, dentists and druggists struck in the provinces of Santiago, Valparaiso, Concepcion, Arica and Magallanes. Hospitals handled only emergency cases, and the national medical college warned it would suspend even those services if the government took reprisals against physicians.

In the capital, the Communist-led Central Labor Federation (CUT) called a general strike for June 21 to support the government. Jorge Godoy, the federation's leader, said workers would paralyze "everything, even lights and telephones, so the reactionaries can gauge the strength of the working class."

President Salvador Allende flew to El Teniente June 20 for a first-hand report on the strike, the longest and costliest of his administration.

Allende had met with six strike leaders June 15 after severe street fighting in Santiago between government supporters and backers of the copper strike. The meeting was denounced by the political commissions of the Communist and Socialist parties, which asserted the government should offer no new concessions to strikers with "fascist and seditious" motives. Allende said June 16 that he had not altered his previous position but simply stressed to the strike leaders "the grave consequences of [this] conflict for the country."

Supporters of the government and the copper strike battled June 15; one person was reported killed and 63 injured. The presidential palace was surrounded throughout the day by chanting workers and students, and by most of Santiago's heavy trash trucks and road scrapers. Nearby, national police and pro-Allende activists fought off anti-government workers and students who sought to welcome a miners' march which had set out from El Teniente the day before.

The government said the miners had no permission to march. When they attempted to enter the city, they were cut down by tear gas and water cannon. Most of the miners gave up the march, but about 2,000 reportedly were smuggled into Santiago in private vehicles.

Police battled striking miners near the presidential palace June 16, breaking up miners' barricades located near the headquarters of the opposition Christian Democratic party, which supported the strike. Ex-President Eduardo Frei, the Christian Democratic leader and newly elected Senate president, charged 50 persons were injured and accused the police of "brutal repression."

Allende June 17 linked the strike to an alleged plot by his opponents to bring down the government. He said the plot would fail because neither Congress nor the armed forces would support it.

(Allende again sought to bring the military into his Cabinet, as he did in November 1972 to help end the nationwide protest strikes, the Washington Post reported June 17. However, the officers reportedly were asking that he abandon his programs for rapid socialization of the country, which Allende found difficult to accept.)

New clashes occurred in Santiago June 19 as riot policemen used tear gas on rock-throwing demonstrators who demanded settlement of the copper strike. The violence followed an anti-government rally near the presidential palace, organized by the Christian Democrats.

At El Teniente, meanwhile, an estimated 50%-60% of the work force was either on strike or manning the emergency maintenance crews which miners provided even in total shutdowns.

A government offer of productivity bonuses and a lump payment, which officials said would cost the state copper company more than the strikers' original demands, had split copper workers into two factions. The majority of unskilled workers, and virtually all card-carrying members of the parties in the ruling Popular Unity coalition (UP), had voted to accept the offer and had returned to work. Virtually all the skilled workers stood by the original demands and continued to strike.

Rancagua, where most of the miners lived, was controlled by the strikers. They received food from sympathetic farmers to the south, brought in trucks provided by the same owners who played a critical role in the October 1972 strikes. Rancagua's radio station was occupied by wives of the strikers, and the local newspaper supported the stoppage.

Milton Puga, a Christian Democrat and leader of the striking skilled workers' union, justified the strike's continuation by noting the government's dismissal of 75 strikers, it was reported June 16. "In the worst struggles of the Yankee epoch, we never saw a strike in which men were fired for striking," he asserted.

Asked if strikers were receiving help from groups that sought the collapse of the government, Puga said strikebreaking efforts were so intense that strikers took help from any source but that it did not imply any political commitment. The military commander of the area, Col. Orlando Ibanez, said he was aware of no subversion by outside agitators in Rancagua.

A high government copper official, Waldo Fortin, admitted June 14 that some striking workers had been fired. However, he said each person had been dismissed for assaulting nonstrikers or damaging government property.

Workers at Chuquicamata, Chile's other crucial copper mine, voted by a narrow margin June 6 not to continue their strike in solidarity with El Teniente, according to the Cuban press agency Prensa Latina.

Strikes, violence continue—Most transportation and commerce were halted in the provinces of Santiago, Valparaiso, Concepcion and Arica June 21, as government opponents struck to support the El Teniente walkout and leftist workers struck in support of the government.

Those striking against the government included doctors, engineers, other professionals and some students, many of whom had struck the day before. Workers supporting the government generally were affiliated with the Communist-led Central Labor Federation (CUT), which called a 24-hour strike to "erase the attempt by fascism to cause a civil war in the country."

Troops were called out to help quell shootings and riots in the capital and other cities. Bombs exploded in Santiago outside a Socialist party office, a government office and a government television installation. A fourth bomb wrecked two cars outside the home of a Cuban embassy official, but no injuries were reported.

In Curico, south of Santiago, shootings and riots left at least six persons wounded, police reported. In Osorno, further south, five persons were injured as Communists and Christian Democrats clashed with rocks and knives.

Allende told workers gathered outside the Government House that he would start court action against Fatherland and Liberty and against the National party. He accused the Nationals of sedition in issuing a statement charging that the government had repeatedly violated the Constitution, thus making itself "illegitimate."

The leading opposition newspaper, El Mercurio, was closed for six days June 21 by court order, for allegedly "inciting subversion" by printing the National statement. The newspaper failed to appear June 22, for the first time in its 73-year history. However, the closure order was overturned by an appeals court later in the day, and El Mercurio reappeared June 23.

Police clashed with government opponents and supporters in Santiago June 26, following the arrival from Rancagua of some 500 wives of striking miners. Police reported no injuries, but at least four ambulances removed injured demonstrators, according to news reports. Allende met with 10 of the miners' wives for about an hour.

More than 1,000 striking miners who arrived in Santiago June 15 despite a police blockade, had remained in the capital and were living in university buildings controlled by anti-government students, the New York Times reported June 27.

El Teniente strike ends. Striking workers at the El Teniente copper mine agreed July 2 to return to their jobs, ending a 74-day walkout that cost the country an estimated $70 million.

The strikers, representing more than half the mine's work force, accepted a government offer of a series of bonuses retroactive to April 1, and a pay increase. One issue, however, remained unresolved: the strike leaders wanted immediate reinstatement of strikers fired during the walkout, while the government wanted a commission created to deal with strikers who had committed illegal acts. The government had charged all those fired had committed such acts.

The state copper concern, CODELCO, said June 3, as strikers began returning to work, that no copper would be available for sale in July.

Economy minister suspended. The Chamber of Deputies voted to suspend Economy Minister Orlando Millas June 20 on charges of responsibility for alleged discrimination in the distribution of scarce food items. An earlier and very similar motion against Millas, introduced by the right-wing National party, had been defeated May 18 when Christian Democratic deputies abstained from the vote on grounds the motion was "unsuitably" worded. Millas was accused by Christian Democrats of violating the law in favor of the government's Price and Supply Boards (JAPs), created to facilitate and control the distribution of scarce food items. Opposition legislators believed the JAPs were illegal and behaved in discriminatory fashion.

Impeachment measures against yet another Cabinet official, Interior Minister Gerardo Espinoza, were introduced in the Chamber by Christian Democrats June 20. Espinoza was accused of responsibility for a police raid the day before on television Channel 6 of the University of Chile. Police allegedly violated university autonomy and destroyed equipment belonging to the channel, which had begun transmission June 17 after left-wing workers occupied the university's Channel 9.

Allende, Supreme Court clash. The 13 Supreme Court justices June 26 accused President Allende of having, "without warning or motive," participated in a "systematic campaign" to destroy the power and prestige of Chile's highest tribunal.

The court made the charge in response to a letter from Allende alleging that "on each occasion that the harsh social and political struggle of our country has become exasperating ... [the court] has been absent, or more exactly, has been present to make observations of doubtful benefit which rarely favor social peace and the re-establishment of democratic dialogue."

The exchange coincided with the publication of articles in the left-wing press criticizing recent Supreme Court decisions, particularly in political cases.

Cost of living up 238%. Official statistics reported June 7 showed the cost of living in Chile had risen by a record 238% in the 12 months ending in May.

Industrial production fell by 5.6% in January-March, compared with the same period in 1972, according to a private sector study reported June 15. Sales were reported down by 4.9%.

The French firm Peugeot signed an agreement with the state development corporation to produce 15,000 medium-sized vehicles in Chile in 1973, rising to 30,000 in 1980, it was reported June 1. The vehicles would contain 65.6% Chilean parts in 1973 and 92.6% in 1975.

Finland contributed a $10.6 million credit to develop Chile's forestry industry, according to a report June 6. Chile agreed to use 80% of the loan to purchase Finnish equipment.

Bulgaria granted Chile a $17 million loan for construction of a sulphuric acid plant, it was reported June 29.

Canada granted an $8 million loan for the purchase of twin Otter 300 planes and for re-equipment of the state telecommunications company, it was reported July 27.

Spain granted Chile a loan equivalent to some $45 million for the purchase of motor manufacturing machinery and equipment, and for imports of wheat, oil and other foodstuffs, it was reported July 20.

The U.S. Commerce Dept. reported Aug. 3 that U.S. exports to Chile had declined by 50% since the election of President Allende in 1970.

Coup attempt crushed. Troops loyal to President Salvador Allende crushed an attempted military coup June 29, the first bid to overthrow an elected Chilean government in 42 years.

About 100 rebel troops attacked the presidential palace and the Defense Ministry in downtown Santiago shortly before 9 a.m. They were held off by the palace guard until loyal troops under the army commander, Gen. Carlos Prats, surrounded them and forced their surrender. Twenty-two persons, mostly civilian passers-by, were reported killed and 34 wounded in the battle, which left the immediate area in a shambles.

The rebels, in four tanks and other armored vehicles, first took control of Constitution Plaza, in front of the presidential palace. They herded some civilians out of the area and then shelled the palace and raked the surrounding streets with automatic weapons fire. Several squads of rebels with tanks broke off to attack the Defense Ministry nearby, breaking down its doors and freeing an army captain held there for alleged implication in a planned coup denounced by authorities the day before.

While the rebels battled the palace guard, Allende, at his private residence, declared a nationwide state of emergency and ordered the revolt crushed. Prats personally led loyal troops in the counterattack. The government was in control of the palace by 11:30 a.m.

Allende later made a nationwide broadcast, announcing that most of the rebels had surrendered and that "the situation in the whole country is one of calm and absolute tranquillity." He said the navy and air force commanders in chief had given him their backing immediately after the outbreak. He added that the aborted revolt would have no impact on his government's policies.

Spokesmen for the main opposition party, the Christian Democrats, called for support of the constitutional order during and after the revolt. Allende also received messages of support from Cuban Premier Fidel Castro, Mexican President Luis Echeverria Alvarez, and Argentine ex-President Juan Peron.

Government supporters demonstrated in the streets of Santiago after the revolt was crushed. Leftists reportedly tried to storm the offices of La Tribuna, an anti-government newspaper, and the headquarters of the right-wing National party, but were turned back by policemen firing tear gas. El Mercurio, the leading opposition paper, was temporarily occupied by police, and other newspaper offices were temporarily evacuated. The pro-government radio station Radio Portales was reportedly bombed.

Allende spoke to a crowd of thousands of supporters from the balcony of the presidential palace in the evening. He denounced the "fascists, traitors and cowards" who he said planned the aborted revolt, and asserted "the people and the armed forces can never be defeated." He said the rebels included civilian members of the extreme right-wing Fatherland and Liberty party, who were now seeking asylum at foreign embassies.

(Five Fatherland and Liberty leaders, including party chief Pablo Rodriguez, were reported July 2 to have taken refuge in the Ecuadorean embassy, where they sought political asylum.)

Allende later sent Congress legislation declaring a 90-day state of siege. Despite a government warning that the nation was "on the brink of civil war," the bill was rejected July 2 by an 81-52 vote in the Chamber of Deputies. Leaders of the four opposition parties maintained Allende had ample powers to preserve order under the state of emergency.

Under the emergency, the armed forces assumed control of the public order, and the government could prohibit public gatherings, censor the news and order curfews. The more extreme state of siege, normally reserved for wartime, would have given the president broader authority in suspending civil rights.

The military authorities banned all "commentary" about the revolt June 30. Newspapers published accounts and photographs of the uprising, but some papers appeared with blank spaces, indicating censored passages. Seven radio stations and La Tribuna were reported closed July 1. La Tribuna reportedly had described the uprising as a vulgar show by the government to obtain greater power and institute a dictatorship. An 11 p.m.–6 a.m. curfew was also imposed.

Meanwhile, the rebels and their reputed leader, Col. Roberto Souper, were under arrest in an army camp.

'Barracks revolt' thwarted—The army had announced June 28 the crushing of a "barracks revolt" against the commanding officers and the government.

Gen. Mario Sepulveda, army commander of Santiago Province, said the effort to "break the institutional processes" had been "totally aborted" with the arrest of several low-ranking officers early June 27, shortly before a bizarre incident which the government described as an attempt on the life of the army commander in chief, Gen. Prats.

According to Government Secretary General Anibal Palma, Prats was being driven to the Defense Ministry when his car was boxed in by several others at an intersection. The general feared he was about to be assassinated, and consequently left his automobile, fired two warning shots with a pistol—one striking the door of a woman's car—and fled in a taxi. This account was roughly corroborated by an early United Press International report.

According to other press accounts and opposition charges, however, Prats became enraged when the woman motorist recognized him and stuck out her tongue. The general allegedly pursued her in his vehicle and fired at her. When she stopped, he allegedly aimed the gun at her head and demanded an apology. An angry crowd gathered, and Prats departed in a taxi.

The incident caused a near-riot as angry motorists and bystanders surrounded Prats' car, painted anti-government slogans on it and deflated its tires. Three busloads of riot police firing tear gas arrived to end the disturbance.

Prats reportedly submitted his resignation to Allende shortly after the incident. Allende, however, rejected it, and declared a state of emergency in Santiago Province, calling it "a necessary measure to confront the excesses of fascism." Gen. Sepulveda was named commander of the emergency zone.

Emergency lifted; Cabinet shuffled— Allende dissolved the nationwide state of emergency July 4 and named a new all-civilian Cabinet the next day.

The emergency, declared during the unsuccessful military coup attempt June 29, was ended because the country had returned to "absolute normality," according to Interior Undersecretary Daniel Vergara.

The Cabinet had resigned July 3 and Allende had announced that day he would not appoint military officers to the new Cabinet. He explained he did not want the armed forces "involved in political disputes"; however, Congressional sources reported Allende had asked officers to join the Cabinet, but they had made unacceptable demands, including appointments to key undersecretary posts in several ministries as well as governorships and other provincial posts.

The new Cabinet preserved the political balance of its predecessor, with four Socialists, four Radicals, three Communists, two independents and one member each of the Christian Left and MAPU parties. There were seven new ministers.

The Cabinet:

Interior—Carlos Briones; foreign affairs—Orlando Letelier; defense—Clodomiro Almeyda; agriculture—Ernesto Torrealba; finance—Fernando Flores Labra; economy—Jose Cademartori; labor—Jorge Godoy; health—Arturo Jiron; justice—Sergio Insunza; mines—Pedro Felipe Ramirez; public works—Humberto Martones; housing—Luis Matte Valdez;

education—Edgargo Enriquez; lands and colonization—Roberto Cuellar; government secretary general—Anibal Palma.

Among the ministers replaced in the new Cabinet were two who had been censured and dismissed by the Senate and two suspended by the Chamber of Deputies. The last to be suspended was Interior Minister Gerardo Espinoza late July 3, on charges of violating university autonomy in authorizing a police raid on television Channel 6 of the University of Chile.

(Jaime Toha Gonzalez, brother of ex-Defense Minister Jose Toha Gonzalez, was sworn in as agriculture minister July 15, replacing Torrealba, who had resigned July 11.)

Upon swearing in the new ministers, Allende announced a 14-point emergency plan developed by leaders of his Popular Unity coalition after the coup attempt.

Among the plan's provisions:

Strengthening of the government's political, economic and administrative authority, and guarantees of public order and "civic coexistence"; economic discipline and austerity to combat inflation; "drastic" curbs to prevent crimes against the national economy; price policies favoring "popular consumption" goods over non-essential and luxury articles; wage readjustment policies favoring sectors with lowest incomes; amplification and "rationalization" of state takeovers of enterprises in the reformed agrarian sector; broader participation by workers in the management of the economy; incorporation of popular organizations in the administration of the state.

Christian Democratic Sen. Aylwin commended Allende July 5 for pledging to govern in "pluralism, democracy and liberty," but expressed disappointment in the absence of the military officers from the new Cabinet.

Allende aide murdered. President Salvador Allende's naval aide-de-camp, Capt. Arturo Araya, was assassinated by unidentified gunmen at his home in Santiago early July 27.

The presidential press office made public a statement describing the assassination as "a typical fascist action of Fatherland and Liberty," the extreme right-wing party linked with the aborted June 29 military coup. Sen. Luis Corvalan, leader of the Communist party, blamed the killing on "sectors that seek the overthrow of the government," including, it was assumed, the opposition parties.

The four opposition groups—the Christian Democrats, National party, Social Democratic (formerly Radical Left) party and Radical Democracy party—issued a statement July 28 condemning the assassination, but also accused the government of responsibility for the nation's current crisis and of using even "the death and pain of others" to vent its "characteristic hatreds and ill will."

Fatherland and Liberty leader Robert Thieme, in hiding in Chile after a brief exile in Argentina, charged July 27 that "Marxist-Leninists" had committed the murder. He volunteered to surrender to the navy to prove his party's innocence.

Thieme had announced July 17 that Fatherland and Liberty would unleash a total armed offensive to overthrow the government. The party had published an advertisement in the Santiago newspaper La Tribuna July 13 claiming responsibility for the June 29 coup attempt. The government had closed La Tribuna for six days as a result.

Five Fatherland and Liberty leaders had flown to Ecuador July 7 after the Ecuadorean embassy in Santiago granted them political asylum and Allende authorized safe conduct out of Chile. Other party members gained asylum July 6 in the Colombian and Paraguayan embassies.

Truck owners strike. Truck owners throughout Chile went on strike July 26, threatening to paralyze the country and precipitate a crisis as grave as the one engendered by their strike in October 1972.

The National Confederation of Truck Owners charged the government had not observed its November 1972 agreement to make available new trucks and spare parts, and had tried to set up a parallel trucking organization. The federation said it was prepared to strike "indefinitely."

The strike immediately affected Santiago and other cities, and by July 31 shortages of food, gasoline and kerosene reached serious proportions. Santiago was reported receiving only 30% of its supplies.

The government requisitioned 950 trucks for the most urgent needs, but many of their operators were victims of stonings and sabotage by presumed right-wing agitators. Rail lines and several bridges were reported dynamited in an apparent attempt to isolate the capital from its seaports and generally disrupt communications. Gas stations throughout the country also were reported attacked.

The National Confederation of Ground Transports, controlling some 86,000 buses, taxis and trucks, threatened to join the strike if an agreement with the government was not reached soon. The Superior National Security Council had issued a "formal and severe warning" July 28 against solidarity strikes by any unions.

Political negotiations. Amid growing tension, the Christian Democratic party acceded to President Allende's often-voiced request for political negotiations to avert a civil war. Allende and the Christian Democratic party president, Sen. Patricio Aylwin, met July 30, but no details of the talks were revealed.

Christian Democratic sources said Aug. 1 that the party had sent a letter to Allende demanding the disarming of paramilitary groups on both the left and the right; restoration of factories and farm properties seized after the aborted military coup; approval of a constitutional reform bill to define the private, mixed and state sectors of the economy; and formation of a Cabinet that would provide "constitutional guarantees," i.e. one including military representatives.

Allende was said to have the backing of the majority of the Popular Unity parties in his talks with Aylwin, but not of his militant Socialist party.

A dozen private businesses and professional associations announced Aug. 1 they had formed a "civic front" to overthrow the Allende administration. The group, including lawyers, teachers, doctors and builders associations, published a full-page advertisement in the opposition newspaper El Mercurio.

Strikes, violence widen. Public transportation in Santiago was virtually suspended Aug. 3 when 60,000 bus, truck, taxi and jitney owners joined the crippling, nine-day strike by private truckers.

The new action was called Aug. 2 by the National Confederation of Ground Transports after President Salvador Allende rejected its demand to fire Transport Undersecretary Jaime Faivovich, whom it held responsible for clashes July 31 in which four truckers were injured. The clashes occurred when truckers resisted authorities ordered by Faivovich to confiscate some 100 striking trucks.

Bus owners did not officially join the stoppage, but only 30% of the capital's private buses were running Aug. 3. State-owned buses continued to operate, but they amounted to only 10% of Santiago's fleet.

Employes of the Santiago water works had struck Aug. 1. Physicians and copper miners threatened to strike Aug. 4; the doctors protested shortages of equipment and medicine and low salaries in state hospitals, while miners demanded the immediate rehiring of co-workers fired during the recent El Teniente strike.

The truckers' strike, which caused critical fuel shortages and sent food prices skyrocketing, was denounced as "seditious" by Allende at a press conference Aug. 3. The president said the stoppage, like the truckers' strike of October 1972, would be defeated by voluntary work by "workers and youth."

Allende declared that "all public services and officials are under a state of emergency, and will work Saturdays and Sundays if necessary to collaborate with the government and the armed forces." He named army Gen. Herman Brady to direct efforts to provide emergency transportation.

Allende asserted he would not bring military officers into his Cabinet, as strike leaders and the opposition Christian Democratic party demanded. He insisted on "the importance of the cooperation" of the armed forces but asserted: "I think it is up to the politicians to solve the country's political problems, and I believe the armed forces agree."

(The Cabinet reportedly resigned Aug. 3 to give Allende a free hand as the strikes widened, but Allende was said to have rejected the resignations.)

Allende charged that certain elements of the opposition, particularly the extreme right-wing Fatherland and Liberty party, were using "all means to try to overthrow the government and regain their old privileges." He asserted there was a "concerted plan" to sabotage his talks with the Christian Democrats.

Christian Democratic officials said after the press conference that the talks were "over" because Allende had not acceded to their "minimum demands."

Allende had agreed Aug. 2 to sign a constitutional reform passed by the opposition-controlled Congress which delineated the state, private and mixed sectors of the economy and prohibited further nationalization of private industry without Congressional approval—provided a general agreement was reached on several other points. These included application of the reform; passing of a constitutional amendment requiring future constitutional reforms to be passed by a two-thirds majority in Congress instead of the present simple majority; and approval of a series of government bills on cooperatives, profit-sharing for workers, and the state's role in the economy.

Allende charged at the Aug. 3 press conference that 180 acts of terrorism against railroads, highways, bridges, pipelines, schools and hospitals had been committed since the assassination of his naval aide-de-camp July 27.

Most of the violence was connected to attempts by strikers to isolate Santiago and other major cities, according to the New York Times Aug. 3. Saboteurs were dynamiting transport routes in strategic areas, and stoning, firing upon or setting fire to strikebreaking trucks.

An estimated 20 workers were seriously wounded Aug. 7 when an oil pipeline exploded about 100 miles south of Santiago. All railroad traffic between the capital and the South had been stopped the day before when a power plant substation was blown up near Rancagua.

Gen. Brady announced Aug. 5 that truckers who returned to work would get armed protection against terrorists. He was authorized by Allende the same day to requisition buses and taxis if they did not resume service.

Soldiers raid factories. Allende asked for the retirement of two air force officers Aug. 7 amid growing acrimony between his left-wing supporters and the armed forces over military raids on factories.

The retirements followed a raid on factories in and near Punta Arenas in which a worker was shot to death when he failed to comply with army orders to halt. The raid had been authorized by air force Gen. Manuel Torres de la Cruz, the regional military commander, who claimed to have acted under the Arms Control Act. The Central Labor Federation (CUT) and Allende's Socialist party had demanded Torres' resignation and the immediate repeal of the law, which allowed the armed forces to conduct raids in search of weapons without authorization from the government.

Leftist naval plots charged. The navy announced Aug. 7 it had quashed a revolt planned by servicemen aboard a cruiser and destroyer stationed at Valparaiso.

A naval communique said 22 persons were under arrest and faced courts martial for plotting to take the vessels out of the harbor while many crew members were on shore leave. It blamed the plot on "extremist groups alien to our institution ... who have been calling for disobedience in the armed forces." The extremist Revolutionary Left Movement (MIR) had issued numerous such calls recently.

The commander of the second naval zone based in Talcahuano claimed Aug. 9 to have detected and halted attempts by "civilians of the extreme left" to infiltrate naval units in the local shipyards.

The London Times reported Aug. 15 that the navy had presented two lawsuits against the MIR, calling its members irresponsible adventurers seeking only to cause chaos by attacking Chile's basic institutions.

(The navy was reported Aug. 24 to have requested the lifting of the Congressional immunity of two government supporters—Carlos Altamirano, secretary general of Allende's Socialist party, and Oscar Garreton, leader of the small, radical MAPU party. The legislators were accused of "intellectual" responsibility for an alleged leftist plan to subvert the navy.)

Military rejoins Cabinet. President Salvador Allende, yielding to pressure from opposition leaders and anti-government strikers, gave Cabinet posts to the commanders of the three armed forces and the national police Aug. 9.

The Cabinet reorganization, the third of 1973, was precipitated by the crippling truckers' strike, other stoppages and related terrorism. Allende entrusted the new ministers with restoring political and economic order in Chile.

Gen. Carlos Prats, the army commander and former interior minister, rejoined the Cabinet as defense minister. Navy commander Adm. Raul Montero Cornejo was named finance minister; air force commander Gen. Cesar Ruiz Danyau, transport minister; and National Police Chief Gen. Jose Maria Sepulveda, lands and colonization minister.

Four civilian ministers resigned, seven retained their posts and four were shifted to new posts. Foreign Minister Orlando Letelier became interior minister; Defense Minister Clodomiro Almeyda, foreign minister; Government Secretary General Anibal Palma, housing minister; and Finance Minister Fernando Flores Labra, government secretary general.

The new Cabinet, aside from its military members, retained roughly the same political composition as its predecessor, with three Socialists, three Communists, two Radicals, one independent, and one member each of the Christian Left and MAPU parties.

Allende called the new Cabinet one of "national security" whose task was to "defend Chile from fascism [and] prevent the separation of the people from the government and from the armed forces." The ministers, he added, would "reject any attempted political, subversive infiltration of the armed forces, national police and civil police."

Allende said the Cabinet had to "end the fascist transport strike and outlaw all fascist groups such as [the] Fatherland and Liberty [party]." In an indirect threat to left-wing extremists, the president added that authorities would act against "any individual or groups seeking to subvert order, whatever their political orientation."

Allende also stressed the necessity of controlling Chile's skyrocketing inflation, which, he said, might "lead to a chaos without exit."

Reactions to the new Cabinet by the opposition were divided. Christian Democratic party President Patricio Aylwin, representing the party's conservative sector, said Aug. 9 that the appointments were not enough, and called for the "real participation" of the armed forces at every level. However, Sen. Renan Fuentealba, leader of the party's left wing, said Aug. 10 he believed the Cabinet would "give security to all Chileans and [meant] a rectification by the government so that the process of change will be normalized but not held back."

The right-wing National party, which had called for the overthrow of the government, warned Aug. 9 that the military officers in the Cabinet ran the risk of "serving as screens for the maneuvers of extremist groups."

On the government's side, the Socialist and Communist parties jointly backed the new Cabinet Aug. 12, following earlier protests against military participation in the Cabinet from the radical wing of the Socialists and the smaller MAPU party. The Central Labor Federation (CUT) held a massive rally in support of the government in Santiago Aug. 9.

The armed forces also were divided by the current crisis, according to the London newsletter Latin America Aug. 10. Senior officers were classed by left-wing politicians as "golpistas" (plotters) or "no-golpistas." The armed forces had recently been denounced by leftists for concentrating in their search for illegal weapons on leftist workers' groups, rather than on right-wing and openly seditious organizations such as Fatherland and Liberty.

Strikes & terrorism. The truckers' strike, related stoppages and terrorism continued despite a government ultimatum to the strikers and the appointment of military commissioners in each province to get the trucks back on the roads.

The government warned Aug. 10 that if the strike did not end Aug. 12, striking trucks would be confiscated and their owners prosecuted. The government agreed to meet strikers' demands for the import and distribution of spare parts and new trucks but refused a demand for the resignation of Transportation Undersecretary Jaime Faivovich.

The truckers rejected the ultimatum Aug. 11, vowing to continue the strike "to the last ditch." They continued to concentrate their vehicles at El Monte, some

30 miles west of Santiago, where they brought in first aid tents and medical equipment to prepare for battle with authorities. More than 500 police backed by three tanks had tried to requisition trucks there late Aug. 10, but Faivovich had called off the operation after they clashed with truckers.

The Christian Democrats declared their support for the strike Aug. 12. Eduardo Cerda, the party's general secretary, said in a radio speech that the truckers were expressing "legitimate grievances " and warned that the government would be responsible for any violence resulting from attempts to break the strike.

The government Aug. 12 appointed a military commissioner in each province to requisition trucks and, if necessary, use soldiers to seize them.

Meanwhile, fuel was rationed, food supplies rotted in warehouses, prices skyrocketed, and 40%–50% of industry and business were paralyzed because of the strike. Some relief was provided by voluntary work organized by the government political parties.

Strike-related sabotage continued, with daily attacks on strikebreaking trucks and buses, and dynamiting of roads, tunnels, railways, bridges and power stations. Electric power was cut off for nearly an hour in the major provinces late Aug. 13, when saboteurs dynamited three high-tension electric pylons outside Santiago. The action interrupted a televised speech by Allende, who was denouncing the strike.

Allende and government spokesmen blamed Fatherland and Liberty for the sabotage, citing a declaration by the party Aug. 12 pledging to renew its offensive against the government. However, the right-wing press attempted Aug. 13 to put the blame on left-wing extremists.

Meanwhile, the left-wing press was accusing the U.S. embassy in Chile of backing the strikes and terrorism. An editorial in the newspaper Ultima Hora suggested Aug. 13 that U.S. Ambassador Nathaniel Davis and the Central Intelligence Agency were helping finance the current right-wing press and radio campaign against the government. The editorial was signed by Hernan del Canto, a former Cabinet official and an influential member of Allende's Socialist party.

The left-wing press campaign against the U.S. and its alleged support of the strikes continued, but the government denied responsibility for it. Bombs were discovered and dismantled late Aug. 15 in the gardens of the homes of three U.S. embassy officials. U.S. Ambassador Nathaniel Davis met Aug. 16 with Foreign Minister Clodomiro Almeyda, who assured him attacks on U.S. diplomats would not be tolerated.

The government requisitioned more than 2,000 striking trucks Aug. 16–18 in an attempt to get food and fuel supplies moving again. Many strikers removed parts from their trucks and deflated their tires, but did not otherwise resist authorities seizing the vehicles.

The government released a report Aug. 17 saying the truckers' strike had cost Chile $6 million a day, and had helped destroy half of the winter's green vegetable crop and half the country's milk production. Planting was reported to be impossible in several provinces without delivery of seeds and fuel, and heavy livestock losses were reported in the extreme south.

National Planning Office Director Gonzalo Martner, who released the report, called the truck stoppage a "political strike aimed at overthrowing the government, with the help of imperialism." Allende charged Aug. 16 that the political opposition had planned and directed the strike, and was "endangering the foundations of the state."

Other strike-related terrorism continued, meanwhile, with more than 360 terrorist attacks and six deaths reported since the strikes began July 26. Strikebreaking trucks and buses were attacked daily by presumed right-wing militants, and land transport routes and high-tension electric pylons were dynamited. A pro-government transport union leader, Oscar Balboa, was murdered Aug. 18 by what the government called "reactionary bands."

The government Aug. 17 sent to Congress draft legislation that would give it broader powers to combat terrorism, particularly attacks against water supplies, electricity and gas installations, factories, and distributors of mining, agricultural, or industrial products.

Officials replaced—The government Aug. 18 granted what appeared to be the truckers' major demand, the removal of Faivovich as transport undersecretary and general commissioner of highway associations.

The truckers said Faivovich's dismissal only allowed a resumption of talks with the government and the stoppage would continue. Army Gen. Herman Brady was given Faivovich's post as highways commissioner, or chief "intervenor" in the truckers' strike.

The public works and transport minister, air force Gen. Cesar Ruiz Danyau, also resigned Aug. 18, claiming President Salvador Allende had not given him sufficient power to end the truckers' strike. Allendé denied the charge, and political sources reported that Ruiz had resigned because of serious differences with the president on ways of ending the strike.

The new transport minister was Gen. Humberto Magliochetti Barahona, the air force operations chief.

Ruiz also was dismissed as air force commander and replaced in that post by Gen. Gustavo Leigh Guzman. An undetermined number of air force officers opposed this action, forcing a postponement of the transfer of command. However, Leigh assumed his post without incident Aug. 20.

(Political observers quoted in the Washington Post Aug. 21 said the incident was a warning to the other military chiefs in the Cabinet that if they proposed projects disapproved by Allende, they might lose their military as well as ministerial posts.)

More than 3,000 doctors in Santiago began a 48-hour strike in solidarity with the truckers Aug. 20, and were joined the next day by colleagues elsewhere in the country. Many physicians protested the shortage of medicine and instruments in Chile's hospitals. Shopowners had begun a strike in the six southernmost provinces Aug. 16. Santiago's shopowners and most organizations of professionals, including lawyers, businessmen, engineers and pilots, joined the strikes Aug. 21. They reportedly demanded a quick solution to the truckers' strike, guarantees to private enterprise, more power for the military, and reinstatement of Gen. Ruiz.

Right- and left-wing militants clashed in Santiago Aug. 21, hurling rocks and in some cases firing on each other. Police using tear gas broke up the fights, with several injuries reported.

Street battles again broke out between right-wing and left-wing students in the capital Aug. 24, and were broken up by national police.

Strike-related terrorism also continued, with daily attacks on strike-breaking trucks and buses, dynamiting of roads and bridges, and sabotage of power installations. In Santiago, the North Korean embassy, several stores and the homes of government supporters were bombed Aug. 22, and the homes of two Cuban diplomats were bombed Aug. 27.

Fourteen members of the neo-fascist Fatherland and Liberty party were reported arrested Aug. 22, and seven others, including party leader Roberto Thieme, were reported seized Aug. 26. The Santiago police chief said that with Thieme's arrest "we have accounted for nearly all recent terrorist acts."

Thieme had admitted that his men had staged numerous terrorist attacks recently, including the dynamiting of a pylon which interrupted a nationwide address by Allende, it was reported Aug. 27. Their purpose, Thieme said, was to "accelerate the country's chaos and provide a military takeover as soon as possible." "If we have to burn this country to save it from [Allende], then we'll do that," Thieme asserted.

The pro-Allende Central Labor Federation (CUT) Aug. 21 ordered its members to stay on their jobs but to "keep vigilant" as the strikes spread. CUT-affiliated employes of the International Telephone and Telegraph Corp. (ITT) seized control of the U.S. firm's Santiago headquarters to assure continuation of telegraph and Telex communications. They kept open cable communications with the outside world, but ITT management instructed its branch offices to refuse cable traffic.

The Communist newspaper El Siglo published a denunciation Aug. 21 of an alleged "foreign conspiracy" against Chile's independence and sovereignty. It specifically accused ITT of backing the transport strike.

The CUT directed its members Aug. 23 to prevent any attempt to overthrow the president. CUT members had occupied at least 100 major industries since the aborted military coup attempt June 29.

Leaders of the striking truckers gave notice Aug. 27 that they would not return to work until the government worked out a constitutional reform providing guarantees for private enterprise. Shops and transportation were shut down in nine provinces Aug. 24, while most of Chile's 7,000 doctors continued their indefinite strike in support of the truckers and in protest against the shortage of medicine and instruments in the nation's hospitals.

In an effort to break the transport strike the Allende regime late Sept. 6 offered some 6,000 new trucks, buses and taxis to persons willing to drive them. A ministerial council said the vehicles could be purchased for 20% down and 24% monthly payments. The government added that it had "never had under consideration as an objective the nationalization of truck transport," as striking truckers had charged.

In another conciliatory move Sept. 7, Labor Minister Jorge Godoy announced plans for legislation setting a general 250% wage increase, effective in October, to keep pace with Chile's skyrocketing cost of living.

Engineers and construction workers joined in the wave of anti-government strikes Sept. 10. Pilots of the national airline, LAN, had declared an indefinite strike Sept. 7, and shopkeepers had extended their previous strike for 48 hours that day.

Prats quits. President Salvador Allende, beset by crippling anti-government strikes and terrorism, received an additional blow Aug. 23 when his staunchest military defender, Gen. Carlos Prats Gonzalez, resigned as defense minister and army commander in chief.

Gen. Augusto Pinochet Ugarte was named army commander Aug. 24, but no one was immediately named to the defense post.

Prats' letter of resignation, released Aug. 24, said he had been forced to step down by a "sector of army officers." He said his participation in the Cabinet had caused a left-right split in the army, and he had resigned "so as not to serve as a pretext for those who seek to overthrow the constitutional government." The newspaper La Nacion added that Prats had told reporters he was influenced by recent demonstrations outside his home in which wives of army officers, including many generals, had demanded his resignation.

Two other army generals, Guillermo Pickering and Mario Sepulveda, resigned Aug. 24, and all other generals reportedly submitted resignations subsequently. Rear Adm. Raul Montero Cornejo, the finance minister, returned to his post as navy commander in chief Aug. 24, leaving in doubt whether he would continue to serve in the Cabinet.

Prats' resignation followed adoption by the opposition-controlled Chamber of Deputies Aug. 22 of a resolution accusing the government of "constant violations of the fundamental rights and guarantees established in the Constitution " and calling on the Defense Ministry to "direct the government's action" as a way of guaranteeing democratic institutions.

In a strong reply Aug. 24, Allende accused the opposition of seeking to provoke a military coup by inciting the armed forces to disobey civil authorities.

It was widely accepted that a mutual allegiance had been hammered out between an important military sector and the leadership of the opposition Christian Democrats, the Washington Post reported Aug. 26. The Christian Democrats did not explicitly favor a military takeover, but their leader, Patricio Aylwin, was quoted as saying he would choose a military regime over "a Marxist dictatorship," the Post reported.

Aylwin said Aug. 25 that only "sufficient military presence" in the government could restore stability and guarantee observance of the Constitution and the law. Such presence meant at least six military men in the Cabinet "with real powers" and military men at the level of undersecretary and at the head of government agencies, Aylwin said.

The New York Times noted Aug. 27 that the Christian Democrats were playing a dual role in the current crisis, calling for a democratic solution while simultaneously supporting the strikes and demonstrations aimed at total capitulation by the government.

Furthermore, the party's newspaper had used blatant anti-semitism in its campaign against the government, charging the government had been taken over by a "Jewish-Communist cell" which allegedly was waging a racial war against the Arab community in Santiago and occupying key posts in government and industry, the Times reported.

Cabinet shuffled. President Salvador Allende named a new Cabinet Aug. 28 as anti-government strikes, related terrorism and sporadic street clashes continued for the fifth week.

The Cabinet shuffle, the fourth of 1973, followed the resignation Aug. 27 of the finance minister, navy Adm. Raul Montero Cornejo, the last of the armed forces commanders in the Cabinet. The government disclosed Sept. 2 that Montero had also offered to give up his naval post, but Allende had asked him to stay on.

The new Cabinet consisted of one officer of each of the armed forces, the commander of the national police, and 11 civilian members of Allende's Popular Unity coalition. Four new ministers were appointed, one rejoined the Cabinet, one shifted posts, and nine ministers retained their portfolios. The civilian ministers included three Socialists, three Communists, two Radicals, one independent, and one member each of the Christian Left and MAPU parties.

The Cabinet:

Interior—Carlos Briones; defense—Orlando Letelier; foreign affairs—Clodomiro Almeyda; finance—navy Rear Adm. Daniel Arellano; economy—Jose Cademartori; mining—army Gen. Rolando Gonzalez; public works & transportation—air force Gen. Humberto Magliochetti; justice—Sergio Insunza; labor—Jorge Godoy; housing—Pedro Felipe Ramirez; agriculture—Jaime Toha; lands & colonization—national police Gen. Jose Maria Sepulveda; health—Mario Lagos; education—Edgardo Enriquez; government secretary general—Fernando Flores.

Allende said the new Cabinet's mission was to "prevent civil war and guarantee security." He denounced the strikes and right-wing sabotage, and asserted he would not resign. He said he represented "a process of revolutionary transformations which will not be stopped either by terror or by fascist threats."

Shopkeepers throughout the nation began a 48-hour strike Aug. 28, joining most of Chile's doctors and thousands of professionals, including engineers, technicians and architects, whose previous stoppages continued. Some 15,000 members of the opposition-dominated Federation of Farmworkers also struck. The pro-Allende Central Labor Federation, which held a rally to support the government, denounced the stoppages as "fascist."

Transport Minister Magliochetti announced Aug. 29 that official negotiations with striking transport workers were "definitively canceled" and that the government was withdrawing legal recognition of the National Confederation of Truck Owners, which began the current strikes. Magliochetti asserted the government would assign 2,000 requisitioned taxis and 2,700 trucks to drivers prepared to return to work.

Shopkeepers extended their strike a third day Aug. 30 as general strikes in several southern provinces entered their third week. The shopkeepers returned to work Aug. 31, but doctors, nurses and pharmacists continued to strike. Pilots of the national airline, LAN, began a 72-hour stoppage Sept. 3.

The Confederation of Professional Employes, claiming more than 90,000 white-collar members, began an indefinite strike Sept. 4, as scores of thousands of leftists marched in Santiago to celebrate the third anniversary of Allende's election. The National Confederation of Retailers announced a 48-hour strike the same evening to protest the wounding of four persons in a clash between truck drivers and police about 60 miles from the capital.

Strike-related terrorism and sabotage continued, meanwhile, although apparently diminished since the arrest Aug. 26 of Roberto Thieme, leader of the neo-fascist Fatherland and Liberty party.

Bombings of several private homes in Santiago and electricity installations in the southern town of Temuco were reported Aug. 28; an army lieutenant was murdered Aug. 30; and two oil pipelines were reported dynamited Sept. 4. Interior Minister Briones said Aug. 30 there had been more than 500 terrorist attacks and eight related deaths since the strikes began July 26.

Street clashes also continued. Left- and right-wing extremists fought in the mining town of Rancagua Aug. 29 after leftists attacked the local opposition newspaper.

The navy, in an independent move criticized by government supporters, joined police in occupying the Catholic University in Valparaiso Aug. 31 to quell disturbances between armed groups of leftist and anti-government students. In Santiago, police used tear gas Sept. 5 to disperse a massive group of women and students marching on the presidential palace to demand Allende's resignation.

The armed forces and even the opposition reportedly remained divided over the strike crisis. Different military factions supported participation in the Cabinet, strict adherence to the armed forces' constitutional role, or seizure of power. The opposition Christian Democrats were divided into conservative and moderate factions, the latter with a less combative attitude toward the president.

The Christian Democratic disunity was made clear in a public letter, reported Aug. 30, in which ex-presidential candidate Radomiro Tomic expressed his support for Gen. Carlos Prats Gonzalez, former defense minister and army commander, who had been denounced by other Christian Democrats for his support of Allende.

The right-wing National party continued to call for Allende's resignation, while the extremist Fatherland and Liberty party was revealed to have worked extensively to try to overthrow the government. Statements by Roberto Thieme to police, reported by the London newsletter Latin America Aug. 31, indicated Fatherland and Liberty had coordinated sabotage attacks with the activities of striking truckers, and had worked with rightist elements in the armed forces to discredit military "constitutionalists." Thieme reportedly asserted the truckers' strike was planned solely to overthrow the government.

The Christian Democrats proposed Sept. 9 that Allende and all elected officials resign and allow new elections to resolve the strike crisis. The party had asserted Sept. 5 it would begin impeachment proceedings against "six or eight" Cabinet ministers it said had broken the law in attempting to end the strikes.

Sources close to the Christian Democratic leadership, quoted in the Washington Post Sept. 7, explained the impeachment proceedings were to help either to "separate the armed forces from Allende's newly formed Cabinet" or to "force the military to accept Cabinet posts only if they can appoint other officers to the civil service."

Tension between the government and the armed forces had been increased by an incident Sept. 7 in which air force troops searching for illegal arms caches had invaded a Santiago nylon factory, opening machine gun fire and wounding three workers and causing damage to the building and machinery. The air force claimed leftist workers occupying the factory had provoked a gun battle and wounded an officer. However, the head of the state development corporation, Pedro Vuskovic, claimed the troops had fired without provocation.

Navy plot charged—The executive committee of the Popular Unity coalition issued a statement Sept. 5 accusing the navy of planning to overthrow Allende and of torturing sailors detained after an alleged attempt to start a left-wing mutiny a month before.

The statement, not a government document, implied the sailors were arrested for refusing to obey orders to involve their ships in a coup maneuver. It alleged the detainees were subjected to "unprecedented tortures" and demanded "correct and just treatment and respect for the [sailors'] human rights."

Military Coup d'Etat, Allende Commits Suicide

Allende regime overthrown. The armed forces and national police ousted the Popular Unity government Sept. 11, in the first successful military coup against a Chilean civilian administration since 1927.

Police officials in Santiago said President Salvador Allende Gossens had committed suicide rather than surrender power. A newspaper photographer allowed to see the body and a military communique Sept. 12 confirmed that the president was dead, but there was some confusion over whether he had taken his own life.

A four-man military junta seized control of the government and declared a state of siege, imposing censorship and a round-the-clock curfew. The junta members were the army commander, Gen. Augusto Pinochet Ugarte; the air force chief, Gen. Gustavo Leigh Guzman; the acting navy commander, Adm. Jose Toribio Merino Castro, and the national police chief, Gen. Cesar Mendoza. Pinochet was sworn in as president of Chile Sept. 13.

The four commanders had demanded early Sept. 11 that Allende resign by noon. The president refused, going on nationwide radio to declare: "I will not resign. I will not do it . . . I am ready to resist by any means, even at the cost of my own life, so this will serve as a lesson in the ignominious history of those who have strength but not reason." He then urged workers to occupy their factories and resist the coup.

Rebel forces attacked moments after the noon deadline; air force jets dropped bombs and fired rockets on the presidential palace in downtown Santiago, severely damaging the building, and also bombed Allende's official residence, about a mile away, after guards there reportedly resisted rebel troops.

Soldiers and police seized radio and television stations and broadcast the following communique:

Proclamation of the military government junta: Bearing in mind
1. The very grave economic, social and moral crisis which is destroying the country,
2. The incapacity of the government to adopt measures to stop the growth and development of chaos,
3. The constant increase of armed para-military groups organized and trained by Popular Unity which will bring the people of Chile to an inevitable civil war, the armed forces and carabineros [national police] declare:
 1. That the president of the republic must proceed immediately to hand over his high office to the Chilean armed forces and carabineros.
 2. The Chilean armed forces and carabineros are united to initiate the historic and responsible mission to fight for the liberation of the fatherland from the Marxist yoke, and for the restoration of order and constitutional rule.
 3. The workers of Chile may be certain that the economic and social benefits they have achieved up to the present will not suffer fundamental changes.
 4. The press, radio transmitters and television channels of the Popular Unity must suspend their informative activities from this moment onward; otherwise they will be assaulted by land and air.

5. The people of Santiago must remain in their homes to avoid [the killing of] innocent victims.

Fighting was heavy between soldiers surrounding the presidential palace and snipers supporting the president, according to a United Press International correspondent. There appeared to be no other organized resistance to the rebel attack. No official reports of casualties were given, but unofficial accounts Sept. 12, as sniper fire continued and scattered resistance to the coup developed, put the number of casualties at 500–1,000.

After the rebels took control of the palace Sept. 11, a police prefect announced that Allende and a close adviser, Augusto Olivares, had killed themselves. Newsmen from the leading opposition newspaper, El Mercurio, were allowed in, and the paper's chief photographer, Juan Enrique Lira, said he saw Allende lying dead, having apparently shot himself in the mouth.

The military junta did not confirm Allende's death until the next day, and did not confirm the police claim of suicide. An official communique said Allende had agreed shortly before 2 p.m. to resign, but when a patrol arrived later in the palace, after a delay caused by sniper fire, it found the president dead. The communique said Allende was buried at noon Sept. 12 "in the presence of his family."

A series of orders was issued immediately after the coup by the military junta. Congress was recessed "until further order," all bank accounts were frozen, foreigners were ordered to the nearest police station to identify themselves, and 68 prominent Socialist and Communist leaders were ordered to appear at the Defense Ministry or face arrest.

More than 100 Communist and Socialist party members were reported arrested Sept. 11 in Santiago and Valparaiso, the port city where naval units made the first moves against the government early in the day. (Allende had gone on the Socialist radio station shortly after 8 a.m. to charge "a sector of the navy" had rebelled in the port, and ask "the army to defend the government.")

The junta announced Sept. 12 that 19 Socialist and Communist leaders had "presented themselves" to the police, including Interior Minister Carlos Briones and Foreign Minister Clodomiro Almeyda. Military sources said some would be released after questioning and others detained. Sources quoted by the Associated Press said 60 officials of Allende's government had sought asylum in the Mexican embassy and others had asked refuge elsewhere.

Explosions were heard in some industrial neighborhoods of Santiago Sept. 12 and snipers barricaded in office buildings exchanged fire with military patrols. The junta declared that "all persons who persist in a suicidal and irresponsible attitude will definitely be attacked. They will be shot on the spot if taken prisoner."

Six hundred leftists reportedly surrendered after a gunfight at the technical university near downtown Santiago. There also were reports of gun battles between soldiers and armed workers occupying factories to protest the coup.

Erratic communications made it impossible to determine conditions outside Santiago, but the junta said in a broadcast Sept. 12 that the country was "returning to normal." Long-distance telephone and telegraph services in Santiago had been shut down during the rebel attacks Sept. 11, but had been reopened at nightfall.

The junta said Sept. 12 it had expelled 150 Cuban extremists. It broke diplomatic relations with Cuba Sept. 13. Leftists from other countries also were being rounded up for expulsion, according to press reports.

(Cuba charged in a complaint to the United Nations Security Council Sept. 12 that the Chilean armed forces had attacked its embassy in Santiago and a Cuban merchant ship off the Chilean coast during the coup Sept. 11. The complaint also said two Cubans in Chile on World Health Organization scholarships had been arrested.)

A military-controlled television station in Santiago broadcast film clips Sept. 12 showing huge arms caches that, according to officers appearing in the films, were seized from the presidential palace and Allende's private residence. The commentators said most of the arms were made in the Soviet Union. Film clips were also shown of Allende's private residence, emphasizing the well-stocked pantry the president kept despite Chile's severe food shortage.

Allende suicide disputed—President Allende's widow, Hortensia Bussi de Allende, asserted Sept. 19 that her husband had not committed suicide but had been "murdered" by soldiers or police invading the presidential palace during the coup Sept. 11.

Mrs. Allende, who took political asylum in Mexico, had asserted Sept. 15, while in the Mexican ambassador's residence in Santiago, and Sept. 16, upon arrival in Mexico City, that military reports of her husband's suicide were true. However, she said her mind had been changed by "eyewitness" reports that Allende's body bore 13 bullet wounds. She added that Allende had told her he would not commit suicide but would resist a coup by force.

The chief Chilean correspondent for Prensa Latina, the Cuban news agency, reported in El Nacional of Caracas Sept. 15 that Allende had died fighting off palace invaders with a submachine gun. The correspondent, Jorge Timossi, added that Allende's former housing minister, Anibal Palma, had been executed in the palace during the coup.

The charge that Allende was murdered was aired in the United Nations Security Council Sept. 17 by the Cuban representative, Ricardo Alarcon. Alarcon denounced the Chilean junta and the U.S., asserting: "It is not difficult to know where the main responsibility lies. The trail of blood spilled in Chile leads directly to the dark dens of the Central Intelligence Agency and the Pentagon."

Alarcon's remarks, interrupted at one point by shouts from angry Cuban exiles in the gallery who opposed the island's Communist government, were subsequently denounced by Chile's new representative to the U.N. and by the U.S. delegate, John Scali. The Chilean delegate, Raul Bazan, charged that Cuba's embassy staff in Chile had been training leftist guerrillas in sabotage. Scali charged Alarcon had "descended" in his remarks to "a new low, even for those who wallow in such words as normal talk."

Charges that Allende was murdered also came from President Tito of Yugoslavia, who said Sept. 14 that "imperialist reaction" had instigated Chile's "hireling generals" to seize power. The

Central Committee of the Soviet Communist party denounced "the actions of reactionary forces in Chile" Sept. 13.

Most Latin American governments declared brief periods of national mourning for Allende, and only Brazil and Uruguay, with governments dominated by right-wing military men, recognized the Chilean junta, both doing so Sept. 13. The governments of Sweden and Finland cut off aid to Chile Sept. 13.

The junta issued an official medical report Oct. 31 confirming its assertion that Allende committed suicide during the coup Sept. 11. The report said the president shot himself twice under the chin with a machine gun shortly after the armed forces and national police attacked the presidential palace. Supporters of the UP abroad, including Allende's wife and daughters, continued to claim the president was killed by the military rebels.

U.S. denies coup complicity—The U.S. State Department and White House Sept. 11–12 declined to comment on Allende's overthrow, asserting it was an internal Chilean matter, and denied charges from Communist and other countries that the U.S. had a hand in the military coup.

However, a State Department official admitted to senators Sept. 12 that the U.S. had advance knowledge of the coup. Jack Kubisch, an assistant secretary of state, told members of the Western Hemisphere Subcommittee of the Senate Foreign Relations Committee that a Chilean officer had told a U.S. official in Chile of the coup some 10–16 hours before it occurred, but officials at "the highest level" in Washington had decided not to intervene in any way.

(State Department and White House spokesmen subsequently denied the U.S. had known of the coup beforehand. Paul J. Hare, State Department spokesman, admitted the U.S. embassy "did receive reports that Sept. 11 was to be the date," but said it had previously been advised of coups planned for Sept. 8 and Sept. 10, and thus considered the last prediction a rumor likely to be false. "There was absolutely no way of knowing beforehand that on any of these dates, including the Sept. 11 date, a coup attempt would be made," Hare asserted.)

The U.S. reluctance to comment on the coup was attributed to sensitivity over charges that the Central Intelligence Agency (CIA) and the International Telephone and Telegraph Corp. (ITT) had previously conspired against Allende.

(A number of large U.S. corporations whose properties had been seized by Allende's government said Sept. 11 they might consider resuming operations in Chile if the new government were receptive to investment. The companies included ITT, Ford Motor Co., and E. I. Du Pont de Nemours & Co., according to the New York Times Sept. 12.)

U.S. critics of the Nixon Administration's policies in Latin America blamed the U.S. Sept. 12 for helping create the conditions in which military intervention in Chile became likely, according to the Washington Post Sept. 13. One critic, Joseph Collins of the Institute for Policy Studies, a Washington research organization, charged U.S. "tactics" in Chile under Allende were aimed at causing "economic chaos."

Charges of CIA involvement in the coup were made in the capitals of several Communist countries and by supporters of Allende in South American and Western European nations.

Some 30,000 leftists marched past the Chilean embassy in Paris Sept. 11, denouncing the CIA for allegedly overthrowing Allende. In Rome, thousands of demonstrators held similar rallies.

The clandestine Chilean news agency Arauco alleged two U.S. airmen, Capts. M. B. Lemmons and D. C. Baird, had helped coordinate attacks by the Chilean air force during and after the military coup, the London newsletter Latin America reported Nov. 30.

Defense of the coup came from leading newspapers in Brazil, where a right-wing military regime held power.

Truckers' leader asks strike end—Juan Salas, a leader of the six-week truckers' strike, which helped cause Allende's downfall, Sept. 12 urged striking truckers to return to work Sept. 13 in compliance with military demands.

Salas, speaking on the official radio network, congratulated the truckers for maintaining the strike until then, asserting: "The effort that all of you made has been crowned with the satisfaction of seeing the fatherland free." Another strike leader, Leon Vilarin, congratulated the armed forces for deposing the president.

Organizations representing doctors, dentists, pharmacists, nurses and other professionals said Sept. 12 that their groups were prepared to return to work immediately.

Valparaiso installations attacked— Navy and army installations in the port city of Valparaiso were reported attacked by supporters of the deposed government Sept. 14. According to reports, the attacks were crushed by the military, with many of the assailants arrested and a few summarily executed. The city was placed under a round-the-clock curfew.

Scattered resistance to the junta continued in Santiago and other localities Sept. 13-17, but was downplayed by military authorities. Heavy shooting between pro-Allende snipers and military and police officers was reported the night of Sept. 13-14, and more shooting and several bomb explosions were reported the next night. Resistance to authorities in the interior of the country was reported Sept. 15. Fighting in the capital persisted Sept. 16, but was said to taper off the next day.

Trucks began delivering supplies to Santiago Sept. 15, and the city was reported returning to normal Sept. 17. The night curfew there was shortened, but the 24-hour curfew in Valparaiso was maintained.

The London newsletter Latin America reported Sept. 21 that most reports from Chile indicated there had been hard fighting between authorities and backers of Allende in industrial and working class areas. According to some reports, the attack by government supporters in Valparaiso Sept. 14 had nearly succeeded in recapturing control of the port from naval and other military authorities, and was beaten off only after heavy casualties on both sides.

The government conceded Sept. 24 that some resistance continued from supporters of the Allende government. Adm. Jose Toribio Merino Castro, navy commander and junta member, said Chile was still in a "state of internal war . . . There are still people killing Chileans, most of them foreigners."

Military sources admitted to the news agency LATIN Sept. 28 that a number of guerrilla groups in the South had not yet been crushed. Most of their members were presumed to be from the Revolutionary Left Movement.

Military opposition to coup reported. Accounts emerging from Chile indicated there had been opposition within the armed forces to the military coup, and hundreds of officers had been killed both before the takeover and in open fighting after it, the London newsletter Latin America reported Nov. 9.

According to Latin America, "well-informed persons now leaving Santiago" said several hundred officers thought likely to oppose the coup had been shot the night before it occurred, and much of the fighting during the first three days after the takeover was among military units. A Santiago school for noncommissioned officers of the national police reportedly had held out against the insurgents for three days, and several regiments supporting the Allende government had fought bloody engagements.

These reports were corroborated by a dispatch by Jorge Timossi, former Santiago correspondent of the Cuban press agency Prensa Latina, Latin America reported. Timossi said many officers were killed or detained the night before the coup, including the then navy commander, Adm. Raul Montero, and air force Gen. Alberto Bachelet, who headed the National Distribution Secretariat under Allende. (Bachelet was to be court-martialed for "sedition" and "inciting to rebellion," according to the Santiago newspaper La Segunda Nov. 13.)

Junta in Office

New Cabinet sworn in. The military junta swore in a new Cabinet Sept. 13, two days after violently overthrowing the Popular Unity government of the late President Salvador Allende Gossens.

The Cabinet consisted of 10 armed forces officers, three national police officers and two civilians. The ministers: Interior—army Gen. Oscar Bonilla; foreign affairs—navy Rear Adm. Ismael Huerta; economy—army Gen. Rolando Gonzalez; finance—Rear Adm. Lorenzo Botuso; education—Rene Tovar; justice—Gonzalo Prieto; defense—Vice Adm. Patricio Carvajal; public works—air force Brig. Gen. Humberto Gutierrez; agriculture—air force Col. (ret.) Sergio Crespo; lands & colonization—national police Gen. (ret.) Diego Barra; health—air force Col. Alberto Spencer; labor—national police Gen. Mario McKay; mines—national police Gen. Arturo Goanes; housing—air force Brig. Gen. Arturo Vivero; and government secretary general—army Col. Pedro Cuevas.

Gen. Augusto Pinochet Ugarte, junta president, said Sept. 14 his government would implement policies of "national unity, not geared to the outdated patterns of the right or left." He charged the deposed civilian government had "gone beyond the limits of the law in a clear and deliberate manner, accumulating in its hands the greatest amount of political and economic power and putting in great danger all the rights and liberties of the inhabitants of the country."

Pinochet asserted Sept. 16, in response to questions by the New York Times, that the coup against Allende had been decided on "unanimously" by the armed forces and national police "when the military intelligence services verified the existence of large arsenals in the power of Marxist elements." He said it was "insolence" to even ask whether there had been U.S. aid or cooperation in the revolt, because "the armed forces and police of Chile, with a pure tradition of respect for legitimate authority, will never accept foreign intrusion."

Asked when parliamentary government might be restored, Pinochet declared: "When the country returns to normality and the unity of all Chileans and of Chile as a nation and a state attains sufficient strength to guarantee return to its traditional and exemplary republican democratic path. Under those conditions, elections—the sooner the better."

The new interior minister, Gen. Oscar Bonilla, asserted Sept. 14 that the coup had been staged to "safeguard the destiny of the country" against 10,000 foreign "extremists" who allegedly entered the country under Allende's government and supported a government plan to violently seize full power and institute a dictatorship. The junta Sept. 19 added the charge that Allende had "sacked and robbed" Chile during his three years in office.

The junta received the support Sept. 13 of the two major political opposition parties, the Christian Democrats and the Nationals. The Christian Democrats made it clear that they expected an early return to constitutional rule.

Ex-President Eduardo Frei, a senator and the acknowledged Christian Democratic leader, said in a phone call to a son overseas Sept. 14 that his party had been guaranteed new elections within 6-12 months. He supported military charges that the Allende government had been preparing its own armed uprising, as did Christian Democratic party President Patricio Aylwin Sept. 18.

The leading opposition newspaper, El Mercurio, one of only two permitted to publish by the junta, praised the coup Sept. 13, declaring: "The intervention of the armed forces saved Chileans from the imminent Marxist dictatorship and from political, social and economic annihilation." Twenty-six newspapers and magazines had been closed by the junta for allegedly opposing its goal to "depoliticize" Chile's mass media.

Marxist parties banned; new Constitution planned. The military junta Sept. 21 outlawed the nation's Marxist political parties and declared the non-Marxist parties "in recess to let the country catch its breath politically." It also announced plans for a new Constitution giving the armed forces a role in future legislative bodies.

Gen. Augusto Pinochet Ugarte, junta president, charged at a news conference that the Marxist parties were responsible for the Sept. 11 military coup "because their behavior, their lack of morals and ethics, the fraud they perpetrated on the people were bringing about chaos and the downfall of the nation."

At a separate news conference, Gen. Gustavo Leigh Guzman, air force commander and also junta member, said a "committee of distinguished jurists" was working on a new Constitution, "based on a general outline indicated by the junta," which would assure the armed forces of a wider role in national affairs and "representation in legislative bodies." Congress had been closed indefinitely by the junta on the day of the coup.

The junta moves, though not the junta itself, were criticized Sept. 22 by Sen. Patricio Aylwin, president of the Christian Democratic party, who had supported the coup. Aylwin told a news conference his party was "categorically and clearly against" any attempt to use the military government "to turn back history and establish the model of a permanent reactionary dictatorship."

"Christian Democrats do not accept directives concerning changes in the constitutional Chilean regime that do not come from the people," Aylwin asserted. "No one can impose a constitutional regime, and certainly not by force of arms." He added that his party did not believe "that political parties can be suppressed by decree, nor do we believe that ideas can be suppressed by governmental decisions."

The junta took other action in a number of areas. Among the developments:

Economy—Pay raises scheduled by the ousted government for Oct. 1, to offset effects of Chile's runaway inflation, were canceled by the junta Sept. 30. Finance Minister Rear Adm. Lorenzo Gotuzzo said the move was necessitated by the nation's "economic prostration." The national currency, the escudo, was devalued by 143% Oct. 1.

Chile asked the International Monetary Fund and the World Bank Sept. 27 to help rescue it from "the brink of bankruptcy." Gen. Eduardo Cano, new president of the Central Bank, told the annual meeting of the two lending agencies in Nairobi, Kenya that Chile would "create the conditions that will form an environment in which external assistance can prove effective."

Foreign Minister Rear Adm. Ismael Huerta said Sept. 28 that "the door is open" for a resumption of negotiations on compensation for U.S. copper companies whose Chilean properties were nationalized by the Popular Unity government. However, he asserted Chile's copper mines would remain in government hands, and the country would "maintain sovereignty over its natural resources" while welcoming foreign investment in other areas.

The massive El Teniente mine was placed under the direction of new managers. Jorge Sibisa, the new general manager, said Sept. 28 that he had fired 316 workers who were "political agents," and another 467 workers hired during the previous six months. A report by the Washington Post Sept. 30 said the mine was operating full-time, with no apparent discord among workers.

The vast majority of state-run factories and businesses were placed back in the hands of the executives who ran them before the late President Salvador Allende was elected, the New York Times reported Sept. 25. Agencies administering food and price controls were abolished, new delegates were named to most state economic agencies, and pledges were made to restore to its owners land that the junta said was illegally expropriated under Allende.

Factories not returned to the private sector, such as the large textile plants, were placed under the control of military personnel.

Labor—The pro-Allende Central Labor Federation (CUT), the nation's largest labor group with some 800,000 members, was abolished Sept. 25. The junta charged CUT had "transformed itself into an organ of political character, under the influence of foreign tendencies alien to the national spirit."

Government—All mayors and city councilmen were removed from office Sept. 25.

Education—The junta obtained the resignations of all university rectors Sept. 29 as part of a plan to eliminate "the grave and conflicting problems that have practically impeded the normal development of academic activities." Concern for the Chilean tradition of university autonomy was voiced Sept. 30 by Edgardo Boeninger, resigning rector of the University of Chile, and by El Mercurio, the nation's leading newspaper.

A new education minister, Rear Adm. Hugo Castro Jimenez, was appointed Sept. 27. He replaced Jose Navarro Tobar, one of two civilians in the Cabinet named by the junta Sept. 13. Navarro, who resigned for "personal" reasons, would become Chile's ambassador to Costa Rica.

U.S., others recognize junta. The U.S. officially recognized the Chilean military junta Sept. 24. Panama, Haiti, Venezuela and South Korea followed suit that day, and other countries did so later.

The Soviet Union and its Eastern European allies refused to recognize the junta, with the Soviet Union breaking diplomatic relations Sept. 21. Moscow accused the junta of "arbitrariness, lawlessness and mockery" toward Soviet institutions in Chile, citing the alleged searching and beating of Soviet sailors during the military coup and hostile acts against Soviet citizens in the country. Yugoslavia broke relations with Chile Sept. 27.

Adm. Merino, junta member, charged Sept. 25 that 16 Soviet citizens, in Chile to help build housing, had been training Chileans in urban guerrilla warfare. The junta continued its campaign against "foreign extremists," urging citizens in radio broadcasts to turn in "foreign extremists who have come to kill Chileans." It broke relations with North Korea Sept. 23.

Casualty reports. The junta claimed Sept. 18 that 95 persons had been killed, 300 wounded and 4,700 arrested since the coup Sept. 11, but other sources asserted the toll was much higher. A government official had said Sept. 17 that 5,200 persons, including foreigners, would receive courts martial under wartime laws for alleged subversive activities.

Amnesty International, the London-based organization working to free political prisoners, charged Sept. 15 that Chilean authorities were systematically arresting and executing backers of the Allende government and that "hundreds" of workers already had been killed. One Chilean doctor reported 5,000 dead and 1,000 wounded at his hospital, Amnesty International asserted.

Unofficial estimates of the number of prisoners taken by the junta varied from 3,500 to 20,000. The high figure came from Jose Gerbasi, correspondent of El Nacional of Caracas, who reported Sept. 18 that 10,000 prisoners were being held in the national stadium in Santiago, 6,000–7,000 in other stadiums, and others in military installations. Those arrested included officials and former officials of Allende's government, including Jose and Jaime Toha, Clodomiro Almeyda and Orlando Letelier, according to a report Sept. 15.

Two British citizens arrested and held for two days said Sept. 19 that thousands of Chileans and foreigners were being subjected to "systematic brutality" in the national stadium. One of the Britons, Adrian Jansen, said there had been "Bolivians, Haitians, Nicaraguans, Brazilians, Uruguayans, Paraguayans and Guatemalans in our cell, and they were terrified." His companion said they saw "prisoners, mostly Latins, kneeling on the ground with their hands up in the air, being kicked and beaten on the calves. Another group came into our cell and appeared to have been badly beaten up."

Jansen said he had heard firing while he was in the stadium "which could only have come from inside." There were numerous reports of executions of foreigners; one Venezuelan student, Enrique Maza Carvajal, had been executed in the first hours after the coup Sept. 11, according to El Nacional of Caracas Sept. 19.

A U.S. Senate subcommittee on refugees held hearings on Chile's refugee problem Sept. 28. Sen. Edward M. Kennedy (D, Mass.), chairman of the subcommittee, deplored the Nixon Administration's "policy of silence" on the human problems resulting from the Chilean coup, and said Washington should be "in no hurry to provide economic assistance to a regime which has come to power through a violent military coup—especially after years of denying such bilateral assistance and impeding multilateral assistance to a democratically elected government."

Chile Sept. 26 released six U.S. citizens taken prisoner during the coup. Two of them claimed at Kennedy's subcomittee hearings to have heard but not seen the execution of several hundred prisoners in the national stadium in Santiago.

The body of a man identified as a missing U.S. student, Frank Teruggi Jr., of Chicago, was reported found in Santiago Oct. 3. Teruggi had been arrested by soldiers Sept. 20.

Foreign embassies in Santiago were reported concerned about the fate of their nationals in Chile under the new government, fearing many would be executed for alleged "extremism." A number of embassies also harbored Chileans seeking political asylum; Mexico, which withdrew its ambassador from Chile Sept. 14, said the next day that 332 Chileans were asking asylum in its embassy, and Argentina said Sept. 18 that 300 Chileans had taken refuge in its embassy. Some governments airlifted refugees out of Chile, but the junta informed them Sept. 23 it would no longer give Chileans safe-conduct passes for political asylum abroad.

The Chilean National Committee for Aid to Refugees, under the auspices of the U.N. high commissioner for refugees, had reached an agreement with the junta to establish 15 reception centers in Santiago and 11 in the provinces where foreign refugees would be assisted in putting their identification papers in order, or in leaving the country, it was reported Oct. 2. U.N. officials emphasized they could protect only foreigners, and not Chileans, who under international law were not considered refugees until they left the country.

Rev. Juan Alcina, a Spanish priest of the Catholic Action Workers Movement, was reported arrested Sept. 18 and found shot to death several days later. A Chilean priest, Miguel Woodward, who worked in a slum district of Valparaiso and taught at the Catholic University, reportedly died after being arrested and beaten "savagely."

The government called on Chileans to turn in all arms, allowing them to deposit them in churches to protect their identities. The Roman Catholic Church had offered to cooperate with the junta in the "reconstruction" of Chile, but was alarmed by the junta's increasing repression, particularly its arrest and expulsion of foreign priests, it was reported Oct. 1.

An office within the church reportedly had been set up to look into abuses of human rights by the junta and acts of violence toward workers, who generally supported the Allende government, and toward religious institutions.

The church hierarchy was reported concerned over the junta's dismissal of the rector of Catholic University, who had been appointed by the pope.

2,796 deaths reported. The U.S. magazine Newsweek reported in its Oct. 8 issue that, according to the daughter of a staff member of the Santiago city morgue, 2,796 corpses had been received and processed by the morgue Sept. 11-25. The junta claimed Sept. 25 that only 284 persons had been killed since the coup, but unofficial death estimates ranged as high as 5,000.

Newsweek correspondent John Barnes reported slipping into the morgue on two separate occasions and seeing at least 270 corpses. On the first occasion he saw 200 bodies, reporting that "most had been shot at close range under the chin. Some had been machinegunned in the body . . . They were all young and, judging from the roughness of their hands, all were from the working class . . . Most of their heads had been crushed."

As for corpses not delivered to the morgue, Barnes reported: "No one knows how many may have been disposed of elsewhere; a gravedigger told me of reports that helicopters have been gathering bodies at the emergency first-aid center in central Santiago, then carrying them out to sea to be dumped. One priest informed me that on [Sept. 15] he had managed to get into the city's Technical University, which had been the scene of heavy fighting . . . He told me he saw 200 bodies . . ."

Barnes reported that nearly all the victims came from the slums around Santiago. National police reportedly raided slums and took away local leaders, who later appeared on death lists issued by the government.

Leftists arrested. Luis Corvalan, secretary general of the Communist party, was arrested in Santiago Sept. 27. The junta announced Oct. 3 that he would be tried before a military court for treason, subversion, infraction of the arms-control law and alleged fraud by Communists in state-controlled industries. Conviction carried a possible death penalty.

(Corvalan's arrest led to widespread fear he would be summarily executed, and caused a shouting and shoving incident at United Nations headquarters in New York between the Chilean and Saudi Arabian delegates to the General

Assembly. The tussle, between Raul Bazan of Chile and Jamil Baroody of Saudi Arabia, followed an appeal to U.N. Secretary General Kurt Waldheim by the Soviet delegate, Yakov Malik, to intercede to save Corvalan's life. Waldheim later contacted the Chilean government and learned that Corvalan had neither been tried nor sentenced.)

Corvalan was one of 17 former government and Popular Unity coalition officials most sought by the junta. The junta Sept. 28 offered to reward citizens turning in any of the officials with the equivalent of $1,500, plus any money carried by the officials. The list included CUT President Luis Figueroa and Socialist party Secretary General Carlos Altamirano.

The junta disclosed Sept. 22 that 30 "very important persons," officials at the upper levels of the Allende government, were being held at a naval base prison on Dawson Island, in the Strait of Magellan. Interior Minister Gen. Oscar Bonilla said Sept. 29 the detainees included Clodomiro Almeyda, Jose Toha, Anibal Palma (previously reported dead), Carlos Matus, Luis Matte, Sergio Bitar, Fernando Flores and Jose Cademartori, all former Cabinet ministers, and Daniel Vergara, former interior undersecretary. Red Cross officials were allowed to visit the Dawson Island prison, it was reported Oct. 2.

Santiago Mayor Julio Stuardo, a Socialist, was arrested Oct. 1. The governor of Talca Province, German Castro Rojas, was executed Sept. 27 for allegedly killing a policeman and attempting to blow up a dam on the day of the military coup.

Meanwhile, soldiers and national police continued what they called Operation Cleanup, intended to eliminate Marxist influence from Chilean life. Left-wing students and workers were arrested, and Marxist literature was burned in Santiago. The manager of the government newspaper La Nacion, Oscar Waiss, was reported under arrest Oct. 4. (La Nacion had been handed over to the Chilean Journalists' Federation, and would resume publication under a new name, La Patria).

The leader of the neo-fascist Fatherland and Liberty party, Roberto Thieme, was released on bail along with four aides Sept. 26. They had been arrested before the coup for admitted terrorism and sabotage against the Allende government.

Radicals, API banned. A decree by the military junta Oct. 14 banned all seven parties of the deposed Popular Unity (UP) government, including the Radicals and the Independent Popular Action party (API), two groups not included in the junta's earlier ban on Marxist parties.

Gen. Gustavo Leigh Guzman, air force commander and junta member, had said Oct. 8 that the non-Marxist parties which had opposed the UP and supported the military coup, would remain "in recess" for the present. "This is not a time for discussions, dialogues, meetings, forums or Congressional debates," Leigh asserted. "We must pull this country out of its present chaos and clean it of undesirable, negative and dangerous elements. Only after achieving this will we study the suitability of authorizing political parties."

The junta's apparent determination not to restore political or civil liberties in the near future reportedly alarmed its moderate civilian supporters, despite a new assertion by ex-President Eduardo Frei that the armed forces had "saved" Chile from a "Marxist dictatorship." Frei, leader of the Christian Democrats, said in an interview in the Madrid newspaper ABC Oct. 10 that "this is a time in which politicians must be quiet."

The junta continued to receive the strong support of the neo-fascist Fatherland and Liberty party and of the rightwing National party, which suggested the regime found its own political movement similar to Brazil's governing ARENA party. The president of the Supreme Court, Enrique Urrutia Manzano, added his support for the junta Oct. 18, saying he trusted "the goodwill of the military leaders" to restore legal norms and institutions after it "re-educated" the "many people who have been led morally astray."

Arrests, executions continue. Arrests and executions of leftists continued during October and November as the junta tried to stamp out all remaining resistance. Executions announced officially included that of Jose Gregorio Liendo

("Comandante Pepe") Oct. 3. Liendo had led peasants and leftists in seizures of private farms in the South.

The junta announced 43 executions Oct. 19–Nov. 5, bringing the official total to 94. Unofficial reports continued to put the total much higher, and to estimate the overall number of deaths since the coup at more than 2,000, roughly four times the number estimated by the junta.

The junta Oct. 24 ordered an end to summary executions, but said military tribunals would continue to hand down death sentences for crimes such as treason, armed resistance and attacks on security officials. More than 30 of the officially announced executions were said to have been summary, and another 100 persons had been killed by police and soldiers while reportedly "trying to escape."

The junta claimed Oct. 6 that 513 persons, including 37 policemen and soldiers, had been killed since the coup Sept. 11. This number too was disputed by numerous sources. The New York Times reported Oct. 12 that more than 2,000 persons might have been killed during the period.

Authorities reported Oct. 6 that 1,094 leftists had been rounded up in southern Chile in massive police and troop raids. Large arms caches were also reported confiscated. The army maintained tight control of Concepcion, the reputed MIR stronghold, where many of the raids took place. In Santiago, the curfew was extended by two hours (to 8 p.m.–6 a.m.) Oct. 4.

The leaders of two of the banned Marxist parties, Carlos Altamirano of the Socialists and Oscar Garreton of MAPU, were declared common criminals by the junta Oct. 8 and denied the right of political asylum. The two and Miguel Enriquez, leader of the extremist Revolutionary Left Movement (MIR), were court-martialed in absentia for allegedly encouraging mutiny in the navy.

MIR Secretary General Pablo Henriquez Barra was reported arrested in Concepcion Province Oct. 12.

(Governments abroad continued to voice concern over the safety of Communist party Secretary General Luis Corvalan, arrested Sept. 27 but not yet court-martialed. Corvalan denied in an interview with the Associated Press Oct. 5 that the UP had planned to eliminate military and opposition leaders and institute a dictatorship. "My conscience is quite clean," he said, "because as the entire world knows, [the UP] organized a revolution without violence, without recourse to arms.")

327 persons were released Oct. 12 from the prison in Santiago's national stadium. Officials said some 3,000 prisoners remained there. The junta announced Oct. 14 that 1,316 persons had been given safe conduct to leave the country, and 386 were still hiding in foreign embassies. An airplane with 116 refugees aboard had left for Mexico Oct. 13.

Military courts began trials Oct. 17 for some 1,200 prisoners accused of "political activism" in factories, illegal possession of arms, resisting the armed forces and police, making personal profits while in public office, and other alleged crimes. Some defendants were sentenced to life imprisonment.

The junta continued to clear out the temporary prison camp in Santiago's national stadium, moving all but some 1,000 prisoners to city jails by Nov. 5. Arrests continued, however, as authorities fought what they called "pockets of resistance" remaining in some parts of the country. A resistance group in Valparaiso was reported smashed Oct. 24.

The junta claimed Oct. 26 that all prisoners remaining in the Santiago stadium were Chileans, the last 200 foreigners having been turned over to the national refugee organization for removal from the country. Foreign Minister Ismael Huerta had asserted Oct. 19 that of 5,000 persons seeking asylum in foreign embassies since the coup, only 119 had been denied safeconducts out of the country; those denied passage reportedly were former high officials in the Allende government being investigated for possible wrongdoing.

The junta confirmed Oct. 19 that a second U.S. citizen, Charles E. Horman of New York, had died since the coup. Horman was reported arrested Sept. 17 was later found shot dead.

The Latin American School for Social Sciences, founded in 1957 by the United Nations Educational, Scientific and Cultural Organization and the Inter-

American Development Bank, disclosed Oct. 21 that it had suspended its activities and sent home its foreign students for fear of their safety under the new regime.

Luis Ramallo, interim secretary general of the school, said two of the school's Bolivian students had been killed while in military custody. Twelve other persons connected with the school had been arrested since the coup and five remained in custody, despite oral assurances from authorities that the school would not be "harassed," Ramallo asserted.

Three foreign priests—two Spaniards and a Frenchman—were expelled from Chile Oct. 20 for alleged "extremist activities." Some 50 foreign clerics had been forced to leave the country since the coup, according to Roman Catholic Church sources in Santiago.

Torture charged—A three-man commission of foreign jurists charged Oct. 13 that an investigation they carried out in Santiago revealed confirmed cases of torture and summary executions since the military coup.

A commission member, Leopoldo Torres Boursault of Spain, secretary general of the International Movement of Catholic Jurists, said: "We have found cases of mistreatment of all kinds. In some cases we have interviewed the victims themselves, and in other cases the information has come from persons of absolute moral integrity, including diplomats and clerics."

Prisoners, often foreigners, were beaten, burned with cigarettes, immersed in water and given electric shocks, the commission reported. Others were summarily executed, with authorities announcing later they had been shot trying to escape.

"We send 30 to 40 missions around the world yearly and we have not seen in recent years a situation so grave as that in Chile—not even Brazil or Greece," said another commission member, Joe Nordmann of France, secretary general of the International Association of Democratic Jurists.

The commission met Oct. 12 with the junta president, Gen. Augusto Pinochet Ugarte, who denied any violation of human rights and asserted: "We must defend ourselves."

The commission also took up the problem of foreign political refugees. More than 800 political refugees had found asylum in United Nations-sponsored sanctuaries, and there was fear the junta might send them back to their own countries, where they faced arrest. The commission pointed out to Pinochet that such action would violate international conventions.

Torres and the third commission member, Muchel Blum of France, secretary general of the International Federation of Human Rights, spoke in Washington, D.C. Oct. 17 with members of the U.S. House Foreign Affairs Committee and with members of the staff of Sen. Edward M. Kennedy (D, Mass.), chairman of a Senate subcommittee on refugees.

The U.S. Senate had passed an amendment to a foreign aid bill Oct. 2 prohibiting aid to Chile until the new government guaranteed the right to seek political asylum, the right to leave the country for political asylum abroad, and humane treatment in jails and prison camps. The Nixon Administration granted Chile a $24 million credit Oct. 5 for wheat purchases, provoking an angry reaction from Kennedy, who noted the loan was "eight times the total commodity credit offered to Chile in the past three years when a democratically elected government was in power."

Criticism of the junta's treatment of both Chilean and foreign prisoners continued in foreign countries despite junta assertions that human rights were being respected and prisoners were being tried for violations of the law and not for their political beliefs.

The Inter-American Commission on Human Rights, an agency of the Organization of American States, disclosed Oct. 25 that it had sent two notes to Gen. Pinochet asking him to respect the human rights of Chileans and foreigners in his country.

The Council of the Inter-Parliamentary Union, meeting in Geneva Oct. 26, unanimously approved a resolution denouncing the junta for allowing summary executions, arresting members of Congress, and "inverting the evolution toward greater economic, social and cultural progress undertaken by the Allende presidency." The Council urged all governments to suspend all political, economic and military assistance to Chile.

Reports of abuse of human rights continued to come from foreign newsmen. Swedish journalist Bo Sourander, arriving in Stockholm Oct. 25 after being expelled from Chile, asserted prisoners in Santiago were beaten savagely and tortured, and Brazilian police interrogators had been allowed into Chile to question Brazilian political refugees arrested after the coup.

A French journalist, Pierre Kalfon of the French newspaper Le Monde, was expelled from Chile Oct. 21. He said he was deported for reporting a press conference in which three international jurists reported extensive abuse of human rights by the junta.

Other junta action. Among other junta actions:

Economy—Prices of essential articles were raised by 200%-1,800% Oct. 15 to allow them to reach their "real" level and help spur an increase in local production.

Regulation of agricultural prices was begun, and subsidies were instituted for tea, bread, noodles, sugar and vegetable oil. Workers were awarded special monthly bonuses and family supplements, but their workweek was increased by four hours.

The economy minister, army Gen. Rolando Gonzalez, was replaced Oct. 11 by Fernando Leniz, president of the El Mercurio newspaper chain, who became the second civilian member of the Cabinet. Gonzalez, who reportedly underwent surgery recently, would become ambassador to Paraguay.

The junta had said Oct. 4 that its principal financial adviser would be Rene Saez, a former general manager of the state development corporation and administrator of Alliance for Progress programs.

The rate of inflation would reach an unprecedented 1,200% by the end of 1973, Gen. Gustavo Leigh Guzman, air force commander and junta member, said Oct. 16. The official inflation rate was 323.5% through July, Guzman said, but this was based on figures falsified by the UP. "We are in for some very, very hard times," Guzman asserted. "Next winter we will undoubtedly have to ration electrical power and face other shortages. We don't want to make false promises."

The Central Bank president, Gen. Eduardo Cano, said Chile's foreign debt stood at $4 billion, it was reported Oct. 26. The country's trade deficit was $500 million.

Gen. Augusto Pinochet Ugarte, army commander and junta president, said Oct. 19 that the regime would return to their previous owners most of the more than 300 Chilean and foreign companies seized without compensation by the Allende government. These reportedly included some 40 firms in which U.S. interests had invested. Pinochet stipulated, however, that the companies must give up claims against the government for damages or losses to their installations while under government control.

Chile's new ambassador to the U.S., retired air force Gen. Walter Heitmann, said Nov. 5 the government was willing to "renegotiate the indemnization" of the major U.S. copper companies expropriated under Allende. He added, however, that compensation to the companies should be fixed by the Chilean government and should be reinvested in Chile. He suggested a compensation payment of $60 million.

Education—Retired military officers Oct. 3 assumed the rectorships of the University of Chile and Catholic University in Santiago. Gen. Cesar Ruiz Danyau, former air force commander and transport minister, took control of the first school, and navy Rear Adm. Jorge Sweet of the second.

Housing—Interior Minister Gen. Oscar Bonilla Oct. 22 called conditions in Santiago's shantytowns, or poblaciones, "a national catastrophe," and announced a program to improve them. He said a "pilot study" of some 200 poblaciones had solved their basic problems in a week, and in one shantytown, formerly called Poblacion Ho Chi Minh, the Housing Ministry had already installed electric lights, telephone service and a water pump, and had begun building a school.

The Chilean authorities were replacing Marxist leaders of the poblaciones with non-Marxist junta supporters, in many cases Christian Democrats, the New York Times reported Oct. 16. Many of the former poblacion leaders had been arrested and some had been reported executed.

The junta also had radically altered delivery of food and medical services in the shantytowns, formerly under left-wing control. Government warehouses that had distributed food and household goods at cheap, subsidized prices had been closed in favor of more expensive private groceries and other shops. The clinic system created by the UP to bring medical facilities into the poblaciones was being dismantled in favor of the large, central hospital system backed by conservative medical authorities.

Civil liberties—A decree Oct. 17 forbade all political activity by individuals, parties or other organized groups.

Pinochet said in an interview with the newspaper El Mercurio Oct. 27 that the state of siege would continue for at least eight more months. He admitted some armed resistance to the junta continued, particularly in the South.

Government—The junta announced Oct. 26 a sweeping reorganization of virtually all public services and enterprises in which the state had a majority interest. Dismissals of thousands of public employes had been reported since the coup, according to press accounts Oct. 17. More than 500 persons, including 155 journalists, reportedly had lost their jobs in the state and private press and broadcasting.

The junta announced its intention Oct. 29 to establish a national youth secretariat to "promote the great moral values of the Chilean nation" and "open broad and renewed horizons to all youth."

Press—Four foreign newsmen were expelled by the junta Oct. 15 for allegedly sending false dispatches abroad. They were listed as Philippe Labreveux, of the Paris newspaper Le Monde, who had left Chile the previous week; Grazie Mary Cervi (believed to be Italian journalist Mario Cervi, who also had left); Leif Person, a Swede; and Peter Sumberd, otherwise unidentified.

(A Brazilian journalist, Flavio Vanderley of the Rio de Janeiro opposition weekly Opiniao, was reported missing Oct. 18. A spokesman for the airline Swissair reportedly said he had been arrested.)

Defense of Coup & Junta

Junta defended at U.N. Foreign Minister Ismael Huerta defended the military junta before the United Nations General Assembly Oct. 10, charging foreign reports of abuse of human rights in Chile constituted a "most false, most malevolent, most vicious and very well-orchestrated campaign."

The delegations of Cuba, the Soviet Union, Algeria, Tanzania and at least 16 other nations walked out of the Assembly as Huerta rose to speak, but there was some applause from Latin diplomats. Eight demonstrators in the public gallery were evicted during Huerta's address after they shouted anti-junta slogans.

Huerta asserted the armed forces had overthrown the late President Salvador Allende and his Popular Unity coalition (UP) to avert what he called a totalitarian takeover largely instigated and supported by Cuba. To support this contention, Huerta read and later distributed to newsmen a handwritten letter which, he said, had been sent to Allende by Cuban Premier Fidel Castro July 29.

In the alleged letter, Castro offered his cooperation "in the face of the difficulties and dangers obstructing and threatening the [Chilean] process." He wrote of the need for Allende to "gain time to organize forces in case the fight breaks out" and urged the president not to "forget for a second . . . the vigorous support offered by the working class."

Huerta charged foreign agents sent principally by Cuba had smuggled into Chile enough Soviet- and Czech-made weapons to equip 20,000 men. He added that more than 13,000 foreign extremists had been admitted to the country under Allende to establish "a parallel army to oppose the regular armed forces." These foreigners, Heurta charged, had become directors of public offices, taken illegal control of factories, and in a few cases, joined Chilean delegations in international negotiations.

Huerta later held a press conference in which he outlined "Plan Z," which, he claimed, had been devised by Cuba and the UP to seize "absolute political power" in Chile. The plan, to have been carried out Sept. 17-19, while troops were occupied in national independence anniversary celebrations, allegedly involved assassination of the armed forces commanders, political leaders, and business and management organization executives.

In response to questions about the military takeover of Chilean universities, Huerta said the junta sought to return the schools to their "teaching and investigative functions." He barred any future participation in the universities by Marxists. In response to questions about the junta's expulsion of several foreign journalists, Huerta said: "Chile opens its doors to newsmen and to all who wish to verify the truth."

Cuban response—Cuban Ambassador Raul Roa returned to the General Assembly after Huerta's address and delivered a bitter denunciation of the Chilean junta and the U.S., which he accused of directing the overthrow of Allende.

He called Huerta "a sergeant of Goebbels," and asserted the Chilean had been telling Nazi-style "big lies" while the junta committed Nazi-style atrocities.

Chilean Ambassador Raul Bazan rose after Roa concluded and repeated Huerta's charges against Cuba. He then attacked Premier Castro personally, asserting Castro had made it his "daily pastime" to watch the execution of political opponents and to invite foreign diplomats to the spectacle.

The attack on Castro caused Roa to shout at Bazan and rush to the podium with a few other Cuban representatives to silence the Chilean. The Cubans were stopped by U.N. guards and other delegates. Eyewitnesses said later that some of the Cubans had carried pistols under their jackets and one had warned, "Be careful, I am armed!"

Junta White Paper justifies coup. The military junta issued a 264-page White Paper Oct. 30 purporting to explain why it overthrew the Popular Unity (UP) government of the late President Salvador Allende Gossens.

The report asserted the armed forces had taken power because Allende had sought to "decapitate" them and because he had presided over the "economic, social, institutional and moral ruin" of Chile.

The bulk of the document was devoted to "Plan Z," the alleged Marxist plot to assassinate military and opposition political leaders during national independence celebrations Sept. 17-19. However, the report provided little actual documentation of the alleged plan, failing to state where it was discovered, to list persons or organizations directly linked to it, or to provide strong evidence of its endorsement by Allende.

Certain documents in the White Paper indicated the Socialist and Communist parties had discussed in detail the possibility of a coup and the armed action to be taken against it. However, one Socialist document asserted a well-organized coup would be impossible because of political divisions among military officers and the presumed impossibility of keeping the revolt a secret during its planning stages.

The report asserted large caches of arms had been discovered in Allende's private residences ("enough to equip without difficulty about 5,000 men"), and that the president had used his home on the outskirts of Santiago as a guerrilla training camp. Photographs of the alleged caches were included in the White Paper.

'72 military plotting revealed. Gen. Augusto Pinochet Ugarte, junta president, revealed that the armed forces had plotted to overthrow the government of the late President Salvador Allende since mid-1972, and had decided to seize power May 28, not immediately before the Sept. 11 coup, as previously claimed, the Washington Post reported Dec. 29.

U.S. policies linked to coup. U.S. Rep. Michael J. Harrington (D, Mass.) said in Santiago Oct. 27 that U.S. economic policies of "deprivation" had set in motion the events that led to the Chilean military coup.

Harrington asserted that three days of intensive contacts in Chile, including a two-hour meeting with three of the four military junta members, had reinforced his view that "United States economic policy was the really damaging part of our relationship" with the deposed government of President Salvador Allende.

He stressed "the enormous pressures [the U.S.] brought to bear" on the late President by curbing credits, expressing "chilling interest" in the private sector, and failing to continue economic programs. "We lost a major opportunity in not trying to deal with the freely elected government," Harrington declared, asserting the U.S. could have demonstrated pluralism by cooperating with Allende's Marxist experiment.

Harrington said the junta members had "tried to convey" to him "a strong sense of legitimacy for what they had done," but had been evasive when he expressed "concern over the suppression of the rights of expression and political parties."

Harrington was a member of the House of Representatives' Subcommittee on Inter-American Affairs, which received secret testimony Oct. 11 on Central Intelligence Agency (CIA) operations in Chile during Allende's presidency. The testimony, by CIA Director William E. Colby and agency official Frederick D. Davis, was obtained by journalist Tad Szulc, who reviewed it in an article in the Miami Herald Oct. 22.

Testimony by Colby and Davis, at times unclear and contradictory, touched on "the CIA's own very extensive role in Chilean politics, but it also helps in understanding and reconstructing the [Nixon] Administration's basic policy of bringing about Allende's fall one way or another," according to Szulc.

"The [CIA] activities described range from the 'penetration' of all the major Chilean political parties, support for anti-regime demonstrations and financing of the opposition press and other groups to heretofore unsuspected agency involvement in financial negotiations between Washington and Santiago in late 1972 and early 1973 when Chileans were desperately seeking an accommodation," Szulc wrote.

"There are indications that the CIA, acting on the basis of its own reports on the 'deterioration' of the Chilean economic situation, was among the agencies counseling the White House to rebuff Allende's attempts to work out a settlement on the compensations to be paid for nationalized American property and a renegotiation of Chile's $1.7 billion debt to the United States," he continued.

"The Nixon Administration's firm refusal to help Chile, even on humanitarian grounds, was emphasized about a week before the military coup when it turned down Santiago's request for credits to buy 300,000 tons of wheat [in the U.S.] at a time when the Chileans had run out of foreign currency and bread shortages were developing," Szulc noted. "On Oct. 5, however, the new military junta was granted $24.5 million in wheat credits after the White House overruled State Department objections. The department's Bureau of Inter-American Affairs reportedly believed such a gesture was premature and could be politically embarrassing."

Colby reportedly told the subcommittee that the CIA and the National Security Council had felt it was "not in the United States' interest" ،or Allende's government to be overthrown. He made the comment in response to a question about a similar statement reportedly made by Jack Kubisch, assistant secretary of state for inter-American affairs.

A letter Oct. 8 from Richard A. Fagen, professor of political science at Stanford University, to Sen. J. William Fulbright, chairman of the Senate Foreign Relations Committee, reported that Kubisch had told a group of U.S. scholars, "It would have been better had Allende served his entire term, taking the nation and the Chilean people into complete and total ruin. Only then would the full discrediting of socialism have taken place. Only then would people have gotten the message that socialism doesn't work. What has happened has confused this lesson."

Arrests, resistance continue. Arrests of supporters of the ousted government continued in Santiago as further resistance to the junta was reported in the South.

The junta announced the arrest of eight "Communists and extremists" in the capital Nov. 14, and of 20 alleged Marxists there Nov. 22.

In the South, some 1,000 specially trained anti-guerrilla troops began operating at the beginning of November in the area between Concepcion and Osorno, it was reported Nov. 17. Seven guerrillas were reported killed in an unsuccessful attack Nov. 11 on an army regiment in the southern city of Temuco.

The junta said Nov. 22 it had awarded safe-conducts out of the country to 4,342 of the 4,480 Chileans who had taken refuge in European or Latin American embassies in the capital. It added it had expelled 487 other Chileans and had allowed out 182 foreigners hiding in facilities of international organizations.

The national stadium in Santiago was reported cleared of prisoners Nov. 11. Red Cross official Robert Gaillard-Moret, allowed to visit the country's major prison camps, said he had found prisoners in good health and under humane treatment.

The Washington Post reported Nov. 8 that Pedro Ramirez, mines and later housing minister in Allende's Cabinet, had disappeared after being held by authorities for a week. Ramirez, a son-in-law of Radomiro Tomic, former Christian Democratic presidential candidate, had been virtually the only high official of the Allende government not arrested during the first month after the military coup.

Another leftist, Dewest Bascunan, director of the bi-monthly magazine Andino, had been found dead after attempting to flee to Argentina, the Santiago newspapers El Mercurio and La Prensa reported Nov. 8.

The junta Nov. 15 announced confiscation of all goods and property belonging to the outlawed Marxist parties and other left-wing groups.

Former Bolivian official abducted—Jorge Gallardo Lozada, former Bolivian interior minister, reportedly was kidnapped from his exile home in Santiago and returned to his country on orders of the Bolivian government.

Gallardo's wife, Maria Eugenia Paz, said Nov. 5 that her husband had been seized the week before by two men in civilian clothes—one armed with a submachine gun—and two soldiers. The Chilean Bureau of Investigations denied knowledge of the incident, but the Bolivian government admitted Gallardo had returned to Bolivia two days after his abduction, according to a report Nov. 23.

Mrs. Gallardo insisted her husband had "retired from politics" and that his abduction was "an act of vengeance" by the Bolivian government for a book he had written in 1972. The book, "From Torres to Banzer—Ten Months of Emergency in Bolivia," treated the overthrow of the government of Gen. Juan Jose Torres, under whom Gallardo served, by Gen. Hugo Banzer Suarez, the current president, and implicated the U.S. Central Intelligence Agency and the Brazilian government.

Universities purged. Thousands of leftist students and professors had been suspended from universities, and many faced possible permanent expulsion, it was reported Nov. 14.

Military rectors had closed whole departments or universities that they considered leftist strongholds, and had encouraged right-wing students and professors to denounce Marxist colleagues. Most departments of the University of Chile had been assigned a "prosecutor," usually a law professor, to receive written or oral denunciations. The denounced were not allowed to face their accusers.

The eastern campus of the University of Chile in Santiago had been closed because of alleged Marxist penetration of its social science and political science departments, and some 8,000 students there, mostly leftists, had been suspended. At the University of Concepcion, the most important academic center south of the capital, some 6,000 of 16,000 students and hundreds of professors had been suspended.

About 70 students and 44 of the 360 professors had been suspended from the University of Chile Law School. Some 1,500 students in the university's schools of fine arts, music and architecture also had been suspended along with about 100 professors.

Teachers' colleges to be reorganized—The junta Dec. 13 appointed a commission to direct the reorganization of the nation's teachers' colleges. The reorganization was to "end the situation of anarchy in the technical, administrative and pedagogic aspects of teacher training," and "re-establish the principles of order, discipline and morality," the official decree said.

Cuban, Soviet ships held in Panama Canal. Freighters owned by the Cuban and Soviet governments were detained by U.S. authorities in the Panama Canal Zone in October and November at the request of Chilean companies demanding delivery of cargo they claimed to have paid for previously.

A Cuban freighter, the Imias, was detained by U.S. federal court order Oct. 2 at the request of Chile's National Sugar Industry and its Vina del Mar Refining Co., which claimed two other Cuban vessels, the Playa Larga and the Marble Island, had failed to deliver more than 18,000 metric tons of sugar purchased for more than $8 million.

The Playa Larga had been unloading its sugar in the Chilean port of Valparaiso Sept. 11, the day of the Chilean military coup, and had escaped with much of its cargo after being bombed and strafed by Chilean air force rebels. It had met the Marble Island a day later in the Pacific and warned it not to proceed to Chile. The Chilean firms had attempted to have the Marble Island detained Oct. 1 in the Panamanian port of Balboa, at the entrance to the Canal, but the vessel had escaped.

Panama officially protested the detention of the Imias Oct. 4, asserting that under international law the U.S. had no legal jurisdiction over a vessel owned by a foreign government.

A Soviet freighter, the William Foster, was detained in the Canal Oct. 13 by order of U.S. federal Judge Guthrie Crowe, at the request of two Chilean firms claiming to have paid $309,000 for some of its cargo, including electrolytic zinc. This was protested by the Panamanian National Assembly Oct. 18.

An out-of-court settlement was reached on the William Foster at the behest of the U.S. State Department, it was reported Nov. 7. The vessel was freed after it agreed to transfer its Chilean-bought cargo to another Soviet vessel for shipment to Chile via Peru.

The Imias was freed by court order Nov. 13, also at the request of the State Department.

Constitution draft approved. The military junta Nov. 29 approved a draft for a new Constitution which would establish an "organic democracy" and assure "the incorporation of all sectors of activity in the process of collective decision-making."

According to Enrique Ortuzar, president of the jurists' commission that drafted the document, the new Constitution would contain a mechanism to prevent the election of a minority government—such as the one overthrown by the junta—and would provide for resolution of conflicts between the executive and legislative branches by plebiscite.

Like the previous Constitutions of 1833 and 1925, Ortuzar said, the new one would "maintain and strengthen public liberties, without discrimination; guarantee equality before the law, and the freedoms of conscience, worship, learning and expression. It will also respect the right to property."

The document would reaffirm the importance of political parties, but these could act "only within their proper orbit," Ortuzar said. Parties would not be allowed to "intervene" in "public administration or in elections or labor conflicts in universities, educational establishments, economic associations or labor unions," he asserted.

Parties which "oppose the democratic system of government will be declared unconstitutional," Ortuzar siad, apparently referring to the now outlawed left-wing organizations. Persons who "agitated against the democratic regime" and "defended crime and political violence" would "not be able to exercise any public function," he added.

The Constitution would guarantee the independence of the judiciary and the comptroller general's office, he said. The armed forces and national police would remain "essentially professional, hierarchical, disciplined, obedient and non-deliberative," always understanding that "their obedience is to the entire institutionality of the country and that it can never mean, as the previous regime intended, a political subjugation to the president of the republic."

The role of the military would continue to be the protection of Chile's internal and external security, in defense of which the armed forces and police had "freed the nation from the international communism which was destroying it," Ortuzar asserted.

Swedish envoy expelled. The government Dec. 4 declared Swedish Ambassador Harald Edelstam "persona non grata" and accused him of exceeding his authority as a foreign diplomat. He was the first non-Communist envoy to be asked to leave Chile since the military coup Sept. 11.

Edelstam had said he and four embassy secretaries had been beaten Nov. 25 by soldiers and police who arrested a Uruguayan woman under their protection.

Edelstam asserted he and his aides were assaulted at a clinic in Santiago as they tried to prevent authorities from seizing Consuelo Alonso Freiria, who had sought asylum three weeks earlier in the Cuban embassy, under Swedish protection since Chile and Cuba broke relations Sept. 13. Alonso had been recovering from an emergency operation when the incident occurred. She was taken by the authorities to a prison clinic.

The Chilean Foreign Ministry denied Nov. 26 that there had been violence at the clinic but criticized Edelstam for trying to prevent Alonso's arrest. It alleged Edelstam had acted "improperly" because Alonso had given up diplomatic asylum in leaving the Cuban embassy. Edelstam asserted the army had approved her move from the embassy, and she thus remained under Swedish protection.

Swedish Foreign Minister Sven Andersson and United Nations high commissioner for refugees, Prince Sadruddin Aga Khan, formally protested the incident Nov. 26.

A high Chilean police official, Jaime Vasquez, alleged Nov. 28 that Uruguayan Interpol officers had identified Alonso as Mirta Ercilia Fernandez, widow of a Tupamaro guerrilla leader, and said she was wanted in Uruguay for "terrorist conspiracy and falsification of public documents."

Alonso was allowed to leave Santiago for Stockholm Dec. 3 after authorities determined that she had not participated in domestic "subversive" activities. The police Dec. 1 had given the press a sworn statement by Alonso confirming that she was actually Mirta Ercilia Fernandez, widow of a Tupamaro leader, as the police had claimed, and had entered Chile illegally.

Edelstam had vigorously defended the rights of political refugees in Chile since the military coup Sept. 11. He was credited with single-handedly preventing troops from storming the Cuban embassy and with protecting the estimated 20–32 Chilean and foreign refugees who had sought asylum there. He also was a major backer of the international effort to win guarantees for the security of opponents of the new military junta.

Troops had surrounded the Cuban embassy Nov. 6 and had arrested a Swedish newswoman and two Chilean chauffeurs of the Swedish embassy attempting to enter the building. Edelstam protested the action the next day and secured the release of the journalist—Margarethe Sourander, wife of Swedish newsman Bo Sourander, arrested and deported earlier—and the drivers. He complained that Swedish embassy automobiles were searched illegally and that he was forced to sleep at the Cuban embassy every night "to protect the refugees."

The Chilean government asserted the Cuban embassy had been surrounded because persons inside it had fired on security forces outside. Edelstam denied this.

Edelstam left Santiago Dec. 9. Arriving in Stockholm the next day, he charged that some 15,000 persons had been killed in Chile since the coup, 7,000 had been arrested and 30,000 left homeless. He noted that arrests were continuing and alleged that political prisoners were being tortured.

Swedish Foreign Minister Sven Andersson Dec. 4 had protested Edelstam's expulsion and commended Edelstam for working "more than any other person [in Chile] to save refugees." Sweden said Dec. 5 it would not name a new ambassador to Chile. Swedish aid to Chile was canceled Dec. 11.

Miriam Contreras, personal secretary to the late President Salvador Allende and one of the 10 persons most sought by the government, had taken asylum in the Swedish embassy, according to government sources Dec. 5. Orlando Cantuarias, a former Cabinet minister and vice president of the Radical party, left the embassy Dec. 9 and surrendered to police.

Estimates of the number of Chilean and foreign refugees remaining in Western European and Latin American embassies in the capital ranged from 500–700, reported by the Washington Post Dec. 11, to some 2,000, reported by the French newspaper Le Monde the same day. Le Monde reported the junta had decided to give no more safe-conducts abroad to refugees in embassies of countries that had not signed asylum conventions with Chile. These reportedly included most Western European nations.

The Geneva-based Intergovernmental Commission on European Migrations said Nov. 30 that some 1,200 refugees of 28 nationalities had been transferred from Chile to 26 countries since the coup. The majority, about 800, went to Western Europe, and the others to Latin American states. Sweden, the Netherlands and France were the European nations most willing to take refugees from Chile, according to Le Monde Dec. 5.

The U.S. had offered to allow foreign refugees stranded in Chile after the military coup to enter the U.S. under a special "parole" arrangement suspending certain immigration restrictions, it was reported Dec. 1. The offer—initially suggested by Sen. Edward M. Kennedy (D, Mass.)—had been made more than a month before, but fewer than 30 persons had accepted it.

The Latin embassies with most refugees were those of Argentina, Mexico and Venezuela. Some reports said the refugees remained there because Chile would not grant them safe-conducts, and others asserted the nations in question were reluctant to admit leftists because of their own domestic conditions. The Washington Post reported Dec. 11 that Chileans in the U.S. said the junta had denied safe-conducts to 200–300 Chilean refugees who had been at one time or another leaders of the ousted Popular Unity coalition.

The Bogota newspaper El Tiempo Nov. 29–30 criticized the treatment by the Chilean junta of refugees in the Colombian embassy in Santiago. It also charged Colombian actions to protect refugees had been "weak and irregular."

The wife of Oscar Garreton, leader of the left-wing MAPU party and one of the junta's 10 most wanted persons, had charged Nov. 29 that the junta had offered safe-conducts to a dozen refugees in the Colombian embassy in exchange for Garreton, who was also in the embassy.

In a related development reported Dec. 6, three persons were wounded and captured when they tried to scale the fence around the Panamanian embassy in Santiago and gain asylum there. Panama, Honduras and Costa Rica reportedly had been the Latin countries most willing to take Chilean refugees.

The junta told European embassies in Santiago Dec. 10 that it would not grant courtesy safe-conduct abroad to persons who took political asylum in the embassies after Dec. 11. Military guards were strengthened outside all embassies Dec. 10 to prevent political refugees from gaining entrance.

The Times of London reported Dec. 12 that more than 2,000 foreign refugees remained in hostels set up by the United Nations High Commissioner for Refugees. Their political background reportedly made them unwelcome in their own countries, and some lacked the official visas necessary to leave Chile.

West German Chancellor Willy Brandt said Bonn would give asylum to more Chilean refugees than any other European nation, it was reported Dec. 11. He said 40 refugees from Chile had arrived in West Germany Dec. 7.

Ex-minister wounded. Ex-Agriculture Minister Rolando Calderon was shot in the head Dec. 19 by a sniper who fired into the Cuban embassy in Santiago, where Calderon had taken refuge after the military coup. He was not wounded seriously, but was taken to a military hospital after receiving safe conduct from the junta.

Torture reports continue. The Mexico City newspaper Excelsior Dec. 7 printed photographs of what it called four separate instances of torture of detainees at the national stadium in Santiago, which until recently was used to hold persons arrested after the military coup.

The French weekly Politique Hebdo, cited by the Cuban press agency Prensa Latina Nov. 9, alleged political prisoners in Chile were forced to walk on hot coals or with broken glass in their shoes, and were subjected to other "scientific" tortures administered with the aid of "specialists" from Brazil and Uruguay.

Prensa Latina also reported that executions of leftists were continuing. (The government later stopped announcing executions to improve its image abroad, the Miami Herald reported Dec. 10.) The junta announced one execution Dec. 1, bringing the official total to 95. Socialist Congressman Luis Espinoza Villalobos was shot to death Dec. 4 while "attempting to escape" from a military patrol transferring him from one prison to another.

The French newspaper Le Monde reported Nov. 29 that at least 18 doctors had vanished, been arrested or executed since the military coup. Five had been executed, including Enrique Paris, a member of the Communist party's central committee; 10 had disappeared, including former Health Minister Arturo Jiron and National Health Service Director Sergio Infante; and three had been arrested, including Alfredo Jadresic, former dean of the medical faculty of the University of Chile at Santiago.

Persecution of leftist doctors had been organized within the medical profession, Le Monde reported. A commission had been named at each health center to classify personnel politically and report to military authorities. Denunciations were encouraged, and all doctors in directorial positions were replaced with supporters of the new government. Many doctors detained during or immediately after the military coup had been abused, and one—Martin Cordero, now living in London—had been tortured, Le Monde reported.

Other arrests continue—The government announced the capture of 10 "extremists" in Concepcion Nov. 28 and of seven "extreme left terrorists" in Curico and Concepcion Provinces Dec. 9. Seven prisoners had been condemned to life imprisonment by a military court in Talca Nov. 8.

Communist party Secretary General Luis Corvalan and several other political prisoners—including former Cabinet minister Pedro Felipe Ramirez, previously reported disappeared, and Anselmo Sule, former Radical party president—had been transferred to the prison on Dawson Island, in the Strait of Magellan, where high officials of the ousted government were held, Le Monde reported Nov. 30.

Other political prisoners were at Chacabuco and Pisagua, in the north, and on Quiriquina Island, in front of the Talcahuano naval base in the south. Some 500 prisoners on Quiriquina were being forced to build their own prison, El Nacional of Caracas reported Dec. 9.

Sources within and outside Chile reported that former Interior Undersecretary Daniel Vergara, held on Dawson Island since the coup, had died Dec. 9 of gangrene from an unattended wound suffered during the coup. The navy asserted Dec. 11 that Vergara was alive at a naval hospital at Punta Arenas, where he was being treated for an infected hand.

Two other former government officials, Werber Villar and Rigoberto Achu Liendo, both Communists, were killed in northern Chile Dec. 14 while allegedly trying to escape from authorities, according to the French newspaper Le Monde. The army announced Dec. 22 that five "terrorists" had died in a gun battle with troops in Santiago after they were discovered trying to blow up a city power supply line.

The navy confirmed Dec. 19 that two more persons had been condemned to death, presumably for "terrorist" activities, bringing the official number of executions to about 100.

Carlos Altamirano, secretary general of the outlawed Socialist party and one of the junta's 10 most wanted men, said in a message broadcast by Havana radio Dec. 18 that all democratic forces in Chile should unite for "a long struggle, inevitably victorious," against the junta. The junta had denied earlier reports that Altamirano had surrendered to undergo medical treatment.

Mrs. Allende sees Trudeau. Hortensia Bussi de Allende, widow of President Salvador Allende, met with Canadian Prime Minister Pierre Trudeau in Ottawa Nov. 30. At a subsequent press conference she urged Canada to aid Chilean political refugees and cut off loans to and trade with Chile's "fascist" military junta.

Since her husband's ouster and death Sept. 11, Mrs. Allende had visited several Latin American and European cities to seek help for Chilean political refugees and political prisoners.

Chileans abroad to lose citizenship. A spokesman for the junta told United Press International Dec. 10 that Chileans abroad who attacked "the essential interests of the state" would lose their citizenship.

The spokesman said there were some 50 persons "directing the campaign against Chile abroad," including Hortensia Bussi de Allende, widow of President Salvador Allende; Volodia Teitelboim, former Communist senator; and Armando Uribe and Carlos Vasallo, former ambassadors to East Germany and Italy, respectively.

Other foreign developments—A Chilean mission led by Leon Vilarin, a leader of the truckers' strike that helped precipitate the military coup, was expelled from Venezuela Dec. 3. The group was on an international tour to explain the current Chilean "reality" and offset bad publicity being given the junta in the foreign press. The mission and the Chilean Foreign Ministry accepted Venezuela's explanation that the expulsion was dictated by security considerations for the Venezuelan presidential election Dec. 9.

Vilarin's group proceeded to the Dominican Republic, where its scheduled press conference Dec. 5 was boycotted by the national newsmen's union. The union denounced the mission for "making propaganda" for Chile's "ferocious and brutal military dictatorship."

The Congo Republic broke relations with Chile Dec. 7.

Private U.S. loans increase. Loans to Chile by private U.S. banks had increased sharply since the military junta overthrew the left-wing government of the late President Salvador Allende, the New York Times reported Nov. 12.

Manufacturers Hanover Trust Co. of New York announced a $24 million loan to the Bank of Chile Nov. 9, and banking sources quoted by the Times said Manufacturers Hanover had extended an additional $20 million loan to the Central Bank. Financial sources in Santiago added that eight to 10 U.S. banks and two Canadian banks had offered Chile commercial loans totaling about $150 million since the armed forces took power.

In a related development, an international bank syndicate including three U.S. banks—Bankers Trust, Irving Trust and First National City Bank—and several Canadian banks had opened a $170 million credit line to Chile, according to the Andean Times' Latin America Economic Report Dec. 14.

U.S. government loans also were made available after the coup. The U.S. Agriculture Department disclosed granting a $28 million loan to Chile to buy U.S. corn, it was reported Nov. 16. The U.S. earlier had provided a $24 million credit for wheat purchases.

Copper negotiator named. The government Dec. 13 named Julio Philippi, a former finance minister, as its representative for projected talks with U.S. copper firms whose property was expropriated by the ousted government.

Economy Minister Fernando Leniz, announcing the appointment, stressed that it meant only that the government was willing "to discuss the issue" of compensation to the U.S. companies.

The U.S. had agreed to renegotiate its share of Chile's foreign debt—whose total, according to the junta, was $3.2 billion—without prior compensation to U.S. copper companies for property expropriated without payment under Allende, it was reported Nov. 16. This concession followed a visit to the U.S. by Foreign Minister Ismael Huerta, who defended the junta at the United Nations and conferred with officials of Kennecott Copper Corp., Anaconda Co. and other firms.

The junta already had offered to compensate the copper companies, but it had virtually no cash to do so; reserves in the Central Bank reportedly totaled only $3.5 million.

U.S. debt repayment pact. The U.S. State and Treasury Departments announced Dec. 21 that the U.S. and Chile had reached agreement on repayment of $124 million in Chilean debts over the next eight years.

Chile reportedly agreed to pay $60 million over a four-year period beginning with a $16 million payment Dec. 28, and another $64 million over six years beginning Jan. 1, 1975, adding a 6% yearly interest rate.

The Wall Street Journal reported Dec. 28 that Chile had sent the U.S. $19.5 million for the first installment, with the extra $3.5 million to be kept in reserve.

Economic developments. The government Nov. 28 devalued the escudo and reduced taxes on imports.

The newspaper La Segunda reported Nov. 23 that the state development corporation CORFO had drawn up a list of 88 businesses and industries to be returned to their owners because they had been "illegally" confiscated by the Allende government.

Military authorities announced that 115 nationalized companies, including 12 controlled by foreign capital, were being returned to their former owners, it was reported Dec. 11. Among the first returned were four U.S.-owned motion picture distributors.

Two U.S. firms, General Tire International and Dow Chemical, said Nov. 7 they had been invited to resume operations in Chile.

The first strike since Allende's overthrow, by some 200 manual workers on Santiago's subway system demanding higher wages, was broken when army troops occupied the site and warned that strikers would be dismissed immediately, it was reported Nov. 23.

The government Dec. 5 decreed a ban on domestic beef sales to last Dec. 8–18.

The junta Dec. 19 announced its 1974 wage policy. It set a single pay scale for public employes, including the armed forces and police, and provided for 500% wage increases, based on salaries earned in January 1973, for private sector employes. Pensions and annuities were similarly increased, and family bonuses were doubled.

The government's special economic adviser, Orlando Saenz, had resigned on grounds he had completed the task entrusted to him, the London newsletter Latin America reported Dec. 14.

October inflation up 87.6%—The cost of living in Chile rose by 87.6% in October, increasing the rate of inflation for the first 10 months of 1973 to 449.2%, according to the National Statistics Institute Nov. 13.

The institute said the October figure reflected price increases ordered by the junta shortly after the military coup to put the economy on a more "realistic" basis. The junta had estimated inflation might reach 1,200% by the end of 1973.

The junta was being forced to print large amounts of new currency to meet many of its financial commitments, despite having criticized the Allende government for doing so and thus adding to inflation, the Andean Times' Latin America Economic Report noted Nov. 16. The 70% increase in the money supply from September to the end of 1973 would be higher than for any period under Allende before May.

Land reform ends—Chile's land reform program, begun in 1960 under conservative President Jorge Alessandri, was ended Dec. 19 when the military junta decreed that land could no longer be expropriated.

Most land designated for agrarian reform by previous governments reportedly was being turned over to peasants with individual deeds of ownership, to be purchased over 30-year periods.

The Agrarian Reform Institute Nov. 16 began returning to their former owners agricultural properties of less than 40 hectares expropriated by the ousted government.

Voting records voided. The junta Nov. 19 nullified all electoral records, including recent voter registrations, while it studied creation of a new system to prevent vote fraud and guarantee the "seriousness and efficiency" of the electoral process.

An Interior Ministry decree announcing the action charged "investigations pursued by public and university organizations have proved the existence of grave and extensive vote fraud," particularly in the March congressional elections, in which the deposed government did better than expected.

The junta had claimed in its recent White Paper justifying the military coup, that an investigative commission of the Catholic University had found the government benefited from numerous irregularities in the elections, including double registration of voters and ballots cast for deceased persons.

The junta Nov. 12 dissolved as "unnecessary" the Constitutional Court, established by the ousted government to resolve disputes between the executive and legislative branches.

The junta announced Nov. 14 that public employes would be barred from participating in politics and would be observed regularly by government inspectors to see that they worked "in a real spirit of discipline."

Santiago elections barred. An edict signed by Gen. Sergio Arellano, commander of the Santiago Province emergency zone, prohibited "elections of any type—be they in unions, economic associations, politics, schools or any other groups." Vacancies in elected offices would henceforth be filled in consultation "with the corresponding representative of the military junta." The edict, issued Dec. 16, applied only to Santiago Province.

Newspaper closed. Interior Minister Gen. Oscar Bonilla said Nov. 28 that the left-wing tabloid Clarin, closed since the coup, would not reappear. Three other leftist papers—El Siglo, Puro Chile and Ultima Hora—previously had been closed permanently.

Colombia

Economic Improvements & Problems

1972 exports high. The Foundation for Development, an independent institute, reported 1972 exports at a high level, with large earnings from coffee (traditionally the principal source of foreign exchange) and an unusually sharp increase in sales of non-traditional exports, the London newsletter Latin America reported Jan. 5. However, the rise in the cost of living was also high, reported at 15%-16%.

According to the figures, non-traditional exports—both agricultural and industrial—rose by more than 60%, accounting for 31% of Colombia's 1972 foreign exchange earnings, compared with coffee's 51%. The new balance reportedly raised hopes that Colombia would soon abandon its excessive dependence on coffee. Foreign reserves reportedly doubled, reaching nearly $300 million.

In 1972, Colombia achieved its first positive trade balance in five years, Finance Minister Rodrigo Llorente reported Jan. 23. The 1972 trade surplus of $1.9 million, compared with a 1971 deficit of $171.9 million, was attributed largely to increased world coffee prices.

Llorente returned from a trip to Japan and the U.S. at the end of January, having negotiated $130 million worth of foreign credits for Colombia, the newsletter Latin America reported Feb. 9.

Financial developments. Among financial developments reported:

The World Bank announced Jan. 8 that it had loaned $56 million to Medellin Public Enterprises, an autonomous public utility, to help finance the second stage of the Guatape hydroelectric scheme. A $25 million Japanese loan to Colombia for development of the Cauca valley, near the western coast, was reported Jan. 12.

Colombia had successfully offered $20 million of 8¼% sinking fund bonds, 50% to U.S. investors and the remainder to European and Japanese purchasers, the Wall Street Journal reported Jan. 19. The 15-year bonds, priced at 100, represented Colombia's initial public offering of long-term debt payable in U.S. currency, according to a spokesman in New York.

The electric power institute ICEL would spend $43 million in transmission networks and connection systems, Latin America reported March 23. Part of the sum would come from the Inter-American Development Bank (IDB).

The IDB would lend the government $20 million toward a $100 million program to open the Caribbean coast to international tourism, it was reported Feb. 16.

The IDB would provide $11 million of a $20 million government expenditure to improve and enlarge the ports of Barranquilla, Buenaventura, Cartagena and Santa Marta over the next five years, according to a report Feb. 23.

COLOMBIA

The World Bank and the Inter-American Development Bank had granted Colombia about $100 million in loans for road building, port improvements and expansion, water supplies, drainage and other projects, according to Bogota Mayor Anibal Fernandez de Soto, the London newsletter Latin America reported May 25. The International Monetary Fund granted Colombia 20 million Special Drawing Rights, or paper gold, June 6.

Congress March 15 approved a bill nationalizing the Bank of the Republic, Colombia's central bank, previously controlled by private bankers. The government would hold 99% of the bank's shares.

Television workers strike. Employes of the nation's three television stations and the government radio station began an indefinite strike March 22 to demand wage increases, overtime pay and classification as public employes. The action followed a record 2% cost of living increase in February.

The government, which owned the television stations, declared the stoppage illegal and adopted "drastic measures" against the striking union, according to El Nacional of Caracas March 24.

Meanwhile, representatives of 70,000 teachers warned March 23 they would strike unless the government abandoned the projected elimination of 6,000 teaching positions. Education Minister Juan Jacobo Munoz said the positions would have to be eliminated because Congress had voted against a bill increasing city housing taxes to finance state education programs.

More than 20,000 employes of the Colombian Social Security Institute, including medical personnel, threatened March 23 to strike unless the government agreed to a 20% wage increase instead of the 7% it had offered. More than one million Social Security recipients would be affected by a strike.

The Cabinet announced March 23 that it would revise its economic policies to halt the constant devaluation of Colombia's currency and the high rate of inflation which were generating price increases and public discontent.

Cost of living up 14%. The cost of living rose by 14% during the first five months of 1973, leading the government to impose a number of anti-inflationary measures, it was reported June 21.

Food prices for blue-collar workers increased by 33.3% and housing costs rose by 12.7% in January–May. A 3% consumer price rise for white-collar workers and 3.8% hike for blue-collar workers in April marked the highest monthly increase in 10 years.

President Misael Pastrana Borrero called the increases "alarming" in a nationwide broadcast May 12. Price controls on essential articles were imposed May 15, and new fines and prison sentences for hoarders and speculators were reported May 25.

The government earlier had announced a series of emergency economic measures, reported May 11. They included restrictions on public spending; an effort to hold down food prices by stimulating production, improving distribution, and authorizing more imports to take advantage of the recent growth in foreign exchange reserves; and the transfer to the recently nationalized Bank of the Republic of funds deposited in private banks by public agencies.

Meat exports had been reported cut by half May 4 in an effort to hold down domestic meat prices. Strict price controls over companies distributing and selling gas were reported June 8.

The government announced it was importing 130,000 tons of cereals, mostly wheat, to offset acute domestic shortages, it was reported June 15. Hundreds of bakeries reportedly had shut down, and bread had been rationed in some towns because of the wheat shortage.

Colombia's largest trade union, the Colombian Workers Union, had urged Jan. 5 that the regime freeze salaries, prices and taxes to curb the "asphyxiating" rate of inflation. The union said wage hikes were usually absorbed by inflation within three or four months.

Transport strike violence. A general transport strike in Bogota and four other cities Oct. 1–3 led to riots and other protests against the high cost of living and the government's economic policies. Two persons were killed, 230 injured and more than 2,000 arrested before the stoppage ended without satisfaction of the strikers' demands.

The strike was called at midnight Sept. 30 by unions representing 150,000 bus, jitney and taxi drivers who demanded a higher minimum wage, an eight-hour day, and better social security. It was initially supported by bus owners, who sought government approval of a 100% fare increase, but the owners dropped out when the government declared the stoppage illegal.

Troops were called into Bogota Oct. 1 when striking drivers, students and teachers (teachers had been on strike since August for higher salaries and other benefits) clashed with police and looters attacked stores in poor sections of the city. Hundreds of persons were arrested, including the principal strike leader, Tancredo Herran, president of the National Salaried Drivers' Union, and other union leaders. The strike spread that day to Cali, Medellin, Barranquilla and Bucaramanga, where additional disturbances were reported.

Full-scale rioting erupted in Bogota Oct. 2, with attacks on police and soldiers, looting and stoning of stores, factories and banks, and destruction of some 110 buses. Two strikers were killed and some 1,000 were arrested. Cucuta, Armenia, Ibague and Villavicencio, like the capital, were virtually paralyzed by the strike, and experienced similar disturbances.

The government refused to grant the strikers' demands, calling the stoppage subversive, suspending the legal status of the striking unions for six months and ordering their funds frozen. It did, however, offer bus owners higher subsidies which would enable them to recover cost of living losses without an unpopular fare increase.

Drivers began returning to work Oct. 3, explaining they could not afford a longer strike.

Drivers' representatives were allowed Oct. 4 to present petitions for higher salaries and an eight-hour day to the Public Works Ministry.

Meanwhile, the teachers' strike continued, with no new government move since the arrest, reported Sept. 28, of 550 strikers across the country for disobeying an earlier government ban on demonstrations and public meetings.

Subversive plot charged—The State Security Department claimed it discovered a subversive plot to have been carried out during the transport strike, according to the Bogota newspaper El Tiempo Oct. 5.

A department spokesman told the newspaper that 25 extreme leftists had been arrested in connection with the plot, and one subversive had surrendered 500 U.S.-made bullets. The spokesman refused to identify the alleged plotters. He said only that the "existence of a subversive plan was evident, since the [damaged] banks and shops had nothing to do with the wage demands of the drivers."

President Misael Pastrana Borrero had charged in a nationwide television and radio address Oct. 4 that in breaking the strike, the government had "broken the tentacles of subversion." He asserted the strike violence had been promoted by "subversive groups that thought the time had come to upset the institutions that govern us and to throw Colombia into uncertainty and chaos."

Pastrana charged that "certain" international news agencies had, in their coverage of the transport strike, tried to "discredit our system, methodically transmitting reports that lacked veracity."

Pastrana also praised recent military successes against the nation's guerrilla groups, asserting the Castroite National Liberation Army (ELN) had been "reduced to impotence" and the Maoist People's Liberation Army (EPL) had been "almost totally destroyed."

New oil policy. Mines and Petroleum Minister Gerardo Silva Valderrama July 4 announced a new government oil policy to readjust prices and deal with the scarcity of fuel and other resources.

Silva also asserted the government would nationalize the gold, silver and platinum mines in Antioquia and El Choco if the foreign companies managing them did not accept 51% state participation.

Business and political leaders meeting in Medellin had concluded March 4 that Colombia would have to invest $480 million in the next 10 years to find new

COLOMBIA

sources of petroleum to overcome the current energy crisis. The government moved to increase investment in oil exploration by saying it would allow foreign firms to increase the price of hydrocarbons extracted from sources found in the next five years.

Other events. President Pastrana had ordered three bids for air navigational aids and traffic control by a British, a U.S. and a French company, to be submitted to the International Civil Aviation Organization for its recommendation, Latin America reported Feb. 2. The action followed press allegations of irregularities in awarding the contract, worth $25 million–$45 million, by the Colombian Civil Aeronautics Administration, which recommended the British firm Imperial Overseas on technical grounds even though its price was the highest and delivery schedule longest.

The government had nationalized the mining concern Choco Pacifico and taken charge of gold production following the rise in the price of gold occasioned by the recent dollar devaluation, Latin America reported Feb. 23.

A nine-month drought affecting three-quarters of Colombia's territory had caused great losses in agriculture and livestock breeding, large forest fires that threatened oil installations, and an acute water shortage, El Nacional of Caracas reported Feb. 26. Antonio Jose Gonzalez, president of the Colombian Farmers Association, estimated peasants had lost $50 million.

The Bogota newspaper El Tiempo said March 21 that cattle smuggling into Venezuela had increased to "uncontrollable" dimensions. Venezuelan officials agreed March 24 it was a serious problem, but claimed the illegal entry of Colombian cattle had decreased by 10% in 1971–72.

Guerrillas Active

Industrialists kidnapped. Members of the left-wing National Liberation Army (ELN) killed one person and kidnapped six others in the northern departments of Antioquia and Cordoba Jan. 6–8, causing nationwide concern and an increase in military operations in the north. One of the captives was released in exchange for $20,000, but the other five, including three wealthy industrialists, were held by the guerrillas.

The government asserted Jan. 9 that it would use "all energies" to combat the ELN, while the press and agricultural and livestock organizations called for severe measures, including the death penalty, against kidnappers. The armed forces offered rewards totaling $20,000 for information leading to the capture of ELN founders Fabio and Manuel Vasquez Castano and their lieutenants, Spanish priest Domingo Lain and ex-student Ricardo Lara Parada, El Nacional of Caracas reported Jan. 19.

The guerrillas offered to exchange their five captives for 18 suspected ELN members held by authorities in Bucaramanga, according to a Havana radio broadcast Jan. 24. The government did not respond to the offer.

Presumed ELN guerrillas assaulted a gold mine north of Medellin Jan. 16, killing a guard, downing a helicopter and making off with gold reportedly valued at $50,000.

Guerrillas in the Santa Barbara emerald region of eastern Boyaca ambushed a police patrol Jan. 25, killing five officers and wounding another 10, police reported.

Armed members of the ELN clashed with soldiers in the department of Santander Jan. 25. First reports said two soldiers had been killed, several guerrillas wounded and one subversive, Maria Teresa Echeverria, had been killed. Echeverria reportedly was the first female guerrilla to die in combat. Later reports from the Defense Ministry said Luis Jose Solano Sepulveda, second in command of the ELN, had also been killed in the clash.

Emergency measures adopted. The government adopted a series of emergency security measures Jan. 26 following a number of bloody guerrilla actions and the attempted kidnapping of a prominent Cali industrialist and publisher. Among the provisions:

■ All persons convicted by military authorities of kidnapping, extortion and related crimes would serve their sentences in the island prison of La Gorgona, in the Pacific Ocean, considered the most secure in the country.

- The governors of the nation's 22 departments (states) were authorized to set rewards for persons who provided information detailing crimes and leading to the capture of criminals.

- Special groups were formed within the armed forces to pursue guerrilla bands operating in rural areas. They would be given new equipment, including helicopters and mobile radio units.

- Unauthorized emerald prospecting was prohibited in the emerald regions of the department of Boyaca, which was placed under military rule.

- The mass media were warned that the government would "regulate information" wherever accounts and rumors did not "conform to reality" and tended to create alarm and anxiety.

The measures were set at a Cabinet meeting called late Jan. 26, only hours after Alvaro Caicedo, a wealthy Cali industrialist and publisher, was wounded in a thwarted kidnapping attempt.

The day before, an estimated 50 guerrillas had taken temporary control of the village of San Pedro de Uraba, in the northern department of Antioquia, sacking stores and granaries, robbing the local bank and killing four policemen. The army immediately launched a land and air search for the subversives, said to belong to the pro-Moscow Colombian Revolutionary Armed Forces.

President Misael Pastrana Borrero Jan. 28 indirectly blamed the Communist party and other "foreign groups" for Colombia's current terrorist wave. He noted that the most recent guerrilla actions coincided with an international meeting of Communist youths at the Capitol building in Bogota.

Gustavo Escobar, a stockbreeder kidnapped Feb. 23, was freed in Medellin March 10 without collection of a ransom, the French newspaper Le Monde reported March 13. Police said two men and two women had been arrested in the case.

Guerrilla cooperation reported. There was strong evidence the country's three main guerrilla groups were trying to coordinate their activities in the face of the government's determined anti-guerrilla campaign, the London newsletter Latin America reported March 9.

Elements of the three groups—the pro-Cuban National Liberation Army (ELN), the pro-Soviet Colombian Revolutionary Armed Forces and the pro-Chinese People's Liberation Army (EPL)—had staged a joint attack March 2 on Florian, a small township in the eastern department of Santander. It was the fifth attack on a rural town in three months, but it was not certain whether the previous four had been joint operations, Latin America reported.

Two guerrillas were reported killed at Florian. Despite this and heavy ELN casualties in February, the guerrillas were making considerable progress, Latin America reported. They were said to be active in contiguous territory, instead of isolated areas, and to be concentrating on agricultural areas in the north and northwest, where peasant discontent was high.

The army was reported March 9 to have captured Jesus Ariza Gomez, an important EPL leader in Antioquia.

The army claimed to have discovered a large cache of ELN arms in Santander, and to have captured an important ELN urban guerrilla leader near Cali, Latin America reported March 16.

Presumed ELN guerrillas killed five soldiers and wounded three others in an ambush in southwestern Santander department April 8.

One person was killed April 6 when guerrillas in the southeastern jungles shot down a helicopter being used for exploration by the oil firm Tennessee Colombia.

Guerrillas kill Liberal leader. German Gomez Pelaez, a landowner, journalist and Liberal party leader in the department of Cordoba, was kidnapped May 6 and later killed by members of the People's Liberation Army (EPL), a Maoist guerrilla group, according to a military communiqué May 11.

The communiqué said two EPL members had been arrested in the case. It asserted Gomez Pelaez' murder "confirms the necessity for all citizens to unite to defend society from the horrendous threat posed by insurgents" kidnapping millionaires and other prominent citizens.

Earlier, another guerrilla group, the Castroite National Liberation Army (ELN), had released five Medellin industrialists kidnapped in January in exchange for large ransoms, the London newsletter Latin America reported May 18.

Forty-five persons held for eight months on charges of collaborating with the ELN had been reported released March 30 in Bucaramanga. The local army commander and military judge, Gen. Ramón Rincon Quinones, ruled they had already served the minimum sentence for the crime of rebellion, despite not having been tried or sentenced.

Another 120 persons accused of helping the ELN were brought to trial in April before a military court in Bucaramanga, but the court's president suspended the trial early in May to study charges of irregularities made by the chief military attorney. A defense attorney had questioned the legality of the trial's conduct by the 5th Brigade, which also investigated guerrilla activities. There were also charges that the prisoners were being mistreated, and that one prisoner had been tortured, it was reported May 18.

Nine alleged ELN members were freed by the army May 19 and five others were released June 3, after military judges ruled they had served, during pre-trial detention, the sentence for rebellion.

About 50 members of the Colombian Revolutionary Armed Forces May 22 temporarily occupied the township of Colombia in the department of Huila. The army admitted that the raid was led by Manuel ("Tirofijo") Marulanda, whose death the army had announced previously, the newsletter Latin America reported June 1.

The Defense Ministry charged June 16 that 21 EPL members had killed five brothers June 14 after sacking their farm in Tierra Alta, Cordoba department.

Guerrillas clash with soldiers. Two army officers were killed and five soldiers wounded June 25 when they were ambushed by guerrillas of the National Liberation Army (ELN), military authorities announced June 26.

The clash occurred near the township of Puerto Berrio, some 124 miles west of Medellin. Military sources said the guerrillas also suffered casualties.

In a development reported July 6, the army confirmed the death of Celso Osma, a reputed ELN leader. Officials speculated Osma may have been killed by other ELN guerrillas, according to the Miami Herald.

There were five deaths in a clash between soldiers and guerrillas of the People's Liberation Army (EPL), according to military authorities in Medellin July 3. The victims reported were three peasants, a soldier, and a guerrilla identified as Cristobal Bejambre.

FARC guerrilla activities. At least six soldiers, one civilian guide and two insurgents were killed when guerrillas of the Communist Colombian Revolutionary Armed Forces (FARC) ambushed a military patrol near the town of La Herrera, 250 miles southwest of Bogota, the Defense Ministry announced Oct. 13.

Some 40 FARC guerrillas had briefly occupied the town of San Fernando, Santander department, and reportedly paid cash for medicine they took back into the mountains, according to the London newsletter Latin America Aug. 17.

FARC leader Manuel "Tirofijo" Marulanda was pardoned Sept. 27 by a superior court in Popayan, Cauca department, which reversed a 21-year prison sentence in absentia against the guerrilla leader for allegedly heading a FARC attack on the town of Inza, northeast of Popayan, in 1965. The guerrillas had killed some 20 persons, looted the local bank and several stores, and burned down the court building where insurgents were prosecuted.

Another FARC leader, Rigoberto Losada, had been reported arrested July 14.

Guerrillas reported smashed. Army Commander Gen. Alvaro Herrera Calderon claimed Oct. 10 that recent military operations had all but destroyed two of the nation's three left-wing guerrilla groups, the EPL and ELN.

Herrera said the EPL had lost 25 guerrillas killed by troops and 68 captured since the beginning of 1973. He alleged the group was "practically wiped out, and only its chief and a small band of combatants" remained at large.

The ELN, Herrera said, had been partly destroyed by an army offensive begun Aug. 25 against the guerrillas' main column in the mountainous Anori region of Antioquia department. The troops, totaling 3,000 by late September, reportedly killed 21 insurgents and captured another 28.

Military sources had claimed July 22 that an estimated 60–75 deserters from the ELN and EPL had surrendered to troops fighting the guerrillas in the Alto Sinu region of Cordoba department.

The commander of the 4th Brigade, Col. Alvaro Riveros Abello, said Oct. 19 that the brigade's 48-day campaign against the ELN in Antioquia department had resulted in the capture of 32 and the death of 42 others including Antonio and Manuel Vasquez Castano, brothers of ELN founder Fabio Vasquez Castano.

The brothers reportedly were killed in a clash with troops Oct. 19. (Earlier reports of Antonio's death apparently were erroneous.) A third ELN leader, Ricardo Lara Parada, was reported arrested Nov. 25. The army claimed that the ELN had been reduced to one small group led by Fabio Vasquez Castano.

Among Colombia's guerrilla groups, only the Communist-supported Colombian Revolutionary Armed Forces (FARC) remained relatively untouched by recent military operations, continuing to control territory in the south where they had established two "independent republics."

In a radio address reported Nov. 28, President Misael Pastrana Borrero urged guerrillas to turn themselves in, promising that their "lives will be respected and [their] acts judged with the full legal formalities."

In a related development Oct. 29, Gen. Carlos Lombana, armed forces' solicitor, rejected charges that concentration camps existed for political prisoners in Colombia and that captured guerrillas or guerrilla suspects were tortured. However, he said the army was investigating reports of abuse of political prisoners.

Political Developments

Agrarian reform bill criticized. Criticism of the government's agrarian reform bill, reported passed by Congress Feb. 16, was increasing despite a plea from Liberal leader Carlos Lleras Restrepo for a "pause" in the debate, the newsletter Latin America reported March 9.

The reform, approved after a year of negotiations between the ruling Liberal and Conservative parties, would bail the Agrarian Reform Institute (INCORA) out of bankruptcy and spur expropriation of poorly farmed estates, the newsletter reported. It reduced from 100 to 30 hectares the amount of land that could be retained by an individual, and gave the individual three years to make the land productive.

Productivity would be measured by a minimum 12% annual return on the land and by output per hectare.

The reform was expected to figure importantly in the 1974 presidential election, with the traditionalist Conservative hopeful, Alvaro Gomez Hurtado, leading the attack on the measure by large landowners. Hernan Jaramillo Ocampo, the "progressive" Conservative contender, was reluctantly defending the reform since it was negotiated while he was agriculture minister, Latin America reported.

Corruption charges denied. President Pastrana Feb. 14 denied charges of administrative corruption in a number of government agencies, including INCORA.

The charges were initiated by the Medellin Chamber of Commerce and echoed by several newspapers. Pastrana earlier had charged his critics had not produced a concrete case of corruption, and had refused his invitation to engage in a public "dialogue" on the subject. The conservative Medellin newspaper El Colombiano had defended the rejection of the dialogue on grounds the invitation constituted a threat to Pastrana's critics.

COLOMBIA

Lleras urges 'progressive' coalition. Ex-President Carlos Lleras Restrepo, leader of the Liberal party, had called for a coalition of "progressive" political groups to nominate a single candidate for the 1974 presidential elections, it was reported Jan. 2.

In a nationwide radio broadcast, Lleras said the proposed coalition should nominate a man who would "look to the country's future." The proposal reportedly was seen as a call for renewal of the Liberal-Conservative National Front coalition—with Lleras as its joint presidential candidate—and a move against ex-Foreign Minister Alfonso Lopez Michelsen, Lleras' presidential rival within the Liberal party.

Lleras lamented in a message from Europe, reported April 22, that "the appetite for power has been reborn in both parties. The national spirit which inspired reform is being abandoned, and there is talk of extinguishing the current system, as if it were a matter of putting an end to an evil. The National Front was not an evil."

Lleras' proposal was rejected by Lopez Michelsen and numerous other Liberals, who reportedly felt they could as easily defeat the Conservatives in any electoral contest, it was reported May 11. Gomez Hurtado ignored the issue.

Cabinet shuffle. President Misael Pastrana Borrero revised his Cabinet April 13, following the resignation April 6 of all ministers except the defense secretary, Gen. Hernando Currea Cubides.

The ministers reportedly resigned to enable some of their number to begin actively campaigning for the 1974 general elections. (The Constitution required all ministers seeking elective office to quit their posts at least one year before the election date.) Gen. Currea was considered "apolitical."

Five ministers were replaced and the others reappointed. The new Cabinet, like its predecessor, consisted of six Liberals, six Conservatives and Currea. However, there was a shift in balance toward the center among ministers of both parties, according to the newsletter Latin America April 20.

Followers of Conservative presidential aspirant Alvaro Gomez Hurtado, representing the party's right wing, lost two ministries and gained one. Among the Liberals, supporters of presidential aspirant Alfonso Lopez Michelsen, of the party's most progressive sector, were represented only by Labor Minister Crispin Villazon de Armas. However, Villazon resigned April 15, apparently over a political dispute in his home department of El Cesar. He was replaced by José Antonio Murgan, a follower of ex-President Carlos Lleras Restrepo, it was reported May 6.

The other new ministers were Jaime Castro (justice), Luis Fernando Echavarria (finance), José Raimundo Sojo (economic development), Gerardo Silva (mines and petroleum) and Carlos Holguin Sardi (communications).

In another presidential appointment reported May 6, Anibal Fernandez de Soto, a Conservative, replaced Bogota Mayor Carlos Alban Holguin, another Conservative, who resigned to run for the Senate.

Pastrana reportedly offended Mariano Ospina Perez, the aging Conservative party leader, by not consulting him before revising the Cabinet. Their rift deepened when the two leaders clashed over who should head the list of Conservative senatorial candidates for Bogota, according to Latin America May 11. Pastrana reportedly favored ex-Finance Minister Rodrigo Llorente, while Ospina wanted Alban Holguin.

Pastrana, who was not a candidate for re-election, sought the Conservative party leadership, according to Latin America. However, Ospina Perez, who remained powerful enough to choose his successor, was thought to favor Gomez Hurtado for the post.

Rojas Pinilla seeks presidency. Ex-dictator Gustavo Rojas Pinilla announced April 25 that he had accepted the presidential nomination of the opposition National Popular Alliance (ANAPO).

The former president, who narrowly lost the disputed 1970 presidential election, issued a call to "all dissatisfied Liberals and Conservatives, compatriots without a party, opposition groups and, above all, the powerful and decisive mass of abstentionists" to support his platform of "Colombian Socialism," which he defined as "aimed at the creation of wealth to raise the economic level of the people, with respect for the freedom of religion of the immense majority of Christians and without dependence on foreign doctrine or ideologies."

Rojas Pinilla's candidacy had been in doubt because of his poor health.

Sen. Hernando Echeverri Mejia, leader of the Colombian Broad Movement, a left-wing offshoot of ANAPO, announced his presidential candidacy May 16.

The Rev. Alfonso Vanegas, coordinator of ANAPO for Bogota, had announced March 11 that he was quitting the party and accused its leaders of putting their own "unscrupulous personal ambitions" above "the interests of the exploited people." Vanegas said in a letter to ANAPO leader Gustavo Rojas Pinilla that "evil forces" had infiltrated the party to prevent "the exploited from organizing their liberation."

Lleras quits Liberal post. Ex-President Carlos Lleras Restrepo resigned as director of the Liberal party June 10, after a stormy party convention balked at endorsing his plan for a renewed alliance with the Conservative party in the 1974 presidential election.

Followers of ex-Foreign Minister Alfonso Lopez Michelsen, Lleras' chief rival in the party, took control of the convention after Lleras' departure, but did not use the opportunity to vote Lopez Michelsen the Liberal presidential nomination. Rather, they called for party unity, urged Lleras to resume his post, and postponed the convention until June 30.

Lleras made it clear subsequently that he would not resume the party leadership. He announced June 23 that he would seek the Liberal presidential nomination, and would also ask the support of certain Conservative sectors.

The Liberal party was split into three factions—Lleras', Lopez Michelsen's, and that of ex-foreign Minister Julio Cesar Turbay Ayala, currently ambassador to Britain. Lleras' defeat at the convention was ascribed in part to the refusal of Turbay's forces to back him. Turbay reportedly also sought the Liberal nomination.

The Conservatives, meanwhile, were split between factions favoring an agreement with the Liberals and ones wishing to stand alone in the election. Rafael Aguero, president of the party's executive board, had agreed to discuss a pact with the Liberals, but presidential hopeful Alvaro Gomez Hurtado, who claimed the backing of the party's majority, strongly opposed such action, it was reported June 15.

Liberals nominate Lopez Michelsen. In an unexpected vote at a late evening session June 30, the Liberal party nominated Lopez Michelsen as its presidential candidate.

Although the convention was not expected to choose its candidate until December, Lopez' rival, Carlos Lleras Restrepo, urged an early vote to end divisions in the party. The convention then voted 162 for Lopez with 88 votes for Lleras. A former president and foreign minister, Julio Cesar Turbay Ayala, considered a "neutral" in the contest between the two candidates, was unanimously elected Liberal party chief.

The Bogota daily El Tiempo reported July 1 that Lleras accepted the Liberals' decision. The London newsletter Latin America reported July 6 that Lleras was still considering heading an alliance of rightist Liberals and moderate Conservatives.

In a letter printed in El Tiempo July 4, President Misael Pastrana Borrero stated that his government would maintain total impartiality in the campaign.

Other candidates—Alvaro Gomez Hurtado won the presidential nomination of the Conservative party Sept. 14. He was considered a hard-line conservative.

Sen. Hernando Echeverry Mejia, considered far left, was nominated Sept. 22 by the National Opposition Union, a coalition of the Communist party, the Revolutionary Independent Labor Movement and Echeverry's Colombian Broad Movement.

(Colombian novelist Gabriel Garcia Marquez said Sept. 29 he would give $7,000 to Echeverry's campaign. The money came from prizes awarded Garcia for his

COLOMBIA

novel, Cien Años de Soledad. Garcia had donated other prize money in 1972 to the presidential campaign of Venezuela's Movement to Socialism.)

Lopez Michelsen opened his campaign Aug. 5, asserting a decisive victory for his party in 1974 would indicate "a shift by the entire nation to the left." A similar victory by Gomez Hurtado, he charged, would mean Colombians preferred "an authoritarian regime and a development policy adverse to certain kinds of reforms, such as agrarian reform, urban reform . . . economic growth before distribution of income."

Lopez vowed, if elected, to "re-establish fiscal equilibrium, arrest the cost of living increase, increase exports, implement administrative austerity, and restore full confidence in our weakened currency." He emphasized the need for a new regional trade policy, asserting Colombia must "exercise the power and the commercial and political influence which corresponds" to it in the Caribbean and in its "bilateral relations" with Central America and the Dominican Republic.

Gomez Hurtado, for his part, was attempting to move closer to the center, according to the newsletter Latin America Aug. 10. He advocated a rise in the minimum wage and its attachment to the cost of living index, and declared he would "make the peasants the owners of their land." Gomez Hurtado traditionally had opposed agrarian reform.

Despite the Liberal-Conservative presidential contest, the two parties were cementing an agreement for mutual control of the government after the elections, Latin America reported. Virtual agreement reportedly had been reached on a division of Cabinet posts, with the offices of interior minister, attorney general and solicitor general going to the losing party.

Meanwhile, Lopez Michelsen was announcing mild reformist proposals, according to the newsletter Latin America Nov. 16. One of his plans—for better cooperation between employers and workers, within current industrial mechanisms for conciliation and dialogue—was attacked by Hernando Echeverry Mejia, who had charged that it would help the government restrict and control the trade union movement, and hold down inflation at the workers' expense, Latin America reported.

ANAPO names new candidate. The opposition National Popular Alliance (ANAPO) Oct. 12 proclaimed Sen. Maria Eugenia Rojas de Moreno Diaz its new candidate for the April 1974 presidential elections. Her father, ex-President Gustavo Rojas Pinilla, had renounced the ANAPO nomination Aug. 2 on grounds of ill health.

Sen. Moreno, 42, was the first woman in Colombia and reportedly in Latin America to run for the presidency. She would campaign on a nationalist and socialist platform approved Oct. 11 by a tumultuous ANAPO convention in Bogota.

The platform called for nationalization of foreign trade, the banking system and education, and socialization of health, medicine and hospital services. Conservative newspapers called the platform Marxist, but ANAPO replied it consisted only of "simple programs to defend the working class."

Sen. Moreno's aims, according to press reports Oct. 13, were essentially to curb Colombia's high rate of unemployment, currently about 12% of the labor force; to arrest the accelerating rate of inflation (30% for the last year); and to convert Colombia into a nationalist and popular state.

Sen. Moreno charged Oct. 4 that there was "no freedom of the press in Colombia." She alleged in a letter to the Colombian Newspaper Association that there was "an absolute and irreducible monopoly over all means of mass communication," and that large subsidies to some newspapers made them "economic and public relations appendages" of the government.

Mrs. Moreno was said to be picking up strength despite the defection to the Conservatives of numerous ANAPO rightists, including seven senators and her brother, Gustavo Rojas Correa. Rojas Correa charged in a public letter of support for Gomez Hurtado Nov. 20 that ANAPO was "currently guided by Marxist ideas and has fallen under the control of leftist agitators."

Gen. Gustavo Rojas Pinilla, Rojas Correa's father and the ANAPO chief, replied Nov. 20 that his party was not Communist but "Socialist the Colombian way." Rojas Pinilla said ANAPO was Christian and nationalist, respected private property, sought to improve the standard of living of all Colombians, and, in agrarian matters, sought to exploit unproductive large farms and increase the holdings of peasants.

Mrs. Moreno had made overtures to the armed forces, El Nacional of Caracas reported Oct. 14. In one speech she charged the present government had left the military out of "progress in the professions."

Fifth presidential candidate. The small Christian Social Democratic party nominated industrialist Hermes Duarte to be its candidate in the April 1974 presidential election, it was reported Dec. 12.

Other Developments

Drug crackdown pledged. President Misael Pastrana Borrero had promised to "commit the necessary economic resources" to combat the narcotics traffic and had named his justice minister, Miguel Escobar Mendez, to coordinate a national drug control board, it was announced Jan. 14.

The announcement followed a two-day visit to Colombia by two U.S. congressmen—Morgan F. Murphy (D, Ill.) and Robert H. Steele (R, Conn.), both members of the House Foreign Affairs Committee—investigating drug routes to the U.S. Steele said appointment of a Colombian coordinator was "a remarkable success, especially since . . . the drugs traffic [in the country] had been lacking effective controls for years." Colombia had become "perhaps the most important transshipment point" for U.S.-bound narcotics, Steele asserted.

According to Steele and Murphy, 100% of the cocaine and 50%–60% of the heroin entering the U.S. was routed through South America. Colombia, where authority was divided because of a multiplicity of law enforcement agencies, was "one of the real holes left" in the international drug control network, Steele said.

About 20 kilos of cocaine, valued at more than $1.5 million, were seized by authorities April 11 in the southern city of Popayan. More than $3.5 million worth of hard drugs had been confiscated in the city since Jan. 1.

Authorities on San Adres Island in the Caribbean May 3 discovered cocaine worth $1.8 million on a private airplane. The plane, registered in the U.S., allegedly was making a fuel stop on the way to Mexico from Nicaragua. Two U.S. citizens and a Colombian were arrested.

The Bogota press had demanded strong government action against drug smugglers after U.S. customs officials discovered more than 1,000 kilos of marijuana on two Colombian freighters in April. The discoveries, called "an international scandal," were made in Wilmington, N.C. April 10 and Savannah, Ga. April 11. No persons were arrested.

Colombia's strategic location near the Panama Canal, with more than 2,000 miles of generally unguarded coastline, had made it a key transshipment point for U.S.-bound drugs.

Drugs ordered destroyed. The government May 12 ordered the destruction of all marijuana plantations discovered and all illegal drugs confiscated by security officials. A decree signed by President Misael Pastrana Borrero and the justice and health ministers also ordered the destruction of all confiscated drugs currently held in vaults of the Bank of the Republic.

The action followed a report May 10 in the Bogota newspaper El Tiempo which alleged that corrupt court and police officials were defeating the government's drug crackdown. Judges took bribes from and gave light sentences to convicted drug merchants, and police were involved in the narcotics traffic, the report said.

An unnamed Justice Ministry official quoted by El Tiempo said only 8% of the drugs confiscated in 1972 had reached the Bank of the Republic. The report added that none of the marijuana and cocaine confiscated thus far in 1973 had been received by the bank. The official charged judges and customs officials would demand to keep confiscated drugs as "proof of the crime," and then return them to narcotics merchants for large bribes.

Colombian law required that all confiscated drugs be transferred to the

Health Ministry's security vaults in the Bank of the Republic, the official said.

The director general of customs, Luis Granada Mejia, said May 12 that $30 million worth of marijuana and cocaine had been confiscated in 1972, but drugs worth only half that amount had reached the bank. He asserted judges demanded marijuana seized by customs officials— threatening to prosecute the officials if they did not comply—and the drugs then disappeared.

Leticia called cocaine center. The Amazon River port of Leticia had become the center of the international cocaine trade, harboring Brazilian and Peruvian as well as Colombian smugglers, according to the Bogota newspaper El Tiempo June 5.

Drug smugglers controlled virtually all activities in Leticia, and all members of the town government were involved, El Tiempo charged. Leticia's top security official had been arrested in Bogota in May and charged with illegal possession of 19 kilos of cocaine.

Cocaine seized. Police in southern Colombia Dec. 6 reported seizing a U.S.-bound shipment of more than 37 pounds of cocaine worth some $2 million. The shipment was transported by land from Ecuador by three men, one of whom escaped after bribing two Colombian detectives.

15,000-mile hijacking. Two armed men seized a turboprop airliner with 87 aboard over Colombia May 30 and forced it to fly 15,000 miles, over 60 hours, around the Caribbean and South America. They finally accepted a $50,000 ransom and escaped, one in Argentina and the other in Paraguay.

A Paraguayan and former soccer player, Francisco Solano Lopez, was arrested June 8 near Asuncion, Paraguay, and confessed to participating in the hijacking. He said he and his partner had not acted out of political motives as they claimed during the hijacking. His partner was reported hiding in Argentina with his half of the ransom. Most of Solano Lopez' share was recovered.

The hijackers seized the plane, belonging to the Medellin airline S.A.M., on a flight from Cali to Medellin. They directed it to Aruba, in the Dutch Antilles, and demanded the release of 47 imprisoned guerrillas and a $200,000 ransom. The Colombian government rejected the demands.

About half of the passengers were allowed to leave the plane in Aruba, and another 11 escaped. The hijackers ordered the plane to Guayaquil, Ecuador and then Lima, Peru May 31, and more passengers were allowed off at each stop. The plane flew June 1 to Mendoza, Argentina, and then returned to Aruba, where an S.A.M. representative turned over $50,000. The plane flew late that night to Resistencia, Argentina, where one hijacker escaped, and early the next day to Asuncion, where the other fled. It ended its journey in Buenos Aires with only the pilot and five other crew members aboard.

Blood export scandal. The government adopted strict measures against private blood plasma exporters following a death caused by lax health regulations at a private blood bank in Bogota, it was reported June 13.

Plasma exports supervised by the Foreign Trade Institute were prohibited, official inspection of Colombia's estimated 100 private blood banks was begun, and a special law on the problem was drafted.

Poor Colombians reportedly sold their blood to private banks at a rate of $2.40 per pint. The blood was immediately processed for plasma, which was exported to the U.S. and Europe where its price reached $18.

Private banks reportedly ignored health regulations observed by the Red Cross, which received and provided plasma free. Failure by a bank to observe one rule— that donations by an individual be at least six months apart—caused the death May 10 of a young man who had sold 1,500 cc's of his blood within two weeks.

The president of the Colombian Red Cross, Jorge Cavalier, charged May 13 that plasma exports were growing while there was a shortage of the substance in Colombia's hospitals.

Student disturbances. Students rioted in Medellin, Bogota and other cities June 8–14, in what press sources called the worst disturbances of President Pastrana's administration.

One student was killed, more than 100 were reported injured, and hundreds were arrested in clashes between security forces and university and high school students. Three universities were occupied by troops and six were closed temporarily.

The troubles began June 8 in Medellin, after meetings called by students at the University of Antioquia to commemorate a 1954 massacre for which Gen. Gustavo Rojas Pinilla, then dictator and currently a presidential candidate, was held responsible. A student was killed by a policeman, leading to riots and the burning of a university building by engineering students. Authorities closed the university and imposed a curfew in the city.

The situation worsened the next day when the governor of Antioquia ordered the student victim buried at dawn. University and high school students throughout the department went on strike, and students at other Colombian universities struck in sympathy. Three universities—Antioquia, the University of Tolima in Ibague, and Santander Industrial University in Bucaramanga—were reported occupied by soldiers June 11 following violent disturbances. About 500 students rioted the next day in Cienaga, a small town on the Atlantic coast, and were subdued after police reinforcements arrived from the provincial capital of Santa Marta.

Student disturbances were reported June 12–13 in Bogota, Medellin, Santa Marta, Barranquilla, Valledupar, Tunja and Sogamoso. The worst clashes occurred June 13 in Bogota, where 47 persons, including 42 soldiers, were reported injured, and 50 students were reported arrested.

The government imposed rigid security measures in the major cities June 14 to prevent further disturbances. However, riots continued, and a student in Sogamoso reportedly was injured by gunfire.

The government charged June 14 that the disturbances were part of a subversive plan devised by students expelled from schools in 1972 for inciting riots. However, the newsletter Latin America, citing anti-hunger chants during the riots, speculated June 22 that the rapid spread of the troubles was caused by widespread discontent with the high cost of living.

Students, police clash. Students and police clashed in the streets of Bucaramanga July 5, a day after Santander Industrial University was closed for the semester due to student disturbances. Thirty-five students were expelled from the school, and 25 were arrested. Four policemen and three students were injured.

The University of Administration and Finances in Medellin was closed July 3 and 30 students were expelled for starting a fire in the school's building.

Cardinal urges church activism. Cardinal Anibal Munoz Duque Nov. 26 urged Colombia's Roman Catholic bishops and archbishops to fight "injustice, inequality, violence and hate."

Speaking at the start of the annual episcopal conference of the Colombian church, one of the most conservative in Latin America, Munoz Duque encouraged the clergy to denounce "the misery of the small farms and the poor neighborhoods, and the contrast between the wasteful spending of a few and the needs of the multitudes."

The conference received from Rev. Lucio Castrillon, bishop of Pereira, a socio-economic report on which it would base its final statement. The report denounced a wide range of injustices and criticized foreign investment in Colombia and the government's agrarian reform program. Among the report's findings:

■ 84.3% of working Colombians earned salaries below $70 a month, while .77% earned more than $400 monthly.

■ 66% of the land was owned by 8% of the landowners, and much of the arable land remained uncultivated. The government's agrarian reform policy had failed to affect this situation.

■ Foreign investment in Colombia was "devoted more to the purchase of cheap labor than to sectors of lasting development." The mining and petroleum sectors employed few Colombians but produced great profits for foreign companies.

■ Unemployment was growing as the population increased and the exodus from the country to the cities continued. Children were forced to work in rural areas; an estimated 247,000 children aged 10–14 were in the nation's work force.

■ There were few educational opportunities for the poor, crime was increasing, and there was apathy among most voters regarding the outcome of the April 1974 elections.

Indians flee to Venezuela. At least 200 Indians from three warring Colombian tribes had fled across the Venezuelan border to escape troops attempting to pacify them, El Nacional of Caracas reported Feb. 19. The tribes—the Uriana, Epiayu and Abshiana—had fought for years over horse rustling. Five persons had been killed and eight wounded in their latest clash.

Indian killers sentenced. A judge in Ibague Nov. 30 ordered 24-year prison sentences for eight Colombians and two Venezuelans convicted of murdering 16 Cuiba Indians in 1967. It was the second trial for the defendants, following a scandal in 1972 when seven of them were acquitted on grounds they did not know killing Indians was a crime.

3 islands claimed. A senatorial commission Feb. 7 ratified Colombia's sovereignty over the keys of Roncador, Quitasueno and Serrana, in the Caribbean archipelago of San Adres-Providencia. Nicaragua also claimed sovereignty over the keys, which the U.S. recognized as Colombian territory in 1972.

East German ties set. Colombia and East Germany agreed March 23 to establish diplomatic relations based on "respect for the principles of juridicial equality among states, non-intervention, and the sovereignty and independence of peoples." The accord was signed in Bogota by Foreign Minister Alfredo Vasquez Carrizosa and the head of a special East German mission.

The agreement followed an appeal Feb. 1 by 68 Colombian senators, representing all political groups, for the establishment of diplomatic relations with Cuba, China, East Germany, North Korea, North Vietnam "and all other nations with which Colombia does not have relations." The government was reported March 16 to have decided to begin negotiations with China for an eventual exchange of ambassadors.

Chinese newsmen expelled. Five Chinese newsmen had been "invited to leave the country" in view of "their activities related to the public order," according to national security sources cited in U.S. press reports May 10.

The journalists had arrived in Colombia several weeks before, with visas extending through the end of May.

Army officers arrested. Army intelligence agents had arrested 22 army officers and 40 civilians on charges of selling arms and ammunition belonging to the armed forces, it was reported Nov. 13.

Cuba

Relations with Communist Countries

New Soviet aid detailed. Premier Fidel Castro Jan. 4 gave details of five agreements through which the Soviet Union would provide "extraordinary" new economic aid to Cuba. The pacts, signed by Castro and Soviet officials in Moscow Dec. 23, 1972, included these provisions:

■ The combined Cuban debt to the Soviet Union through 1972, including trade deficits and unpaid credits, would be deferred until 1986, and then repaid in Cuban products over the next 25 years. Interest charges would be frozen as of Jan. 1.

■ The Soviet Union would provide new credits to cover Cuba's 1973–75 trade deficits, to be repaid in Cuban goods and services over 25 years beginning in 1986.

■ The two countries agreed on the amount of goods to be exchanged in 1973–75.

■ The Soviet Union would provide up to $390 million worth of economic and technical aid to Cuba for capital development in 1973–75, the total to be repaid as of 1976 at a "low" interest rate.

The aid would help finance development of textile and nickel production, oil refining, electric power, transportation, communications, electronic computers, mechanization of the sugar harvest, irrigation, hydraulic resources, auto repair plants and factories to produce transistor radio and television sets.

■ From 1973 until 1980 the Soviet Union would pay 11¢ a pound for Cuban sugar—reportedly 2¢ more than the current high world market price—and $5,000 a ton for Cuban nickel, compared with the recent world price of $2,000–$3,000 a ton.

Castro said the initiative for the agreements had come from the Soviet Union, which he called "a true friend, who has acted toward us with a high degree of generosity, unselfishness and fraternity." He termed the pacts "a clear response" by a rich nation to the problems of a poor and underdeveloped country, adding: "I believe it is unprecedented in the history of [Latin American] countries."

According to the London newsletter Latin America Jan. 12, the agreements would assure Soviet industry of vital nickel supplies for the foreseeable future from Cuba, which held 40% of the world's known reserves. They might also make Cuba economically viable, and thus a showcase for the Soviet version of communism in the Third World, the newsletter commented.

Czechoslovak credits. Cuba and Czechoslovakia Jan. 6 signed an accord in Prague under which Czechoslovakia would supply Cuba with credits for an electric power plant, sugar refinery machinery, and equipment for constructing pipe and tube fittings.

Polish agreement. Cuba and Poland signed a credit agreement April 2 covering the sugar industry and Havana shipyards, among other sectors. Polish President Henryk Jablonski made an official visit to Cuba at the end of April, reported in Granma's weekly edition May 6.

Husak visits. Czechoslovak Communist party Secretary General Gustav Husak visited Cuba April 3–7, conferring with Premier Castro in what he called an atmosphere of "profound mutual understanding and agreement." He became only the second person, after Chilean President Allende, to be awarded the National Order of Jose Marti, given to heads of state and political leaders who had done "outstanding work in the struggle for solidarity and against imperialism."

Ceausescu visits. Rumanian President Nicolae Ceausescu visited Cuba Aug. 29–Sept. 1, on the first leg of a Latin American tour to gain support for Rumania's independent foreign policy.

He was met at the Havana airport Aug. 29 by Premier Castro, First Vice Premier Raul Castro, and President Osvaldo Dorticos. Ceausescu and his delegation subsequently discussed with Cuban officials economic and commercial cooperation, and Latin American politics, according to El Nacional of Caracas Aug. 31.

Soviet thermoelectric contract. The government signed a $30 million contract with the Soviet Union to expand the Mariel thermoelectric installations west of Havana, aiming at an increase in capacity from 200 megawatts to 500, it was reported Aug. 24.

The U.S. & Western Hemisphere

Resumption of U.S. ties asked. Twelve U.S. congressmen urged President Nixon and Congress Jan. 29 to take immediate steps to normalize U.S. relations with Cuba. They said such action "would eliminate an apparent policy contradiction which strives for friendship with Russia while concurrently condemning Cuba for harboring Soviet presence."

The representatives, all Republicans, proposed at a Washington news conference that Nixon make every effort to reach an agreement with Cuba on airliner hijacking and use talks on that subject as a starting point for discussion of other issues.

The congressmen also urged Nixon to support a recent Peruvian proposal to the Organization of American States (OAS) that would permit any member state to resume normal relations with Cuba. They further recommended that the House Foreign Affairs Committee and the Senate Foreign Relations Committee hold hearings on U.S. policy toward Cuba.

The congressmen said Premier Castro had indicated a new attitude toward the U.S. by agreeing to negotiate a hijacking pact, and Cuba had reduced its aid to local insurgents throughout Latin America. They added that Cuban leaders had privately indicated the U.S. naval presence in Guantanamo Bay would not be a major issue in any effort to normalize relations.

Galo Plaza, secretary general of the OAS, had declared that the current isolation of Cuba was "not constructive," and that OAS member states should "examine, coolly and calmly, the possibility of lifting the sanctions imposed on Cuba" in 1964, the newsletter Latin America reported Jan. 12.

In related developments: A bomb explosion in San Juan, Puerto Rico Jan. 22 destroyed two automobiles belonging to Cuban exile leader Alberto Rodriguez and damaged his residence.

Five legislators from Puerto Rico's Popular Democratic party Jan. 16 urged Premier Castro to free the estimated 60,000 political prisoners allegedly held in Cuba. They said the prisoners included 58 newsmen.

Hijacking curbs set. The U.S. and Cuba Feb. 15 signed a five-year agreement, effective immediately, to curb the hijacking of aircraft and ships between the two countries. The U.S. insisted, however, that the accord did not foreshadow any improvement in its relations with the Cuban government.

The agreement, officially a "memorandum of understanding" rather than a formal treaty requiring Senate confirmation, was signed simultaneously by U.S. Secretary of State William P. Rogers in Washington and Cuban Foreign Minister Raul Roa in Havana. It committed both countries to either try hijackers "for the offense punishable by the most severe penalty" or extradite them.

The accord also permitted both nations to grant political asylum to hijackers under carefully defined terms, but committed each to punish anyone who used its territory to organize attacks against the other. The latter provision was of particular importance to Cuba because U.S.-based Cuban exile groups had conducted raids against their former homeland, and had committed random violence against Cuban citizens.

The agreement stated that each country would promptly return stolen airplanes or vessels and protect innocent persons and goods on board, and would send back "without delay" any ransom collected by the hijackers. Cuba previously had not returned hijacking ransom money, and was still holding $2 million, taken by hijackers from Southern Airways in November 1972, for use as

Text of U.S., Cuban Agreement Signed Feb. 15

The government of the United States of America and the Government of the Republic of Cuba, on the basis of equality and strict reciprocity, agree:

FIRST: Any person who hereafter seizes, removes, appropriates or diverts from its normal route or activities an aircraft or vessel registered under the laws of one of the parties and brings it to the territory of the other party shall be considered to have committed an offense and therefore shall either be returned to the party of registry of the aircraft or vessel to be tried by the courts of that party in conformity with its laws or be brought before the courts of the party whose territory he reached for trial in conformity with its laws for the offense punishable by the most severe penalty according to the circumstances and the seriousness of the acts to which this article refers. In addition, the party whose territory is reached by the aircraft or vessel shall take all necessary steps to facilitate without delay the continuation of the journey of the passengers and crew innocent of the hijacking of the aircraft or vessel in question, with their belongings, as well as the journey of the aircraft or vessel itself with all goods carried with it, including any funds obtained by extortion or other illegal means, or the return of the foregoing to the territory of the first party; likewise, it shall take all steps to protect the physical integrity of the aircraft or vessel and all goods carried with it, including any funds obtained by extortion or other illegal means, and the physical integrity of the passengers and crew innocent of the hijacking, and their belongings while they are in its territory as a consequence of or in connection with the acts to which this article refers.

In the event that the offenses referred to above are not punishable under the laws existing in the country to which the persons committing them arrived, the party in question shall be obligated, except in the case of minor offenses, to return the persons who have committed such acts, in accordance with the applicable legal procedures, to the territory of the other party to be tried by its courts in conformity with its laws.

SECOND: Each party shall try with a view to serve punishment in accordance with its laws any person who, within its territory, hereafter conspires to promote, or promotes, or prepares, or directs, or forms part of an expedition which from its territory or any other place carries out acts of violence or depredation against aircraft or vessels of any kind or registration coming or going to the territory of the other party or who, within its territory, hereafter conspires to promote or promotes, or prepares, or directs, or forms part of an expedition which from its territory or any other place carries out such acts or other similar unlawful acts in the territory of the other party.

THIRD: Each party shall apply strictly its own laws to any national of the other party who, coming from the territory of the other party, enters its territory, violating its laws as well as national and international requirements pertaining to immigration, health, customs and the like.

FOURTH: The party in whose territory the perpetrators of the acts described in Article First arrive may take into consideration any extenuating or mitigating circumstances in those cases in which the persons responsible for the acts were being sought for strictly political reasons and were in real and imminent danger of death without a viable alternative for leaving the country, provided there was no financial extortion or physical injury to the members of the crew, passengers, or other persons in connection with the hijacking.

Final provisions:

This agreement may be amended or expanded by decision of the parties.

This agreement shall be in force for five years and may be renewed for an equal term by express decision of the parties.

Either party may inform the other of its decision to terminate this agreement at any time while it is in force by written denunciation submitted six months in advance.

This agreement shall enter into force on the date agreed by the parties.

Done in English and Spanish texts, which are equally authentic.

evidence in the trial of the hijackers in Havana.

Rogers told a news conference after he signed the accord that "nothing in this agreement is inconsistent with the traditional and strongly felt American view of the right to emigrate freely nor does it constitute a change in our overall policy toward Cuba." He said the U.S. would not ease its diplomatic and trade boycott of Cuba until "the policies and attitudes of the Cuban government" changed.

U.S. State Department spokesman Charles W. Bray 3rd had announced Feb. 13 that an agreement between the two countries was virtually concluded. Bray said details of the pact would not be disclosed pending consultation with Congress, but asserted that agreement had been reached on all substantive issues.

State Department confirmation followed a disclosure by President Nixon Feb. 13 that three months of indirect negotiations between Cuba and the U.S. on a hijacking agreement had been successfully concluded. Nixon told a few newsmen at the White House that he had just spoken to Secretary of State Rogers about "the hijacking agreement with Cuba." Rogers told newsmen in Miami later that day that the agreement could be signed in "a few days."

Accord signed with Canada—A bilateral agreement requiring Cuba and Canada to prosecute hijackers or return them to the country in which the crime was committed was signed Feb. 15 in Ottawa by External Affairs Minister Mitchell Sharp and Cuban Vice Foreign Minister Rene Anillo. The accord was identical to the one with the U.S.

Pact signed with Mexico—Cuba and Mexico reached an agreement June 7 to curb the hijacking of airliners and ships between their borders.

The treaty, signed in Havana by Foreign Minister Raul Roa Garcia and Mexican Ambassador Victor Alfonso Maldonado, obligated countries to which planes or ships were hijacked, to either prosecute the hijackers or return them to the country of departure. However, it allowed both countries to grant asylum to hijackers when they appeared "in real and imminent danger of death or of being deprived of their liberty for clearly political reasons, and had had no other way of gaining safety."

The agreement also required each country to "punish severely according to its laws" any person who, from its territory, conspired or took part in an attack on ships or planes traveling to or from the other country.

Figueres urges 'dialogue.' Costa Rican President Jose Figueres told a gathering of Cuban exiles in Puerto Rico Jan. 29 that they should begin a "dialogue" with Premier Fidel Castro, and offered himself as an intermediary. His proposal reportedly outraged the exiles, but received the support of Puerto Rico Gov. Rafael Hernandez Colon, who called it "very realistic."

Despite his offer to mediate between Castro and Cuban exiles, Figueres said Costa Rica could not re-establish relations with Cuba, "at least not until the current Cuban regime meets two conditions: freedom for political prisoners and freedom for Cubans to return to their homes and leave them whenever they wish." During a visit to Panama Jan. 30, Figueres evaded questions from newsmen concerning his ability, as a long-standing opponent of communism in Cuba, to mediate successfully with Castro.

Puerto Rico's ex-governor, Luis Ferre, had urged the U.S. to "find a formula that leads to the normalization of its relations with Cuba... [and] that would make possible [Cuba's] return to the Organization of American States," the Miami Herald reported Jan. 28. Carlos Sanz de Santamaria, president of the Inter-American Committee of the Alliance for Progress, said Feb. 5 that "any hemispheric movement to be prepared for the future must include Cuba" and "other countries that are going to have political liberty in the coming years."

U.S. airlift ends. The Cuba-Miami airlift, which had taken nearly 261,000 Cuban refugees to the U.S. since 1965, ended with two flights April 6.

Cuban boat attacked. A Havana radio broadcast said a Cuban fisherman was wounded in a machinegun and hand grenade attack on his boat by "counter-revolutionaries" operating from the U.S., the Washington Post reported Feb. 2. The attack was said to have occurred in Bahamian waters, where a similar attack was reported in October 1972.

Ships sent to Panama—The government handed over to Panama two freighters owned by the Miami-based Bahamas Line and seized by Cuban gunboats in December 1971 for allegedly participating in subversive activities against Cuba.

The Johnny Express arrived in Panamanian waters April 23 and the Layla Express the next day. The ships, which had flown the Panamanian flag when captured, were entrusted to the Panamanian government on the condition that they not be returned to their owners, Cuban exiles opposed to the Communist regime.

The captain of the Johnny Express, Jose Villa, was reported in custody in Panama April 29.

Castro speeches. In his traditional May Day speech, Premier Castro said Cuba had not abandoned Latin American revolutionaries trying to overthrow "reactionary oligarchic governments." He was particularly critical of Brazil, which he called "the No. 1 ally of the United States in Latin America." Castro also promised Cuban support for Venezuela if its oil dispute with Washington became more acute.

Castro assailed the U.S., the Organization of American States (OAS) and several right-wing Latin American governments in his speech July 26 commemorating the 20th anniversary of the revolutionary assault on the Moncada barracks.

Speaking before 20,000 persons outside the old barracks in Santiago, Castro accused the U.S. of using "the most corrupt, unpopular and discredited governments in this continent"—Brazil, Bolivia, Paraguay and Uruguay—to isolate the "progressive and revolutionary states"—Cuba, Chile, Peru, Argentina and Panama.

Castro reiterated Cuba's proposal for a new inter-American organization excluding the U.S., but admitted it was not yet viable "because the U.S. still controls many [Latin] governments." He dismissed current attempts to restructure the OAS, saying "it makes no sense to revive it. Let us allow it to die a natural death."

Castro criticized "certain leaders who consider themselves part of the Third World" who drew parallels between Soviet foreign policy and U.S. imperialism. He called such comparisons "reactionary," stressing that the U.S.S.R. had provided arms to revolutionaries in Cuba, Southeast Asia, Africa and the Middle East.

Dorticos in Chile, Peru. President Osvaldo Dorticos visited Chile and Peru May 31–June 4, after attending Argentina's presidential inauguration and sealing the resumption of Cuban-Argentine relations. He was received warmly in all three countries.

Dorticos arrived in Chile May 31 and met June 2 with President Salvador Allende. At a press conference June 3, he attacked the U.S. for not recognizing major changes in Latin America and merely continuing to play its role of hemispheric "policeman." He said there would be no contacts to improve U.S.-Cuban relations until the U.S. "unilaterally halts the blockade of Cuba."

Dorticos continued to Peru June 4, where he conferred with President Juan Velasco Alvarado on "continental and Latin American problems." The two presidents praised their countries' processes of change, with Dorticos asserting: "Our revolutions travel different roads, but both point toward the beautiful horizon of continental liberation."

Velasco thanked Premier Fidel Castro for his friendship toward Peru and his concern over Velasco's health. Castro had sent specialists and orthopedic equipment to help Velasco recover from his recent leg amputation, according to a report April 14.

Castro had hailed Velasco as a "revolutionary of firm convictions" during a visit to Cuba by the head of the Peruvian social mobilization agency SINAMOS, it was reported May 18.

Argentine relations resumed. President Osvaldo Dorticos went to Argentina for the inauguration May 25 of Hector Campora as Argentine president.

Campora met Dorticos May 28 and announced afterwards that Argentina and Cuba had established diplomatic relations. Dorticos hailed the resumption of ties between the two nations as "a gesture of sovereignty and independence."

Emilio Aragones Navarro, a member of the Communist party's Central Committee and director of the National Fisheries Institute, was appointed Cuba's ambassador to Argentina, it was reported June 15.

Cuba June 5 purchased from Argentina 27,000 tons of corn in the first commercial transaction between the two countries in 13 years. Cuba agreed two days later to import another 31,000 tons of Argentine corn, according to the official newspaper Granma June 9.

The new government of Argenina Aug. 24 granted Cuba $200 million in credits to purchase trucks, tractors, agricultural machinery and other items manufactured in Argentina.

Other Developments

Economy shows gains. Recently published statistics for 1972 showed most sectors of the economy had reached, and some had exceeded, their annual production targets for the second year in a row, the New York Times reported Feb. 4. Despite continuing problems of mismanagement, the economy was recovering from the disatrous drops in production in 1970, which stemmed from the effort to produce a 10 million ton sugar crop, the Times reported.

The gains, however, had not yet affected the average Cuban, for whom most consumer goods remained strictly rationed, the Times reported. The government Feb. 1 had further reduced meat quotas in view of a shortage attributed to higher prices of imported feed grass, a shortage of fishmeal, droughts during the past three years and the 1971 epidemic of African porcine fever, which necessitated the killing of 600,000 pigs and hogs.

According to the Times, the gains followed a reorganization of the economy, with a greater emphasis on production costs. The government decided to expand or modernize existing plants whenever possible before building new ones, and waged an all-out effort against worker absenteeism. Cubans were encouraged to work harder through a scheme that partially restored material incentives and gave better workers a priority for receiving consumer goods. In several sectors factories and production centers were encouraged to compete with one another in reaching production targets, the Times reported.

Sugar harvest ahead of '72. Foreign Trade Minister Marcelo Fernandez told an international sugar conference in Geneva that Cuban sugar production for 1973 had already passed 5 million tons, 1.2 million tons ahead of the 1972 pace, it was reported May 18. Fernandez was quoted June 15 as predicting the harvest would reach at least 5.4 million tons.

Sugar production had been reported behind schedule early in April because of industrial breakdowns, irregular cane supplies and bad weather.

Troops aid in economic development. Cuba was increasing armed forces reserve training to free regular troops for sectors of the economy that were short of manpower, according to the head of the armed forces, First Vice Premier Raul Castro, April 16.

Among other economic developments:

Cuba had become the world's second leading exporter of lobster, after Australia, and the rapidly expanding fishing industry had become a major source of foreign income, it was reported July 7. Living and working conditions in Cuba's fishing ports had also improved dramatically.

The government announced production in the basic industry sector had reached 101% of its target for the first half of 1973, an increase of 16% over the same period of 1972, it was reported Aug. 3.

Laws offered for public discussion. Five draft laws had been submitted for public discussion at work places, in rural communities, committees to defend the revolution, military units and elsewhere, it was reported Feb. 2. The laws concerned crimes against the economy, against the family and children and against "the normal development of sexual relations," and covered the improper use of military uniforms and criminal responsibility at age 16.

Party unit enlarged. The Political Bureau had decided to add four members to the Secretariat of the Central Committee of the Cuban Communist party, El Nacional of Caracas reported Feb. 8. The new members, added to "strengthen the activities" of the party unit, were: Maj. Antonio Perez Herrero, head of the army's political section; Isidoro Malmierca, subdirector of the National Fishing Institute; Raul Garcia Pelaez, ambassador-designate to the Soviet Union; and Labor Minister Jorge Risquet. The Secretariat had previously had only seven members, including Premier Fidel Castro, First Vice Premier Raul Castro and President Osvaldo Dorticos.

Ordoqui freed. Authorities had released Joaquin Ordoqui Mesa, a former armed forces deputy minister placed under house arrest in 1965 for maintaining "questionable cultural contacts with an enemy agent" in Mexico, the London newsletter Latin America reported May 4.

Ordoqui's suspension from the Communist party was confirmed despite official admission that there was no conclusive proof of his "collaboration with the enemy." Ordoqui had consistently denied such collaboration.

Judicial reform set. A sweeping reform of the judiciary, to go into effect later in 1973, was reported by the London newsletter Latin America Aug. 17.

There would be a new People's Supreme Court, with four chambers dealing with criminal, civil and administrative and military offenses, and crimes against state security. Below these would be the People's Provincial Courts, with civil and criminal chambers to deal with cases warranting sentences of up to six years' imprisonment. At the local level, People's Basic Courts would deal with offenses warranting up to six months' imprisonment.

Those convicted of crimes against the state would be sentenced according to their participation in or responsibility for the crimes if they were civilians, and would receive the death penalty if they belonged to the armed forces, according to Raul Amaro Salup, a prospective judge of the chamber on crimes against state security. All those convicted would have the right of appeal, and would be able to engage a lawyer or conduct their own defense.

The private practice of law would be banned, and lawyers would be compelled to join collective offices, of which there were currently 50, Latin America reported.

Arab state relations. Cuba and Algeria reached a new trade agreement June 7 in which, among other points, Cuban sugar exports to Algeria were fixed for 1974–76.

The Washington Post reported that Cubans were training South Yemeni pilots to fly MiG-21 jet fighters, according to the newsletter Latin America June 29.

Dominican Republic

Guerrilla Action Fails

Guerrillas land, battle troops. A small band of guerrillas landed on the southern coast Feb. 4 and moved quickly into the central mountain range, military sources reported. The group was spotted by an army patrol Feb. 6, and "very intense" fighting ensued. One guerrilla and three soldiers reportedly were killed.

The army said Feb. 5 that the guerrillas—nine or 10 men in olive green uniforms—had landed in Azua province from Cuba to prepare a coup against President Joaquin Balaguer. Although it denied the guerrillas constituted any "danger to the people," the government sent 2,000 troops to pursue them. It also closed Santo Domingo's public schools, university and radio stations, and ordered the arrest of a number of opposition leaders, including ex-President Juan Bosch, who were accused of supporting the guerrilla operation.

Bosch, the leader of the Dominican Revolution party (PRD), was not present when police raided and occupied his home. He issued a statement from a hiding place somewhere in Santo Domingo denying PRD leaders knew of the guerrilla operation, and accusing the government of using the operation to oust him from the country.

Police also surrounded the home of Luis Amiama Tio, who had been promoting a united opposition front against Balaguer in the 1974 elections. Amiama Tio complained to newsmen that he was "virtually under house arrest." The government said other unidentified opposition leaders would be tried for alleged involvement with the guerrilla operation.

A military spokesman Feb. 5 denied reports circulated outside the country that the guerrillas were led by Francisco Caamano, who headed the pro-Bosch forces in the 1965 Dominican civil war. (A Venezuelan newspaper, El Mundo, reported Jan. 21 that Caamano had died in Cuba. The report was denied by PRD Secretary General José Francisco Pena Gomez.)

Security measures set. Tanks and armored cars moved into Santo Domingo Feb. 8 as the government instituted a series of strict security measures following the guerrilla landing.

The measures, amounting to a state of emergency, included tight military surveillance of the major cities, censorship of broadcasting, raids on hundreds of homes and the detention of "suspicious" persons. The French newspaper Le Monde reported Feb. 10 that hundreds of persons were arrested. Other sources reported that the raids on homes were ordered to insure the capture of ex-President Juan Bosch and José Francisco Peña Gómez, leaders of the opposition Dominican Revolutionary party (PRD), who were in hiding.

The measures were announced Feb. 7 by President Joaquin Balaguer, who gave details of the alleged guerrilla landing in Azua province Feb. 4. Balaguer said the subversives—10 men, all "uniquely experienced, trained in Cuba and other Communist countries"—had split into two groups, with eight men heading into the central mountains to divert military attention while the other two entered the capital to promote urban guerrilla warfare. He charged the operation was part of a plot against his government, of which Bosch and Peña Gómez—whom Balaguer refrained from naming—were implicitly the ringleaders.

Bosch issued a message late Feb. 7 denying that he or any other PRD leader knew anything of the alleged guerrilla operation and demanding that the government publish alleged documents implicating the PRD in the operation, which the government claimed to have found in the boat in which the guerrillas were said to have landed. A message from Peña Gómez charged the police wanted to kill him and deport Bosch.

Opponents of the government abroad also questioned the reports of the guerrilla operation and criticized the new security measures. Gen. Elias Wessin y Wessin, former air force chief, said in Madrid Feb. 7 that according to his "contacts" in Santo Domingo, the guerrilla operation was "theater organized by the Balaguer government itself to dispose of the political opposition," which was allegedly "united" against the president for the first time. Wessin's contention was supported by Manuel Jimenez Rodriguez, a former mayor of Santo Domingo living in Puerto Rico, the Miami Herald reported Feb. 8.

In Santo Domingo, meanwhile, newspapers received a communiqué Feb. 10 in which an organization calling itself Commandos of the Resistance took credit for the guerrilla operation, which it claimed was led by former Col. Francisco Caamano. Wessin had said Feb. 7 that Caamano was in Cuba, adding: "I don't believe that in the present situation of [Cuba] it would interest Fidel Castro to become involved in an affair" like the guerrilla operation.

Fresh troops were dispatched to the central mountains Feb. 10 to pursue the alleged guerrilla band. The government had claimed Feb. 7 that troops had surrounded the subversives, but other sources said later that the guerrillas had broken through the encirclement.

The army Feb. 9 confirmed earlier reports that three soldiers had been killed in a battle with the guerrillas. Police had announced the day before that a police officer in Santiago had been shot to death by unknown assailants.

Eight professional organizations in Santo Domingo Feb. 12 asked Balaguer to lift the emergency security measures he imposed Feb. 8. Balaguer said Feb. 15 that the measures would remain in effect while "the current emergency situation lasts." He admitted for the first time, however, that his government had no concrete evidence that Cuba was connected with the guerrilla operation.

Norwegian ship strafed—Dominican fighter-bombers Feb. 9 strafed a Norwegian ship by mistake after taking it for a vessel carrying guerrillas, President Balaguer disclosed Feb. 16. Balaguer said his government had apologized to Norway over the incident, in which the ship sustained slight damages.

Caamano reported killed. Former Col. Francisco Caamano, leader of the constitutionalist forces in the 1965 civil war, was killed by soldiers in the central mountains Feb. 16 and buried there Feb. 17, according to military reports.

Caamano reportedly had been leading a small guerrilla band in the mountains since Feb. 4, when the group was said to have landed on the southern coast. Two other guerrillas reportedly were killed with him, and the rest of the band—an estimated six or seven men—was said to be "completely disbanded."

Two newspapermen were permitted to see Caamano's body, but only military personnel witnessed the burial. One of the newsmen, Antonio Garcia Valoy of Santo Domingo's Listin Diario, said Feb. 17 that Caamano was "easily recognizable."

However, Caamaño's father, a retired army general, said Feb. 18 he could not be certain his son was dead until the body was turned over to his family.

A statement by Caamaño's family reported by El Nacional of Caracas Feb. 24 said the family "never doubted the version of the armed forces" about the former colonel's death. However, Caamaño's father, retired Gen. Fausto Caamaño, was reported Feb. 25 to have disavowed the statement and asked President Balaguer to exhume the body identified as his son. Balaguer had said Feb. 19 that the body would be exhumed "at the opportune time," after military officials and the elder Caamaño had "jointly" considered "the impact which the exhumation . . . might have on public order."

An official PRD statement reported Feb. 20 pointed out "contradictions and inconsistencies" in the armed forces' account of the guerrilla landing and Caamaño's death. It said, among other things, that Caamaño would not have initiated a guerrilla campaign as poorly equipped as the military report said it was, and that he would not have left the hills to try to fight on a highway.

A man identifying himself as a guerrilla told the Santo Domingo newspaper Ultima Hora March 4 that Caamaño had led the guerrilla invasion, but that only Alfredo Perez Vargas had been killed by troops. Caamaño and Herberto Lalane, he said, were still alive. Authorities later claimed that the alleged guerrilla, Toribio Pena Jaquez, was actually a police agent "pressured" by Communist elements to deny Caamaño's death.

The Santo Domingo radio station Radio Comercial was closed March 4 after broadcasting Pena Jaquez' interview with Ultima Hora. The station was reported reopened March 16. Industry and Trade Minister José Antonio Brea Peña, who owned Radio Comercial, resigned to protest the closing March 4, but said March 5 that he would withdraw the resignation if the officials who ordered the closing were publicly reprimanded.

In the central mountains, air force fighter planes bombed and strafed the area where the remnants of the guerrilla band were hiding, the Miami Herald reported March 2. At least two guerrillas were reported killed in the attack, according to the Santo Domingo newspaper El Nacional. Two soldiers were reported killed in a clash with the guerrillas March 17.

Guerrillas reported crushed. Troops in the north central mountains had killed or captured all but one of the guerrillas who landed in Azua province Feb. 4, the armed forces announced March 28.

Seven guerrillas were reported killed, the last two in a clash with soldiers near Bonao March 22, and one was reported captured March 25.

The captive guerrilla was identified as Hamlet Herman Perez, 39, a former university professor. He was reported March 28 to have confirmed the death of Francisco Caamaño. The remaining guerrilla was reported to be Caamaño's cousin, Claudio Caamaño. A third surviving guerrilla was later identified.

Herman Perez also told authorities the insurgents had arrived in the Dominican Republic by a circuitous route from Cuba, where they had been trained in guerrilla warfare, the Herald reported.

Five soldiers had been killed and seven wounded in clashes with the guerrillas, according to El Nacional of Caracas March 28.

Juan Bosch disputed the claim of Herman Perez that Bosch had "betrayed" the invasion. Bosch asserted he had broken with Francisco Caamaño in 1968.

Bosch charged May 29 that the military ruler of Panama, Gen. Omar Torrijos, had warned Balaguer beforehand of the guerrilla operation. "Nevertheless, the guerrillas got through into the mountains without encountering any opposition. Could it have been a plan to let them enter?" he asked.

Claudio Caamaño escapes—Claudio Caamaño, safe in Mexico City, said that the invasion had been launched from the island of Guadeloupe after the insurgents picked up arms "somewhere in Venezuela," the London newsletter Latin America reported June 1. Caamaño, who had taken refuge in the Mexican embassy in Santo Domingo, had been given safe-conduct to leave the country in late May. Caamaño, whose transfer to Cuba was reported June 8, was later quoted by a

Mexican magazine as saying his late uncle Francisco Caamano had been captured alive by the army in February and perhaps tortured before being shot, Latin America reported Aug. 3. Dominican authorities claimed Caamano was killed in battle.

Herman Perez also had been allowed to move to Cuba, according to Latin America June 15. The third surviving guerrilla, Toribio Peña Jaquez, had left the Dominican Republic with safe-conduct to Chile, it was reported July 6.

Politics & Violence

Cabinet shuffle. In a significant Cabinet shuffle, Interior and Police Minister Enrique Perez y Perez had switched posts with the army commander, Gen. Rafael de Jesus Checo, and ex-National Police Chief Neit Nivar Seijas had been named secretary of the presidency and promoted to major general, La Prensa of Buenos Aires reported Jan. 8.

The changes were seen as evidence of President Balaguer's complete control over the armed forces and the fall from favor of Nivar Seijas, the newsletter Latin America reported Jan. 19. Nivar Seijas, the newsletter said, had grown too ambitious for Balaguer and was no longer essential to the president as a right-hand man within the military. His promotion following his dismissal as national police chief was seen as a move to check the new power of Perez y Perez and thus maintain a balance in the armed forces.

According to the Santo Domingo weekly Ahora, the Cabinet shuffle showed "Balaguer can now remove the head of the police, the air force, the army or the navy, and nothing will happen in this country. Whether we like it or not, this is the most stable government of the past decade." Latin America, which cited the Ahora commentary, noted that it was the first time since the rule of dictator Rafael Trujillo that the president had controlled the armed forces so absolutely.

Balaguer's current power contrasted with the weakness of the opposition, which could not be expected to seriously challenge the president in the 1974 elections, Latin America commented. Leaders of at least five opposition parties had met in an attempt to unite against Balaguer in the elections, but the PRD, the strongest of the group, had withdrawn from the deliberations, La Prensa reported Feb. 1.

PRD leader wounded—Arturo Guzman, secretary general of the Santiago construction workers union and a leader of the PRD labor faction, was shot and wounded by unidentified assailants Jan. 2. The government ordered an investigation of the attack, the second on Guzman in less than three months.

PRD Secretary General Peña Gomez charged Jan. 4 that right-wing terrorism had increased in 1971–72 and would continue to spread with the acquiescence of "the repressive and corrupt Balaguer government." Ex-president Bosch had said Jan. 2 that official corruption was "rampant," and that President Balaguer's "uncontrollable desire to continue in office for the rest of his life" had led to "the wholesale purchase of men."

Massive PRD arrests charged. Some 1,400–1,500 members of the Dominican Revolutionary party (PRD), the country's largest opposition group, had been jailed during the previous three weeks "without justification," according to a leader of the party's U.S. branch Feb. 21.

The PRD official, Winston Arnaud, spoke at a news conference in Washington, where he sought the help of sympathetic U.S. congressmen and others in protesting what he called Dominican government repression of his party. Arnaud charged the government had used the landing of a guerrilla band Feb. 4 as a pretext for widespread arrests and other types of pressure against leaders of the PRD and other opposition groups, which had formed a coalition to prevent the reelection of President Joaquin Balaguer in 1974.

Arnaud said that despite PRD denials of any involvement with the guerrillas, party offices throughout the country had been occupied by troops, and the homes of many party members had been searched. Noting that the PRD's top leaders, ex-President Juan Bosch and party secretary general José Francisco Peña Gomez had gone into hiding, Ar-

DOMINICAN REPUBLIC

naud warned: "Every day our leaders' lives are more in danger."

(A spokesman for the Dominican embassy in Washington responded that there was "no reason" for Bosch and Peña Gomez to fear for their lives, noting that "no charge has been brought against them publicly." Justifying the government's strict security measures, the spokesman said: "Every government has the right to take precautions when it is endangered. All the precautions have been taken in accordance with the constitution and its laws." The regime Feb. 11 had denied was persecuting the PRD, saying it did "not know why" Bosch and other party leaders were in hiding. Former Vice President Francisco Lora Feb. 12 urged Bosch to bring the PRD into an opposition coalition against Balaguer in the 1974 elections.

(Bosch Feb. 12 said the party was going underground to escape the "persecution" ordered by Balaguer.)

Arnaud also charged that the government had produced no convincing evidence that the guerrilla invasion actually had taken place, nor that former Col. Francisco Caamano had been killed. He noted that Wellington Ascanio Peterson, whom the government said had been killed along with Caamano, had turned up alive in Cuba the previous day.

(The Dominican armed forces said Feb. 21 that the body identified as Peterson was actually that of Alfredo Perez Vargas, a member of the June 14 Revolutionary Movement who had disappeared in January 1969. Perez Vargas' body reportedly was identified by his mother following disclosure by the Cuban press agency Prensa Latina that Peterson was alive and studying in Havana.)

Sen. Edward M. Kennedy (D, Mass.) told the U.S. Senate Feb. 21 that he was concerned over the "serious deterioration of political liberties" in the Dominican Republic. Kennedy, quoted in El Nacional of Caracas Feb. 23, said he understood "the political directors of the legal opposition party are jailed and held without the filing of charges or accusations of any kind against them."

Kennedy said the Dominican government had taken "repressive actions"— including the closing of all schools and several radio stations, and imposition of broad censorship and a de facto curfew —in response to reports that "a single ship, of little size, had been discovered and fears that guerrillas had landed on the island. All formal parties denied any connection with the supposed invasion and there were serious doubts whether an invasion actually had taken place." Nevertheless, arrests were ordered which seemed "out of all proportion to any reasonable worry over national security," Kennedy said.

President Balaguer Feb. 27 denied the PRD and Kennedy charges, asserting the current security measures were "minimal and a mere nuisance to the people." He accused opposition leaders of using "their relations with international communism . . . to distort the image of the Dominican Republic abroad."

In an apparent response to Balaguer, Bosch came out of hiding briefly March 12 and urged the PRD to "fight relentlessly to establish in the country a government that will not serve the whims of one man but follow the mandate of the law." Appearing at PRD headquarters in Santo Domingo, Bosch accused the government of abusing its power and urged its replacement by "an honorable government, which will act with dignity and speak with respect to our people and the world."

The presidential press secretary declared March 13 that Bosch's statement had placed him and the PRD "outside constitutionality and the law."

In New York, meanwhile, the PRD Feb. 15 presented documents to the United Nations Secretariat and Human Rights Commission, and asked the U.N. to send an international commission to investigate the situation in the Dominican Republic. The PRD again denied government charges that it supported the "supposed [guerrilla] invasion," and accused the government of "open dictatorship, [with] hundreds of crimes committed and an unbroken line of violations of human rights."

Two members of the PRD executive council, Euclides Gutierrez and Diomedes Mercedes, March 9 were the first PRD members to be formally charged with complicity in the guerrilla landing. The two had been held in Santo Domingo since mid-February. Two PRD offices were reported raided and damaged by Santo Domingo police March 9.

Editor slain. Gregorio Garcia Castro, editor of the Santo Domingo newspaper Ultima Hora and a critic of the government, was shot to death by unidentified persons as he left his offices March 28.

President Joaquin Balaguer immediately appointed a high-level commission to find the killers. The commission, headed by Gen. Neit Nivar Seijas, secretary of the presidency, March 31 interrogated one of Balaguer's military aides, Maj. Socrates Pichardo, who had been cited as a suspect by the National Professional Newspapermen's Union. Pichardo was temporarily stripped of rank and duties, but was later reported cleared of suspicion. His brother and a number of friends were reported detained for questioning.

Garcia Castro, one of the most widely read columnists in the country, was said to have sharply criticized not only the government but most political groups. He had reportedly warned Balaguer that there was a police plot to kill him, according to the London newsletter Latin America April 6.

Police chief ousted—Gen. José Ernesto Cruz Brea, the national police chief, was reported replaced April 19 by Gen. Salvador Llugeres Montas, a former air force chief and interior minister. The action was linked to the official investigation of Garcia Castro's murder.

Cruz Brea's replacement reportedly followed disclosure that he had personally ordered Col. Carlos Peguero de la Cruz, head of the police secret service, to accuse Pichardo. Pichardo later was restored to his post, but as a civilian without military rank. The secret service chief reportedly was dismissed.

A police lieutenant and two army privates had been jailed on charges of shooting Garcia Castro, it was reported April 20.

Bosch emerges from hiding. Ex-President Juan Bosch emerged from three months of hiding May 4, following an appeal by his badly split Dominican Revolutionary party (PRD) and a guarantee of safety by the government.

Bosch appeared at the PRD's Santo Domingo headquarters, where he was cheered by hundreds of supporters. He declared he was more prepared than ever to continue the "struggle" against President Joaquin Balaguer, which would end only when "the people [are] in power."

President Balaguer had asserted April 27 that Bosch could return to political life with impunity.

The PRD's permanent commission had appealed to Bosch May 2 to emerge and resume leadership of the party, which was split following the expulsion April 30 of six party leaders and the subsequent resignation of the party's secretary general, José Francisco Peña Gomez.

According to the London newsletter Latin America May 18, the expulsions stemmed from a dispute over the advisability of forming a coalition of all opposition parties to oppose Balaguer's expected bid for a third presidential term in 1974. Negotiations between the PRD and three groups—the Democratic Integration Movement (MID), the Social Christian Revolutionary party (PRSC) and the Quisqueyan Democratic party (PQD)—had begun in January, but had been called off in April, largely at the instigation of Bosch. The expelled PRD members reportedly opposed the suspension.

Peña Gomez, Latin America reported, had favored a closer relationship with the PQD, which like the PRD did not represent upper-class interests. Bosch, however, reportedly rejected this because of the right-wing history of the party and its leader, ex-Gen. Elias Wessin y Wessin. There were also reports that Peña Gomez had been in touch with Gen. Neit Nivar Seijas, secretary of the presidency and leader of an influential military faction, and this, too, Bosch regarded as dangerous, Latin America reported.

Bosch said April 28 he would not run for president as long as the Dominican Republic was "ruled" by the U.S. "Power in this country is held first by . . . the United States. Secondly, by the . . . Dominican army as a subsidiary of the Pentagon. And thirdly, by Balaguer," he asserted.

Bosch was again accused of complicity in the aborted guerrilla operation May 8. Hamlet Herman Perez, one of the two surviving insurgents, said the guerrillas' leader, the late Francisco Caamano, had told him that he trusted Bosch and that half of the guerrillas were PRD members.

A joint communiqué by the armed forces leaders, reported Sept. 28, charged right-wing groups had offered money to extreme left-wing groups to "throw the country into chaos." The message was denounced by opposition leaders, who asserted it constituted interference in politics and was an attempt to head off a possible opposition coalition against Balaguer. Luis Manuel Campillo, a congressman from the Democratic Integration Movement, charged Oct. 1 that the communique was "an attempt to intimidate the people and a prelude to a campaign of repression."

Bosch quits PRD. Ex-President Juan Bosch resigned Nov. 18 as leader of the Dominican Revolutionary party (PRD) and said he would organize a new opposition group, to be called the Dominican Liberation party (PLD).

Bosch's resignation, following a bitter split among PRD leaders, reportedly dealt a serious blow to efforts by opposition parties to form a united front against the re-election of President Joaquin Balaguer in May 1974. At least 12 political groups had been meeting for several months on Bosch's initiative to achieve such a coalition. The groups reportedly accepted the PLD as a new party to the talks Nov. 21.

According to the Miami Herald Nov. 29, Bosch's resignation was designed to force the ouster from the PRD of his opponents. However, the move backfired as only nine of 24 key party officials left with Bosch, the Herald noted. The remainder reportedly said they would remain in the PRD and work for Balaguer's defeat.

At a news conference Nov. 18, Bosch said the PLD would "fight on all political fronts, and particularly against the corruption and abuses of the current government." He said he continued to support "the unity of all parties" against the government and "in defense of the democratic rights of the people, and of national sovereignty."

Before the PLD could operate as a political party and participate in the presidential campaign, it would have to be declared legal by the Central Electoral Commission.

Publication canceled—The government had canceled a new afternoon newspaper, La Razon, because the company which was to distribute it allegedly was illegally constituted, the Miami Herald reported Feb. 16. Newspaper employes reportedly claimed the cancellation was ordered because La Razon's owner had publicly attacked President Balaguer.

Broadcast bill opposed—The Association of Dominican Dailies and the Dominican Radio Broadcasters Association asked the government March 15 to withdraw a new broadcasting bill they said restricted freedom of the press.

The bill, announced by President Balaguer March 6, would create the position of assistant to the attorney general to monitor the nation's radio stations and corrupt officials. It would also give the director of communications authority to suspend any news program on radio or television which he believed incited rebellion or disturbed the peace.

The bill stated that before a news program was broadcast, its producer, director or assistant director must send a statement of intent to the police and Interior Ministry if it was in the capital and to the provincial governor if it was outside.

The bill was also protested by the Inter-American Press Association (IAPA) March 16. The IAPA Feb. 28 had opposed two other government bills which it said limited press freedom, but these were withdrawn March 6. Balaguer assured the IAPA March 14 that the Dominican press would be free so long as he was president.

Later, the regime briefly closed a Santo Domingo radio station, Radio Pueblo, Sept. 4 after it broadcast statements by opposition leader Pablo Rafael Casimiro Castro attacking Balaguer. The station was ordered closed for 30 hours by General Telecommunications Director Victor Justo, but Balaguer voided the order following protests from the national media.

Students, police clash. Hundreds of students armed with rocks and sticks fought police in Santo Domingo June 1. The disturbances closed most public educational institutions in the city. An undetermined number of students were arrested.

The students reportedly protested the fatal shooting by police of a student in the southern town of Barahona, during a student demonstration demanding that a local school be built and that more state funds be allocated for the Autonomous University of Santo Domingo (UASD).

Police had ended a 57-day occupation of UASD April 3.

One student was killed and others injured Nov. 15 when police tried to break up a march by 500 students in downtown Santo Domingo. The demonstrators, who joined state university authorities in demanding higher allocations, left the area a shambles.

Strike called off. An anti-government general strike scheduled for Nov. 4 was called off after business groups reached an agreement with President Balaguer, it was reported Oct. 26. The agreement followed several days of partial walkouts and shutdowns of businesses in the interior, protesting alleged government discrimination against business interests, the Journal of Commerce reported.

Leftist abductor reaches France. Leftwing revolutionary Manfredo Casado, who took political asylum in the Mexican embassy in Santo Domingo in 1972, was given safe-conduct to travel to France Sept. 27 after he kidnapped the 12-year-old son of Mexican Ambassador Francisco Garcia and threatened to kill himself and the boy.

The government, which had denied Casado safe-conduct before, acceded when Casado threatened to use a gasoline cache and a grenade to blow up the room in which he held the boy. Casado released the boy unharmed at the Santo Domingo airport. He arrived in France Sept. 28.

In a related development, police in Santo Domingo announced the arrest Nov. 2 of Plinio Matos Moquete, leader of the outlawed leftist "January 12" movement, the Cuban press agency Prensa Latina reported Nov. 4. Matos was sought on charges of bank robbery, illegal possession of arms, and "political subversion." His brother Manuel had been arrested in June on similar charges, according to Prensa Latina.

Economic Developments

'72 exports up. The Center for Promotion of Exports, a government agency, said the nation's 1972 exports totaled $348.1 million, $107.3 million higher than the 1971 figure, the Miami Herald reported March 1.

OAS development loan. Galo Plaza, secretary general of the Organization of American States, had signed an $11 million aid agreement with President Balaguer to develop the northwest, the London newsletter Latin America reported Feb. 9.

IDB provides financing. The Inter-American Development Bank Jan. 27 announced approval of a $24.8 million loan to promote agricultural development in the Dominican Republic. The International Development Association, an affiliate of the World Bank, Jan. 19 announced approval of a $13 million credit to finance irrigation in the Yaque del Norte river valley.

The IDB Nov. 21 lent $18.8 million to help finance an irrigation and agricultural development project in the Cibao Valley, in the northwest.

The bank had approved an $18.6 million loan Nov. 1 to help finance a $23.3 million government project to expand and improve Santo Domingo's water supply system.

Ecuador

Oil Developments

Oil concessions returned. The government Jan. 1 took back 1.27 million acres of oil concessions granted to the U.S.-based Texaco-Gulf consortium during the administration of ex-President Jose Maria Velasco Ibarra.

The action conformed with a June 1972 decree ordering oil companies to return 60% of their concessions to the state upon completion of exploration. A Texaco-Gulf request for "adequate compensation" was rejected Jan. 10 on grounds that the consortium, as stipulated in the decree, had selected the acreage to be returned.

Natural Resources Minister Gustavo Jarrin Ampudia said Jan. 4 that the returned concessions contained proved reserves of 35 million barrels of crude, representing at least $70 million in revenues for the government.

(Ecuador's ambassador to the U.S. had said his government's November 1972 cancellation of another U.S. consortium's oil concessions in the Gulf of Guayaquil was an "isolated" action designed to facilitate investigation and determination of the circumstances under which the concessions were granted, it was reported Jan. 10. He said there had been no discussion of compensation to the consortium because its concessions had only been "revoked," not "expropriated" or "confiscated.")

The government would receive 80% of income from oil exports as of Jan. 1, the Times of the Americas reported Jan. 10.

Production income tax imposed. The government May 31 decreed an 86% tax on the oil production income of firms which had obtained exploration rights to Ecuadorean concessions and then transferred the concessions to other companies for exploitation.

Natural Resources Minister Capt. Gustavo Jarrin Ampudia said the measure would prevent companies from making large profits on concessions after they stopped work on them.

Among the firms affected were Phoenix Canada Oil Co. of Canada and Norsul Oil & Mining Ltd. of the U.S. (not Canada, as previously reported.

Each held a 1% production participation in the Coca concession in Oriente Province, one of two which supplied the more than 200,000 barrels of oil produced daily by the Texaco-Gulf consortium.

The government raised the reference price for crude from $2.60 per barrel to $3.61 per barrel April 1–May 23. The high price was offered by a Japanese concern, Sumitomo Shoji Kaisha, according to El Nacional of Caracas May 25.

New Texaco-Gulf contract. The government and the U.S.-based Texaco-Gulf consortium had signed a new concession contract which would give Ecuador nearly 80% of the gross profits of its petroleum exports, a Gulf spokesman announced Aug. 7.

The 20-year contract, signed in Quito Aug. 6, reduced by half, to about one million acres, the consortium's oil exploration area in the Amazon basin in northeastern Ecuador. Ecuador won the right to purchase for its own merchandising up to 51% of the consortium's total production, currently averaging 200,000 barrels of crude per day.

The new contract was the third between the two sides in less than 10 years. The previous one, signed in 1969 and scheduled to last 40 years, gave Ecuador some 60% of the gross profits.

Ecuador Sun, a subsidiary of Sun Oil Co., signed a new exploration contract with the government covering 438,000 acres in the Amazon region, it was reported Aug. 8. The contract renewal deadline for other companies seeking exploration and exploitation rights was extended from Aug. 6 to Oct. 6, it was reported Aug. 13.

Revenue from oil exports had multiplied Ecuador's monetary reserves six times in the past 14 months, making it the only country in Latin America in which the Central Bank gave foreign currency sellers a better rate than foreign exchange dealers, the London newsletter Latin America reported Aug. 3.

Ex-president ordered arrested. The military government ordered the arrest of ex-President Otto Arosemena Gomez Oct. 4, a few hours after Arosemena denounced a civil court which tried him on charges of involvement in the awarding of illegal oil concessions to a U.S. consortium in 1968.

Arosemena was acquitted, but several other persons including three former Cabinet ministers were convicted and given jail sentences. The ex-ministers were Augusto Barreiro Solorzano (sentenced to six years), Galo Pico Mantilla (five years) and Nestor Vega Moreno (one year), according to the newsletter Latin America Sept. 28.

Oil prices raised. The government Nov. 10 raised posted prices for crude oil by an average of $2.05 a barrel, to $7.30 a barrel for a key grade. It was the seventh time posted prices were raised since Ecuadorean petroleum production began.

In a speech reported Nov. 14, President Guillermo Rodriguez Lara said Ecuador was now earning $1 million daily from oil exports, and that most of the money was earmarked for development.

The government granted rights to construct a $92 million state petroleum refinery to the Japanese firms Sumitomo Shiji Jaisha and Chiyoda Chemical Engineering, it was reported Nov. 21. The refinery, to be completed by 1976, was expected to produce 50,000 barrels a day in its initial stages.

The government had signed, after long negotiations, a contract with the U.S. oil firm OKC for exploration over 291,150 hectares of land in eastern Ecuador, it was reported Oct. 26.

Other Events

IDB provides financing. The Inter-American Development Bank had approved an $18.8 million loan to help finance expansion and improvement of Quito's drinking water system, the Times of the Americas reported Jan. 10.

Later, the IDB July 12 approved a $14.3 million loan to help finance a comprehensive development plan for Quito, including expansion of the sewage system, construction of arterial streets, expansion of retail and wholesale market facilities, and construction of a slaughterhouse.

'72 exports up—Ecuadorean exports reached record levels in 1972, but the balance of payments deficit remained at $33.6 million, it was reported May 25.

The government had raised the proportion of their capital that foreign companies operating in Ecuador must deposit in local banks from 25% to 100%, Latin America reported Jan. 5.

Aulestia out. President Guillermo Rodriguez Lara accepted the resignation of Defense Minister Victor Aulestia, submitted as a matter of courtesy Dec.

29, 1972 to enable the president to name a new Cabinet for 1973. Aulestia's dismissal, like the return of the oil concessions, was seen as a victory for the military regime's nationalists over its right-wing, pro-Brazilian members. (Another conservative officer, Gen. Alejandro Romo Escobar, had resigned as president of a special tribunal trying 28 leftists on charges of subversion, the London newsletter Latin America reported Jan. 26.)

Former official ordered arrested. A special tribunal in Quito Jan. 31 ordered the arrest of ex-Defense Minister Jorge Acosta Velasco for allegedly making personal use of public funds during the administration of ex-President Jose Maria Velasco Ibarra. Acosta, considered Velasco's most powerful minister before his dismissal in 1971, resided in Europe.

New ministers named. Rear Adm. Alfredo Poveda was appointed government (interior) minister June 6, replacing Gen. Galo Latorre Sierra, who resigned.

Poveda was commander of the first naval zone, based in Guayaquil. In the Cabinet, he was expected to side with President Rodriguez Lara against the armed forces' conservative, or "Brazilian" faction, according to the newsletter Latin America June 15. Latorre belonged to the right-wing New National Order group.

In another appointment reported June 22, Col. Luis Guillermo Duran, commander of the second military district (Guayaquil), became education minister, replacing Gen. Vicente Anda Aguirre, whose death after a heart attack was reported June 15.

Student violence. One person had been killed and several others wounded in student violence in Guayaquil, and three students had received gunshot wounds during clashes in Loja, the Miami Herald reported March 9.

The student killed in Guayaquil had been "executed" for political discrepancies with rival student groups, according to police sources. Students voted March 8 to elect a new rector of Guayaquil University.

Quito police used tear gas June 4 to disperse more than 1,000 students protesting government controls over the nation's universities.

The demonstrators, who came from different parts of the country, were driven back from the presidential palace, where they had planned to send a delegation to President Guillermo Rodriguez Lara.

Press law signed. President Guillermo Rodriguez Lara March 14 signed a law setting conditions under which newspapers and magazines would have to reserve free space for government announcements. The law stipulated that the space granted the government could not exceed 2% of the overall space in the publication.

The law had been protested by a number of press groups when it was announced in November 1972, but the government had asserted it did not threaten freedom of the press. Some representatives of the press participated in the final formulation of the law, but others refused to participate in protest against government interference in the news media.

In a related development reported March 7, the National Newspapermen's Union protested the seven-day imprisonment and fining of a television commentator, Francisco Darque Moreno, for alleged "disrespect for state authorities." Darque Moreno reportedly had criticized the length and style of speeches by some government officials.

The same union asked the government to abolish the National Information Secretariat and other instruments that allegedly limited press freedom, it was reported Nov. 25.

Opposition leaders arrested. Two political leaders were jailed following the formation in late July of the Democratic Restoration Front, a coalition of parties which criticized the military regime and demanded an early return to constitutional rule.

Gonzalo Oleas Zambrano, head of a faction of the Ecuadorean Socialist party, was held July 31–Aug. 3 on charges of "spreading false rumors." He had denounced the government upon assuming the front's weekly rotating chairmanship, and had demanded the regime hand over power to the front so it could hold new elections.

Manuel Araujo Hidalgo, head of the National Velasquista Federation, was arrested without explanation Aug. 6, after he assumed the front's chairmanship and criticized the government. Two Guayaquil university professors were suspended for criticizing government education policies, it was reported Aug. 9.

The front included, besides the Socialists and Velasquistas, the Conservative and Radical Liberal parties, and the populist Concentration of Popular Forces of former Guayaquil mayor and presidential candidate Asaad Bucaram. The small, Moscow-line Communist party continued to support the government.

Government communiques denounced front leaders as "political schemers" and their parties as "unpopular minorities." They warned that the phase of "excessive tolerance" was over, and that subversion and obstruction of government programs would not be allowed.

Francisco Huerta, leader of the opposition Radical Liberal party, was arrested and banished to the remote Amazon region, it was reported Aug. 15.

Strike disturbances. Street fighting erupted in Guayaquil and Quito in August and September in connection with strikes by teachers and by industrial and municipal workers. The government ordered the arrest of the teachers' strike leaders, calling them subversives, but later it named mediators to investigate the teachers' complaints and settle the other strikes.

A teacher and two students were killed in Guayaquil Aug. 10-15 in disturbances growing out of a teachers' strike to protest irregularities in distribution of free school materials in the coastal provinces. The strikers also demanded the resignation of Education Minister Col. Guillermo Duran, whom they held responsible.

The disturbances spread to the nearby city of Milagros, where several persons were injured Aug. 14, and to Quito, where a student was reported killed Aug. 16.

The government offered Aug. 20 to hold talks with the National Teachers' Union (UNE), which led the strike. UNE leaders said they welcomed the talks, but would remain in hiding until the order for their arrest was lifted. They repeated their demand for Duran's removal.

Students and teachers supporting the strike were reported arrested in Guayaquil Aug. 27. Disturbances were reported in the coastal city of Machala Aug. 27 and in Guayaquil Aug. 27-28. The strike finally was reported settled Sept. 7 after President Rodriguez Lara agreed to a government investigation of UNE's complaints.

Trouble broke out again in Guayaquil schools in mid-September, coinciding with a strike at the local cement plant which paralyzed the government's public works program for the port, the newsletter Latin America reported Sept. 28. The cement workers were joined in solidarity strikes by the Guayas Province Workers' Federation, which included municipal, hospital and some farm workers. A textile plant in Quito was reported occupied.

The government reportedly blamed these strikes too on a subversive conspiracy. However, it appointed mediators to settle the stoppages, according to Latin America.

According to Latin America Oct. 26, the immediate cause of recent public discontent in Ecuador was inflation, estimated officially at 15% but in reality probably higher. Inflation reportedly was fueled by the oil boom, [See above] which had had little impact on the income of the average Ecuadorean ($249 a year in 1971).

Guayaquil, with some of the worst urban conditions in the world, had been severely affected by the government's crackdown on smuggling, an important part of the port's economic life, Latin America reported. The government also had reduced the political and economic influence of Guayaquil's merchants, who had protested preferential treatment given to Quito, the center of the oil companies' operations.

ITT aid obstruction reported. The U.S. magazine Business Week reported in its Aug. 11 issue that the International Telephone & Telegraph Corp. (ITT) had had

ECUADOR

$15.8 million in U.S. aid withheld from Ecuador until the Ecuadorean government settled a claim for an expropriated ITT subsidiary.

The subsidiary, All American Cables & Radio, was expropriated in 1970. According to Business Week, ITT initially demanded $1.3 million in reparations but finally agreed to about $600,000 plus some valuable land. When Ecuador was within $25,000 of the ITT figure, the company balked, and asked the U.S. State Department to invoke seldom used sanctions calling for a cutoff of U.S. loans and aid to countries that nationalized U.S. concerns without paying "prompt, adequate and effective compensation."

Jack Neal, an ITT Washington representative, reportedly put pressure on officials of the State Department, the Agency for International Development (AID) and the Treasury Department to "bottle up all aid to Ecuador," threatening to complain directly to Secretary of State William P. Rogers and then-Treasury Secretary John B. Connally Jr. "The net result," Business Week reported, "was that $15.8 million of assistance authorized in June 1970, was held up for two years by AID. And a $14.3 million Inter-American Development Bank (IDB) loan was threatened with cancellation by U.S. representatives on the lending institution if Ecuador did not cave in on the $25,000 difference with ITT."

Ecuador acceded to ITT's demands in January 1972. It paid the $600,000, but immediately began to retake the land it had offered as part of the expropriation package. It also awarded to other bidders a satellite relay station contract sought by ITT, according to Business Week.

After the overthrow of ex-President Jose Maria Velasco Ibarra in February 1972, the new military government began "good faith" negotiations with ITT over the remaining disputed land, Business Week reported. Restrictions on U.S. loans and aid to Ecuador were subsequently lifted.

Haiti

U.S. envoy held, ransomed. U.S. Ambassador Clinton E. Knox was seized by three armed Haitians in Port-au-Prince Jan. 23 and freed unharmed the next day in exchange for the release of 12 Haitian prisoners, safe conduct to Mexico and a $70,000 ransom.

Knox's captors, two men and a woman, were not identified but were said to have links with exile groups that had opposed the Haitian government for years. They said the persons released were political prisoners. The abductors and freed prisoners reportedly reached Mexico safely.

In Washington, a State Department spokesman said Knox's captors had demanded a $500,000 ransom, but this had been refused by Secretary of State William P. Rogers. The spokesman said he did not know who paid the final ransom, but newspapers reported the $70,000 had been offered by French mediators during the tense all-night negotiations that preceded Knox's release.

Knox was seized as he drove to his residence in Port-au-Prince Jan. 23. He was forced at gunpoint into another car, in which he and his captors entered the residence grounds. Knox then telephoned the U.S. consul general in Port-au-Prince, Ward L. Christensen, who joined him at the residence and was held until the final agreement was reached with the kidnappers.

In New York, a Haitian exile group called the Coalition of National Liberation Brigades said that the released "prisoners have been under constant threat to be eliminated in case of any disorder in the country. And disorder there will be. ... The actual, archaic, farcical government, led by Clinton Knox and the State Department, must go."

Exiles leave Mexico for Chile. The three kidnappers and 12 freed prisoners flown to Mexico following the abduction of Clinton Knox were refused asylum by the Mexican government Feb. 1 and flown to Santiago, Chile. The Chilean government gave them transit visas while deciding whether to let them stay in the country.

The exiles had wanted to remain in Mexico, which they said they had selected for asylum "because of [its] great liberal tradition." However, diplomatic sources in Mexico City said the Mexican government felt allowing the Haitians to remain in the country would jeopardize its current negotiations for extradition of three Mexicans who had hijacked an airliner to Cuba after securing the release of six political prisoners and a ransom of $340,000. Cuba returned the ransom Jan. 31 but refused to extradite the hijackers. Mexico had also returned to Haiti the $70,000 paid for the release of Knox.

HAITI

The Haitian exiles—four men and a woman, most of them teachers—said Jan. 24 that they belonged to the National Antiduvalierist Movement, an organization without ideology or international political affiliations which sought only to free Haiti from the dictatorship of President Jean-Claude Duvalier. They said they had the support of all students and intellectual groups in Haiti.

The Haitian ambassador in Mexico City charged the exiles included common criminals and some Communist criminals, but no political leaders of any importance, El Nacional of Caracas reported Jan. 26.

Prisoner release hoax revealed. The opposition newspaper Haiti-Observateur of New York said nearly all the 72 political prisoners the government claimed to have freed in December 1972 had in fact been released in 1969, the London newsletter Latin America reported Feb. 16. The paper said many of the 72 had contacted it to say they had been living in the U.S. or Canada for several years.

A later Haiti-Observateur report, cited in Latin America March 9, said 60 persons had died of disease and torture in Haiti's main political prison, Fort Dimanche, since President Duvalier came to power in 1971. A message smuggled out of the jail said there were about 400 prisoners there, including Fred and Reneld Baptiste, veterans of the abortive 1964 and 1968 invasions to overthrow the president's late father, Francois Duvalier.

Hubert Legros, an anti-Duvalier lawyer released in December 1972 after two years in jail, had been reported re-arrested in Port-au-Prince, according to Latin America Feb. 9.

U.S. to send aid envoy. The U.S., encouraged by developments under President Jean-Claude Duvalier, would send an aid official to Haiti for the first time since 1963, it was reported Jan. 13.

U.S. military embargo ended. The U.S. had placed Haiti back on its list of countries eligible for foreign military sales and credit programs, ending an 11-year embargo, the Washington Post reported April 16. Inclusion of Haiti on the list, submitted to Congress in December 1972, had gone unnoticed, the Post reported.

Most aid to Haiti had been cut off in 1962 to protest misuse of funds and other abuses by the regime of the late President Francois Duvalier. Since Duvalier's death in 1971 and the accession to the presidency of his son, Jean-Claude, the U.S. and several international aid organizations had gradually resumed economic aid, and the U.S. State Department had approved sales of arms to Haiti by private U.S. companies.

Haiti had submitted various requests for U.S. military aid since 1971 to replace "obsolescent" armed forces equipment. While awaiting U.S. government approval of the requests, Haiti had purchased rifles, ammunition, helicopters and patrol boats from private U.S. companies, the Post reported.

Haitian Foreign Minister Adrien Raymond said the U.S. Agency for International Development had approved a $3.5 million loan for road maintenance in Haiti, the Post reported.

Lafontant dismissed. Roger Lafontant, interior and defense minister since November 1972, was dismissed by President Duvalier Jan. 16 and replaced by Breton Nazaire, a strong Duvalierist.

Lafontant's dismissal reportedly was linked to an editorial in the government newspaper Le Nouveau Monde Jan. 10 which attacked associates of the president's late father, Francois Duvalier. The editorial, for which Lafrontant reportedly was responsible, denounced persons "who in the recent past got rich on allowances, concessions and pillaging the national exchequer."

The editorial reportedly offended the president's mother, Simone Duvalier, who reportedly persuaded her son to fire Lafontant. Former ministers reportedly had been trying to persuade the Duvaliers to reshuffle the Cabinet at the time the editorial appeared.

Lafontant had gained his Cabinet post after the dismissal of Lt. Col. Luckner Cambronne, the former strongman of the Haitian government. Cambronne, who had fled to Colombia after his downfall, had taken up residence in Miami, the Miami Herald reported Jan. 20.

Elections held. Elections to fill the 58 seats in the National Assembly were held

Feb. 11. Although an official count was not immediately released, it was assumed supporters of President Jean-Claude Duvalier had won most if not all of the seats. Some 300 candidates, most openly committed to the government, ran in the elections, the first since 1969.

Staples prices cut. President Duvalier announced March 27 that the prices of rice, beans and corn had been cut 40%–50%. He said the action had been taken after "some businessmen" had attempted to hoard rice and beans to create an artificial shortage and gain "high profits."

Lebert ousted. Industry Minister Jean-Pierre Lebert, the longest-standing Cabinet member, had been dismissed after eight years in office, it was reported April 27. His replacement by Deputy Finance Minister Serge Fourcand followed growing public complaints against rising prices. Ex-Interior and Defense Minister Luckner Cambronne reportedly had been named inspector-general of Haitian embassies and consulates in the Americas.

Port project halted. A free port and resort project begun on the Ile de la Tortue by a Texas entrepreneur, Don Pierson, had been halted by the government and placed under judicial control until Pierson proved he had "fulfilled contractual obligations to the state," the Miami Herald reported March 27.

Pierson reportedly had signed a 99-year contract with the government of the late President Francois Duvalier. However, the current government claimed Pierson's development company, the Dupont Caribbean Freeport Authority, had "neglected all . . . obligations and wanted to exploit the island without consulting the state and without forwarding documentary proof for government control," the Herald reported.

The Haitian Supreme Court Aug. 27 upheld the government's March cancellation of Pierson's contract.

OAS unit criticizes regime. The Inter-American Commission on Human Rights of the Organization of American States had condemned the Duvalier government for not answering its inquiries concerning former soccer star Joseph Gaetjens, allegedly held by the regime for nine years, the New York opposition journal Haiti-Observateur reported July 6.

The commission urged the government to investigate Gaetjens' disappearance and invoke "sanctions against those who are responsible for this illegal detention." It also recommended that the regime pay "reparations and adequate indemnification" to Gaetjens' family.

In another foreign development:

President Duvalier recalled his ambassador from Santo Domingo amid rumors of worsening relations with the Dominican Republic, it was reported June 21. The Dominican newspaper Listin Diario said the recall followed the closing of the border between the two countries by Duvalier in response to a decision by the Dominican Republic not to sell foodstuffs to Haiti.

French official visits. French Planning and Housing Minister Olivier Guichard paid a three-day visit to Port-au-Prince, it was reported July 13. He was the highest-ranking French official to visit Haiti since it declared its independence from France in 1804.

Guichard said upon returning to Paris that France would give Haiti $1.25 million in aid in 1973 and considerably more in 1974, under the terms of a 10-year scientific, cultural and economic agreement signed without publicity in June. The French government reportedly pledged to compensate French investors in Haiti for any losses in the event of Haitian nationalizations or political upheaval.

A French road-building firm recently had won a contract to improve Haiti's road system, it was reported July 13.

Development loan. The Inter-American Development Bank Aug. 2 approved a $22.2 million loan to help the government build a highway from Leogane to Les Cayes in the mountainous southern peninsula. Total cost of the project was estimated at $25.1 million.

The government signed an agreement guaranteeing West German investments in Haiti, it was reported Aug. 24.

HAITI

Government, army shake-ups. President Jean-Claude Duvalier dismissed 49 government and military officials Aug. 9–14, in the biggest shake-ups of his 2½ years in office.

The dismissals, affecting four Cabinet ministers and the army chief of staff, among others, followed a mysterious fire two weeks before which damaged the presidential palace and destroyed virtually all of Haiti's ammunition. (A second fire in the palace, also unexplained, was reported Aug. 31.)

The changes also followed, by hours, the departure from Haiti of Marie-Denise Duvalier Dominique, sister of the president, who re-entered the country at the end of June and had reportedly made another unsuccessful attempt to wrest power from her brother. She was rebuffed by the military establishment led by her old enemy Gen. Gracia Jacques, commander of the presidential guard, according to the London newsletter Latin America Aug. 17.

The president Aug. 9 dismissed Finance Minister Edouard Francisque, Information Minister Fritz Cineas, Health Minister Alix Theard and Public Works Minister Max Bonhomme. They were immediately replaced, respectively, by Emmanuel Bros, Paul Blanchet, Daniel Beaulieu and Pierre Petit. Blanchet had been information minister under the late President Francois Duvalier, while Cineas, appointed ambassador to Italy, was considered an ally of ousted Interior and Defense Minister Luckner Cambronne.

Duvalier also replaced the ambassador to the United Nations, the security chief at the Port-au-Prince airport, the army chief of staff, the military commander of the Nord department, and 21 other officers. Other government and military dismissals were reported in the following days.

The five-hour presidential palace fire July 23 was caused by explosions of unknown origin in the basement munitions depot.

A second fire of mysterious origin, reported by police July 27, killed at least 10 persons as it swept through a Port-au-Prince baseball factory.

Refugees reach U.S. Eighteen persons claiming to have fled Haiti in June were picked up by a U.S. fishing boat July 16 as their rickety vessel limped toward Marathon in the Florida Keys.

Guerrilla landing reported. Sources in the Dominican Republic, quoted by the Associated Press, reported Sept. 12 that about 20 guerrillas opposed to the Duvalier regime had landed on Haiti's northern coast, and said Sept. 13 that another 60 cohorts had joined them. The government disputed the reports, but canceled all internal airline flights until further notice.

The Haitian ambassador in Santo Domingo, Clement Vincent, said Sept. 11 that an undetermined number of armed men had attempted to land that day at Baye St. Nicholas, on Haiti's northwest coast, but had been repulsed by a coast guard vessel which engaged them in an "intense shootout." Vincent said the guerrillas had abandoned a boat containing arms, ammunition, dynamite and "Marxist propaganda."

Information Minister Blanchet said in Port-au-Prince Sept. 14 that there was "nothing" to the reports of a guerrilla invasion, and that the coast guard vessel actually had driven off "smugglers" mistaken for subversives. The government later claimed that the Sept. 11 action involved discovery by security forces of a yacht containing 660 pounds of marijuana. The Foreign Ministry said the coast guard had exchanged fire with the yacht's occupants, and later arrested three U.S. citizens on the vessel.

Haitian police reported Sept. 14 that a man identified only as Guy Jackson Harewood had been killed Sept. 11 in an exchange of gunfire between police and guerrillas in a wooded area near the alleged invasion site. There was no mention of the report in the Foreign Ministry statement.

Mexico

Guerrilla Activity

U.S. envoy kidnapped, ransomed. The U.S. consul general in Guadalajara, Terrance G. Leonhardy, was kidnapped by left-wing guerrillas May 4 and freed unharmed May 7 after the Mexican government agreed to a number of demands, including freedom and safe conduct to Cuba for 30 alleged political prisoners.

The freed prisoners, 26 men and four women, arrived in Havana on a Mexican airliner May 6, and they said that they would return to Mexico to fight the government. Mexican authorities called them "common delinquents," but press sources said most of them belonged to urban guerrilla groups, which had carried out other kidnappings and bank robberies. The best known of those released was José Bracho Campos, an associate of the late guerrilla leader Genaro Vasquez Rojas.

Leonhardy was kidnapped by members of the People's Revolutionary Armed Forces, who demanded May 5 that the government: free the prisoners and transport them to Cuba; order the national press to publish a guerrilla communiqué; suspend the police and military search for Leonhardy; and allow the Cuban ambassador to go on television to confirm the safe arrival in Havana of the prisoners.

President Luis Echeverria Alvarez quickly agreed to meet the demands, saying his government prized human life highly. The U.S. reiterated its stance against yielding to extortion or blackmail for the release of officials abroad and left the matter in Mexican hands.

The demands were met May 6, but Leonhardy was not released for another day, leading to speculation the guerrillas had asked other concessions from the government. The governor of Jalisco state, Alberto Orozco Romero, said May 8 that Leonhardy's wife had paid the guerrillas $80,000 ransom, which she borrowed from a local bank. The U.S. had reportedly endorsed the loan, but the State Department denied this May 8.

The guerrilla communique published in the press May 6 and broadcast over television and radio, denounced Mexico's low health standards, its illiteracy and exorbitant credit rates, blaming the misery of impoverished workers and peasants on the concentration of wealth in the hands of a few, the outflow of Mexican capital abroad, and government repression of students, workers and peasants who tried to organize against authorities.

The guerrillas denounced the government for trying to "convince the people that we are common delinquents, hired killers, cattle rustlers, enemies of the country. Today, for the first time and not voluntarily, the mass media are serving the proletarian cause."

Leonhardy reportedly was the first foreign diplomat kidnapped in Mexico.

Jalisco state Gov. Alberto Orozco Romero said May 9 that Leonhardy would be responsible for paying back the $80,000 ransom money provided by a local bank.

Guerrillas kill policemen. Three policemen were shot to death in a clash with guerrillas commanded by Lucio Cabanas near the Pacific resort of Acapulco, it was reported April 6.

Police were reported March 23 to have announced the arrest of 10 guerrillas in Guerrero state and seizure of a large cache of arms. Guerrillas said, however, that an even larger consignment of arms had already been sent into the mountains.

Six peasants in the village of Peloncillo were executed by soldiers April 25 after being accused of sending food supplies to Cabanas' guerrilla group, the mayor of the village reported. The official said the victims' wives and relatives had been forced to dig graves for them.

The executions reportedly followed the murder of a kidnapped local landowner by the Cabanas group after his family refused to pay $240,000 ransom. The army, which had launched a strong anti-guerrilla offensive in Guerrero, said it had arrested Cabanas' cousin, Manuel Garcia Cabanas, it was reported May 4.

Student Unrest

University classes resume. Classes at UNAM, the national university in Mexico City, resumed Jan. 16 following a three-month student strike.

The strike, in support of striking university employes, ended when the university granted the employes a 30% wage increase, a five-day workweek and other benefits. The university did not, however, grant the employes' union a closed shop, leaving many students, lecturers and workers at odds over whether the employes' strike should continue.

Guillermo Soberon, a U.S.-educated scientist, was chosen rector of UNAM Jan. 4, replacing Pablo Gonzalez, who resigned in November 1972 after failing to curb student disturbances and resolve the employes' strike. Soberon's inaugural, reported Jan. 19, was marred by the occupation of his offices by students, teachers and workers.

The Mexico City newspaper Excelsior said Jan. 5 that during its recent crisis UNAM had fallen "to the lowest level. Everything said about [UNAM] in terms of negativity and frustration was valid. Irresponsibility and gangsterism joined hands from the campus to the classrooms." Excelsior said Soberon was an "intelligent, diligent" man recommended by a number of research institutes.

More violence. In Puebla, two policemen posing as university students were kidnapped by students, who tortured and fatally shot one of them and wounded the other, the newsletter Latin America reported Feb. 9. The Puebla University rector blamed police and the Puebla state governor for infiltrating the university with secret agents and held them responsible for the assassination of two university lecturers in 1972.

A Puebla student had been reported killed Feb. 2 in clashes between students and police or right-wing strong arm groups. A student was killed in similar clashes in Villa Hermosa, and another student was killed in Monterrey, according to the same report. Three other Monterrey students had been wounded in clashes with police, reported Jan. 19.

Officials in Guadalajara said they feared a student war following the murder of four local student leaders by other youths, the Miami Herald reported Feb. 17.

In another development reported April 13, right-wing gangs of thugs known as "porras" reappeared in Mexico City, attacking and injuring the director of the National Polytechnic Institute and beating up a number of high school students and teachers.

Puebla students killed. Four students were killed and about 20 persons wounded May 1 in a shootout between police and students at the Autonomous University of

Puebla. Students and authorities blamed each other for the incident.

The violence began when police tried to stop about 300 students from joining the Labor Day march in downtown Puebla. The students reportedly fought with officers in the streets near the university and then seized a university building, taking three police hostages with them. A five-hour shootout ensued in which four students were fatally wounded. Students later released the police hostages in exchange for six youths arrested by police, but continued to occupy the building.

Students hijacked 14 city buses May 2 and used them to blockade all streets leading to the university. Police sealed off the area, but did not move against the students. Another student was killed the next day after attending a massive funeral service for the May 1 victims; police claimed he was run over by a bus, but doctors said he had been struck repeatedly with "a pipe or other blunt object."

Puebla state Gov. Gonzalo Bautista O'Farrill was sharply criticized after the May 1 incident. Students accused him of direct responsibility for the killings. The university rector, Sergio Flores, charged May 2 that authorities had "provoked" the incident by posting police sharpshooters near the main university building. There were numerous calls for the governor's resignation.

Bautista charged May 3 that students sought his resignation "in order to continue dedicating themselves to vandalism and pillage. They don't want me because I haven't allowed them to go on murdering, robbing and kidnapping." He alleged that student violence in Puebla was instigated by the Mexican Communist party, but said he was not personally anti-Communist.

A week later Bautista quit his post "so that the life of my beloved state" can return to normal." His predecessor had also resigned over student conflicts.

Meanwhile, the government in Mexico City banned a student march scheduled for May 9 to protest the Puebla killings. The traffic police chief, Gen. Daniel Gutierrez Santos, said the demonstration had been organized by "students and other groups, especially the Communist party, which are trying to alter the public order."

Students killed. A student was shot dead at the University of Guadalajara Aug. 6. He was the third youth killed in student gun battles there in less than a week.

Two students were reported shot to death May 25 in disturbances in Culiacan. Similar disturbances, but no casualties, were reported in Durango and Mexico City.

University entry restrictions set. Sergio Dominguez Vargas, secretary general of the Autonomous National University of Mexico (UNAM), said at least 12,000 of the 36,000 students taking UNAM's entrance exams in April would have to be failed to avert a collapse in academic standards, it was reported March 23.

Dominguez asserted that unless restrictions were imposed on entrance to the massive Mexico City university, there would not be "enough human resources to meet the needs of students." The school was designed 25 years before for 25,000 students but currently had 80,000 undergraduates plus 95,000 students in affiliated preparatory colleges and 14,500 lecturers and professors. If current growth rates were maintained, UNAM would have 240,000 students by the end of 1973 and 516,000 by 1975, according to the London newsletter Latin America March 23.

Restrictions on entry to UNAM reportedly had been instituted before but never seriously enforced because of political pressure in favor of a higher education for anyone desiring it. The new policy was said to be the work of UNAM's new rector, Guillermo Soberon.

New university promised. Authorities in Torreon (Coahuila state), under pressure from students, announced they would establish a new regional university in the city, the Miami Herald reported April 4.

Students demanding a regional university had seized Torreon's public transportation system March 30 and blocked main roads out of the city. Their demand followed the failure of a professor from the Torreon campus of the University of Coahuila to accept the university's rectorship in view of objections by students on the main campus in Saltillo, 170 miles east.

Torreon authorities said local state university facilities would become part of the new regional university, to be called the Autonomous University of La Laguna.

Police raid UNAM campus. An estimated 600-1,000 policemen raided the Autonomous National University (UNAM) campus in Mexico City early Aug. 10 at the request of Rector Guillermo Soberon. Some 45 persons were arrested, but only one was charged with a criminal offense, according to reports.

Police said Soberon had called them in to help end a wave of violence on the campus. More than 700 crimes—mostly robberies and burglaries—had been reported there in the previous two months, and a student had been shot dead the preceeding weekend.

University officials also claimed there had been an attempt by students some two weeks before to kidnap Soberon and hold him until authorities released a peasant leader and some 50 students arrested earlier. Militant students organized in self-styled Committees for Struggle charged the kidnap story was invented by university authorities to justify the unprecedented call for police intervention.

(According to the newsletter Latin America Aug. 17, the alleged kidnap attempt involved not Soberon but an official in his office, and the assailants were said to have been "porras," mercenary thugs usually employed by right-wing elements. Soberon's office reportedly admitted porras had been involved but claimed they had been working for leftists.)

Soberon's resort to police action was protested Aug. 10 by the UNAM professors' union, which warned the incident "could give the authorities a pretext to bring repression to the university."

Politics & Government

Election law reform. Congress had approved a number of reforms in the national election laws, the Times of the Americas reported Jan. 24.

The reforms included awarding of free radio and television time to all parties, reduction of the minimum age for election to the Senate from 35 to 30 and to the Chamber of Deputies from 30 to 21, and provisions for awarding more seats in the lower house to the small and virtually powerless opposition groups.

Under the old proportional representation law, any political party gaining 2.5% of the national vote received a block of five Chamber seats. Every additional half per cent entitled the party to another seat, to a maximum of 20. Under the reformed law, the maximum was raised to 25 and the base required for the first five seats was reduced to 1.5%.

Opposition parties charged the reform was only token, since it did not give them an opportunity to have a reasonable constituency in the Chamber. The ruling Institutional Revolutionary party (PRI) controlled all 178 Chamber seats elected in individual districts, leaving for the opposition only the few seats awarded by proportional representation. The PRI also controlled the presidency and all 60 seats in the Senate.

Ex-president scores corruption. Ex-President Emilio Portes Gil broke a long political silence April 11 to criticize government corruption and call for strict application of the law against "those who defraud the people [and] oppress the peasants."

"The immorality we have reached has no parallel in our national history," Portes Gil said in a speech to some 2,000 peasants in Morelos, 62 miles from Mexico City, commemorating the 54th anniversary of the assassination of revolutionary leader Emiliano Zapata. "The flag of the Mexican revolution is used for illegal enrichment, while the entire country remains poor and exploited," Portes Gil asserted.

The ex-president specifically attacked officials of state agrarian banks, who allegedly "robbed and defrauded the impoverished peasants of the republic." He said numerous cases of corruption, including a recent $1.6 million fraud in the Yucatan Agrarian Bank had been denounced to authorities, but officials had not pressed any investigations.

Ex-presidents had traditionally refused to make political statements, El Nacional of Caracas reported April 12.

Another former president, Miguel Aleman, had angrily denied reports that in 1948 he had planned with his foreign minister, Jaime Torres Bodet, to allow U.S. oil companies to return to Mexico and compete freely with the state concern Pemex, set up with an oil monopoly when the industry was nationalized 10 years earlier. The reports, cited Feb. 2 with Aleman's denial, had arisen from publication in the U.S. of State Department papers for the period.

Economist Jesus Silva Herzog, said to be largely responsible for drafting the nationalization documents, said Aleman had signed exploration contracts with U.S. companies which had cost Mexico $24 million to rescind 20 years later. These contracts allegedly were a substitute for Aleman's original plan, which was stopped by nationalist opposition in Mexico. The Mexico City newspaper Excelsior had published other documents purporting to show that another ex-president, the late Manuel Avila Camacho, in office before Aleman, was also implicated in plans to allow U.S. oil companies to return to Mexico, it was reported Feb. 2.

PRI wins elections. The ruling Revolutionary Institutional party (PRI) won an overwhelming majority July 1 in elections for 194 federal deputies, seven state governors and 87 mayors.

The final count gave the PRI 69.55% of the total vote and the major opposition group, the conservative National Action party (PAN), 14.74%. The PRI took 189 of the 194 elective seats in the Chamber of Deputies, to four for the PAN and one for the Authentic Party of the Mexican Revolution. The PAN was entitled to the maximum 25 additional Chamber seats awarded by proportional representation, since its share of the vote exceeded 11½%.

Initial reports said voter abstention was low, but a report by the newsletter Latin America July 13 asserted it may have been as high as the 35% recorded in 1970. The government had tried to stimulate interest by a series of electoral reforms and a vigorous voter registration drive.

PAN leader José Angel Conchello charged July 4 that "electoral chieftainism has gained control of the entire republic, and the elections were characterized by disorganization and anarchy." PAN officials said they would contest results in 30 election districts.

Finance minister replaced. Finance Minister Hugo Margain, reported to be at odds with President Luis Echeverria, resigned for "health reasons" May 29 and was replaced by Jose Lopez Portillo, an administrator considered loyal to the president.

The development caused an outcry from private business, which charged the government's "vague" policies had caused agricultural production to fall and inflation to accelerate. The Chamber of Commerce accused the government June 2 of "buying inflation" with its recent importation of $320 million worth of wheat, corn, powdered milk and other food items. There were reports June 9 of hoarding of U.S. dollars, leading to fears of a devaluation of the peso. Lopez Portillo charged the hoarding was the work of "cowards, catastrophists and satanists."

Margain was reported to have disagreed strongly with the government's policy of intervening in the private sector by purchasing shares in private firms.

Lopez Portillo, a former aide to ex-President Gustavo Diaz Ordaz, was replaced as director of the National Electricity Commission by Arsenio Farel, president of the Sugar Chamber and a former law partner of Echeverria's brother, it was reported May 29.

Margain was reported June 22 to have been named ambassador to Great Britain.

Tabasco, Yucatan riots. Troops moved into two southern communities—Comalcalco in Tabasco state and Merida in Yucatan state—to restore order after bloody weekend riots over political disputes, the Miami Herald reported Sept. 26.

The mayor's office in Comalcalco reported three persons had been killed Sept. 23 when demonstrators stormed government offices to protest a nomination for the mayoral election in

November. In Merida, weekend rioters had protested the removal of the local mayor for alleged mishandling of government funds.

Foreign Relations & Trade

Echeverria on world tour. President Luis Echeverria Alvarez visited six countries on three continents March 29-April 26, on what he called a "mission of peace" to promote Mexican political and economic interests and to defend the position of Third World countries against pressure from the great powers.

He visited Canada, Great Britain, Belgium, France, the Soviet Union and China. The highlight of the tour was said to be the agreement of France and China to sign the second protocol of the Treaty of Tlatelolco, under which nuclear powers pledged not to use or threaten to use nuclear arms in Latin America.

The tour reportedly was calculated to assert Mexico's independence from the U.S. by including visits to the three major world groupings outside it—the Soviet Union, China and the European Economic Community (EEC).

(Echeverria met with U.S. Presidential adviser Henry Kissinger shortly before beginning his trip but did not release details of the talks.)

The tour was also intended to build support for Echeverria among Mexican leftists and strengthen the president in his battle for reform against the right, the London newsletter Latin America reported March 30. Echeverria was the first Mexican chief executive to visit Moscow and Peking, and the first Latin American president to visit China since the Communist takeover there in 1949.

Echeverria was in Canada March 29–April 2, conferring with Prime Minister Pierre Elliott Trudeau and other officials on ways to strengthen ties between their countries, particularly through increased trade and economic cooperation. He urged the Canadian Parliament March 30 to work for coordination of Mexican and Canadian efforts to control foreign investments and curb the powers of multinational corporations. Echeverria urged in Toronto March 31 that Canada and Mexico jointly oppose any attempts by the U.S. Senate to erect protectionist trade barriers.

A joint communiqué issued by Echeverria and Trudeau April 2 supported Mexican initiatives for a United Nations charter of economic rights and duties for all countries. Before departing for Europe, Echeverria said that Cuba should be readmitted to the Organization of American States (OAS).

Echeverria arrived in England April 2 and was greeted officially by Queen Elizabeth the next day. He conferred April 4 with Prime Minister Edward Heath, reportedly urging closer ties between the EEC and Latin American regional trade organizations, and asking British support for his proposed U.N. charter. Echeverria said April 6 that Mexico supported other Latin American nations claiming 200-mile offshore territorial limits.

Echeverria toured Belgium April 6-9. He met with Premier Edmond Leburton, other Belgian officials and EEC aides, asking for closer trade relations and gaining Belgian support for the proposed U.N. charter.

During his visit to France April 9-12, Echeverria conferred with President Georges Pompidou, who agreed with unspecified "reservations" to sign the Tlatelolco protocol. However, observers noted that the French Cabinet had not yet approved the move. France also agreed April 10 to grant Mexico an unspecified loan, but stressed the credit would be consistent with EEC investments in Latin America and would not give Mexico special privileges that might alienate other countries.

Echeverria met April 11 with Argentine ex-President Juan Perón, who flew to Paris to confer with him. Perón said he shared Echeverria's dissatisfaction with the structure of the OAS and supported his call for international control of multinational corporations.

(The Spanish government issued a formal protest April 14 against assertions by Echeverria in Great Britain and France that Mexico would continue to deny recognition to the Franco government. Mexico recognized the Spanish republican government in exile, which had its seat in Mexico City.)

Echeverria visited the Soviet Union April 12-19, talking with Communist party General Secretary Leonid Brezhnev and other officials on ways to increase the dwindling trade between the two countries. He reportedly asked for Soviet adherence to the Tlatelolco protocol, but did not obtain it.

Echeverria toured China April 19-24, conferring with Premier Chou En-lai and other officials. The two countries signed a one-year commercial treaty April 22 which granted mutual seaport facilities and gave Mexico most-favored-nation trade status with China. China also agreed to sign the Tlatelolco protocol.

Foreign investment bill passed. Congress had approved the government's moderate but controversial bill regulating foreign investment, it was reported Feb. 23. U.S. investors had opposed some of the bill's provisions, but the government claimed they entailed no substantial change in economic policy.

The bill reportedly required that foreign investors complement Mexican capital rather than displace it; open new fields of business and industrial activity; mix their capital with Mexican capital; give Mexican citizens first opportunity for available jobs and use foreign techniques and employes on a limited basis; share advanced technology and improved technical methods with Mexico; produce goods for export; use domestic products and raw materials as much as possible; and use foreign financing rather than make demands on limited Mexican credit.

The non-retroactive bill was the first to control the extent and nature of foreign capital invested in Mexico. Foreign investment was currently estimated at $3.2 billion–$3.5 billion, about 80% of which was U.S. capital. Mexico said foreign capital represented about 8% of its private investment and about 5% of its total investment, the Wall Street Journal reported March 21.

Mexican authorities had charged the projected withdrawal from Mexico of H. J. Heinz Co., the U.S. food processing firm, was a reaction against the foreign investment bill, the London newsletter Latin America reported Feb. 9. Heinz, however, said it would withdraw because of "low returns." Mexico charged Heinz had bought its way into the country at a "ridiculously low price" nine years before, and had neglected the land on which it grew its crops.

Trade relations. President Arturo A. Molina of El Salvador had visited Mexico and agreed with Mexican officials to form a joint mixed commission to conduct a thorough review of bilateral trade relations, it was reported Jan. 17. A group of Mexican industrialists had subsequently visited El Salvador and pledged to manufacture products not presently produced in Central America.

The Foreign Trade Institute said exports had risen by 22.9% in 1972, it was reported March 3. Mexico again had a large trade surplus with other Latin American Free Trade Association countries in 1972, with exports of $140.7 million and imports of $119.7 million, it was reported March 9.

The National Bank said Mexican industry would spend $670 million to import machine tools over the next decade unless a local machine tool industry began to develop, it was reported Feb. 16.

The private firm Cementos Anahuac del Golfo, in which the state firm Somex had had a large holding, had signed a contract to export cement to the U.S. over the next six years, it was reported March 2. Anahuac would triple its capacity and earn more than $80 million a year in foreign currency.

Mexican private businessmen had been negotiating with Uruguayan businessmen over possible investment of $100 million in Uruguay, it was reported March 9. A Mexican trade mission reportedly had made a discreet visit to Uruguay in December 1972 but had refused to talk to Cabinet ministers because it considered the current government there "only transitional."

A Mexican trade delegation had been visiting Cuba to sell more agricultural and industrial goods in exchange for Cuban nickel and rum, it was reported March 16. Under a signed agreement, Cuba would buy $6.4 million worth of Mexican exports.

A new company had been formed with West German and Mexican capital to market public sector products internationally, the newsletter Latin America reported March 16. The new firm, Exmex, would concentrate on basic commodities and railway rolling stock. It would operate on a worldwide basis, but would be concerned first with solving the imbalance of trade between Mexico and West Germany.

Japan's Mitsubishi Corp. said in Tokyo that it had purchased Exportadora de Sal, a salt manufacturing company in Mexico, from National Bulk Carriers Inc. of the U.S. for about $20 million, the Wall Street Journal reported April 11. Mitsubishi said Exportadora had an annual production capacity of 4.5 million tons of salt, of which 2.8 million tons had been exported to Japan.

Industry and Commerce Minister Carlos Torres Manzo said exports of live cattle would be reduced by 24% and exports of dressed beef by 50% because of domestic shortages and rapidly rising local prices, it was reported June 19. Nearly all the exports went to the U.S. Mexican wholesale meat prices had risen by 11.8% since January.

U.S. immigration controversy. A furor had been touched off in the government and press by a U.S. news report describing an apparently illegal system under which Mexicans seized illegally entering the U.S. were removed to the interior of Mexico against their will, it was reported May 4.

The report, which appeared in the New York Times April 15, disclosed how Mexican and U.S. border officials put thousands of illegal emigrants annually on privately owned Mexican buses and airplanes which took them to the Mexican interior at their own expense. The report also disclosed that if the aliens paid off the bus and airline operators they were released at the Mexico-U.S. border or near it.

According to federal grand jury testimony in California and immigration authorities on both sides of the border, the aliens violated no Mexican law and thus should not have been transported hundreds of miles into Mexico before being released.

Mexican government sources said President Echeverria had ordered an investigation of the removal program, and had discussed the issue with President Nixon in Washington in June 1972.

U.S. plans desalination plant. The U.S. had decided to build the world's largest desalination plant to improve the quality of Colorado River waters flowing into Mexico, the Wall Street Journal reported June 4.

Planning of the plant, to cost an estimated $60 million–$70 million, was indirectly confirmed to U.S. congressmen by Interior Undersecretary Jack Horton, the Journal reported. The plan reportedly had been approved by Mexican officials, and enjoyed wide support in the U.S. Congress as the best solution to Mexico's decades-old complaint that farming in the Mexicali Valley in Baja California was being damaged by salinity in the lower Colorado.

As currently envisioned by the Interior Department's Office of Saline Water, the plant would remove about 90% of the salt from water in the channel draining the Wellton-Mohawk irrigation project of southern Arizona. It would be capable of treating 130 million–140 million gallons of water daily.

Mexico and the U.S. Aug. 30 signed an agreement to reduce the Colorado's salinity.

The pact, signed in Mexico City, called for the U.S. to build a $67 million desalting plant in southern Arizona and a $36 million drainage system to dump extracted salt into the Gulf of California. The project's overall cost, $115 million, was substantially higher than earlier estimates.

The project, which required approval by the U.S. Congress, would not be completed before 1978. In the meantime, the U.S. would supply clean water to the 75,000 acres of Mexican land needing Colorado River irrigation, by diluting the normal flow of the river with fresh water from storage basins.

200-mile sea limit pledged. President Echeverria reiterated his intention to extend Mexico's 12-mile offshore territorial limits to 200 miles, it was reported

June 29. Seafood industry officials in the U.S. said the move would cost the industry $35 million–$40 million a year, since it would place most of the rich shrimp beds off Mexico's southern coast off limits to foreign boats.

Guyana ties set. Mexico agreed to exchange ambassadors with Guyana, the last independent country in the Western Hemisphere with which it did not have diplomatic relations, it was reported March 16.

East German ties. Mexico and East Germany established diplomatic relations June 5.

Economic & Other Developments

Inflation at 8½%. Inflation during the first four months of 1973 had reached 8½%, more than the rise planned for the entire year, the newsletter Latin America reported June 8.

The government Feb. 12 had devalued the Mexican peso to maintain parity with the devalued U.S. dollar. The move was followed by an increase in food prices, with some items rising 50% or more. According to news reports March 23, food-price patrols of policewomen had begun to operate in Mexico City to keep shopkeepers from raising prices excessively.

Old economic problems were simultaneously emerging, including rising foreign indebtedness and a chronic trade deficit, now about $1.25 billion a year, according to the newsletter.

Government statistics reported May 25 showed 45%–50% of Mexico's families had incomes of less than $80 a month. Statistics published by the Autonomous National University reportedly showed that 9.6 million of the 24 million citizens of working age were unemployed.

Anti-inflation measures announced—The government had announced a "second phase of its economic policy," effectively an anti-inflation program, at the end of July. The 16-point plan, reported by Latin America Aug. 3, called for a redirection of public investment into short-term projects, particularly in agriculture; stricter control over prices, especially of basic necessities; and a tighter grip on monetary policy.

The immediate causes of Mexico's inflationary spiral were external, according to Latin America. The Mexican peso had been adversely affected by the devaluation of the U.S. dollar (the U.S. was Mexico's most important trade partner). In addition, Mexico had suffered a poor wheat harvest and had to import grain at a time of soaring world prices; it had become a substantial oil importer for the first time as the world energy crisis developed; and it had undergone an economic boom when the price of capital goods from abroad was surging upwards.

U.S., other firms struck. More than 200,000 workers in some 1,000 concerns across Mexico struck early in October, gaining 20% wage increases. The firms affected included such U.S.-based companies as General Motors, Coca-Cola, PepsiCo, General Tire and Uniroyal.

The settlement, reported by the London newsletter Latin America Oct. 19, was backed by the government, which publicly supported union demands for 33% increases but privately urged employers to grant the 20% hike. The wage demands were based on Mexico's annual inflation rate, officially estimated at 11%, but unofficially estimated at 40%, Latin America reported.

Other economic developments. Among 1973's economic developments:

The automotive industry, including the assembly of trucks and manufacture of components, grew by about 20% in 1972, it was reported Feb. 16.

The Mexican Workers Confederation, affiliated with the governing Revolutionary Institutional party, held a demonstration in Mexico City Feb. 25 as part of a campaign to establish a five-day, 40-hour week. Most Mexican workers worked six days a week.

The state oil concern Pémex had found large oil deposits in the Gulf of Mexico off the coast of Tabasco, according to a report June 8.

MEXICO

The government planned to develop the coal mines of Oaxaca and Veracruz states and to increase production at other mines in hopes that coal could replace oil as Mexico's main fossil fuel source of electric power, it was reported Aug. 17.

The World Bank granted Mexico loans of $90 million for a Mexico City water supply project and $110 million for agriculture and livestock programs, it was reported June 19.

The World Bank Sept. 6 lent Mexico $70 million to help finance the huge Lazaro Cardenas-Las Truchas steel plant, on Mexico's Pacific coast, which would have an annual production capacity of 1.1 million tons of light finished steel products. A $54 million loan for the plant by the Inter-American Development Bank (IDB) was reported Oct. 26.

The IDB Aug. 30 had announced a $14 million loan toward a $30 million government project to rehabilitate the Juarez Valley irrigation district, raising its net arable area from 42,000 to 60,500 acres, with an increase in the water supply from 199 million to 355 million cubic meters.

The Wells Fargo Bank of San Francisco and the U.S. Export-Import Bank had signed a $54.2 million loan to pay for a $60.2 million sale of U.S. equipment to Mexico for construction of Mexico's first nuclear power plant at Laguna Verde, on the Gulf of Mexico, it was reported Sept. 21.

The European Bank of Tokyo, the Bank of Tokyo, the Industrial Bank of Japan and several European banks had granted the state oil concern Pemex a $50 million loan for unspecified projects, it was reported Sept. 28. (Trade between Mexico and Japan had increased by 23% in the past three years, according to a report Aug. 6.)

The government had acquired full control of Perkins Motors, among the nation's largest manufacturers of diesel engines, by purchasing 60% of its stock held by Chrysler of Mexico, an affiliate of the U.S.-based Chrysler Corp., it was reported Oct. 2.

527 die in Mexican quake, rains. A severe earthquake Aug. 28, preceded by torrential rains Aug. 17-27, killed at least 527 persons in central Mexico.

The quake, measuring 6.5 on the Richter scale, demolished hundreds of buildings and left thousands homeless. Unsafe buildings in a 300-square-mile area were being razed Aug. 30. Hardest hit by the quake were the States of Puebla, Veracruz and Oaxaca.

The heavy rains, worst in 30 years, left 200,000 homeless in north and central Mexico.

Nicaragua

Quake toll 6,000. An official U.N. report on the Managua earthquake of Dec. 23, 1972 said that a "realistic" fatility figure was 6,000, Latin America reported Feb. 9. The estimate contradicted a Jan. 7 assertion by a government spokesman that more than 10,000 people had been killed.

The spokesman, Ivan Osorio, said 10,000–12,000 victims had been buried by relatives or by municipal and military authorities, and "as workers clear the rubble, they keep finding more and more bodies."

The U.N. report said 20,000 persons had been injured in the quakes, 300,000 left homeless, and 60,000 without work. About 90% of the city's commercial distribution capacity was reported destroyed, and total damage was put at $772 million. The report said the earthquakes would also be disastrous for Central American trade and the Central American Common Market.

Galo Plaza, secretary general of the Organization of American States, said after studying the effects of the quakes Jan. 10 that 50% of Managua's commercial establishments had been destroyed, leaving 60,000 persons unemployed. He estimated that more than 70% of the city's housing had been destroyed, and that the remainder had suffered varying degrees of damage. The Housing Bank calculated the cost of rebuilding in the housing sector at $600 million.

Most of Nicaragua's industry, located outside the capital, remained unaffected by the earthquakes. The agricultural sector also suffered little damage, but it had been in crisis at the time the quakes struck. According to the New York Times Jan. 3, drought had destroyed 80% of the corn crop, 35% of bean and rice production and 20% of the country's cotton.

Despite Managua's history of earthquake disasters, the capital would be rebuilt in the same area, according to Gen. Anastasio Somoza Debayle, Nicaragua's military ruler, Jan. 9. However, the city's commercial center would be moved about six miles from its former location. Maurice J. Williams, coordinator of the $10.6 million U.S. relief program, said Jan. 9 that it would be three years before the country returned to normal.

Steps taken by the government to facilitate the capital's reconstruction included extension of the workweek from 48 to 60 hours, adoption of a 10% export duty and a two-year rent freeze, abolition of tax exemptions for two years, and a levy of one month's wages on public employes during 1973, according to a Jan. 8 report.

Fewer than a quarter of Managua's inhabitants remained in the capital as workers continued to clear the rubble and bury the dead. Some essential services were gradually restored. Some looting continued, with police reporting Jan. 3 that National Guard troops had killed 16 looters during the previous five days.

Most aid entering Nicaragua was said to be from the U.S., and most of the U.S. citizens at work in the capital were military personnel, according to a Jan. 10 report. U.S. experts had repaired the city's water, electricity and communications systems, and both the Air Force and Army had flown in field hospitals.

In an appeal before the U.N. Economic Commission for Latin America reported Jan. 19, Labor Minister Juan Jose Martinez asked foreign governments and international agencies to donate $1 billion for the reconstruction of Managua. The U.S. Agency for International Development Feb. 9 announced approval of a $15 million loan for cleanup and repair work in the city.

Quake stirs political dispute. Political tension mounted in January as opposition leaders charged that Somoza had used the disaster to consolidate his hold on the country, and that his regime's traditional corruption had extended to distribution of relief supplies from abroad. The controversy eventually centered around the powerful office created Jan. 6 to direct national reconstruction, which Somoza was expected to assume.

Officially, Nicaragua was ruled by a civilian triumvirate and a constituent assembly, both controlled by members of Somoza's Liberal party, in accordance with a pact reached in 1971 by the Liberals and the opposition, the Conservatives. Since stepping down as president in May 1972, however, Somoza had remained in effective control of the country as commander of the National Guard, the only armed force.

Immediately after the earthquakes, Somoza had appointed himself president of the National Emergency Committee and declared martial law, officially making himself the country's chief executive. He and his wife had subsequently directed all relief operations, leaving the civilian branches of government in the background.

According to La Prensa of Buenos Aires Jan. 2, Conservative leaders had complained that Somoza had deliberately excluded them from relief and reconstruction operations, using the earthquake tragedy to bolster his popular support for the projected 1974 elections. They also charged that relief operations were slow and inefficient.

Conservative leader Fernando Aguero threatened Jan. 10 to resign from the civilian triumvirate and his followers threatened to quit the constituent assembly if the assembly named Somoza to head the National Reconstruction Ministry, which it created Jan. 6 to act as Nicaragua's highest authority during its period of reconstruction. The ministry would not only direct the reconstruction but hold executive power in domestic and foreign affairs. Aguero charged Somoza's nomination to the post would "institutionalize a dictatorship, in violation of the Constitution."

Police chief fired—Somoza had fired the commander of the Managua police force, following reports that policemen and National Guardsmen had been seen looting in the capital's destroyed downtown business district, the Washington Post reported Jan. 10. El Nacional of Caracas Jan. 14 cited reports linking the commander's dismissal to an alleged attempt on Somoza's life, but the reports were denied by the government.

Somoza Jan. 19 heatedly denied foreign news reports that National Guardsmen were stealing relief supplies sent from abroad. "The help a country gives us does not permit it to humiliate this country," he asserted.

According to the London newsletter Latin America Feb. 9, there had been some black marketeering of relief supplies, but this had been limited because of the international attention focused on Nicaragua. However, the National Guard had made large profits reselling in the provinces goods looted from wrecked Managua shops, the newsletter reported.

The government had also rejected help from other Nicaraguan institutions in organizing relief work, thus insuring for itself and the Liberal party all credit for the work, the newsletter reported.

Newspaper censored—Gen. Somoza imposed strict censorship on the Managua newspaper Novedades after it published a report criticizing the quality of construction in Managua, the Miami Herald reported Jan. 23. The censorship was considered surprising because Novedades was directed by one of Somoza's nephews.

U.S. envoy a suicide. The U.S. consul in Managua, James P. Hargrove, had committed suicide Jan. 6, police reported Jan. 8. He had reportedly been under medical supervision, suffering from depression since the earthquakes struck.

Aguero replaced in triumvirate. The National Assembly March 1 dismissed Fernando Aguero, leader of the opposition Conservative party, from the triumvirate which nominally had ruled Nicaragua for nearly a year. Aguero was replaced by Edmundo Paguaga Irias, a leader of a dissident Conservative faction who had been expelled from the party 10 days earlier.

Aguero's dismissal, decided by a 63-27 vote, effectively though not formally ended the 1971 pact between the Conservatives and the ruling Liberals, which established the Liberal-dominated triumvirate and National Assembly to govern until a new president was elected in 1974. Ex-President Anastasio Somoza Debayle had transferred power to the two bodies in May 1972, but had effectively continued to run the country as commander of its only armed force, the National Guard. He had ruled openly since the December 1972 Managua earthquake disaster.

Aguero earlier had threatened to resign from the Conservative seat in the triumvirate and refuse to name a replacement—thus rendering the body ineffective—if Somoza were named to head the new, powerful National Reconstruction Ministry. The Assembly, however, had undercut the threat by voting itself, instead of the individual parties, the power to dismiss or replace members of the triumvirate.

Paguaga Irias and other dissident Conservatives had been expelled from the party because the party reportedly "lost confidence in them." The Assembly, however, refused to recognize their dismissal, and approved their resolution to remove Aguero from the triumvirate on grounds that he had illegally called the meeting at which they were expelled. The Assembly also banned all political meetings or acts during the current state of emergency, effectively barring the Conservative national convention scheduled April 1.

Aguero had been reported censured by the Assembly Feb. 22 for "sending false information abroad." The charge presumably referred to his publicly stated contention that the government had improperly administered relief funds following the earthquake disaster.

'74 elections reaffirmed. The Liberal and Conservative parties reaffirmed their 1971 pact establishing three years of ostensible rule by triumvirate and setting presidential elections for 1974, it was reported June 8.

The new agreement, reached by Gen. Anastasio Somoza, the military dictator, and Edmundo Paguaga Irias, the new Conservative leader, followed the dismissal from the triumvirate of Fernando Aguero and his replacement, both in the triumvirate and the Conservative leadership, by Paguaga Irias.

Aguero formed the new Popular Conservative Movement, taking a large section of his old party with him. Another Conservative offshoot, National Conservative Action, was led by Pedro Chamorro, publisher of the opposition newspaper La Prensa.

The Conservative split left the Liberals, under Somoza's leadership, as the only strong political movement in Nicaragua. Somoza, whose family controlled much of the Nicaraguan economy, was virtually assured of victory in the 1974 elections, according to most sources.

However, some opposition to Somoza was surfacing due to the reported corruption of the Liberal party and of the National Guard, which Somoza commanded. Reconstruction of Managua, the earthquake-ravaged capital, was said to be proceeding very slowly, and refugee camps outside the city were reported becoming permanent slums.

The government had failed to rebuild, even temporarily, the city's business center. A long drought ended in late May, but the torrential rains that followed it brought increased misery to the thousands of citizens living in tents.

The International Development Association, a member of the World Bank Group, May 10 approved credit equivalent to $20 million to help support Managua's reconstruction. The International Monetary Fund had authorized a

$14.4 million loan, reported May 10, and the Inter-American Development Bank a $16.7 million credit, announced April 26.

Reconstruction profiting charged. National Guard Commander Gen. Anastasio Somoza Debayle, the nation's strongman, and a number of his associates were accused of personally profiting from reconstruction work in Managua, the Miami Herald reported Aug. 23.

Local construction firms complained the government had awarded a contract to build a prefabricated children's home to the Miami company Panelfab and its Nicaraguan affiliate, formed recently by a member of the ruling triumvirate, for about $1 million, although local firms had bid less than half that amount. Somoza reportedly took responsibility for awarding the contract.

Other firms claimed they were not given a chance to bid when a Brazilian government credit for heavy equipment was used to buy trucks from a company owned by Somoza. (Somoza also owned a construction company, established after the earthquakes.)

Still other complaints followed a land sale by Cornelio Hueck, president of the National Assembly. Official records showed Hueck purchased the land for less than $20,000 and sold it less than two months later to the National Housing Bank for about $1 million.

Port loan set. The World Bank Feb. 1 announced approval of an $11 million loan for the expansion and modernization of the Pacific port of Corinto, Nicaragua's only deep water port and its main outlet for agricultural exports.

IDB loan. The Inter-American Development Bank Sept. 27 approved an $8.3 million loan to Nicaragua to help finance a land settlement project in a 123,-500 acre zone of the department of Zelaya, on the Atlantic coast.

The IDB had allocated $54 million toward reconstruction of Managua, according to a June 29 report.

Press law passed. The National Assembly approved a controversial new press law imposing stiff fines on newsmen who "defamed" government officials or institutions, it was reported Oct. 6.

The law, denounced as an attack on press freedom by the opposition, the national press, the Central American Association of Journalists and the Inter-American Press Association, was passed 52-0 as legislators of the opposition Conservative party refused to vote. The ruling Liberal party held 60 of the Assembly's 100 seats.

The legislation reportedly was introduced by the government after the principal opposition newspaper, La Prensa, published details of how certain public officials made private fortunes following the December 1972 earthquake disaster.

Luis Palais Debayle, editor of the Somoza family's newspaper Novedades, resigned as president of the Central American Association of Journalists after the group criticized the press law, it was reported Oct. 12.

Guerrilla leader killed. Carlos Fonseca, leader of the Sandinista Liberation Front, a left-wing guerrilla group, was killed in a clash with troops in September, according to his father, reported Oct. 21, and President Somoza, reported Nov. 9. (The Sandinistas reportedly had been inactive for the past three years.)

Fonseca's body reportedly had been in the Managua morgue since Sept. 18. The army had announced Sept. 19 that six guerrillas, including an unidentified member of the Sandinista group, had been killed in recent clashes.

Panama

U.S.-Panamanian relations. A report released Jan. 4 by the U.S. House of Representatives Panama Canal subcommittee charged the U.S. had failed to react decisively to "hostile" actions by the Panamanian government and said it might be necessary to halt economic aid to Panama to guarantee continued U.S. operation and control of the Panama Canal.

The subcommittee chairman, Rep. John M. Murphy (D, N.Y.), said in releasing the report that "a series of hostile actions against the U.S. including the armed takeover of American businesses are symbols of the loss of American rights and the deterioration of our position on the Isthmus of Panama."

The report noted that the U.S. had given the current Panamanian government more than $200 million in aid since 1968 and that "loans and other economic aid in the tens of millions are presently in the works to help Panama" despite "federal laws which explicitly forbid economic assistance and loans to countries" that seize U.S. property or fail to take adequate steps to prevent drugs from being smuggled from their territory into the U.S.

The U.S. State Department, the report charged, had "put a higher priority on placating an increasingly hostile and demanding regime in Panama than it [had] on taking a firm stand against a government that is a major factor in allowing the international flow of heroin and cocaine presently inundating the U.S." There was "overwhelming" evidence that the Panamanian government "has not only failed to stop the transshipment of drugs but is, in part, part of the conspiracy to do just the opposite," the report alleged.

The report said the subcommittee would study "all current aid and loan programs to Panama to determine if the laws of the U.S. have been violated and the will of Congress thwarted. If this is found to be true, the subcommittee will consider recommending to Congress the reduction or termination of all aid programs to Panama as well as other sanctions. The continued operation and control of the Panama Canal by the U.S. may well depend on such actions."

In a related development reported Jan. 27, Panama announced it would no longer refund the duty paid by Canal Zone residents buying foreign (non-U.S.-made) automobiles. The action was allowed by a previously unenforced agreement between Panama and the U.S.

Canal talks renewal asked. Panama had asked the U.S. to resume negotiations on the future of the Panama Canal and Zone, deadlocked for more than a year, the U.S. State Department announced July 3.

A State Department spokesman said the U.S. was studying an invitation by Panamanian Foreign Minister Juan Antonio Tack to continue the talks. U.S. officials were reported encouraged by the tone of Tack's letter and by the recent decrease in anti-U.S. editorials in the controlled Panamanian press.

Chief U.S. negotiator Robert B. Anderson had resigned July 2.

A preliminary report to the Western Hemisphere Affairs Subcommittee of the U.S. Senate's Foreign Relations Committee recommended that the U.S. grant Panama sovereignty over the Canal Zone to demonstrate a "new spirit of global cooperation," La Prensa of Buenos Aires reported Aug. 6.

The report, prepared by James D. Grant, an aide to Sen. Gale McGee (D, Wyo.), the subcommittee chairman, stressed that the canal was not vital to U.S. security in either military or economic terms. To Panama, however, sovereignty over the canal represented freedom from foreign domination, the report asserted.

McGee said he did not agree with every position in the report, but considered it important.

Prospects for a resumption of the talks had been hurt by the Watergate scandals, particularly by reports in the U.S. press (later discredited) that a Central Intelligence Agency plot had been considered in the White House to assassinate Gen. Omar Torrijos, Panama's military ruler, the Miami Herald reported Aug. 7.

3-day canal-pilot walkout. Ship traffic through the Panama Canal was virtually halted Aug. 25-27 as U.S. pilots remained off their jobs to protest the dismissal by the Panama Canal Co. of five officers of the Panama Canal Pilots Association, the pilots' bargaining agent.

The Panama Canal Co., a U.S. government agent, had asked a federal court to find the association and its officers in contempt for failing to obey a company-obtained restraining order against an ongoing slowdown by the pilots. The pilots agreed to return to work after the company withdrew the court action.

The slowdown, begun in mid-August and preceded by another slowdown in early June, protested alleged company extension of working hours, changing of operating procedures, and failure to recruit qualified pilots to meet the current pilot shortage.

U.S. canal talks resume. U.S. Ambassador at Large Ellsworth Bunker conferred with Panamanian officials in Panama City Nov. 27-Dec. 3, resuming the deadlocked talks on a new treaty for the Panama Canal and Zone.

Bunker and Panamanian Foreign Minister Juan Antonio Tack said in a joint statement Dec. 3 that their contact constituted "a significant effort on the part of both parties to try to achieve a just and equitable agreement." Bunker would return to Panama later in December to continue the talks.

During his visit to Panama, Bunker also met with the military ruler, Gen. Omar Torrijos, and President Demetrio Lakas, Vice President Arturo Sucre, and Panama's major canal negotiators, Carlos Lopez Guevara and Diogenes de la Rosa.

The sessions were regarded as orientation for Bunker, with no immediate effort toward achieving a new canal treaty.

Bunker had said on arrival in Panama Nov. 26 that he hoped for "the promptest possible negotiation of a new and modern treaty arrangement," which would "require flexibility ... on the part of the negotiators and understanding on the part of the public." Torrijos had been less conciliatory, telling the press the same day: "This is the last chance. This will be the last peaceful negotiation. If it fails we will have no other recourse but to fight."

Panamanian officials reportedly felt a new confidence regarding the canal, attributed to the success of the U.N. Security Council's meeting in Panama City in March, the appointment of Henry Kissinger as U.S. secretary of state and a conviction that Washington could not long delay decisions on building a new sea-level canal and renovating the existing one.

However, the U.S. and Panamanian negotiating positions were still far apart, according to the Washington Post Nov. 28. Among the major disagreements:

■ Panama demanded full jurisdiction over the Canal Zone within five years,

while Washington proposed a 15-year gradual handover.
■ Panama requested the progressive elimination of U.S. military presence in the zone and immediate Panamanian participation in defense of the waterway. It also sought a drastic reduction in the area used by the military—particularly in such valuable urbanized areas as Balboa—and U.S. payment for the privilege of maintaining troops on Panamanian territory.
■ Panama sought a role in deciding where and how the U.S. might build a new sea-level canal, and prior agreement on how long the U.S. should administer it.
■ Panama wanted U.S. rental of the canal raised sharply from the current $1.9 million a year.

Drug curbs successful. U.S. Drug Enforcement Administration sources said recent Panamanian anti-narcotics efforts had been so successful that heroin merchants had begun to avoid Panama City, once a major transshipment point for U.S.-bound narcotics, the New York Times reported Sept. 23.

Panama authorities had made major seizures of marijuana and cocaine, reversing what U.S. officials had seen as a policy of indifference toward the narcotics traffic. Panama was stung by allegations in the U.S. that high government officials, including Foreign Minister Juan Antonio Tack, were engaged directly or indirectly in drug smuggling.

(U.S. officials had admitted there was no actual evidence linking Tack to the narcotics trade, and had apologized to the foreign minister.)

Chiriqui leftists dismissed. Commercial and landed interests in Chiriqui, alarmed at what they called an attempted Communist takeover, had forced Gen. Torrijos to replace the governor, the mayor of the principal city, and virtually every official with any authority in the province, the Miami Herald reported Aug. 17.

Torrijos claimed the restructuring was due to a "complete absence of authority" in the provincial administration, which he claimed had failed to follow his government's guidelines. However, the crisis actually stemmed from unease over Communist influence in provincial government departments and schools, and recent clashes between rival student groups, the Herald reported.

Conservative and left-wing students clashed in June in the province's four high schools and the branch of the National University at David, the provincial capital, over a youth festival promoted annually, the Herald reported. The problem worsened in July as leftist students prepared for a massive rally in support of Cuban Premier Fidel Castro July 26, the anniversary of the revolutionary assault on the Moncada barracks.

Torrijos reportedly intervened after the David chamber of commerce adopted a strongly worded resolution supporting the "movement of students, parents, teachers, workers and the general public against the attempt of Communist elements to undermine the government and the free enterprise system." The July 26 parade was canceled and the sweeping administrative changes were ordered.

The Roman Catholic Church, in an episcopal declaration read Aug. 4 from pulpits throughout the country, noted the contrast between the "freedom of action and expression" enjoyed by Panamanian leftists and the "serious and lamentable limitations on other groups to express their viewpoints before public opinion." The church called on Torrijos to "protect the rights of all citizens."

Mineral deposits discovered. Recent discoveries of copper, zinc, gold, silver and other metals promised to revolutionize Panama's economy, further divorcing it from its previous dependence on the Panama Canal, agriculture and banking, the Miami Herald reported July 17.

Pavonia S.A., a wholly owned subsidiary of the Canadian firm Canadian Javelin, Ltd., confirmed the discovery in Chiriqui Province of the world's richest copper deposits—an estimated 2.2 billion tons of ore assaying at an average of .81% copper for the first 15 years of mining. Canadian Javelin reportedly was assembling the $600 million capital needed to develop the deposits.

The government and the Canadian firm Canadian Javelin, Ltd. disagreed over whether Panama had granted a Javelin subsidiary, Bison Petroleum and Minerals Ltd., an exploration concession over an area Javelin said contained gold, silver and other metals, it was reported Oct. 25. The government denied Javelin's claim that the concession had been awarded June 21.

Bison Petroleum had said that it had acquired a 200,000 acre concession to explore and exploit gold, silver, zinc and other mineral deposits in Veraguas Province. Bison announced the concession contained at least 115,000 tons of gold-bearing ore at El Remance and about 30,000 tons of base metals at Hatillos.

The government had signed a four-year copper exploration contract with a Japanese consortium, Cobre Panama, for a 40,000 hectare area at Petaquilla in Colon Province, the London newsletter Latin America reported Nov. 2.

Other economic developments—The government Oct. 31 assumed control of Empresas Electricas de Chiriqui S.A., a utility in western Chiriqui Province, and its subsidiary Comunicaciones S.A., following a deadlock in negotiations for government purchase of the companies. A new state agency called the National Telecommunications Institute would operate the internal microwave telephone system and Telex service run by the firms.

The Inter-American Development Bank lent Panama $7.5 million to finance construction of drinking water and sewage systems.

Panama got a $115 million loan from an international banking consortium led by Citicorp International Bank, a subsidiary of the First National City Bank of New York, to be used primarily to refinance Panama's foreign debt, it was reported Oct. 26.

The World Bank lent Panama $30 million Nov. 29 to help finance electrification projects.

The Bank of Tokyo had opened a branch in Panama City in May to aid Japanese investments in mining, fishing, and car and electronic goods sales.

The government was involved in a dispute with local and foreign private businesses, particularly foreign banks, over a series of housing decrees which froze rents and banned evictions for three years and obliged the construction industry to build more low-cost rather than luxury housing, it was reported Nov. 28. More than $100 million in construction reportedly had been paralyzed due to the dispute.

Peru

U.S. tuna boats seized, fined. The navy seized 22 U.S.-owned tuna boats Jan. 10–22 for fishing within Peru's declared 200-mile offshore territorial limits. The boats were fined according to weight, forced to buy Peruvian fishing licenses and then released. The penalties were said to average $30,000 a boat, but one vessel, a California boat seized Jan. 20, reportedly paid $100,000 in fines and license fees.

A U.S. State Department spokesman said Jan. 19 that the U.S. had formally protested the seizures and put military sales to Peru under review. The U.S. recognized only a 12-mile territorial limit, and reimbursed boat owners who were fined for fishing within the 200-mile limit.

U.S. Rep. John M. Murphy (D, N.Y.) charged Jan. 18 that Peru had seized some of the tuna boats with destroyers and other ships leased from the U.S. Navy, and said he was introducing legislation in Congress directing the U.S. to take back ships used by foreign nations to seize other U.S. vessels. Ecuador used converted U.S. patrol boats to seize U.S. tuna vessels, Murphy charged.

Peruvian Fisheries Minister Javier Tantalean denied Jan. 20 that U.S.-leased ships were used to capture tuna boats. He said Murphy's proposed legislation reflected the thought of "a person who still believes in the 'big stick' policy." He added that 21 foreign vessels, including ones from Canada, the U.S., Ecuador, Japan and France, had voluntarily bought Peruvian fishing licenses in January.

Fishing industry nationalized. The government May 7 announced creation of a state monopoly, Pescaperu, to take control of the major portion of the ailing fishing industry.

Production of fishmeal and fish oil, the country's major source of export revenue, was nationalized, but the relatively minor food fishing sector was not.

The nationalized sectors involved some 90 private companies employing 27,000 fishermen and plant workers and operating 1,486 boats and 105 factories. Included among them were subsidiaries of such U.S. firms as International Proteins Corp., which listed its Peruvian assets at $11 million; Cargill Inc., with $7.3 million; and General Mills Inc., with about $1 million.

A government decree published May 8 said owners of expropriated property would receive 10% of the value in cash and 90% in nontransferable bonds, redeemable in 10 years at 6% interest. However, a spokesman for International Proteins in New York said it was unclear how the government would value the properties and whether the foreign companies would be compensated.

In announcing the nationalization, Fisheries Minister Javier Tantalean said the move was the only solution to the fishing industry's current indebtedness and to the crisis brought on by the disappearance of anchoveta from Peru's coastal waters in 1972.

Privately owned fishing and processing firms owed state banks the equivalent of $200 million, Tantalean asserted. He agreed with other officials that the industry's basic problem was overexpansion, and that it could get along with fewer fishmeal plants and only half as many fishing boats.

The nationalization reportedly caused alarm in other industries, particularly mining. The mining industry was troubled by another government decree, directing the larger companies to present programs for improved worker housing and welfare by June 30, it was reported May 10.

The government began gradually reducing the nation's fishing fleet following nationalization.

Cuba had bought 110 fishing vessels from Peru worth about $30 million, Latin America reported Jan. 12.

Exports of fish meal and oil earned $322 million in 1972 despite the drop in production caused by the disappearance of anchovy shoals, it was reported March 2. Manufactured goods earned a record $32.5 million, double the 1971 total.

Anchovy fishing was reported resumed March 9, but only from Monday to Friday and with a temporary catch limit of 50,000 tons for the entire fleet.

The government was using a Dutch credit of $13 million to build a pilot plant for experimenting with the processing of anchoveta, the anchovy found off the Peruvian coast, in a form suitable for human consumption, the newsletter Latin America reported Feb. 2. Anchoveta currently was used only to produce fishmeal. The government hoped tinned anchoveta might compete on world markets with sardines.

A new tuna fishing company with participation of both private and state capital had been set up to operate from the northern port of Zorritos, Latin America reported March 23.

Cerro de Pasco nationalized. The government Dec. 31 nationalized all properties of Cerro de Pasco Corp., the local affiliate of the U.S. copper firm Cerro Corp.

A government decree said Cerro de Pasco's mines were of "public and social interest" and charged that during its 55 years of operation the firm "systematically did not fulfill its obligations concerning the sanitary conditions, housing and safety of its workers." The decree alleged that Cerro was "incapable of financing projects of expansion which would assure future profitability" of its undertakings.

The decree, signed by President Juan Velasco Alvarado and all 15 Cabinet members, established a new state enterprise, Centromin-Peru, to take over Cerro de Pasco's mining, smelting and refining operations. The concern would be headed by retired Gen. Victor Miro Quesada.

The decree did not indicate whether Cerro would be compensated.

Cerro President C. Gordon Murphy had charged Sept. 24, when Cerro had initially withdrawn its offer to sell the subsidiary, that Peru had made only "impossible demands tantamount to expropriation." Cerro also had been subjected to "legalistic harassment" and "public vilification," Murphy charged.

According to Murphy, Peru had said earlier in 1973 that it wanted 100% ownership of Cerro de Pasco but had offered only to take possession of the firm after a sale was agreed to, leaving the price to be determined later on the basis of certain nonnegotiable evaluations made by government appointees. Cerro valued its Cerro de Pasco assets at $175 million, while the government's negotiating figure was about $12 million, Murphy alleged.

The government, Murphy continued, wanted Cerro to retain responsibility for Cerro de Pasco liabilities for an open-ended period, and wanted power to review and renegotiate all contracts made by Cerro de Pasco since Dec. 31, 1971.

The government also had impounded $27 million in Cerro cash by refusing to grant currency export permits to the company, Murphy charged. None of Cerro de Pasco's profit had been remitted to the U.S. since April 1972, he said.

Murphy noted government charges that Cerro de Pasco maintained inadequate and improper housing for its Peruvian workers, and replied that the company had complied with Peru's housing laws until new standards were "arbitrarily" established in May. "The company has spent $66 million on housing and related expenditures in the past 20 years, and it has faithfully submitted a program to meet the requirements of the new law by offering to invest an additional $65 million during the next five-year period," Murphy said. "In the opinion of Cerro's representatives the attack on its housing is not only an effort to bring down the selling price but also an attempt to divert public attention from the government's failure to improve the slums around Lima, among the world's worst."

The government Sept. 25 accused Cerro of trying to "falsify and distort" its conduct "with the clear purpose of damaging the well-earned prestige of Peru in the international financial world." It did not threaten to expropriate the company, saying it would analyze the situation "in a revolutionary spirit" and urging Cerro's Peruvian employes to "remain serenely vigilant" in light of the company's "provocation."

Peru charged Cerro de Pasco had been cited repeatedly for housing, security and pollution violations, and the housing violations dated back to 1950.

Gen. José Graham Hurtado, a key presidential adviser, said in a speech Oct. 8 that Cerro de Pasco would be nationalized "at the moment the government judges convenient." President Juan Velasco Alvarado noted the government's problems with Cerro the same day and said the armed forces would "fully support the government in whatever course of action it takes."

Velasco had told newsmen Aug. 29 that the government might seize Cerro de Pasco if negotiations for its purchase failed. The statement, which surprised Cerro executives, was interpreted as a maneuver to lower the company's asking price. Velasco also charged "the miners are disgusted with the company and the company in turn is afraid to deal with the workers. The miners have nowhere to sleep. Housing conditions are downright inhuman."

According to the London newsletter Latin America Sept. 14, Cerro wanted to sell Cerro de Pasco because publicity of its problems in Peru had depressed its share price over the past four years. The government wished to buy because Cerro's presence was anachronistic. The miners' unions and many nationalist army officers were militant advocates of expropriation.

Mines & minerals. Among other developments involving mines and minerals:

A government official announced May 3 that huge copper deposits with reserves estimated at 300 million tons, had been discovered in the northeastern jungle area near the Maranon River. The state mining firm Minoperu and the Rumanian concern Geomin had formed a joint venture to explore and exploit the copper deposits of Antamina in Ancash department, it was reported May 4. Peru would hold 51% of the capital.

The government's mining plans for 1973–74 provided for investment of $540 million, $240 million of it by Minoperu.

Minoperu, the state mining concern, signed an agreement with a Mexican firm to increase from 112,000 tons to 300,000 tons a year the amount of lead concentrates sent to Mexico for refining, it was reported June 22.

U.S. oil firm loses suit. Standard Oil Co. of California lost a refinery and associated service stations in Peru in a dispute with the government over tax claims, the Wall Street Journal reported March 26.

The unit, operated by the Standard subsidiary Conchan Chevron, was auctioned for alleged back taxes and fines of $5.5 million dating to 1967. The state oil concern Petroperu was the high bidder with $2.6 million, well below the $3.9 million value given the unit by a government-appointed evaluation team.

A spokesman for Standard in San Francisco said the company disagreed with Peru's tax claims and felt its properties had been "unjustly" taken from it. Standard claimed it had been exempted from the disputed taxes by contracts signed with former governments in 1962 and 1963.

Earlier, the International Petroleum Corp., a wholly owned subsidiary of Standard Oil of New Jersey which had ceased to operate in Peru in 1968, had been declared bankrupt at the request of the International Bank of Peru, it was reported Feb. 14.

In other oil developments:

Companies involved only in oil prospecting and exploration in Peru were exempted from tax and tribute payments by a government decree Feb. 22.

The government newspaper La Nueva Cronica announced Feb. 26 that an exploratory well dug by the Occidental Petroleum Corp. near the Ecuadorean border had begun producing more than 2,800 barrels daily.

A number of U.S. companies, including Oceanic Exploration Corp., El Paso Natural Gas Co. and Signal Oil & Gas Co., had signed petroleum operations contracts with the state oil concern Petroperu, it was reported June 5. The government had predicted April 18 that crude production would reach 200,000 barrels daily in 1980, an increase of 135,000 barrels a day over current production.

Petroperu signed service contracts with two U.S. firms and a consortium of French, Spanish and West German interests, it was reported June 15. Petroperu was reported June 1 to have agreed to sell Brazil 4,000 barrels of oil daily from the Trompeteros fields.

World Bank credits. The World Bank granted Peru credits worth $470 million, sealing the end of a long boycott by international financing institutions controlled or influenced by the U.S., the London newsletter Latin America reported June 29.

The award followed a meeting in Paris June 19-20 of the bank's Consultative Group for Peru, which examined plans for 87 Peruvian projects requiring almost $2 billion in foreign financing. The group commended the Peruvian government for its recent achievements—particularly for its "continuing efforts to combine economic growth with social justice"—and recommended that external assistance be provided "on as favorable terms as possible."

The Inter-American Development Bank (IDB) ended a long embargo of Peru April 26, approving a $6 million loan to foster mining development. A $23.3 million IDB loan for Peruvian agricultural development was reported confirmed May 25.

Finance Minister Gen. Francisco Morales Bermudez announced net capital inflow in 1972 totaled $452 million—a new record—and an international consortium headed by the Wells Fargo Bank of the U.S. would lend Peru another $135 million, it was reported May 11.

Japan had granted Peru a $19.3 million loan to build a 275-mile high tension power line between Lima and Chimbote, it was reported Feb. 23. The previous line was destroyed by the May 1970 earthquake.

A $25 million World Bank agricultural development loan to Peru was reported Aug. 24. A $12.3 million loan for Peruvian agrarian and health programs was approved by the Inter-American Development Bank Sept. 6.

A consortium of European and South African banks agreed to lend Peru $100 million for an irrigation project in the south to bring 150,000 acres of land into cultivation, the Miami Herald reported Oct. 6.

A Eurodollar loan worth $200 million for the Southern Peru Copper Corp., a U.S. firm partly controlled by Cerro, was reported approved Dec. 7 by a consortium of 29 banks from the U.S., Canada, Europe and Japan.

Petroperu announced the discovery in Talara of two oil wells jointly capable of producing nearly 4,000 barrels a day, it was reported Dec. 7.

The granting of the credits followed a marked improvement in U.S.-Peruvian relations, spurred by secret talks between Peruvian officials and U.S. special negotiator James Greene to settle disputes concerning Cerro and two other U.S. firms, W. R. Grace & Co. and Exxon Corp. The talks, which began Aug. 17-18, were reported continuing Dec. 26.

The credit lines to Peru were blocked by the U.S. after Peru nationalized Exxon's subsidiary International Petroleum Corp. in 1968.

Government spending to rise. The 1973-74 budget proposed by Finance Minister Francisco Morales Bermudez provided for a 35% rise in government expenditures to build up private industries, diversify production and reduce the country's dependence on rich nations, the London newsletter Latin America reported Jan. 12.

The largest rise would be in capital expenditure, which would be reflected in higher imports, likely to cost more than $1 billion a year. The present rate was about $800 million annually. The government also planned to create 500,000 new jobs, with the most important expansion in the white-collar, middle-class sectors, which reportedly provided the political base for the current regime.

Velasco leg amputation. President Juan Velasco Alvarado underwent two operations for a ruptured abdominal aneurism Feb. 23 and had a leg amputated March 9 after circulatory problems developed. Medical reports issued after the amputation indicated Velasco was recovering satisfactorily.

The operations spurred speculation about a successor to Velasco despite official assertions that the president remained in full control of the government. Government meetings were temporarily directed by Gen. Edgardo Mercado Jarrin, who became the no. 2 man in the military regime Feb. 1, when he assumed the posts of army commander, president of the council of ministers and minister of war. Mercado, a former foreign minister, took over the posts from Gen. Ernesto Montagne Sanchez, who retired.

According to the newsletter Latin America March 16, Mercado was probably the effective ruler of Peru, having had a year as army chief of staff to place his own men in key military posts.

Independent policy reaffirmed. President Juan Velasco Alvarado June 7 reaffirmed his government's independence from "the interests of the warring great powers," asserting there was a "final, deep incompatibility" between the regime and any form of capitalism or communism.

Speaking to a crowd of thousands in Lima, Velasco described Peru's "revolutionary" process as "conceptually and ideologically autonomous, characteristic of our people and entirely remote from any influence originating in the foreign centers of ideological, political, economic and cultural power."

It was the president's first public appearance since his leg amputation.

Soviet military men visit. Seven high-ranking Soviet military officials arrived in Lima for a five-day visit aimed at "strengthening friendly ties between the two countries," the Miami Herald reported March 15. The visit followed a denial by President Velasco Jan. 24 that Peru was buying arms from the U.S.S.R. (The Navy Ministry announced Peru would soon receive three refurbished vessels purchased from the Netherlands and Great Britain, the Herald reported March 15.)

The Soviet Union would give financial and technical aid for the first stage of large-scale irrigation and agricultural schemes in the northern department of Lambayeque, which were expected to require a total investment of about $375 million, the newsletter Latin America reported Jan. 19.

Cuban relations. Cuban President Osvaldo Dorticos June 4 visited Peru, Velasco Alvarado on "continental and Latin American problems." The two presidents praised their countries' processes of change, with Dorticos asserting: "Our revolutions travel different roads, but both point toward the beautiful horizon of continental liberation."

Velasco thanked Premier Fidel Castro for his friendship toward Peru and his concern over Velasco's health. Castro had sent specialists and orthopedic equipment to help Velasco recover from his recent leg amputation, according to a report April 14.

Castro had hailed Velasco as a "revolutionary of firm convictions" during a visit to Cuba by the head of the Peruvian social mobilization agency SINAMOS, it was reported May 18.

In a related development reported Feb. 2, Education Minister Alfredo Carpio Becerra visited Cuba, the fourth Cabinet official to do so since Peru and Cuba resumed diplomatic relations in July 1972.

Brazilian visits. Brazilian Foreign Minister Mario Gibson Barboza visited Lima July 13–15.

Peru's left-wing military government and Brazil's rightist regime agreed to unite in defense of their declared 200-mile offshore territorial limits, and to press jointly for a greater share in world cargo traffic for the merchant marines of developing countries. Brazil also joined Peru in voicing concern over "the protectionist policies of certain industrialized nations"—presumably, the U.S.—in an apparent expression of independence from Washington.

Ties with France cut. Following France's resumption of nuclear tests in the atmosphere July 21, Peru severed relations with the French government July 24.

Chile. Chilean Education Minister Jorge Tapia announced in Lima that Peru and Chile had agreed to a large-scale exchange of teachers, the Miami Herald reported Jan. 18. Tapia said the exchange would help Chileans learn "the reforms implanted by Peru's revolutionary law."

'Barbie' freed. Klaus Altmann, a former Nazi war criminal sought by France under the name Klaus Barbie, was released from a Bolivian prison Oct. 29 following the rejection Oct. 24 by the Bolivian Supreme Court of a Peruvian government extradition request. Altmann had served nearly eight months in jail pending decisions on Peruvian and French extradition requests.

Peru had wanted Altmann's extradition on currency fraud and smuggling charges. He was formally charged, in absentia, in a Peru court Dec. 7 as being a leader of a currency-smuggling ring.

Newsman exiled. Luis Rey de Castro, a prize-winning columnist for the Lima newspaper La Prensa, was exiled to Panama Jan. 30 for writing an article that offended the government.

The Peruvian Journalists Federation protested Rey's expulsion Feb. 1. The Inter-American Press Association Feb. 3 called it "an arbitrary and despotic act."

Workers at Lima's newspaper El Comercio, the nation's oldest, struck Jan. 8–13 to demand resumption of publication of an evening newspaper, suspended early in 1972 during a newspaper workers' strike.

After the strike El Comercio March 24 criticized a government decision to control directly the importing and distribution of newsprint. The paper said the action would neither improve distribution nor lower the price of newsprint, but would threaten freedom of the press.

Labor unrest. Constitutional guarantees were suspended in two departments and a province in April and May to curb strikes and related disturbances.

The government suspended guarantees in the southern department of Moquegua April 25, to prevent a second strike by a federation of unions demanding a new local university, more doctors and nurses at the Moquegua and Ilo hospitals, electricity for the entire department, water and sewage services for shantytowns, and repatriation of all persons exiled for political reasons. A 72-hour strike had been held the week before to demand reinstitution of the first year of studies in the teachers' college, abolished by the Education Ministry.

The repatriation demand referred principally to Hernan Cuentas, general secretary of the Workers Union at the massive Cuajone copper mine, who was secretly deported to Panama April 20. The union had been demanding the rehiring of 450 workers fired by the mine's principal developer, the Southern Peru Copper Corp., on grounds they were construction workers and not miners. The union's protest reportedly had led to violent disturbances.

Strikes began again in Moquegua May 7 and spread to the neighboring department of Arequipa, where the Arequipa Departmental Labor Federation called a general strike to support the Moquegua workers' demands and to protest a government decree setting back by five years the age at which workers were entitled to pensions. Guarantees were suspended in Arequipa May 8. Police using tear gas broke up a solidarity march by railway workers in the city of Arequipa May 9.

The navy minister, Vice Adm. Luis Vargas Caballero, charged May 9 that the strikes were promoted by "small groups with strictly political interests," and said the government would not tolerate any further "agitation." He said he supported strikes for "just" demands, but not ones whose motives had "nothing to do with labor."

Strikes virtually paralyzed Arequipa and Moquegua May 10, and a 48-hour solidarity strike began in the department of Puno. The country's largest labor federation, the Communist-led Peruvian General Labor Confederation (CGTP), expressed solidarity with the Arequipa strikes and urged the government to adopt a "flexible attitude." The 20,000 members of the Federation of Bank Employes struck across Peru May 11 and 14 to protest the new pension plan.

The Peruvian Labor Confederation, dominated by the opposition American Popular Revolutionary Alliance, called a nationwide general strike against the pension plan May 21, but was not joined by the other three labor federations—the CGTP, the government-inspired Peruvian Revolution Labor Confederation, and the Christian Democratic National Labor Confederation. Students in Lima who tried to force shops and businesses to join the strike were dispersed by police using tear gas and fire hoses.

A general strike was called May 24 in the northern port of Chimbote, where the Ancash Department Labor Federation protested the government pension plan and alleged government interference in the fishing industry.

A youth was shot to death in clashes between demonstrators and police. The violence continued the next day, leading the government to suspend guarantees throughout Santa Province.

3,000 workers at the state steel complex in Chimbote walked out in a demand for punishment of those responsible for the death of the youth and the critical wounding of a union executive in clashes with police May 24 during a 24-hour general strike. But they ended their 18-day strike June 11 after the government threatened to fire them. (The subsequent death of the labor leader, Cristobal Espinola, occasioned a one-hour general strike June 15 by Espinola's group, the Peruvian Revolution Labor Confederation.)

The Ancash Department Labor Federation, whose 30 unions struck in solidarity with the steel workers June 6, also ended its stoppage June 11.

The Amazonian town of Pucallpa was partially paralyzed June 6 by a general strike called to support a week-old teachers' strike.

Government-backed candidates were soundly defeated in elections to the complex new teachers' cooperative system, designed to put an end to union militancy in the schools, the newsletter Latin America reported June 22. The government, charging electoral fraud, annulled the vote in Lima, where the opposition coalition SUTEP won 95% of the votes. However, the government reversed this decision when it became clear there would be a nationwide strike as a result, Latin America reported.

4 more die in strikes. At least four persons were killed and 50 injured Nov. 20-28 in strike-related clashes in Arequipa, Puno, Cuzco and Ayacucho. The trouble stemmed from a dispute between the government and the Peruvian Education Workers Union (SUTEP).

Arequipa had been virtually paralyzed after Nov. 15, when transport and other workers struck to demand release of SUTEP leaders and teachers arrested after a 24-hour SUTEP strike Oct. 24. The arrests had been confirmed Oct. 31 by the government, which did not recognize SUTEP as legal and which SUTEP openly opposed. The union estimated Nov. 7 that arrests exceeded 400.

Clashes between police and strikers and students erupted Nov. 20 in Arequipa and Puno, prompting the government to impose a state of emergency, with suspension of union rights and an eight-hour curfew, in both provinces. The Washington Post reported Nov. 24 that according to a foreign observer, as many as a dozen might have been killed.

President Velasco charged Nov. 21 that the disturbances were caused by subversives who were "well armed, have economic resources, and are helped by foreign people." He said his government would "hit [the subversives] with everything."

The Arequipa and Puno strikes continued, however, and spread Nov. 23 to Cuzco, where clashes between students and police left one person dead and some 30 wounded. Students reportedly set fire to an office of SINAMOS, the government social mobilization agency, and burned at least five shops. The regional military commander, Gen. Jose Villalobos, blamed the clashes on left- and right-wing extremists, the U.S. Central Intelligence Agency, and other foreigners.

An end to the Arequipa strike was negotiated subsequently by that region's military commander, Gen. Augusto Freire, it was reported Nov. 30. However, more clashes were reported afterwards in Ayacucho, where a student was killed Nov. 28.

Other economic developments. Among other economic developments of 1973:

Prices of basic articles and public services were frozen Jan. 9.

The government had postponed until June 1974 the deadline, originally set for December 31, 1972, by which foreign companies must sign contracts with the state, it was reported Jan. 5. Under the 1970 industrial law such contracts were to provide for gradual transfer of foreign capital into Peruvian hands, but would also allow the companies to make "reasonable" profits.

Agriculture Minister Enrique Valdez Angulo said the government had expropriated more than 12 million acres of farmland and 1.7 million head of livestock under the agrarian reform program enacted in 1969, the Miami Herald reported March 6. Government plans for the 1973–74 period called for expropriation of nearly 10 million more acres and 400,000 head of livestock, with compensation awarded to the owners.

Valdez Angulo said June 24, on the fourth birthday of the government's agrarian reform program, that small- and medium-sized agricultural property would be respected as long as farmers managed it personally and observed laws protecting workers.

The government announced March 20 it would soon create a new national airline, to be called Aero-Peru. It would initially handle domestic flights and 12–18 months later international flights. The announcement coincided with the arrival in Peru of the first of three Fokker-28 jets purchased in the Netherlands. Peru had lacked an international airline since the bankruptcy of the airline APSA more than two years before.

The navy's industrial services installations May 9 launched a 25,200 ton grain ship, considered the largest ever built in Latin American yards. Peru planned to build even larger ships for sales abroad.

Japanese interests and two Peruvian concerns signed an agreement June 9 to invest $10 million to establish a metallurgical complex in Iquitos.

The state steel concern Siderperu had signed an agreement with the West German firm Hosch Handel for joint construction of a steel tube manufacturing plant in Chimbote, it was reported June 15. The tubes would be used for the planned trans-Andean oil pipeline.

Rumanian government agencies and state companies signed a package of equipment supply, financing, mining and industrial deals with Peru worth some $100 million, it was reported Oct. 12.

The Japanese firm Toyota would build an auto complex in northern Peru valued at $120 million, it was reported Nov. 30.

Use of death penalty expanded. The government Jan. 31 decreed the death penalty for a wider range of offenses—mainly certain types of murder and attacks on police—to combat what it called "the alarming increase in crime."

Capital punishment had been abolished in most cases in September 1971, remaining in force only for treason and certain crimes against police and minors. Under the new decree it would also apply to murder of policemen, killing during a robbery, and endangering the lives or health of large numbers of persons.

Prison reforms set. The government announced a penal reform program designed to eliminate the widespread crime and "promiscuity" among Peru's 15,000 prisoners, it was reported June 14.

Gen. Pedro Richter, interior minister, said the reforms included creation of a national "reorientation center" to which convicts would be assigned for their initial weeks of confinement. During this time experts would study their personalities and determine the appropriate prison for them, eliminating grouping of political prisoners with common criminals, and of first-time offenders with hardened criminals.

Other reforms included awarding of vacations from prison for good conduct, creation of "open jails" run by prisoners, and construction of facilities where prisoners could be alone with their wives or husbands.

Supreme Court justices dismissed. Five Supreme Court justices were dismissed Oct. 25 by the National Council of Justice (CNJ), a suprajudicial organization created by the military government.

The CNJ charged the justices had rendered a verdict of "evident partiality" in acquitting Vicente Ugarte del Pino, dean of the Lima bar, of libel charges against a CNJ member, Alfonso Montesinos. Ugarte had signed a document, co-signed by a fellow bar director, Juan Bautista Bardelli, alleging Montesinos used his position in the CNJ to put pressure on two judges presiding in cases in which he was counsel. Bardelli was convicted.

Puerto Rico

Hernandez Colon inaugurated. Rafael Hernandez Colon, whose Popular Democratic party swept the November 1972 elections, was sworn in as Puerto Rico's fourth elected governor Jan. 2.

The inaugural in San Juan was marked by tributes to Roberto Clemente, the Puerto Rican baseball star killed in an airplane crash two days before, in whose honor all but one of the inaugural social functions were canceled. Referring to Clemente at the end of his inaugural speech, Hernandez Colon said: "Our youth have lost an idol and an example. Our people have lost one of their glories. All of our hearts are saddened by his tragic parting."

In his address, Hernandez Colon mapped an ambitious program for his first term in office that included reform of an inefficient electoral law and sweeping tax changes based on a reduction in tax evasion. He also set as priorities a universal health system and an expansion of industrialization to provide more jobs and keep Puerto Ricans from leaving the island in search of employment.

Six women in new Cabinet. Gov. Hernandez Colon named six women to his new Cabinet, the Miami Herald reported Jan. 13. They held the posts of secretary of education, director of the Civil Defense Office, director of the Personnel Office, director of the Right to Employment Administration, director of the Office of Economic Opportunities and special aide to the governor in charge of long-term policy.

Independence party wins 3 seats. The Puerto Rican Independence party had won three seats in the island's legislature, it was reported Jan. 2. The elections board validating results of the November 1972 balloting said the party's president, Ruben Berrios, had won an at-large seat in the Senate, and two other party members had won at-large seats in the lower house.

The party, which had received a bare 5% of the votes in the 1972 elections, ousted its unsuccessful gubernatorial candidate, Noel Colon Martinez, the Miami Herald reported Feb. 15.

According to the Herald, Colon Martinez was considered less radical than most of the party members who wanted to sever all ties with the U.S.

Anti-inflation measure signed. A bill aimed at curbing inflation through creation of a public corporation to import and distribute public commodities, was signed into law by Gov. Rafael Hernandez Colon April 24.

A companion bill converting Puerto Rico's consumer services administration into a Cabinet-level department with broader powers was also signed. Both measures had been opposed by local businessmen, who charged they gave the government dictatorial powers and undermined the free enterprise system and import trade.

The new corporation represented the first major attempt in Puerto Rico to stabilize food prices by influencing those market conditions that caused instability, the Wall Street Journal reported April 25. The consumer price index had risen in the first quarter of 1973 at an annual rate of almost 6%, reflecting in large measure the sharp increase in food prices on the U.S. mainland, which supplied most of the food consumed in Puerto Rico.

The corporation would also be used to stimulate local food production that could substitute for imports, the Journal reported.

Retail prices of more than 100 basic food items were currently frozen. Under a government plan, growers and middlemen would be eligible to receive government subsidies if they could show that rising costs prevented them from realizing a "reasonable profit margin."

Japanese investment eyed. The Japanese consul to Puerto Rico, Manuel San Juan Jr., said Japanese firms were considering investments totaling $100 million in Puerto Rico, the Miami Herald reported Feb. 6.

Gov. Rafael Hernandez Colon had said in his State of the Commonwealth message that U.S. efforts to restore its balance of payments position with Japan should make Puerto Rico an attractive locale for Japanese investment, the Herald reported.

The Economic Development Administration April 24 announced plans to attract Japanese manufacturing investment to Puerto Rico.

The plans offered Japanese companies setting up plants in Puerto Rico tariff-free access to the mainland U.S., and tax and industrial incentives. Puerto Rico in turn would gain badly needed jobs.

Pardon asked for attackers. The Miami Herald reported Feb. 3 that the Puerto Rican House had asked President Nixon to pardon five Puerto Ricans serving long sentences for an attempt on President Harry S. Truman's life and an attack on U.S. congressmen in 1954.

The resolution, presented by Rep. Carlos Gallisa, vice president of the Puerto Rican Independence Party, was approved unanimously.

More than 1,000 Puerto Rican nationalists marched on the White House in Washington, D.C. Oct. 30 and demanded independence for the island and release of the five prisoners.

The prisoners were Oscar Collazo, sentenced to life imprisonment for killing a White House policeman in an assassination attempt on the late President Harry Truman in 1950; and Lolita Lebron, Rafael Cancel Miranda, Andres Figueroa Cordero and Irving Flores Rodriguez, each sentenced to more than 55 years in prison for opening fire in the U.S. House of Representatives in 1954 and wounding five congressmen.

Industry critics scored. Teodoro Moscoso, head of the Economic Development Administration, charged that an anti-industrial attitude had developed on the island which seriously threatened Puerto Rico's economic growth, it was reported June 23.

Moscoso's criticism reportedly was aimed at environmentalists and independence advocates protesting a government-supported plan to build a superport for giant oil tankers on Puerto Rico's west coast.

Simultaneously with Moscoso's statement, Puerto Rico's Environmental Quality Board ordered three local industries to take immediate action to end air pollution. The board had issued an order two weeks before barring new industries from locating in Catano and Guayanilla, two of the island's most highly industrialized areas, due to the high pollution levels there.

Independence & superport in dispute. Cuba asked that a U.N. committee studying the status of Puerto Rico demand immediate independence for the island, dismantling of U.S. military bases there, and abandonment of plans to build an oil superport on its western coast, it was reported Aug. 18.

Ricardo Alarcon, Cuba's ambassador to the U.N., charged at a session of the Special Committee on Decolonization that under Puerto Rico's U.S. commonwealth status, "Yankee exploiters" invaded the island and forced natives to emigrate to "the ghettoes of New York and semi-forced labor camps of New Jersey and Florida." He described the planned superport as part of a "genocidal process" in which "greedy minorities" settled in Puerto Rico, "threatening to engulf the people and threatening them with extinction."

The U.N. committee was studying whether to list Puerto Rico as a colony entitled to independence. The U.S. refused to participate, claiming Puerto Rico was not a proper subject for U.N. deliberations. The U.S. maintained the island already enjoyed self-determination and was free to change its status to either statehood or full independence.

Leaders of two Puerto Rican pro-independence groups asked the U.N. June 7 to intervene against the proposed construction of the superport.

Juan Mari Bras, secretary general of the Puerto Rican Socialist party, and Ruben Berrios, a senator and president of the Puerto Rican Independence party, made the request before the Special Committee on Decolonization, which they said had jurisdiction over Puerto Rico by virtue of a 1972 resolution asserting the island had a right to self-determination. The committee had voted to set up a working group to consider Puerto Rico's status regarding the U.S.

Mari Bras and Berrios asked that the working group grant them an informal hearing; that it recommend asking the U.S. not to set up the port until the U.N. examined Puerto Rico's case "on its merits"; and that the committee hold hearings in Puerto Rico on the port in 1973. The committee's chairman said he would consider the request.

The Puerto Ricans charged the port would upset the island's ecology, harm agriculture and fishing, and turn Puerto Rico into "an appendage of the international oil cartels." The port was supported by the island's new governor, Rafael Hernandez Colon.

The committee heard further testimony from Mari Bras and Berrios Aug. 23–24. Mari Bras Aug. 23 accused the U.S. of violating international law and the U.N. Charter by exercising political, economic and military control over Puerto Rico. Ruben Berrios asserted Aug. 24 that the island's U.S. commonwealth status did not change its basic colonial nature.

The U.N. committee then voted Aug. 30 to keep the status of Puerto Rico under its "continuous review," deferring for another year the classification of the island as a U.S. colony.

However, the committee's resolution, passed 12–2 with nine abstentions, reaffirmed the "inalienable rights" of Puerto Ricans to "self-determination and independence," and warned the U.S. against obstructing the "full and free exercise" of these rights. It also defended the "economic and social rights" of Puerto Ricans. This apparently was a criticism of the superport proposal.

The resolution was attacked by John Scali, U.S. ambassador to the U.N., who called it "not only irrelevant but ludicrous." Scali noted that the General Assembly had decided in 1953 that Puerto Rico had achieved a self-governing status and should be dropped from the list of colonies examined by the U.N. each year.

Puerto Rico Gov. Rafael Hernandez Colon also attacked the resolution, asserting it had "no legal or moral value whatever and is completely meaningless as far as Puerto Rico is concerned."

The U.N. General Assembly Dec. 15, over U.S. objections, approved the committee's report on its resolution.

Superport OKd. Gov. Hernandez Colon had given the go-ahead for construction of the controversial oil superport on the island of Mona, off Puerto Rico's western coast, it was reported Sept. 28.

The port would handle two million barrels of oil daily by 1977. It would increase Puerto Rican refinery capacity from 250,000 barrels daily to 750,000.

For Puerto Rico, the port's purpose would be to switch development emphasis from light industry to processing oil and other minerals. For the oil industry, the aim would be to facilitate shipment of Persian Gulf oil to the U.S. to help ease the energy crisis.

Puerto Rican officials estimated construction costs at $560 million, but independence advocates put the initial investment at $1.3 billion and the final cumulative investment at $16 billion, according to the Washington Post June 13.

Economic events. The International Telephone and Telegraph Corp. (ITT) said Oct. 4 it had signed a "memorandum of understanding" with Gov. Rafael Hernandez Colon whereby the commonwealth government would purchase ITT's Puerto Rico Telephone Co. for about $125 million in cash, notes and bonds.

The purchase reportedly was motivated by the government's desire to keep telephone rates down. ITT had sought a 50% rate increase over the next four years to meet expansion demands.

Owens-Illinois Inc. Aug. 13 announced plans to build a multi-million dollar plant in Puerto Rico to manufacture glass containers. The plant would employ 300 persons, almost all hired locally.

Puerto Rico's Economic Development Administration had warned that firms elsewhere in the Caribbean and in the Far East were attracting labor-intensive industries away from the island by offering more favorable wage rates, according to a report Sept. 2.

A baseball manufacturing plant in Cayey had decided recently to move to Haiti, where wage rates were lower, it was reported Aug. 25.

Culebra pullout set. Elliot L. Richardson, in one of his last acts as defense secretary, ordered the Navy to end its controversial use of the offshore island of Culebra as a practice gunnery range.

Richardson May 24 ordered gunnery and air bombardment training shifted to Desecheo and Monito, two small uninhabited islands off Puerto Rico's west coast, by mid-1975. The cost of the transfer was estimated at $10 million.

In a letter to Sen. John Stennis (D, Miss.), chairman of the Senate Armed Services Committee, Richardson said that while there were "some operational and cost advantages" to remaining on Culebra, the two smaller islands were "also suitable and would meet military requirements."

The Puerto Rico House of Representatives had unanimously adopted a resolution demanding the Navy's immediate withdrawal from Culebra and Vieques, another off-shore island used for target practice. A similar measure had been adopted by the Commonwealth Senate.

Beauty contest contract canceled. Cancellation of a five-year contract to host the Miss U.S.A. and the Miss Universe beauty pageants was announced by the Puerto Rican Office of Tourism.

According to the New York Times Feb. 18, the tourist office's controller ruled that the contract was signed illegally in 1971 by the administration of Gov. Luis A. Ferre, who was defeated in his bid for re-election.

Under the contract, the government was to pay the pageant's owners $200,000 over five years. The controller, however, said additional costs, including hotel rooms, would bring the government's expenses to $650,000 annually.

Marijuana seized. Police seized marijuana valued at $15 million dollars near San Juan, El Nacional of Caracas reported Feb. 20. The shipment was apparently destined for the U.S. mainland.

Drug unit formed. The government had established a Department of Anti-Addiction Services, with Cabinet-level status, to deal with the persistent problem of drug addiction, it was reported June 23. The unit would be headed by Rafael Santos Del Valle, who would leave his present post as assistant justice secretary.

Authorities estimated as many as 100,000 addicts among Puerto Rico's 2.7 million inhabitants.

Information law protested. The Inter-American Press Association (IAPA) May 18 urged Gov. Hernandez Colon to veto a public information law because it might lead to press censorship.

The law, passed by the legislature, contained an article allowing the government to maintain secret certain unspecified information. The IAPA said the provision "violates the spirit of the constitutional guarantee of freedom of the press."

Mainland unit established. Twenty-seven Puerto Ricans living in the U.S. were sworn in June 23 as members of a new government council formed to look after the interests of two million island natives on the U.S. mainland.

The 27, living in 10 different states and the District of Columbia, took their oaths in Chicago from Puerto Rican Attorney General Francisco DeJesus.

Uruguay

Government-Military Clash

Institutional crisis. As government relations with the armed forces deteriorated, the commanders of the army and air force Feb. 8 publicly demanded the removal of retired Gen. Antonio Francese, who had been appointed defense minister Feb. 7 to replace Armando Malet.

The commanders, Gen. Cesar Augusto Martinez of the army and Brig. Jose Perez Caldas of the air force, made clear in a communique read over nationwide radio and television that their demand was a reaction to Francese's earlier demand for their own resignations. They said they would not heed any of Francese's orders if he remained in office.

President Juan Maria Bordaberry went on radio and television after the communique was read to announce that he would not dismiss Francese and to call on civilians and members of the armed forces to defend Uruguayan institutions. Officials of the Montevideo television station said later that the army had occupied their building and seized the recordings of Bordaberry's message.

Following his public appeal Bordaberry held late-night consultations with advisers and political associates, while the navy, which apparently supported the president in this confrontation, sealed off streets leading to its garrisons in the Montevideo harbor area.

Gen. Martinez and Brig. Perez Caldas had issued a communique Feb. 7 denying charges by a senator that the armed forces were plotting a coup and asserting the military would prevent politicians from making public accusations against them in the future.

The senator, Amilcar Vasconcellos of Bordaberry's Colorado party, had said in a radio message Feb. 1 that "no one, save out of cowardice ... or blindness to history" could ignore the existence in Uruguay of "a movement that seeks to replace legal institutions with the all-embracing will" of the armed forces. He denounced military commanders for allegedly trying to justify armed subversion in Uruguay by pointing to government corruption and charged that "corruption exists not only when public funds are misused ... but also when there are attempts to replace normal administrative organisms by those who have neither the ability nor the authority to do so, but assume these solely because they have force in their hands." (Bordaberry rejected these charges Feb. 2 expressing confidence in the military.)

Vasconcellos also condemned the military for indirectly criticizing Bordaberry, without first consulting the president or his defense minister, in a communiqué calling for "exceptional measures" to investigate charges of corruption in the Montevideo departmental government. The appeal, disclosed Jan. 24, was subsequently supported by then Defense Minister Malet, whose continuation in office Vasconcellos found "incredible." Malet reportedly offered to resign Jan. 26, but was retained by Bordaberry. He resigned Feb. 7 and was immediately replaced by Francese.

The attorney general Feb. 6 received the corruption charges from the National Court prosecutor's office. They included alleged violations of the law by 31 magistrates of the Montevideo Departmental Council, encompassing misuse of funds for private entertainment, abuse of official transportation, hiring of relatives and other charges.

Pact ends military defiance. A six-day challenge, begun by the army and air force Feb. 7 and joined by the navy Feb. 11, ended May 12 when President Bordaberry and the armed forces commanders reached an agreement that formally maintained Uruguay's constitutional system but provided for virtual military control of the government.

Under the agreement, according to press reports Feb. 14, the armed forces pledged to support the Constitution and democratic institutions and to guarantee general elections in 1976. However, the military also gained supervisory control over the civilian administration through creation of a National Security Council. The council would include the three armed forces commanders and the ministers of defense, interior, foreign affairs and economy, with the armed forces controlling the nomination of the defense and interior ministers.

(The new defense and interior ministers, appointed Feb. 13 with military approval, were ex-Interior Minister Walter Ravenna and ex-Interior Undersecretary Col. Nestor Bolentini. The entire Cabinet had resigned Feb. 9 to give Bordaberry a freer hand in resolving the institutional crisis, but only the resignation of Defense Minister Antonio Francese—around whom the crisis had centered—had been immediately accepted. Ravenna's resignation as interior minister was accepted later, but the rest of the Cabinet was confirmed Feb. 13.)

The agreement also called for a crackdown on government corruption and other "economic crimes," and even a "housecleaning" within the armed forces. Management of public utilities would be reformed to eliminate inefficiency and corruption, and several ambassadors and other foreign service officials would be recalled to face charges of making unlawful financial gains.

The agreement was announced following a meeting, at an air base near Montevideo, between Bordaberry and the rebel military leaders—army Gen. Hugo Chiappe Posse, air force Brig. José Perez Caldas and navy Capt. Conrado Olazabal. Chiappe Posse effectively controlled the army following the resignation Feb. 8 of its commander, Gen. Cesar A. Martinez, and the resignation Feb. 10 of his replacement, Gen. Alfredo Verocay. Bordaberry confirmed Olazabal as navy commander shortly before the agreement was announced, replacing Rear Adm. Juan Jose Zorrilla, who had supported the president in the crisis but had lost control of the navy to rebel forces.

According to the New York Times Feb. 14, other officers leading the military challenge to the civilian government were Gen. Esteban Cristi, commander of the crucial first military district; Col. Ramon Traval, head of the joint military command's intelligence service; and Gen. Gregorio Alvarez, chief of the armed forces' joint staff. The military leaders reportedly insisted that they were engaged in a nationalist movement and looked neither to Peru nor to Brazil for an ideological model.

Sen. Wilson Ferreira Aldunate, leader of the majority faction of the opposition Blanco party, said Feb. 14 that the accord between Bordaberry and the military leaders was not a lasting solution to Uruguay's problems, and called for early elections for a new government. Before the agreement was announced, Ferreira had joined other politicians—including members of Bordaberry's Colorado party—in calling for the president's resignation, asserting only new elections could resolve the crisis.

Retired Gen. Liber Seregni, leader of the left-wing Broad Front coalition, had called for Bordaberry's resignation Feb. 9 but had been more conciliatory toward the military than the Blancos and Colorados. Seregni and leaders of the Communist party, a member of the Broad Front, reportedly were receptive to a "Peruvian" solution, in which a military government instituted broad social and economic reforms. The army and air force issued a communique Feb. 9 calling for measures to stimulate production and exports, reorganization of the foreign service, public administration and the tax system, elimination of the foreign debt, redistribution of the land and creation of new jobs.

Navy joins 'rebellion'—A military communique said Feb. 11 that the navy had joined the army and air force in their demands for government reforms and a greater military voice in national affairs, and that Rear Adm. Zorrilla, a firm supporter of civilian control of the armed forces, had "resigned" as navy commander. The navy had supported Bordaberry at the beginning of the crisis, but had been reported seriously divided Feb. 10. (Support for the army and air force by the police had been announced Feb. 9.)

The navy Feb. 9 had sealed off the Montevideo harbor area and the "old city," the capital's banking, commercial and government center, and stationed a destroyer near the harbor. The army sent a squadron of 14 tanks into the city's Prado Park, near the presidential residence, and began taking control of Montevideo's radio and television stations, over which it broadcast frequent messages. Both the army and navy forces withdrew from their positions later the same day, after Bordaberry began negotiations with the rebel commanders through three of his Cabinet ministers.

National Security Council approved. The Cabinet Feb. 23 approved creation of the National Security Council, which, under military direction, would henceforth supervise the civilian government. Establishment of the council was among provisions of the agreement between President Bordaberry and the military.

According to Bordaberry, the council would be the "advisory" board to oversee fulfillment of a 19-point "national reconstruction program" demanded by the military, the Miami Herald reported Feb. 25. The program called for continuation of the armed forces' anti-corruption campaign, restructuring of land tenure and credit, anti-monopoly legislation, an end to military intervention in labor and student disputes, worker participation in company management, stricter state control of private banks, control of inflation and unemployment, and other measures.

The London newsletter Latin America noted Feb. 16 that some provisions of the program contradicted each other—the military probably could not, for instance, simultaneously supervise the government and remain out of student and union disputes—and observed Feb. 23 that Bordaberry's conservative Cabinet, most of which was confirmed after the political crisis, was not likely to implement such reforms.

The renomination of Foreign Minister Juan Carlos Blanco, Industry and Commerce Minister Luis Balparda Blengio and Public Works Minister Angel Servetti surprised observers, according to Latin America. Blanco had been criticized for his close connections with the U.S. embassy and his soft line in the dispute with Argentina over territorial waters. Balparda Blengio and Servetti had been under fire for their private business activities while holding office. Their confirmations reportedly left doubts about the unity and determination of the armed forces.

Contradictions were also apparent in the appointment to the Defense Ministry of Walter Ravenna, formerly a close colleague of ex-President Jorge Pacheco Areco, to whom responsibility for much of the current government corruption was laid, Latin America noted Feb. 16. Gen. Hugo Chiappe Posse, confirmed as army commander Feb. 14 after leading the army rebels in the crisis, had also been close to Pacheco. As head of the ex-President's military household, he had been the link between Pacheco and the hard-liners in the army, the newsletter noted.

Meanwhile, the civilian left was divided in its reactions to the reconstruction program. The Christian Democrats announced "critical approval" for the program because it attacked a number of fundamental issues, but the Communists were dissatisfied with its clause condemning Marxist-Leninist political ideas. However, the Communist-led National Labor Confederation (CNT) had, at a critical moment in the crisis, announced workers would not be ordered to occupy their places of work and begin a general strike in the event of a military coup, Latin America reported Feb. 23.

The major opposition to the reconstruction program came from Colorado Sen. Amilcar Vasconcellos, who charged Feb. 18 that Uruguay was faced with a choice between civil war and a virtual military dictatorship. He condemned Congress for not acting decisively in the crisis, and said he would call the new defense and interior ministers before the legislature, seeking their impeachment if necessary.

Education bill passed. Congress had approved the government's controversial general education bill despite a two-month strike by teachers, continuous student protests and massive opposition from the trade union movement, the London newsletter Latin America reported Jan. 12.

The bill, described by the government as restructuring education and tending to eliminate political influences in the universities, was supported by the ruling Colorado party and right-wing members of the opposition Blanco party and opposed by the liberal majority faction of the Blancos and the left-wing Broad Front coalition.

According to Latin America, opposition to the bill centered on the control it gave the president over all branches of education. School administrators and inspectors, previously chosen by merit in open competition, would henceforth be appointed by the goverment, and their posts would provide new opportunities for political patronage. A vaguely worded prohibition of actions which "might impede or deny the right of study" seemed to outlaw all types of strike action by students or teachers, the newsletter added.

A study of the bill by the National Federation of Secondary School Teachers commented that it read more like a penal code than an education law, Latin America reported. One of the bill's provisions, the newsletter noted, removed certain family allowances from parents whose children did not conform to the disciplinary norms of their schools or colleges.

Teachers lifted their strike after the bill was passed, but since the school year was over the decision did not affect classes.

Drug unit established. Montevideo police said they had set up a special narcotics brigade because of evidence that Uruguay was a "bridge" for U.S.-bound drugs from Europe, the Miami Herald reported Jan. 21. The Herald said Jan. 24 that Uruguayan authorities would freeze all assets in the bank accounts of several suspected narcotics smugglers, all of whom had fled the country.

River Plate naval incident. Uruguayan naval vessels attempted Jan. 26 to seize an Argentine ship and a Norwegian freighter carrying out unloading operations in River Plate waters claimed by Uruguay but were rebuffed by the Argentine ship's captain and Argentine naval forces, according to reports by the Argentine armed forces Jan. 26 and La Prensa of Buenos Aires Jan. 27–30. The Argentine Foreign Ministry said Jan. 29 it had received an "energetic and formal protest" from Uruguay but had rejected it.

According to the Argentine captain, Horacio Luque, his ship was unloading coal from a Norwegian freighter in deep waters about 12 miles from the Uruguayan coast when an armed Uruguayan naval vessel approached. Two Uruguayan officers came aboard the ship and said both the Argentine and Norwegian vessels were under arrest and should follow the Uruguayan ship into Montevideo. The Argentine crew reportedly refused to obey the order, whereupon the Uruguayan ship withdrew, returning later with a destroyer escort to renew the demand. The Argentines again refused—this time supported by the presence of Argentine naval aircraft—and the Uruguayans withdrew.

Following the incident, Argentine and Uruguayan officials met to try to resolve the dispute over territorial waters in the River Plate. Uruguay claimed the demarcation line should be halfway between the two coastlines, while Argentina claimed it should be the deepwater channel, near Uruguay, which its ships needed to use for unloading operations before they could enter the shallower waters of Argentine ports. Uruguay reportedly considered goods unloaded in the deep waters contraband and was annoyed that the unloading took place within sight of its beaches. Uruguayan Sen. Wilson Ferreira Aldunate also maintained the channel had been moving closer to Uruguay as a result of Argentine dredging operations, the London newsletter Latin America reported Feb. 2.

Peso devalued. The peso was devalued by 3.94% Jan. 5, by 5.04% Feb. 4 and by 2.8% Feb. 21. The devaluations, the 11th, 12th and 13th since President Bordaberry's inauguration in March 1972, followed price increases of 5% to 50% on all public services and many essential commodities. A 35% wage increase for private sector workers and employes had gone into effect Jan. 1.

The National Labor Confederation (CNT), which had opposed the 35% increase as insufficient, Jan. 5 called on its 400,000 members to fight Bordaberry's social and economic policies "with serenity and firmness." Virtually all Montevideo state employes, whose labor federation was affiliated with the CNT, struck Jan. 18 to protest Bordaberry's veto of certain provisions of the new government budget.

Bordaberry had promised that Uruguay would meet its foreign debt repayment schedule for the first quarter of 1973 without seeking refinancing, the newsletter Latin America reported Jan. 5. Finance Minister Moises Cohen had said export earnings should be about $100 million during the period, enough to insure the payments.

The Inter-American Development Bank had approved a $10 million loan toward the government's controversial $16.38 million scheme to build an offshore oil terminal near Punta Jose Ignacio, Latin America reported Jan. 12. The project had been opposed by nationalists in the navy and the opposition in Congress, who wanted to spend the money on building up Uruguay's merchant marine.

Agriculture Minister Benito Medero announced a new beef ban would be imposed Aug. 15–Nov. 15 in an effort to boost exports, Latin America reported Feb. 2. Meat exports in 1972 totalled 113,-000 tons, worth $102 million, compared with 80,000 tons worth $58 million in 1971, and 132,000 tons worth $74 million in 1970.

Banks commission named—A military commission was appointed Feb. 19 to oversee the operations of private banks, in cooperation with the Central Bank.

Arrests, warning vs. guerrillas. A wave of arrests took place in January after an announcement by security forces that a new offensive by left-wing Tupamaro guerrillas was imminent, according to Latin America. Left-wing circles were said to doubt the truth of the announcement and fear it was an excuse to round up opponents of the education law and union leaders who might be preparing to mobilize against the government's economic policies.

(The government had closed the left-wing newspaper Ultima Hora for three days for printing in its Jan. 10 edition statements by a former army captain about the torture of Tupamaros by army interrogators.)

Guarantees suspension extended. The Permanent Committee of the Executive Power, acting for Congress while both houses were recessed, voted 6–5 Feb. 15 to extend the suspension of individual guarantees for 45 days. The extension, requested by President Bordaberry, was the fifth since guarantees were suspended in April 1972 to help authorities combat left-wing Tupamaro guerrillas.

Interior Minister Nestor Bolentini admitted that "to eliminate subversion with measures of force is impossible. It can be done only by capturing [the subversives'] banners, and thus winning over youth, so that youth will not be fooled." A congressman of the opposition Blanco party interrupted Bolentini to assert Blancos had been saying such things for years, but a legislator from the left-wing Broad Front coalition said the minister deserved "critical support" for recognizing for the first time that Tupamaros were not merely "mafiosos or criminals."

The National Labor Confederation had held a two-hour strike earlier Feb. 15 to demand the immediate restoration of individual guarantees.

The suspension of individual guarantees was extended by Congress March 31 for another 60 days.

The extension, requested by President Bordaberry, was approved 65-63 after more than 30 hours of debate. As in previous votes, it was supported by most Colorado factions and the right-wing minority Blanco faction, and opposed by certain Colorado sectors the moderate Blanco majority faction and the Broad Front.

The government's case was presented March 30 by Defense Minister Walter Ravenna and Interior Minister Nestor Bolentini. In a four-hour speech, Bolentini argued that although the urban guerrilla movement was practically defeated, it should not be given an opportunity to reorganize. The most vigorous rebuttal was delivered by Colorado Sen. Vasconcellos, who again castigated the armed forces, warning them to "stay within the constitution and the law" and to "aim their threats elsewhere."

Tupamaro jail break—Four Tupamaros, including guerrilla leader Gabino Falero Montes, escaped from a Montevideo military prison Feb. 27 after overpowering a guard.

Mitrione killers reported seized—Security officials March 20 announced the capture of four of the men involved in the 1970 kidnap-murder of U.S. police specialist Dan A. Mitrione. A fifth accomplice had been killed in a clash with police, the officials said.

Antonio Mas Mas, identified as a Spanish student who joined the Tupamaros while attending Montevideo University, was said to have killed Mitrione. His accomplices were identified as Henry Engler, Esteban Pereira and Rodolfo Wolf, arrested with him, and Armando Blanco, killed by police. Engler was said to have directed the abduction and ordered the killing.

Anti-corruption campaign. The federal prosecutor Feb. 19 asked for the lifting of the parliamentary immunity of two congressmen, Edgar Guedes and Carmelo Cabrera Giordano, both ex-presidents of the Montevideo Departmental Council, which was under investigation on extensive corruption charges. The resignations of both were accepted by the Chamber of Deputies Feb. 21. Cabrera was already in prison, but Guedes had disappeared.

The armed forces had announced Feb. 14 that a retired army colonel, Amilcar Feola Casella, would be tried by a military court on charges of illegally importing and selling foreign automobiles.

Pereyra recalled on corruption charge—Ulises Pereyra Reverbel, Uruguay's representative to the Inter-American Development Bank in Washington, was recalled to Montevideo to face military charges of corruption during his tenure as head of the state telephone company UTE, under the administration of ex-President Jorge Pacheco Areco, Latin America reported March 9.

Pereyra and associates were accused of accepting a commission of $500,000 for placing a UTE equipment order with a Spanish firm. Others allegedly involved in the scandal, named by Montevideo newspapers, were a cousin of Pacheco, a brother of ex-Defense Minister Federico Garcia Capurro, and President Bordaberry's campaign manager, Miguel Paez Vilaro. Pereyra denied the more serious allegations, but admitted receiving a racehorse from the Spanish firm, Latin America reported.

Pereyra had long been accused of corruption by opposition congressmen and by the Tupamaros, who held him captive for more than a year in 1971-72.

Military attack on Vasconcellos. The armed forces March 9 asked President Bordaberry to request abrogation of the parliamentary immunity of Colorado Sen. Amilcar Vasconcellos, one of the military's most outspoken critics in the legislature.

The request was based on a speech by Vasconcellos Feb. 1 which was deemed "an attack on the moral integrity of the armed forces." Vasconcellos had charged the military was planning to seize power.

Gold sale & security bill assailed. Opposition groups were reported infuriated by the government's disclosure March 15, at the insistence of the military, that it had secretly sold $65 million worth of Uruguay's gold reserves in 1972 to meet pressing obligations to international creditors.

The Blanco majority faction immediately instituted impeachment proceedings against President Bordaberry, Economy Minister Moises Cohen, who disclosed the sale, and ex-Economy Minister Francisco Forteza, who was in office when the sale was negotiated. The Blancos and other opposition groups—which also called for Bordaberry's resignation—were said to be incensed less over the sale itself than the secrecy under which it was negotiated.

Another call for Bordaberry's resignation was made March 29 by 150,000 members of the National Labor Confederation at a demonstration in Montevideo. The union protested the secret sale of the gold reserves and a government security bill pending in Congress that would suspend many of the constitutional guarantees of Uruguayan citizens.

According to the London newsletter Latin America March 30, the bill, known as the Consolidation of the Peace Law, allowed military tribunals to order the indefinite detainment of persons whose conduct suggested they might be inclined to commit crimes against the state, persons who had legally or illegally assisted others accused of planning to commit crimes against the state, persons who frequented the same places as persons accused of committing crimes against the state, and persons who might be associated with subversive elements through possession of some object which had belonged to the subversive elements.

The preamble to the bill, according to Latin America, equated the left-wing Tupamaro guerrilla movement with common criminality by referring to "instincts of special ferocity, genuine criminal delirium, the flowering of inherited tendencies, subhuman fear and vengeance peculiar to psychopathic personalities." This specific denial of the political basis of Tupamaro activities contradicted an earlier admission by Interior Minister Nestor Bolentini that armed subversion would exist as long as the social and economic conditions that gave rise to it persisted.

Armed forces score Congress, parties. The armed forces commanders charged in a nationwide radio and television broadcast March 23 that Congress and "certain political parties" were obstructing reforms approved by the military and President Juan Maria Bordaberry in February.

The charge, endorsed by Bordaberry, and subsequent denials by most political leaders marked the second major confrontation in two months between the military and civilian political sectors. Military personnel seized Montevideo radio and television facilities to broadcast the attack and simultaneously placed troops in the capital on alert. The troops were reported off alert the next day, however, and the city was reported calm.

The armed forces commanders—army Gen. Hugo Chiappe Posse, navy Capt. Conrado Olazabal and air force Brig. Jose Perez Caldas—blamed political leaders for what they called "the moral deterioration of public administration and the loss of faith by the population at all levels." They charged that reforms demanded by the armed forces to "rebuild" Uruguay were being blocked in Congress by certain "privileged" sectors seeking to protect "a situation that brought them power and personal benefits over a long period of time."

Among the alleged benefits cited by the commanders were campaign loans to political parties by the National Savings and Discount Fund, and housing loans to political leaders provided under a special law. Documentary proof of these was offered to the press.

The commanders also charged that in recent years when armed subversion was "at its highest," representatives of the same corrupt political sectors had "initiated secret negotiations with certain leaders of the clandestine movement. They did this to create the proper conditions for themselves in the event the subversives won, instead of joining ranks to fight sedition and save the institutional system."

The commanders' statement was criticized by politicians of most parties, including the three major political forces—the ruling Colorado party, the opposition Blanco party and the left-wing Broad Front coalition. The military was accused of taking special privileges, including duty-free imports and subsidized housing, and of merely paying lip service to reform. The Christian Democrats, who welcomed military intervention in the government in February, were reported particularly critical of the government's subsequent failure to send reform laws to Congress.

Jorge Batlle, leader of an important Colorado sector, criticized the armed forces March 24, albeit in conciliatory terms. He said his faction too wanted "an honest and efficient administration [and] a profound reform that will modernize Uruguay," and noted that Congress had acted moderately since February to keep from deepening the rift between the military and the civilian administration. He admitted, however, that his faction had outstanding campaign loans from the National Savings and Discount Fund, for which he was "ashamed."

A stronger denunciation of the military was issued by the liberal majority faction of the Blanco party March 27. The group rejected the military charges, asserting it was "not intimidated by [this] show of force nor by the threats of those who wish to control the political sector, overriding the popular will."

Blanco leader in controversy—The national directorate of the opposition Blanco party declared June 5 that any attack on its president, retired navy Capt. Homar Murdoch, was an attack on the entire party.

Murdoch had been accused of "attacking the moral dignity of the armed forces" in a declaration signed by him and other Blanco leaders, which pledged resistance to "any attempt ... to return Uruguay to the era of government by force." Murdoch's arrest reportedly had been ordered, but had not been carried out. Current divisions within the navy and uncertainty over the legality of prosecuting only Murdoch—and not all who signed the declaration—were cited by Latin America June 8 as reasons for Murdoch's continued freedom.

Military Precipitate Crisis, Constitutional Rule Suspended

Minister quits in protest. Commerce Minister Luis Balparda Blengio resigned May 17 amid a new political crisis resulting from military pressure on the Senate to remove the parliamentary immunity of a left-wing senator.

The senator, Enrique Erro of the Broad Front coalition, was accused by the armed forces of cooperating with the Tupamaro guerrilla movement. He denied the charge. President Juan Maria Bordaberry had asked the Senate to lift Erro's immunity so he could be prosecuted before the military supreme court.

Despite considerable military pressure, including the posting of extra troops outside Congress, the Senate did not approve Bordaberry's request in its deliberations May 13–17. The measure required a two-thirds majority but was backed by only about half of the senators. The Senate instead approved a resolution early May 18 "declining competence" in the case and passing it to the Chamber of Deputies. According to La Prensa of Buenos Aires May 18, Erro would be given a "political trial" in the Chamber of Deputies. If the Chamber found him guilty, the case would go back to the Senate, which then could, by a two-thirds majority, remove him from office. Erro could then be tried, but only by the civilian supreme court.

A resolution for Erro's trial was introduced in the Chamber May 17 by Carlos M. Fleitas, a pro-government deputy.

The Senate resolution also asked Bordaberry to call off the surveillance to which Erro recently had been subjected. The senator had been followed, and extra guards had been placed outside embassies where he might take refuge, particularly those of Chile and Peru. Chile reportedly protested the increase in police May 9. Despite the Senate request, police and soldiers remained outside Erro's home May 19.

The armed forces gave Bordaberry their charges against Erro April 10. The military had sought to prosecute the senator in October 1972, but Bordaberry had declined to ask abrogation of his immunity on grounds the evidence against him was insufficient. Bordaberry requested the abrogation April 25.

Erro was accused of maintaining contacts with a number of Tupamaros and allowing a doctor to treat wounded guerrillas in his home. He denied the charges, alleging testimony linking him to subversives was "extracted through torture" from the guerrillas. Observers noted the evidence against Erro came from known Tupamaro defectors, such as Hector Amodio Perez, or from prisoners who had been tortured severely, the London newsletter Latin America reported May 4.

The Senate Constitution and Legislation Committee, which investigated the Erro case before it went to the full Senate, asked to interrogate the Tupamaros who testified against the senator, but permission was denied by the military May 7. However, Bordaberry interceded May 8 to allow Amodio Perez to be questioned. The interrogation was boycotted by Sen. Martin Echegoyen, who demanded to see all the guerrillas testifying. Sen. Zelmar Michelini walked out because the chief of military intelligence, Col. Ramon Trabal, insisted on being present.

Amodio Perez repeated his charges against Erro to the senators and then briefly appeared before the press. The questioning was marked by an incident between Trabal and Sen. Dardo Ortiz of the opposition Blanco party, which occurred when Ortiz obtained a sample of Amodio Perez' handwriting and Trabal demanded it. Trabal ordered Ortiz detained until he handed over the sample, but the order was rescinded.

Ortiz said he wished to compare the sample with handwriting attributed to Amodio Perez in a document in his possession. The senator said the document described an agreement between armed forces officials and some captured Tupamaros to discredit prominent politicians by falsely linking them to the guerrilla movement.

The confrontation between the military and the Senate sharpened May 13 with reports in the press of a military document which accused unnamed legislators of "corrupt practices." In apparent reference to Congress, the document asked: "Who allowed the destruction of the economy and of public morality, creating, fomenting and defending the cause of subversion, closing its eyes to the grave process of deterioration and corruption in the country in the last decades, sustaining a tired and criminal liberalism?" The document declared the military would "maintain measures of force in order to act at any moment."

Senators subsequently tried to reach a compromise with armed forces officers on the Erro case, but the military rejected their efforts. Legislators were reported to be disturbed by reports May 16 that Bordaberry would order Erro's arrest even if his immunity were upheld.

Balparda Blengio, one of three conservative Blancos in the Cabinet, resigned the next day. He said the "current national juncture" constituted a "substantial alteration" of the principles under which he and his colleagues had agreed to join the government.

Colonel arrested—An army lieutenant colonel, Luis Lalo Vasquez, had been arrested for alleged connections with the Tupamaros, the police announced May 25.

Emergency measures imposed. President Juan Maria Bordaberry decreed emergency security measures June 1, after he lost his majority in Congress and the suspension of individual guarantees expired.

The measures, imposed indefinitely to combat alleged subversion, could be overturned by Congress. They allowed detention without trial, searches and arrests without court order, and partial press censorship. They were in force during most of the rule of Bordaberry's predecessor and political mentor, Jorge Pacheco Areco, when the Tupamaro guerrilla movement was much stronger.

The presidential decree chided Congress for failing to pass a government security law that would have replaced the suspension of guarantees. It alleged Congress had "consequently left the nation ... defenseless" against "subversives," who were forming new organizations and continuing their program of "infiltration and development" among "the masses." Observers noted the decree conflicted with frequent government assertions that the Tupamaros had virtually been wiped out.

Bordaberry asserted in a nationwide radio and television address later June 1 that subversion was "always latent" in Uruguay, and that guerrillas were currently regrouping in "hostile" countries. He did not name the countries.

Interior Minister Nestor Bolentini alleged in a newspaper interview June 10 that there was evidence of "new" subversive groups whose members were "trained abroad." He said the groups were distinct from Uruguay's "traditional" guerrillas—presumably the Tupamaros and the Popular Revolutionary Organization-33—but resembled them in wanting to reach power by force.

Bordaberry decreed the emergency measures after the Lista 15 faction of his Colorado party withdrew its support from the government, making an extension of the suspension of guarantees impossible. The faction reportedly defected because of repeated attempts by the armed forces to implicate its leader, Jorge Batlle, in corruption under Pacheco Areco's administration.

Batlle indirectly attacked the armed forces at a political meeting June 2, charging: "Instead of political parties, someone, or some persons elected by no one, trustees of all knowledge, of all honesty, of all genius, [have come] to represent or to replace everyone who votes and thinks, saying: We are the political party, we elect, we rule, we are perfect, honest, unimpeachable, the only ones who are capable, who can resolve everything." This, he asserted, "is dictatorship, dictatorship, it is not democracy."

A stronger attack was delivered June 4 by Sen. Amilcar Vasconcellos, also a Colorado. Vasconcellos asserted Uruguay was on an "accelerated path to militarism. This is a government imposed and directed by the officers." He urged Congress to overturn the emergency security measures, asserting they were designed to prevent the disclosure of "facts that would make everyone's hair stand on end."

"We are entering a period of torture the like of which the republic has never seen," Vasconcellos charged. He had headed a commission investigating police torture a few years back.

Another senator, Juan Pablo Terra of the left-wing Christian Democratic party, had charged in a newspaper editorial June 4 that a young worker recently had been tortured to death at a military installation in the central department of Durazno. The charge was rejected by the army commander, Gen. Hugo Chiappe Posse, who accused Terra of indirectly aiding subversion.

The Senate June 4 summoned Defense Minister Walter Ravenna to answer the torture charge, but he refused to appear unless Terra retracted personal criticism of him in the editorial. Terra had asserted that "Ravenna is nothing and we can expect nothing of him. [He] represents the president." He added that Bordaberry would not aid torture victims.

Congress dissolved. President Juan Maria Bordaberry yielded to intense pressure from the armed forces and dissolved Congress June 27, ending 40 years of Uruguayan constitutional rule.

The action followed a series of increasingly sharp confrontations between the military and civilian politicians. The latest developments were the rejection by the Chamber of Deputies June 21 of impeachment proceedings against leftist Sen. Enrique Erro, accused by the military of aiding the Tupamaro guerrilla movement; and the decision by the Senate June 26 to investigate charges of torture at a military installation in Paysandu state.

The dissolution decree, signed by Bordaberry, Interior Minister Nestor Bolentini and Defense Minister Walter Ravenna, charged the Chamber had ignored "fundamental principles of the Constitution" in rejecting the charges against Erro. It alleged Uruguayan governmental, labor and educational institutions had been undermined by a "conspiracy against the fatherland, aided by the complacency of political groups without national spirit."

The decree announced creation of a Council of State, with members yet to be designated, to "independently" perform congressional functions, oversee the president's activities, and formulate constitutional reforms for a national plebiscite.

The nation's news media, already partially censored, was barred from imputing "dictatorial goals" to Bordaberry, and the armed forces and police were authorized to take "the necessary measures" to prevent disruption of essential public services. Schools were later ordered closed until July 20 to avoid student disturbances.

Uruguay's 19 municipal councils were dissolved June 28. Officials said they would be replaced by boards of appointees working directly under the new government.

Bordaberry claimed in a radio and television broadcast June 27 that he was acting in defense of Uruguayan institutions, alleging the nation had been "heading toward disaster under the appearance of institutionality." He reaffirmed his "profound democratic vocation," rejecting "all ideology of Marxist origin," and vowed elections would take place as scheduled in November 1976.

The president severely criticized Congress, particularly for its refusal to impeach Erro, whom he called a traitor.

A warrant for Erro's arrest was issued June 27, but the senator was in Buenos Aires, where he asked political asylum. Erro again denied any connection with the Tupamaros but asserted: "The Uruguayan government has just created thousands of Tupamaros, for it opened the eyes of those who thought we could, through peaceful change, extract the country from its position of dependency and submission to the dictates of organisms such as the IDB [Inter-American Development Bank], OAS [Organization of American States] and the United States."

Erro and another leftist senator, Zelmar Michelini, who also asked Argentine asylum, denounced the U.S. for aiding Uruguay's security forces and for allegedly providing training and equipment for the torture of political prisoners.

Cabinet officials quit in protest—Education and Culture Minister José Maria Robaina and Public Health Minister Pablo Purriel resigned June 26, after Bordaberry decided to close Congress.

Other officials of both Bordaberry's Colorado party and the opposition parties denounced the government June 27, when troops locked up the Chamber and Senate.

Colorado Sen. Amilcar Vasconcellos, one of the military's most strident critics, asserted "the Uruguayan people cannot be governed by any kind of dictatorship."

Sen. Wilson Ferreira Aldunate, leader of the majority faction of the opposition Blanco party, said he would "openly fight those who subdue the Constitution," particularly the president. "We are at war with Mr. Juan Maria Bordaberry, enemy of our country," Ferreira asserted.

Ferreira reportedly flew to Buenos Aires and sought political asylum there June 27. Two other Blanco leaders—Chamber of Deputies President Hector Gutierrez Ruiz and Sen. Carlos Julio Pereyra—also reportedly fled to Argentina.

General strike. The Communist-led National Labor Confederation (CNT) called an indefinite general strike June 27 to demand restoration of the right to political and labor union activity and of all constitutional guarantees; immediate economic reforms, including nationalization of the banks and restoration of the buying power of wages; and disbanding of "the fascist bands that act with impunity in the schools."

Commerce and transportation gradually stopped in Montevideo June 27. Buses and taxis disappeared from the streets and were replaced by patrolling army and police vehicles. Newspapers shut down in protest, and radio and television stations were forced to broadcast only government announcements, military marches and folk music.

Workers occupied most banks in the capital and an undetermined number of factories, government offices, public services and state utilities June 28. Essential articles became scarce, and fuel reserves dropped to a critical level. Students occupied the National University to "repudiate the gorilla coup."

Government officials and CNT leaders negotiated fruitlessly June 29. Bordaberry met afterwards with the National Security Council and later ordered workers to relinquish all occupied installations. The CNT was outlawed the next day, and troops were sent to break the strike.

Police, navy and army units cleared factories, banks, government offices and the main oil installations June 30, arresting an undetermined number of strikers. Soldiers raided CNT headquarters, confiscating records and arresting union leaders. The government said all strikers would be "submitted to criminal justice"; the CNT asserted, however, that it was prepared for this and would continue to operate underground.

Troops cleared the main building of the National University June 30, arresting about 100, but students later reoccupied it. Police dislodged workers from the offices of the newspapers La Manana and El Diario, but employes occupied the Colorado daily El Dia.

Despite the police and troop operations, the strike continued, with large textile, metallurgical and tire factories still occupied, CNT sources said late June 30.

(A CNT general strike for 65%-80% wage increases had virtually paralyzed Uruguay June 21. The stoppage, the eighth of Bordaberry's administration, was accompanied by student disturbances in which 230 youths were arrested.)

The government made a number of moves to end the strike as critical food and fuel shortages developed. It placed employes of the state alcohol and combustibles administration under military rule July 3 to reopen the state oil refinery. Wage increases were declared the same day.

The increases—31.48% for private sector workers and 25% for civil servants—were accompanied by price rises for more than 100 products and services. The CNT deemed them insufficient, standing by previous demands for 65%-80% wage hikes to regain buying power lost over the previous six years. (The cost of living had risen by 33.1% during the first five months of 1972, according to official statistics reported June 15.)

Bordaberry declared July 4 that striking civil servants would be fired, and that striking employes in the private sector could be fired without compensation. Troops and police simultaneously sought 52 union leaders said to be in hiding, including CNT President José D'Elia, and Enrique Pastorino, president of the World Federation of Trade Unions and a winner of the 1973 Lenin Peace Prize. Union sources had said July 3 that at least 400 workers had been arrested.

The Montevideo newspaper Accion closed in protest July 3, after troops seized its July 2 edition, and three other dailies shut down July 4 to protest censorship. All newspapers were reported back in circulation July 8.

Strikers July 9 staged a Montevideo protest march that was crushed violently by the authorities.

About 5,000 protesters, parading down the city's July 18th Avenue, were set upon by armed police and soldiers. Mounted police with drawn sabers charged the crowd while other police fired tear gas and beat fleeing demonstrators. More than a dozen tanks were sent into the heart of the city, crashing through half-built barricades and taking up positions around Bordaberry's official residence. At least two persons were reported killed, at least 20 wounded and 300 arrested.

Two others persons were killed as a result of the strike—a high-school student was shot by police late July 8 as he painted anti-government slogans on a wall, and a young man was killed by an army patrol July 6. A demonstration by some 3,000 persons, mostly women, was broken up July 3 by police firing tear gas and water cannon.

Strike broken. After 15 days the CNT conceded defeat and called off the general strike July 11.

The federation's underground leadership, depleted by arrests, issued a communique admitting the strike had not "achieved the desired victory." It asserted the "battle" against Bordaberry and the armed forces "must continue, but it is necessary to change the form of struggle."

Interior Minister Col. Nestor Bolentini told newsmen the CNT's dissolution was "irreversible" and announced a new government labor policy to make the unions nonpolitical. Bolentini suggested a new labor organization would be formed which would not "be permitted to intervene in political questions that distort the true sense of union association."

The end of the general strike reportedly resulted from secret contacts between the government and union officials. The government reportedly offered to release all political prisoners, restore union and political rights, review salaries and lift other restrictions on civil liberties in exchange for a 180-day truce. Union leaders said they had not accepted the offer but had agreed to end the strike.

The military commanders, accused by the strikers of seizing power, asserted July 11 that they were "completely subordinated" to Bordaberry and that Uruguay remained under civilian rule. They reaffirmed their adherence to the "national reconstruction" program accepted by Bordaberry in February.

Cabinet revised. The strike over, Bordaberry swore in four new Cabinet ministers July 11, replacing officials who resigned to protest the dissolution of democratic institutions. Two ministers had quit the day before Congress was closed, and three others—Public Works Minister Angel Servetti, Industry and Commerce Minister Jorge Presno, and Planning and Budget Office Director Ricardo Zerbino—had resigned July 3.

The new ministers were all conservative civilians but not politicians. Edmundo Narancio, a historian, was named education and culture minister; Jose Etcheverry Stirling, a literature professor, industry and commerce minister; Eduardo Crispo Ayala, an engineer, public works minister; and Juan Bruno Iruleguy, a physician, public health minister.

Meanwhile, secret negotiations were under way among the government, the military, politicians and union leaders to try to resolve Uruguay's political stalemate, according to most sources. Negotiators included ex-Defense Minister Armando Malet, talking with the armed forces, law professor Adolfo Gelsi, dealing with the government, and attorney Ramón Valdez, consulting political parties, the London newsletter Latin America reported July 13.

The two major opposition groups, the moderate Blanco party and the left-wing Broad Front coalition, had issued a joint statement July 5 calling for Bordaberry's resignation and establishment of a representative provisional government. They called for re-establishment of "legal and constitutional liberties, rights and guarantees to their full extent," and for a "minimal program of social and economic change which, eliminating the privileges currently enjoyed by economically powerful sectors and freeing the nation from external dependence, creates a real possibility for progress."

A resistance committee in exile had been formed in Buenos Aires by Broad Front Sen. Enrique Erro, Blanco Sen. Wilson Ferreira Aldunate and four other opposition legislators, it was reported July 16. The group would coordinate resistance within Uruguay and abroad because many other opposition leaders had been arrested.

Government opponents jailed recently included Broad Front President Liber Seregni, Blanco President Homar Murdoch, Socialist party leader José Cardozo, Broad Front leaders Gen. Victor Licandro and Col. Carlos Zufriategui, and six congressmen, it was reported July 10.

Erro charged July 15 that Uruguay's "military commanders aim to set up a Brazilian-type regime." He asserted the committee had the "solidarity and hospitality" of Argentina's Peronist government. Erro said the military had accused him of supporting the Tupamaro guerrillas "because I refused to condemn them and I pointed out that even Pope Paul has justified the use of violence in the struggle against tyranny."

Labor unions curbed. The government Aug. 1 decreed a law designed to end the autonomy of the nation's once progressive labor unions.

The measure, called the Job Security Law, required all unions to obtain official recognition, forbade union involvement in politics, and allowed strikes only to press wage claims and protest working conditions. It provided for "supervision" of union elections by the official electoral court, government monitoring of the use of union funds, and establishment of government tribunals to deal with labor disputes.

The law also prohibited members of the outlawed National Labor Confederation (CNT) from standing for union posts, forcing the group's Communist leadership to remain underground. The government and the armed forces had explained in a recent television campaign that the CNT must be liquidated to rid the unions of foreign influence, according to the newsletter Latin America July 27.

The CNT, which claimed 400,000 members before it was banned June 30, Aug. 1 called off a general strike scheduled for the next day, reportedly because the union leadership feared the stoppage would be a complete failure.

Bordaberry, Sapelli clash. President Bordaberry, in a letter made public Aug. 1, criticized Vice President Jorge Sapelli for publicly refusing a seat on the projected Council of State and calling for an early return to constitutional rule.

Sapelli had declared July 29 that he was not responsible for the recent dissolution of Congress, and would not sit on the council until freedom of expression and political activity were restored. His statement was praised by members of the different political parties and the Roman Catholic Church hierarchy, and, according to a report Aug. 10, by Interior Minister Nestor Bolentini.

Bordaberry defended the government's recent repressive actions, calling them necessary to defend Uruguayan institutions from "bad politicians" and "enemies of the fatherland." He charged that some of the praise for Sapelli's statement came from persons who had used "all means, from treason to murder, to calumny, threat and conspiracy," to discredit Uruguay abroad.

Press restrictions. Severe restrictions on the press continued with the closing of the leftist newspaper Ultima Hora for 20 days Aug. 9, of the Broad Front daily Ahora for 10 editions Aug. 14, of the Communist newspaper El Popular for 10 days Aug. 27, and of the prestigious left-wing weekly Marcha for six editions Aug. 27. Both El Popular and Marcha had been closed temporarily in July, Marcha for printing the government's repressive decrees under the headline, "This Is Not a Dictatorship."

Ultima Hora was closed for revealing the contents of mysterious anonymous letters, left in a number of newspaper offices, addressed to senior officers of the armed forces. The writers, apparently junior officers, called for implementation of the military program of far-reaching social and economic reforms accepted by Bordaberry in February.

Murdoch & others released. The president of the opposition Blanco party, retired navy Capt. Homar Murdoch, was reported released Aug. 31 after being held for more than six weeks in a military garrison. Five Blanco legislators were freed July 23 after two weeks in jail, and four leaders of the left-wing Broad Front coalition were released July 26 after four days in prison.

The Broad Front president, retired Gen. Liber Seregni, remained in prison along with his top aides, retired Gen. Victor Licandro and retired Col. Carlos Zufriategui. The government Aug. 20 banned circulation of a public petition for Seregni's release.

Some 4,000 political prisoners currently crowded Uruguay's prisons, and persons were arrested daily who had never taken part in revolutionary activity and were merely suspected of "links with sedition," according to the newsletter Latin America Aug. 24. There was little doubt that detainees were routinely tortured at military garrisons and police stations, the newsletter reported.

Chamber head ordered arrested. A warrant was issued Sept. 7 for the arrest of Hector Gutierrez Ruiz, president of the Chamber of Deputies, for alleged collaboration with the Tupamaro guerrilla movement. Gutierrez was in Buenos Aires, Argentina, where he fled immediately after President Bordaberry dissolved the Chamber in late June.

Charges against Gutierrez included changing into national currency $300,000 worth of gold and pounds sterling stolen by Tupamaros in 1971; and pretending to have been kidnapped by Tupamaros and given evidence of police "death squads" in 1972.

A second Chamber member, Hugo Batalla of the Broad Front, had been arrested Sept. 3 for alleged links to the Tupamaros but released Sept. 5 for lack of evidence. Military officials had claimed in announcing the arrest that arms and subversive literature had been found in Batalla's Chamber office.

The armed forces claimed in a radio and television broadcast Sept. 7 that the Tupamaros were reorganizing and currently attempting to infiltrate labor and student organizations. Newsmen were shown a basement hideout in a house under construction outside Montevideo, which officers said would have been used to print subversive literature.

Authorities charged Sept. 22 that some 500 subversives from Bolivia, Peru, Argentina, Chile and Uruguay had been meeting in Santiago, Chile under the leadership of fugitive Tupamaro Raúl Bidegain Creissing and said they planned to slip into Uruguay within two years to promote guerrilla warfare.

6,000 political prisoners reported—The exile Committee for the Defense of Uruguayan Political Prisoners charged in the Buenos Aires newspaper El Mundo Nov. 8 that there were about 6,000 political prisoners in Uruguay, all "continually harassed and living in subhuman conditions."

The Communist Party newspaper El Popular of Montevideo had reported the detention of numerous union leaders, including Felix Diaz, leader of the outlawed National Labor Confederation, according to Prensa Latina Nov. 8. Ramon Caceres, secretary general of the Textile Union, was reportedly seized in October.

In a related development Nov. 14, the committee for political prisoners reported that Raúl Sendic, a founder of the Tupamaro movement, and eight other guerrillas had been sentenced to death by a military court in Montevideo. But they reportedly would be executed only if the Tupamaros continued to operate.

Beef ban imposed. The government Aug. 14 decreed a three-month ban on domestic beef sales to stimulate beef exports. The measure, in effect Aug. 19, followed a four-month beef ban in 1972. Beef and wool exports were Uruguay's major sources of foreign earnings. The ban ended as scheduled Nov. 15. After the ban was lifted, local beef prices rose about 30% to 40% Nov. 16.

The World Bank Oct. 25 had announced a $13.5 million loan to help finance the second stage of a fourth livestock development program in Uruguay. (The bank's livestock loans in the country totaled $54.7 million.)

Meanwhile, the economy continued to stagnate, with a 104% cost of living increase recorded for the year ending July 31. Government figures reported Aug. 25 showed the increase for July alone was 13.2%. The wheat crop was among the worst in history, forcing Uruguay to import wheat from the U.S. while world market prices were rising, it was reported Aug. 24.

President Juan Maria Bordaberry and the national cattle and meat interests maintained Uruguay would be better off if its weak economy were "rationalized" and integrated with the booming Brazilian economy, the London newsletter Latin America reported Aug. 3. Their position reportedly was supported by the U.S. and Brazilian embassies in Montevideo but was opposed by Uruguayan industrialists, who feared having to compete with goods from Brazilian cities.

Foreign Minister Juan Carlos Blanco said Aug. 5 that it was "monstrous to think that Uruguay might cease to be independent," in response to a recent speech to the Brazilian Chamber of Deputies by a Brazilian geopolitician, Enrique da Rocha Correa, who outlined the "conveniences" of having Uruguay united with or economically dependent on Brazil.

Many Uruguayan landowners believed the process of Uruguayan-Brazilian economic integration was already under way, and were investing confidently in machinery, fertilizers and pasture improvement schemes, Latin America reported. Extensive Brazilian purchases of land in Uruguayan border states had been reported in July 1972.

Peso devalued. The government devalued the peso by 1.76% Sept. 7 and by another 2.15% Sept. 28, bringing the total devaluation since the beginning of 1973 to 21.95%. The cost of living increased by 62.4% during the first eight months of 1973, according to a report Sept. 21, and the government estimated unemployment at 15% of the labor force.

The Central Bank announced Nov. 11 that Uruguay had met all its foreign debt payments for 1973, a total of $100 million.

Foreign news agencies to be monitored. The government issued a decree Oct. 15 establishing government monitoring of Uruguayan news sent abroad by foreign news agencies. It was the first restriction on the agencies in the 40 years they had operated in the country.

The decree, signed by President Bordaberry and three Cabinet ministers, charged "the foreign press often publishes news about Uruguay that does not conform to reality," and asserted "national public opinion" needed "informative elements to permit it to control the truth of news sent from our country."

The decree ordered the news agencies or their correspondents to submit to the Interior Ministry copies of news dispatches sent abroad. The copies, to be submitted the day they were filed, must be signed by "representatives" of the agencies concerned. Failure to comply with the order would result in "appropriate legal sanctions," according to the decree.

The order was protested Oct. 16 by the Foreign Press Club in Montevideo, which asked the Interior Ministry for "immediate clarification" of the decree's "scope and consequences." Interior Minister Bolentini denied Oct. 20 that the decree implied "any restriction. Each correspondent can file whatever he honestly thinks or believes. But public opinion and government authorities must know who is informing about Uruguay abroad."

The decree would take effect whenever the news agencies received official notification of its issuance.

Meanwhile, strict censorship of the national press continued, with more closures of newspapers and magazines. The Christian Democratic newspaper Ahora was reported closed Oct. 19 for the third time in a month, this time for reporting alleged differences between Education Minister Narancio and the army. The Communist daily El Popular and the leftist weekly Respuesta were closed Oct. 25 for two months and three weeks, respectively, for unspecified violations of official press restrictions.

El Popular, Ahora, the leftist radio station Radio Nacional and the right-wing weekly Azul y Blanco had been closed Sept. 19 for periods ranging from one to six weeks for their reports on the Chilean military coup. Radio Nacional was the first radio station shut down by the government since 1955.

A new weekly newspaper, 9 de Febrero, had recently appeared, according to the newsletter Latin America Oct. 26. The paper reportedly was supported by the Communists and Christian Democrats and appealed to the nationalist-reformist sectors in the armed forces, bitterly criticizing the Tupamaros and maintaining a distance from Bordaberry. Its name recalled the date, Feb. 9, when the military called for implementation of a program of social and economic reforms.

A frequent contributor to early editions of 9 de Febrero was Gen. Cesar Martinez, the ex-armed forces commander, reportedly sought by Communists and Christian Democrats to replace the imprisoned Gen. Liber Seregni as head of the Broad Front constituencies. The Christian Democrats in particular had consistently been willing to ally with reformist military sectors in an arrangement similar to Peru's, Latin America reported.

University closed. The government closed the University of the Republic in Montevideo Oct. 28 and announced the arrest of at least 150 students, professors and administrators, including the rector and deans of nine of the 10 faculties.

A decree turned over administration of the university to the Education Ministry for an indefinite period. It accused the former university authorities of allowing the faculties to become "a refuge for the conspiracy against the fatherland, its institutions and the security of its inhabitants."

The decree alleged police and military raids on university buildings Oct. 27 had uncovered arms, explosives and subversive literature which showed the faculties were being used for "indoctrination of youth in the Marxist ideology" and for "incitement to armed struggle."

The raids had been ordered by military authorities, Education Minister Edmundo Narancio, Defense Minister Walter Ravenna and Interior Minister Nestor Bolentini after a homemade bomb exploded in the engineering faculty building, killing a university student. The decree said university authorities were "ultimately responsible" for the student's death.

Bolentini said Oct. 28 that the rector, deans of eight faculties and acting dean of a ninth were being held under emergency measures adopted by the government in June. The dean of the law faculty was in Argentina.

The university, the only one in Uruguay, was considered the last center of strong resistance to the regime of President Bordaberry. The rector and the deans recently had made great efforts to curb antigovernment activities within the faculties, but Bordaberry had seized the pretext of the explosion to end the long Uruguayan tradition of university autonomy, according to the French newspaper Le Monde Oct. 31.

The London newsletter Latin America Nov. 16 printed what it called a well-authenticated report suggesting that the slain student, Marcos Caridad Jordan, had been killed not while assembling the bomb, as authorities claimed, but when he opened a door to which a bomb had been rigged by someone else.

Latin America also pointed out that Caridad was a leading member of the Unifying Action Groups, a student organization which had been working with the university rector to prevent any provocative act that might allow the government to seize the university. Yet the Communist party, in a presumed effort to reach an understanding with the government, accepted the government's account of the incident and attacked Caridad as an "ultra-leftist Tupamaro provocateur."

(The Cuban press agency Prensa Latina had reported Nov. 8 that the rector and most deans of the university had been bound over for military trials on charges of concealing subversives, violating state security laws and not reporting crimes.)

Elections to the university council and assembly Sept. 13 had been won by leftist opponents of the regime despite a government decree making voting in the elections compulsory, a move the government had hoped would increase the right-wing vote. Results reported by the London newsletter Latin America Sept. 21 gave 54% of the vote to the slate backed by the left-wing Broad Front coalition, 27% to candidates of the moderate opposition Blanco party, and 19% to a right-wing slate.

The agronomy faculty board had charged before the elections that agronomy student Hugo Leonardo de los Santos, arrested on charges of subversive activities, had died after being tortured by police. The board alleged de los Santos' body showed bruises, a skull fracture and internal injuries. But police, calling the student a Tupamaro guerrilla, said he had died of a stroke, according to the Miami Herald Sept. 12. De los Santos had been arrested Sept. 1, and his family had been notified of his death Sept. 4.

Residency requirement decreed—The government had decreed that university graduates must remain in Uruguay for a number of years after receiving their degrees, it was reported Oct. 12. The decision reflected growing concern in the government because many university graduates had been leaving the country to settle abroad.

Echegoyen to head Council of State. President Juan Maria Bordaberry announced Oct. 27 that Martin Echegoyen, leader of the minority conservative faction of the Blanco party, had agreed to become president of the projected Council of State.

Most prominent politicians, including Vice President Jorge Sapelli, had refused to sit on the Council, which was to replace Congress as Uruguay's major legislative body. The government's inability to form the Council also reflected the continued split between the nationalist-reformist and more conservative sectors of the armed forces, according to the newsletter Latin America Oct. 26.

Sapelli was dismissed in December by Bordaberry and was replaced as vice president by Echegoyen.

Council takes over. The 25-member Council of State was sworn in Dec. 19 to replace Congress as Uruguay's major legislative body.

The appointment of ex-Health Undersecretary Mario Arcos Perez and ex-

Salto department official Jose Antonio Varela to the Council of State was reported by La Prensa of Buenos Aires Nov. 12.

Leftist groups banned. The government Dec. 1 declared illegal 14 left-wing organizations, including the Communist and Socialist parties and several labor and student groups. At least 150 persons were arrested in the following three days.

The decree banning the groups also permanently closed the Communist newspaper El Popular and the new daily Cronica, published by El Popular's staff since October, when El Popular was closed by the government for two months. The decree also banned newspapers or magazines that "represent the continuation" of El Popular and Cronica.

The decree accused the Communist and Socialist parties of receiving "orders, assistance and support from entities outside the country" and of "simultaneously inspiring and carrying out subversion, promoting an artificial class struggle." It added that "literature and documents" found in the University of the Republic after its occupation by police and soldiers Oct. 27 showed student groups had aided the "different Marxist groups" in their activities.

Extra security details were posted in Montevideo and principal roads leading out of the city Dec. 1 as authorities occupied the offices of the banned groups and publications. A list of 80 leftist leaders "to be detained" was published the next day. The government initially confirmed only the arrest Dec. 1 of Eduardo Viera, director of El Popular.

Interior Minister Nestor Bolentini said Dec. 5 that 150 persons were arrested after the Dec. 1 decree, some under the government's emergency security measures and others simply for questioning.

The government newspaper La Manana reported Dec. 3 that Communists and other leftists who had acted against "national interests" would receive military trials.

The banned political parties belonged to the Broad Front coalition. Only the Colorado, Blanco and Christian Democratic parties, the last also a Broad Front member, remained legally active.

Peron visits; River Plate pact signed. Argentine President Juan Perón visited Montevideo briefly Nov. 19 to witness with President Bordaberry the signing of a treaty ending the two countries' century-old dispute over jurisdictional limits in the River Plate.

The pact, signed by Foreign Minister Juan Carlos Blanco and his Argentine counterpart, Alberto Vignes, followed months of negotiations. It combined the Uruguayan demand that the territorial demarcation line in the river be halfway between the two coastlines, with the Argentine demand that it be the deepwater channel nearer Uruguay. Part of the channel would be under Argentine jurisdiction despite remaining part of Uruguayan waters, but would be open to free international navigation.

The pact confirmed Argentine possession of the island of Martin Garcia, near the Uruguayan coast, but provided for a bi-national river administrative commission to operate there. The islet of Timoteo Dominguez was declared Uruguayan.

The pact also treated a number of other issues, including jurisdiction over the river bed and continental shelf, operation of Argentine and Uruguayan fishing boats in the river, port facilities and safety regulations.

Uruguay declared a national holiday Nov. 19 in honor of the treaty. Peron reportedly was given a tumultuous reception by Montevideo citizens.

Venezuela

Latin American Relations

Early in 1973 Venezuela completed arrangements for joining the Andean Group economic bloc. Venezuela and the world's other oil-producing nations continued their record-breaking oil price increases. Student unrest and guerrilla activity continued to trouble Venezuela. In the December elections, the opposition Democratic Action party won the presidency and control of both houses of Congress and most state assemblies and city councils.

Venezuela joins Andean Group. An accord on Venezuelan entry into the Andean Group was signed by President Rafael Caldera in Lima, Peru Feb. 13 as the climax of a tour that took him to Colombia, Ecuador, Chile, Argentina, Bolivia and Peru.

(Caldera's tour was also to have included a stop in Uruguay, but this was canceled Feb. 9 in view of the Uruguayan military rebellion.)

An agreement on Venezuelan entry called the "Lima Consensus" was signed by representatives of Venezuela and the Andean Group nations—those visited by Caldera except for Argentina—as Caldera and Peruvian President Juan Velasco Alvarado looked on. Terms of the pact were not disclosed, but were reported Feb. 23 to include removal within six months of Venezuela's tariffs and restrictions on numerous items from Bolivia and Ecuador—the group's poorest countries—and on a limited list of goods from Chile, Colombia and Peru. Six months after ratification the Andean commission would present a special proposal on Venezuelan participation in the group's joint program for the metal working industry.

According to the Washington Post Feb. 14, Venezuela's entry could almost double the market for many area-wide industries since most Venezuelans participated in the consumer society, unlike large portions of the populations of the more economically backward members of the Andean Group. Venezuela's stable currency and extensive foreign exchange reserves were also regarded as a prime source of capital for the other nations of the group.

The Lima Concensus ended 11 months of negotiations on Venezuelan entry, clouded most recently by Venezuelan concern about potential currency devaluations, the number of tariff exceptions to be given Venezuela, and voting procedures. The negotiations were temporarily halted Feb. 10, but the impasse was broken through the personal intervention of Caldera and Velasco Alvarado.

Caldera, accompanied by other government officials and a technical mission, visited Colombia Feb. 5, Educador Feb. 5–7, Chile Feb. 7, Argentina Feb. 7–11, Bolivia Feb. 11–12, and Peru Feb. 12–13. He conferred with the head of state of each country and with other government officials.

According to the London newsletter Latin America Feb. 16, Caldera made it clear throughout his tour that the continent's Spanish-speaking countries saw their roles in the world very differently from Brazil. He expressed numerous views opposed by the Brazilian regime, including approval of ideological "pluralism" and support for Chile "in any situation." Caldera implied his government eventually would resume relations with Cuba—also opposed by Brazil—saying "we cannot assert that Cuba has interfered in Venezuelan affairs." The Brazilian press criticized Venezuelan entry into the Andean Group Feb. 16.

Caldera held a cordial meeting with Brazilian President Emilio G. Medici in the Venezuelan border town of Santa Elena de Uairen Feb. 20.

A Venezuelan negotiating team returned from Rio de Janeiro Feb. 1 after completing preliminary talks with Brazilian officials on the sale of Venezuelan crude oil to Brazil in exchange for refined derivatives.

Colombian talks. Talks between Venezuela and Colombia on sovereignty over the oil-rich Gulf of Venezuela resumed in Rome in March but were called off by Colombia April 17.

The Colombian Foreign Ministry said May 4 that Venezuela should choose the means to resolve the conflict, but observers noted that Venezuela's preference, negotiations at the foreign ministry level, had previously been rejected by Colombia. Colombia reportedly favored international arbitration, preferably by the International Court of Justice.

Pastrana's visit—Colombian President Misael Pastrana Borrero visited Venezuela July 22–25 and conferred with President Rafael Caldera. A joint communiqué issued at the end of the visit praised "representative democracy" and "pluralist solidarity" among Latin American peoples, but made no reference to the dispute between Venezuela and Colombia over the Gulf of Venezuela.

Foreign Minister Aristides Calvani and his Colombian counterpart, Alfredo Vasquez Carrizosa, met in Bogota Oct. 15–17 and again in Caracas Nov. 6–7 to discuss border and territorial waters disputes between the two countries.

Dutch talks held. Dutch and Venezuelan officials began a second round of talks in Caracas June 29 on demarcation of territorial waters between Venezuela and the Netherlands Antilles. Venezuela claimed a 12-mile limit and the Netherlands only a three-mile limit. The first round of talks, in The Hague in April, led to the establishment of ferry service between Venezuela and the islands of Aruba and Curacao.

Unrest, Terrorism

Student riots. At least 65 persons were injured and more than 150 arrested during disturbances by high school and technical school students in Caracas and other cities Jan. 31–Feb. 27. A youth was killed Feb. 22 in a Caracas neighborhood riot reportedly growing out of the student unrest. Among highlights of the disturbances:

Students in Valencia rioted for the third consecutive day Feb. 7, looting stores, blocking traffic and stoning policemen. Youths in Caracas and Maturin burned vehicles and damaged businesses, while students in Barquisimeto blocked streets and burned buses in support of a strike by educational workers demanding an acceleration of collective wage bargaining.

National Guard troops were called into Barquisimeto Feb. 19 after students burned a bank and stoned several stores. Five policemen were injured in clashes with the rioters. Youths also rioted in Caracas and in Maracaibo, where they supported strikes by teachers and jitney drivers.

Students from 12 high schools and technical schools in Caracas burned vehicles and clashed with police Feb. 20. Nineteen persons, including 13 policemen, were reported injured, some by Molotov cocktails. Teachers at one school charged police had invaded their building and attacked students indiscriminately.

Students rioted in Caracas, Maracaibo, Maturin, Barcelona, Puerto La Cruz, Valera and Barquisimeto Feb 21. Teachers in Maturin charged police were provoking some disturbances.

Businesses in downtown Caracas closed and classes at 30 intermediate schools were suspended Feb. 22 as student riots entered their fourth day. Residents of the "January 23rd" district rioted Feb. 22–24, looting stores and burning vehicles. A youth was killed in that neighborhood Feb. 22 and at least 30 persons were injured Feb. 22–24.

The Caracas police commander, Gen. Hernan Delgado Sanchez, had charged Feb. 2 that student disturbances were being directed by clandestine armed groups as part of "an insurrectional plan in which students would participate." However, President Caldera was reported Feb. 24 to have denied the possibility of links between leftist revolutionary movements and student rioters.

Riots in May—Disturbances by high school and university students continued in Caracas and other cities May 17–25, following riots May 15–16 sparked by the visit to Venezuela of U.S. Secretary of State William P. Rogers.

Students occupied school buildings, stoned motor vehicles and businesses, and clashed with police May 22 in Barinas, Coro, Barquisimeto, Merida, Cumana, San Fernando de Apure and Caracas. The University of the Andes in Merida and the Sucre branch of the Western University in Cumana were closed to prevent further riots. The Coro disturbances reportedly protested the killing by police of a young woman in earlier riots.

Rioting continued May 23 in Barcelona, Puerto La Cruz, Cumana, Puerto Cabello and Caracas. Police in Caracas cleared a high school occupied by students three days before, but students reoccupied it later while other students seized seven other high schools. Soldiers circled the Central Univerity in Caracas to prevent disturbances there.

Disturbances were reported diminished May 25, although 10 intermediate schools in the capital remained in student hands.

Venezuela's frequent student strikes and riots, by now a serious problem for the government, were due not to political motives but to overcrowding, rigid, old-fashioned teaching, harassed teachers and lack of educational funds, the London newsletter Latin America reported May 25.

Student's death protested—National guardsmen surrounded the University City in Caracas Aug. 23 to prevent students from massing in the streets to protest the death of a law student, Noel Rodriguez, at the army's Cocollar antiguerrilla camp. Students protested the death the same day in Barcelona, with some clashes with police reported.

A group of 45 lawyers in Caracas had charged Aug. 22 that Rodriguez had been tortured to death at Cocollar, and named five persons as the student's "murderers."

Communist Deputy Hector Mujica had said Aug. 3 that he and a pro-government lawyer, Jose Rodriguez Iturbe, had learned from a captured guerrilla leader, Carlos Betancourt, that Rodriguez had been seen at Cocollar "badly beaten and almost in a state of coma."

Betancourt, leader of the Red Flag guerrilla group, had been arrested in Caracas July 28.

Guerrillas ambush police. Urban guerrillas in Caracas ambushed a police patrol Feb. 22, wounding seven civilians and four policemen, one of whom reportedly died later. Pamphlets left by the assailants said the attack was "an energetic response by the national Liberation Armed Forces and the Venezuelan Revolution party to the police aggression against workers and students."

Guerrillas attacked an army convoy in the eastern state of Anzoategui Jan. 17, killing four soldiers. The subversives reportedly belonged to the "Jose Felix Rivas" group led by Carlos Betancourt, Julio Escalona and Gabriel Puertas.

Venezuela Feb. 28 received a group of U.S. "Bronco" turboprop fighter planes to use in its campaign against rural guerrillas. The delivery of about 30 U.S. army tanks to Venezuela was reported April 30.

Plane hijacked to Cuba. Four professed members of the People's Revolutionary Army (Zero Point), a left-wing guerrilla organization, hijacked an Avensa airliner with 42 aboard May 18 and flew it on an erratic course to Cuba, where they asked political asylum.

The hijackers, led by Zero Point leader Federico Bottini, seized the plane on a domestic flight from Valera to Barquisimeto. They claimed to have a bomb, and threatened to blow up the aircraft unless the government released 79 "political prisoners," including the leading leftist guerrillas in captivity. They also accused security officials of torturing detainees.

The plane was ordered first to Curacao, where it refueled, then to Panama City, where five passengers were allowed to deplane, and then to Merida, on the Yucatan peninsula in Mexico. It continued early May 19 to Mexico City, where an official told the hijackers the Venezuelan government refused to discuss their demands.

The Mexican official, Miguel Nazar, persuaded the guerrillas not to destroy the plane and offered them either political asylum in Mexico or whatever assistance they needed to reach Cuba. They chose the latter, and the plane, with Nazar aboard, proceeded to Havana, where the hijackers were taken into custody by Cuban police. The plane and passengers were returned to Venezuela May 20.

Mexican Security Minister Mario Moya said May 19 that President Luis Echeverria Alvarez had kept in close touch with the situation, and had "emphasized that every effort should be made to preserve the lives of the innocent people aboard the plane." Mexico consistently had granted demands by hijackers and kidnappers to save lives but had dealt firmly with the culprits if they were caught.

An important Venezuelan police official, Remberto Uzcategui, said May 21 that Bottini had been expected to try to flee the country in some "desperate" fashion but that he had slipped through because of lax ? security measures. Uzcategui claimed Zero Point had virtually been destroyed, and its remaining members were common criminals.

The Cuban and Venezuelan Foreign Ministries announced May 30 that the two nations would soon begin talks toward a bilateral agreement to prevent further hijackings. The talks were seen as a step toward resumption of diplomatic relations.

Cuba hijack pact. Venezuela and Cuba signed a five-year treaty July 6 to prevent the hijacking of airplanes and ships between their borders. Cuba earlier had signed similar agreements with the U.S., Canada and Mexico.

The pact, signed simultaneously in Havana and Caracas, required each country to prosecute or extradite persons who hijacked vessels to it from the other. Hijacked vessels and their passengers would be protected and returned to the country of origin, as would any ransom money obtained by the hijackers.

The signatories were allowed to "take into consideration purely political motives and the circumstances under which the [hijackings] were perpetrated, in order to abstain from returning or prosecuting [hijackers], save when there has been economic extortion or damage to the crew members, passengers, or other persons."

The signing followed an incident June 28 in which a Venezuelan air force pilot, reportedly angered by a charge of reckless flying, flew a jet bomber to Havana and asked political asylum. The plane was returned to Venezuela June 30, but no decision on the asylum request was reported.

Relations between Venezuela and Cuba were improving steadily. Negotiations for the sale of Venezuelan oil to Cuba were reported under way June 8, and a Cuban education mission was reported visiting Venezuela June 7.

Kidnapped West German consul freed. The honorary West German consul in Maracaibo, Kurt Nagel, was kidnapped Nov. 20 and freed two days later when four farmers accidentally discovered him and his abductors some 18 miles from the city. One farmer was seriously wounded and two of the kidnappers were captured in the ensuing clash.

The abductors, later identified as members of the Red Flag guerrilla group, were scheduled for military trials.

The Red Flag had been held responsible for the ambush murder Sept. 30 of three national guardsmen protecting oil installations of the U.S.-owned Creole Petroleum Corp. in the eastern state of Monagas. Remberto Uzcategui, chief of police intelligence, said Oct. 3 that two of the estimated 15 assailants had been identified as Tito Gonzalez Heredia and Miguel Salas Suarez. The attack was the first in the region in three years.

The Defense Ministry announced Oct. 3 that alleged guerrilla Alejandro Rivero had been killed in a clash with soldiers west of Monagas.

East German tie established. Venezuela Aug. 2 established diplomatic relations with East Germany, the 11th Latin American nation to do so.

Oil & the Economy

Oil prices to rise. The government announced it would increase oil prices by as much as 10% to compensate for the U.S. dollar devaluation, it was reported Feb. 21. It also revalued the bolivar by 2.2%, bringing its exchange rate to 4.30 to the dollar.

Announcement of the price hike, the second in four months, followed the release Jan. 6 of a Mines Ministry report showing that oil production had dropped in 1972 by 9.27%, or 330,000 barrels daily, compared with 1971 production. U.S. companies had reportedly decreased production in protest against certain provisions of the 1971 oil reversion law. But the president of Creole Petroleum Corp. had announced that his company would increase production in 1973.

Mines Minister Hugo Perez La Salvia asserted Jan. 15 that Venezuela would not sign a treaty with the U.S. for development of the Orinoco tar belt without assurances of preferential treatment for all Venezuelan oil on the U.S. market. The Orinoco belt contained oil reserves estimated at 700 billion barrels.

As a result of President Rafael Caldera's recent visit to Buenos Aires, Venezuela and Argentina would coordinate their policies on hydrocarbons, with Venezuela providing oil and gas products not produced in Argentina and purchasing Argentine equipment and machinery for its oil industry, it was reported Feb. 16.

Congress May 28 overwhelmingly approved a law nationalizing Venezuela's internal hydrocarbons market by 1976. Only 23% of the $200 million annual market was currently controlled by the state oil firm CVP. Most gas stations were owned by U.S. and other foreign companies.

Soviet oil delivery aid. The Washington Post reported May 23 that Soviet tankers that supplied oil to Cuba were picking up Venezuelan crude oil for delivery to Scandinavian clients on their return trip to the U.S.S.R. A Venezuelan embassy spokesman in Washington said that if the report was true, it would be a private agreement between the oil companies and the Russians. The Organization of American States recommended in 1967 that member states not allow ships that traded with Cuba to call at their ports to pick up certain types of cargo.

Ceausescu visits. Rumanian President Nicolae Ceausescu visited Venezuela Sept. 5–10 on his tour of nine Latin American nations. He exchanged decorations with President Caldera Sept. 6 and the two signed a joint declaration and an agreement for economic, technical, scientific and cultural cooperation Sept. 10.

Mines Minister Hugo Perez La Salvia and his Rumanian counterpart, Bujor Almasan, signed an agreement Sept. 10 to study a wide range of possible oil deals, ranging from supply of crude and refined oil products to Rumania, to establishment of a joint plant to manufacture oil equipment in Venezuela.

Ceausescu announced after leaving Venezuela that Rumania had agreed to supply equipment for exploration and exploitation of oil in Venezuela, in exchange for oil imports to begin soon, it was reported Sept. 14.

Oil export prices boosted. The government increased its posted prices for crude oil and petroleum by-products by 56% effective Nov. 1, to a record $7.24 per barrel. Then, before the month had passed, the government Nov. 30 raised its posted prices for crude oil and oil products by an average 50¢ a barrel, to a record $7.74 a barrel. Residual fuel shipped to the U.S. East Coast was increased by 98¢ a barrel to $8.46 a barrel.

The increase would boost the government's income from oil to an average $4.57 a barrel, compared with $1.62 a barrel at the beginning of 1973. According to one official calculation, Venezuela would earn an extra $1.8 billion in oil revenues in 1974, the Andean Times' Latin America Economic Report noted Nov. 30.

The Nov. 30 raise was the sixth price increase of 1973 and the seventh since October 1972.

The ministers of mines and hydrocarbons had published a joint resolution July 27 increasing the basic export value of both crudes and products by 3%, adding a "variable adjustment" of 9% for crude and of .5%-9% for different products. The two ministries were authorized by a government decree Aug. 29 to totally or partially modify export values whenever they judged it necessary. Posted prices were then increased again Aug. 31 and Oct. 1.

The posted price, or tax export value, was an artificial figure used to calculate tax payments to be made by oil companies to the government.

The price increases were expected to strike particularly hard on the U.S. East Coast. Venezuela was the U.S.' second largest foreign oil supplier, sending 926,000 barrels of crude per day—5.3% of the total U.S. consumption—and an estimated 600,000 barrels of refined products daily. Venezuela also sent a large portion of its exports to eastern Canada.

Oil industry analysts quoted by the New York Times Oct. 27 said the Venezuelan increases should be seen as part of the general attempt by oil producers to obtain maximum profits while consumer nations were in a state of disarray. However, an official of the U.S.-owned Creole Petroleum Corp. was quoted in the Wall Street Journal Oct. 29: "We weren't surprised at the magnitude of the increase in view of what has gone on in the Mideast."

Mines Minister Hugo Perez La Salvia had announced Nov. 15 that foreign oil companies operating in Venezuela had signed an agreement with the government, effective Nov. 1, raising royalty payments on oil production by about one-third. The pact would give the government an additional $230 million in oil revenue over one year, providing production and prices remained at current levels.

Perez La Salvia had said Nov. 5 that Venezuelan oil production would remain at the current level of 3,360,000 barrels a day despite the world energy crisis, the Cuban news agency Prensa Latina reported. Former Mines Minister Juan Pablo Perez Alfonso continued to call for a decrease in production to protect dwindling oil reserves, according to the Washington Post Dec. 5.

Other economic developments—Official 1972 statistics showed industrial output (excluding oil refining) was up by 7% over 1971, power generation rose by 11% and the construction sector grew by 16.5%, it was reported Jan. 17.

The steel firm Siderurgia del Orinoco had sold 3,500 tons of steel to the Soviet Union in what was said to be the first commercial transaction of any importance between Venezuela and a Communist country, it was reported Feb. 9.

The Inter-American Development Bank had announced approval of an $18.5 million loan to Siderurgica del Oriente, Venezuela's largest steel producer, to help increase production at its Matanzas plant and improve facilities at its nearby port on the Orinico River, it was reported Jan. 12.

The government had announced a shift in tariff policy, substituting the system of granting licenses to import goods with a more flexible policy of ad valorem duties, the newsletter Latin America reported Jan. 19. Only milk, wheat and a number of other basic commodities would remain subject to the old system.

The Venezuelan Guayana Corp. announced Feb. 26 that it would build a $154 million aluminum plant in Ciudad Guayana with an initial production capacity of 150,000 tons.

The government planned to import 200,000 tons of corn from Africa in 1973, El Nacional of Caracas reported Jan. 31. The newspaper noted that African corn imported in 1972 had brought a weevil which currently posed a serious threat to large agricultural areas.

The Agriculture Ministry said Feb. 28 that coffee exports would be restricted until domestic coffee prices were reduced to a "reasonable" level.

Three Japanese firms would contribute the bulk of the $11.3 billion required to develop Venezuela's aluminum industry, it was reported Sept. 14.

Venezuela's foreign currency reserves had increased from $878 million to $1.73 billion in 1970-73, it was reported Nov. 2.

The Orinoco Mining Co., an affiliate of U.S. Steel Corp., had put into production its new $85 million high-iron briquette plant at Ciudad Guayana on the Orinoco River, it was reported Nov. 9. The plant, the first of its type, had an annual production capacity of one million tons of briquettes with an iron content of 86.5%, to be used in pig iron production.

A $53 million fertilizer complex run by the Venezuelan Petrochemical Institute had begun operation at Moron, Carabobo state, in north central Venezuela, it was reported Nov. 23.

AD Wins Elections

The December elections, in which the Democratic Action (AD) party scored almost a clean sweep, were preceded by a year of political activity.

Villalba heads URD ticket. Jovito Villalba, leader of the Republican Democratic Union (URD), accepted his party's presidential nomination April 1. The URD had withdrawn from the center-left New Force coalition in December 1972.

Villalba, who lost his bid for the New Force presidential nomination to Popular Electoral Movement (MEP) candidate Jesus Paz Galarraga, had asserted Jan. 10 that the URD was justified in withdrawing from the New Force because independents in the coalition had broken an alleged agreement to vote for his candidacy at the New Force nominating convention. Villalba added that he had not kept a promise to campaign for Paz Galarraga—made immediately after the New Force nominated Paz—because his presence at "a Paz Galarraga meeting would turn it into a Jovito Villalba meeting."

Meanwhile, the URD executive council in Zulia state announced its resignation Jan. 31, asserting the party's withdrawal from the New Force had "further divided the Venezuelan left and handed a right-wing candidate victory on a silver platter." A New Force campaign director said Feb. 7 that a URD sector "of great proportions" would continue to work for a New Force victory.

The Popular Democratic Force proclaimed Jorge Dager its presidential candidate Feb. 18. Dager vowed that if elected he would build a "socialist" government similar to that of his native Egypt.

Pedro Segnini La Cruz, a congressman and secretary general of the Democratic National Front (FND), was proclaimed the FND's presidential candidate at its national convention Feb. 24.

A young official of the Movement toward Socialism (MAS) was knifed to death early Jan. 15 by a member of Democratic Action party. MAS presidential candidate Jose Vincente Rangel called the youth "the first victim of [1973] electoral violence."

Antonio Hernandez Fonseca, MEP secretary general in Caracas, charged Feb. 17 that metropolitan police had broken up an MEP meeting the previous day, throwing tear gas canisters into party headquarters and attacking MEP members.

Perez Jimenez candidacy barred. Congress May 9 ratified a constitutional amendment which effectively barred the presidential candidacy of ex-dictator Marcos Perez Jimenez.

The measure barred anyone sentenced to more than three years in prison for crimes committed while in public office, from election to the presidency, to Congress or to any court. Perez Jimenez had served four years in prison in the 1960s for embezzling state funds during his presidency in the 1950s.

The amendment, the first in Venezuela's history, was approved by Congress in

November 1972 and then passed by 16 of the nation's 20 state assemblies. President Rafael Caldera, whose COPEI party was a main proponent of the measure, said May 10 that it was juridically and morally "irreproachable."

The Nationalist Civic Crusade (CCN), the major party backing Perez Jimenez, said May 10 that it would still try to register him as a presidential candidate before the supreme electoral council, and, if this failed, appeal to the supreme court to declare the amendment unconstitutional. However, Perez Jimenez noted that both the electoral council and the supreme court were dominated by his political enemies.

In an interview with the news agency EFE May 12, Perez Jimenez charged the amendment had been passed because the government and the major opposition party, Democratic Action (AD), feared he would win the December election. He asserted the measure would not have passed in a plebiscite. Public opinion polls continued to show the ex-dictator running slightly ahead of the COPEI and AD candidates.

Perez Jimenez said Venezuela was a "turbulent" country. He expressed doubt that the election would be peaceful. He asserted student and other unrest would continue as long as the nation's "democratic" governments failed to resolve the serious problems of poverty, unemployment and underemployment and dependence on "foreign monopolies that turn us into an economic colony."

The ex-dictator said he could not return soon to Venezuela (he lived in Madrid) because there was a warrant for his arrest in connection with the murder of a police lieutenant in 1954.

He asserted the warrant was illegal because he could not be prosecuted for offenses other than those that motivated his extradition to Venezuela from the U.S. in 1963.

Perez Jimenez' candidacy was submitted June 6 by the Nationalist Civic Crusade and rejected June 14 by the Supreme Electoral Council as barred by the new amendment. The Supreme Court upheld the rejection Aug. 14.

Three other presidential candidates—Pedro Tinoco of the Desarrollista Movement, retired Gen. Martin Garcia Villasmil of the Democratic Socialist party, and independent Miguel Angel Burelli Rivas—reportedly were vying for Perez Jimenez' endorsement. However, the ex-dictator was reported July 18 to have told his followers to support the man they felt best represented his ideals.

The secretary general of the pro-Perez Jimenez United Nationalist Front charged the government had banned broadcast of a taped political statement by the ex-dictator, it was reported July 20.

The London newsletter Latin America reported Nov. 2 that Perez Jiminez had told his closest political aides he would not support any presidential candidate in the December general elections.

Perez Jimenez asserted Nov. 1 he had made "no accord of any kind" with the ruling COPEI party or any other party. Members of the ex-dictator's Nationalist Civic Crusade (CCN) had claimed Oct. 26 to have reached an agreement with COPEI candidate Lorenzo Fernandez, who reportedly promised, in return for their support, to allow Perez Jimenez to return to Venezuela without facing further legal prosecution.

Pedro Tinoco, presidential candidate of the Desarrollista movement and the reported favorite of big business, had claimed upon returning from a visit to Spain Oct. 20 that he had received written assurances of support from Perez Jimenez.

Perez Jimenez followers seized, freed—
Seven leaders of Perez Jimenez' political movement were arrested Nov. 3 and held until Nov. 10 for their connection with a telegram, published in a Maracaibo newspaper Nov. 4, asking President Rafael Caldera to resign and "allow constitution of a government of impartiality and national salvation that will guarantee the upcoming electoral process."

In addition, Sen. Oscar Hurtado Diaz, CCN president, was detained briefly until police realized he had parliamentary immunity, party leaders charged Nov. 5.

The chief of police intelligence, Remberto Uzcategui, charged Nov. 7 that followers of Perez Jimenez were promoting "a coup in Venezuela." However, his evidence for the assertion consisted only of the telegram and a recent declaration by a Perez Jimenez spokesman that the upcoming elections were a "fraud," perpetrated by COPEI and AD, before which "the people will take patriotic positions."

Interior Minister Nectario Andrade Labarca, confirming the arrests Nov. 5, did not accuse followers of the ex-dictator of fomenting a coup but asserted "there is nothing that can compromise our democratic peace nor the stability of [our] system."

The arrests caused protests by political groups opposed to Perez Jimenez, most prominently the Popular Electoral Movement, a member of the left-wing New Force coalition.

Voting machines scandal—The comptroller general May 9 recommended the annulment of a contract between the supreme electoral council and a U.S. firm for 10,000 voting machines.

The firm, the American Voting Machines Corp. (AVM), had charged in court that middlemen had promised commissions totaling $3 million to council members belonging to the MEP and URD, and to two deputies. The company also alleged AD was involved in the scheme, but did not mention any names. The opposition parties denied AVM's charges, and some party members accused COPEI of responsibility for the affair in an attempt to discredit its opponents.

The contract had also been criticized on grounds that no one in Venezuela would be able to maintain the machines, that the old paper ballots were adequate, and that the country could better spend its money elsewhere.

José Vicente Rangel, presidential candidate of the Movement to Socialism, charged April 28 that AD and COPEI were directly responsible for the scandal and for the "immorality and corruption" which he said characterized public administration in Venezuela.

The Supreme Electoral Council voted June 7 to annul the contract and hold the elections with the traditional paper ballots.

Opposition sweeps elections. The opposition Democratic Action party (AD) swept the general elections Dec. 9, winning the presidency and control of both houses of Congress, all but one state assembly and most of the nation's city councils.

AD presidential candidate Carlos Andres Perez won 48.6% of the 4.1 million valid votes, a landslide by Venezuelan standards. Lorenzo Fernandez of the ruling COPEI party was second with 36.78% —giving the two major parties an unprecedented 85.38% of the total vote— and two left-wing candidates, Jesús Paz Galarraga of the New Force coalition and José Vicente Rangel of the Movement to Socialism (MAS), were third and fourth with 5.1% and 4.23% respectively. Eight other presidential candidates trailed.

AD won 28 of 42 Senate seats and 102 of 183 Chamber of Deputies seats at stake in the voting, and COPEI won the second largest total in each house. Seats awarded by proportional representation would increase the Chamber's membership to 203, and proportional representation plus life membership for ex-President Romulo Betancourt and incumbent President Rafael Caldera would raise the number of senators to 49.

AD completed its sweep by winning control of 19 of the 20 state assemblies and 157 of 181 municipal councils.

In claiming victory Dec. 11, Perez said he would use oil policy as "a great instrument to break down trade barriers —it will be a Latin American weapon against the totalitarian trade policies of the industrialized nations against the developing countries." He added, however, that Venezuela would never impose an oil embargo like that of Arab oil exporters.

Perez asserted he would not "join in any effort to generate hate against the United States," but said he would "ask for its respect and better treatment in economic policies."

"Venezuela will fight to have good relations with all countries of the world, above all with the U.S.," Perez said. "Whether we like it or not, the U.S. is the main customer for our oil."

As for recognition of Cuba, Perez said: "it does not seem to me to be an urgent national problem." He was expected to reverse Caldera's policy of moving toward recognition, favored by Fernandez.

COPEI had charged, and U.S. oil executives had privately conceded, that Perez was preferred by the foreign oil firms. However, there was little difference between Perez and Fernandez, even on oil policy, and their campaigns emphasized their images rather than substantive issues.

Rangel, who advocated a redistribution of the national wealth and an oil conservation policy, said choosing between Perez and Fernandez was like choosing "between Pepsi-Cola and Coca-Cola."

The campaign was the longest and most expensive in Venezuelan history, lasting two years and costing the two leading parties an estimated $20 million–$32 million. In the last weeks it had degenerated into false charges and character assassination so offensive that private television stations curtailed campaign advertisements and the Supreme Electoral Council ordered a cut in newspaper advertisements.

El Nacional, Caracas' leading newspaper, which printed page after page of political advertising, said Dec. 3: "Never in this country has there been an electoral campaign so noisy and with such puerile slogans; never have so many millions been spent to shake walls, rattle eardrums and slash nerves. The party that has not done this has not had enough money to."

A columnist in the Bogota newspaper El Tiempo, Enrique Santos Calderon, wrote Dec. 16: "The surprising triumph of the two [major] parties of the Venezuelan system is also the triumph of the inexhaustible publicity resources at their disposal. The consolidation of the two-party system is the consolidation, too, of money in politics. And the weak showing of many of the minority parties cannot be separated from their scant [resources]."

Observers were surprised by the poor showing of MAS, which had been expected to win about 15% of the vote. Many observers said the biggest loser in the elections was ex-dictator Marcos Perez Jimenez, who, after seeing his presidential candidacy barred by a constitutional amendment, instructed his followers not to vote for any presidential candidate. Congressional candidates of the Nationalist Civic Crusade, endorsed by Perez Jimenez, won only four Chamber seats in the direct voting.

The Popular Democratic Force (FDP) and its presidential candidate, Jorge Dager, had decided to give their support to Fernandez. A joint declaration by FDP and COPEI leaders June 2 attacked AD.

Other Areas

BAHAMAS

Andros livestock project. The Bahamas and the U.S. had signed an agreement to develop a $10 million livestock production project on Andros Island in the Bahamas, it was reported Jan. 20. U.S. specialists would provide training for Bahamians in economics, sociology, animal husbandry, agronomy, soil science, horticulture and agricultural engineering.

Bahamas ministers lose key roles. Two Bahamas government officials under attack by business interests and the political opposition had been stripped of key assignments but retained in the Cabinet, it was reported Feb. 23.

Finance and Development Minister Carlton E. Francis gave up his finance post, and Arthur D. Hanna, deputy prime minister and home affairs minister, surrendered his responsibility for immigration policy. Prime Minister Lynden O. Pindling took over immigration duties and said he would direct the Finance Ministry "for the time being."

Hanna, the No. 2 man in the government, had been sharply attacked by businessmen, who claimed his immigration policies had restricted importation of skilled workers from the U.S., Canada and Great Britain, making it difficult for businesses to operate successfully. The government had replied that it sought to make more jobs available for the 85% of Bahamians who were black and mainly poor. Hanna's policies were generally interpreted as contributing to a slowdown of foreign investment in the Bahamas, according to the Wall Street Journal Feb. 23.

Francis had been criticized for his economic policies, particularly, according to one source, for allowing government expenses to exceed revenues.

Ministries reassigned—Pindling was reported Feb. 26 to have taken over the new ministry of economic affairs and Hanna the additional post of finance minister.

The moves were part of a Cabinet shuffle in which Hanna surrendered responsibility for immigration policy and the Home Affairs Ministry, Pindling gave up responsibility for external affairs, and Development Minister Carlton E. Francis surrendered direction of the Finance Ministry. Immigration policy duties were assumed by Pindling, and the Home Affairs Ministry by F. R. Anthony Roberts, a member of the House of Assembly. Nassau attorney Paul Adderley, government leader in the Senate and minister of state, was named external affairs minister, and would become attorney general when the Bahamas gained independence from Great Britain July 10.

Opposition leader quits party. Kendal Isaacs resigned as head of the opposition Free National Movement (FNM) June 9, after failing to control the votes of a few party members on a resolution before the House of Assembly.

Four of the FNM's nine representatives defied Isaacs June 6 and voted for a resolution demanding that residents of Great Abaco Island be given the right to vote for continued status as a British colony after the rest of the Bahamas became independent. The measure, introduced by Errington Watkins, an FNM representative from Marsh Harbour on Great Abaco, was defeated.

Isaacs' resignation reportedly left Prime Minister Pindling's Progressive Liberal party (PLP) virtually without opposition in the Assembly. The PLP held 29 of the body's 38 seats.

Colonial rule ends. The Bahamas became an independent nation early July 10, emerging from three centuries of British colonial rule.

The Bahamian flag was raised in place of the Union Jack shortly after midnight at a ceremony attended by Prime Minister Lynden O. Pindling, Prince Charles of Great Britain, and representatives of 52 countries, including the U.S. and Cuba.

Independence was made official at a second ceremony 10 hours later, when Prince Charles handed Pindling the independence order and the new Bahamian Constitution. Charles read a message from Queen Elizabeth welcoming the Bahamas as the 33d member of the Commonwealth of Nations.

Pindling had said at a press conference July 8 that he expected tourism to continue to be the Bahamas' largest single source of foreign exchange in the immediate future. The islands had earned $285 million from 1.5 million tourists in 1972. Pindling added, however, that he wished to diversify the economy, and was giving serious planning effort to the development of fishing.

Tim B. Donaldson, nominated by Pindling to head the Central Bank, had said in an interview earlier that the government would continue to encourage international banking organizations to establish offices in the Bahamas, a traditional tax haven, it was reported July 11.

The banking industry—with one bank for every 600 Bahamian residents—generated some $12 million annually in salaries and fees.

U.N. entry asked—The Bahamas applied July 10 for membership in the United Nations, through a letter from Pindling to U.N. Secretary General Kurt Waldheim.

BELIZE

Guatemala renews claim. The Guatemalan delegate to the recent United Nations Security Council meeting in Panama had reiterated Guatemala's claim to to British Honduras and had criticized Britain for failing to settle their dispute over the territory, it was reported March 23.

The statement responded to criticism from the Jamaican and Guyanese foreign ministers, who had told the meeting a "neighboring country" had been obstructing Belize's desire for independence. The Guayanese delegate said Belize was not seeking early independence from Britain because it feared being absorbed by the "neighboring country."

New name. British Honduras, a British colony, was officially renamed Belize June 1 following approval of implementing legislation by the territory's House of Representatives in March.

COSTA RICA

Presidential nominees. Manuel Mora Valverde was nominated by the Socialist Action party as its 1974 presidential candidate, the Miami Herald reported Feb. 2.

Mora, a government deputy, had repeatedly traveled to the Soviet Union to negotiate Costa Rican-Russian trade agreements for President José Figueres.

Daniel Oduber resigned his position as president of the Senate to begin campaigning as presidential candidate of Figueres' National Liberation party, it was reported May 11. His major opponents were Jorge Gonzalez Marten of the National Independent party and Fernando Trejos Escalante of the National Unification party. Oduber, favored to win the election, was dissociating himself from Figueres and his acknowledged involvement with fugitive U.S. financier Robert Vesco.

A record eight presidential candidates were reported legally qualified by Nov. 2 after five opposition parties had failed to unite behind a single candidate to run against Oduber.

Negotiations for a united opposition had failed despite the efforts of three former presidents—Otilio Ulate, Mario Echandi and Jose Joaquin Trejos.

Court rules it lacks jurisdiction. The Costa Rican Supreme Court ruled that it did not have jurisdiction over charges that President Figueres violated the constitution by leaving the country in 1972 without permission from Congress.

The court recommended that the case be turned over to the National Assembly which it said had jurisdiction, the Miami Herald reported Feb. 17.

That path was quickly blocked by leaders in the Assembly where Figueres's National Liberation Party had nearly two thirds majority.

National emergency declared. In the face of a prolonged drought that had caused serious power shortages, the Costa Rican government declared a state of emergency April 5.

To conserve power, electrical service was suspended across the country from 7 a.m. to 7 p.m. and companies were authorized to give their employes vacations beginning April 9.

Authorities also reported that drinking water reserves were low and that crop losses from the drought, which started in 1972, had reached $20 million. According to the Miami Herald, the entire crop of corn and 85% of the rice crop were lost in the northern Pacific region and Guanacaste Province.

Economists estimated that the cost of living in Costa Rica had increased by 20% since Jan. 1, the London newsletter Latin America reported Nov. 16.

The government was reported Oct. 9 to have suspended meat exports to the U.S. to insure an adequate domestic supply. Deliveries were resumed Oct. 29.

Bank strike. Economic activity was virtually halted July 14 by a partial strike by bank employes demanding a five-day work week and other benefits, the Cuban newspaper Granma reported July 16.

Soviet ties discussed. Controversy was building in Costa Rica over diplomatic and trade ties with the Soviet Union.

Under terms of a trade agreement, the Soviets were to buy 6,000 metric tons of surplus coffee between 1972 and 1976. Costa Rica was obliged to spend 50% of the coffee receipts on Soviet goods.

The Miami Herald reported April 12 that the Soviets had fulfilled their part of the bargain, buying some 4,500 tons of surplus coffee in the first year worth more than $2.5 million.

But it also cited the newspaper La Republica which said trade between the two countries had declined since the early 1972 opening of the first Soviet embassy in San Jose, the nation's capital—also the first in Central America. It reported that while the Soviet Union purchased $10.8 million worth of coffee between June 1968 and October 1970, it bought only $4 million worth from October 1970 to August 1972. The newspaper also predicted that Soviet purchases would continue to decline in 1973.

For its part, Costa Rica was having difficulty finding Soviet-made goods to purchase. Purchase of Soviet tractors which had been reported several years before had not materialized, the Times of the Americas reported Jan. 31.

Since 1968, the urgency of selling coffee to the Soviet Union had lessened, according to the Herald. Costa Rica then had a 700,000-bag surplus, but coffee shortages had cut that figure.

Although the reduced dependence on coffee sales had opened the government to criticism, President Figueres maintained there is "nothing to regret," acccording to the newsletter Latin America Feb. 2.

Criticism in the Costa Rican press, however, had been sharp. "If the Soviet Union is going to reduce its purchases of coffee and seemingly is not in a position to supply equipment acceptable to our economy, what is the objective of relations struck up with said country?" La Republica asked in an editorial cited by the Herald.

Figueres talks about Vesco. President José Figueres of Costa Rica told a nation-wide radio and television audience May 23 about his financial dealings with Robert L. Vesco, an American accused of a mutual funds swindle by the Securities and Exchange Commission (SEC) and with conspiracy to commit fraud and obstruct justice by a federal grand jury in New York.

(Vesco had fled to Costa Rica where he had substantial investments to avoid U.S. prosecution and had met with Figueres in April to express "officially" his intention to renounce U.S. citizenship, according to the Wall Street Journal May 3.)

Domestic political considerations in Costa Rica forced Figueres to make the disclosures. His opponents based charges that Vesco-owned companies had placed $300,000 in Figueres' personal bank account in the National Bank of North America in New York City on a May 16 Journal report. According to the newspaper, SEC documents showed that Figueres' account had increased by $325,000 between August 1972, when Vesco increased his operations in Costa Rica, and early 1973. The information indicated that Figueres had acted as a conduit, transferring $255,000 from companies in Costa Rica and the Bahamas which were linked to Vesco, to a Vesco-controlled bank, Bahamas Commonwealth Bank. The bank previously had been identified by the SEC as a transfer point for $224 million diverted from four mutual funds controlled by Vesco.

The Journal also reported that SEC documents showed that $70,000 in Figueres' New York bank had been released to the account of a Costa Rican company in which Vesco held 30% ownership and the Figueres family 10% ownership.

In his televised address, Figueres accounted for funds totaling $436,000 in the New York account. "Some of this money" originated with the Bahamas Commonwealth Bank, Figueres admitted.

Figueres said other funds in the personal account were intended for endowment of a national symphony for Costa Rica, "interesting scientific experiments" in Phoenix, Ariz., and a Costa Rican factory producing prefabricated houses.

Figueres also explained the Watergate scandal and defended Vesco's right to make a political contribution to the Nixon re-election campaign.

A special committee of the Costa Rican Congress, established to investigate Vesco's investments there, cleared him of charges of wrongdoing May 16. "There was no doubt cast on the legality of Mr. Vesco's operations," the report declared. The study showed that Vesco had invested $5.25 million in Costa Rican nationalized banks; $1.5 million in a government housing institute; $1 million in a government waterworks institute; and an undisclosed amount in private homes, a coffee plantation, timber works and low-income housing construction. Vesco claimed his Costa Rican investments totaled $25 million since 1969.

Former President Otilio Ulate, a political foe of Figueres, said May 25 that he had written President Nixon May 17 asking that the U.S. release all available documents regarding Costa Rican involvement in Vesco's alleged illegal activities. Ulate said he requested the information "to restore the good name of Costa Rica, compromised by the Watergate scandal, because of the business relationship existing between Figueres and Vesco."

EL SALVADOR

Leftists arrested. About 100 left-wing politicians and trade union leaders had been arrested following the government's alleged discovery of an international terrorist plot led by the Salvadorean Communist party, it was reported Feb. 16. In Congress the opposition National Union party complained that the National Guard had broken into one of its party headquarters, halted a meeting and arrested several party leaders.

President Arturo A. Molina's government exiled veteran Communist leader

Jacinto Castellanos March 13. Officials claimed to have confiscated $50,000 with which Castellanos proposed to finance the plot. In Paris, a student committee charged the Salvadorean government Feb. 12 had killed a former labor leader, Tito Dimas Alas, and exiled 26 leftists to Guatemala, the French newspaper Le Monde reported March 8.

Economic developments. Molina visited Mexico and agreed with Mexican officials to form a joint mixed commission to conduct a thorough review of bilateral trade relations, it was reported Jan. 17. A group of Mexican industrialists had subsequently visited El Salvador and pledged to manufacture products not presently produced in Central America.

Molina had denied charges that his five-year economic and social development plan—which provided, among other measures, for government intervention in the foreign marketing of coffee, sugar and cotton—was in any way socialist, it was reported Feb. 9.

Drought's effects—The Coffee Growers Association estimated the prolonged Central American drought would cut Salvadorean coffee production by 30%-40% in 1973, it was reported May 15. Coffee was the nation's major source of export earnings.

In the face of increasingly serious water shortages in San Salvador, water supplies in most parts of the city were being turned on for only one hour a day, it was reported Jan. 19.

The drought created shortages of maize, rice and beans, pushing up their prices, but rain came in time to avert a severe shortage of electricity, it was reported June 8.

International loans—The Inter-American Development Bank had approved a $38.1 million loan to help El Salvador build the first stage of a hydroelectric power plant at Cerron Grande, it was reported Jan. 12. The government planned to spend $80 million building the plant, which had a projected generating capacity of 270,000 kilowatts. In related developments:

The Inter-American Development Bank Sept. 13 announced approval of an $8 million loan to help finance an irrigation and agricultural development project north of San Salvador.

The International Bank for Reconstruction & Development (World Bank) approved April 30 a $27.3 million loan for expansion of Salvadorean electric power and transmission facilities, including construction of the first geothermal power plant financed by the bank in Latin America.

Torture probe set. Congress voted to investigate police methods in response to charges that police tortured two Christian Democrats arrested after a bomb exploded outside an army barracks in Santa Ana, it was reported June 16. The Catholic news agency Latinamerica Press suggested June 21 the explosion was a pretext for the government to arrest political opponents.

A terrorist group calling itself the Popular Liberation Front claimed responsibility for earlier explosions which caused some $500,000 damage to the San Salvador offices of the U.S.-owned International Business Machines Corp., it was reported May 11.

Arms from Israel. El Salvador was reported Sept. 28 to have bought arms and 25 jet fighters from Israel.

Resignations. Economy Minister Salvador Sanchez and Agriculture Minister Enrique Alvarez had resigned without explanation, it was reported Oct. 12. They were the first Cabinet officials to quit since President Arturo Molina's inauguration 14 months before.

GUATEMALA

Parties pick 1974 tickets. The National Liberation Movement (MLN) and the Democratic Institutional party (PID), which composed the ruling right-wing coalition, had named Gen. Kjell Laugerud as their presidential candidate for the 1974 elections, it was reported Jan. 26.

Laugerud resigned as defense minister to begin the campaign. His running mate would be Mario Sandoval Alarcon, the MLN leader and president of Congress, who shelved his own presidential ambitions in the interests of coalition unity.

The Revolutionary Democratic Unity Front (FURD), a semi-dissident sector of the Christian Democratic party, had chosen Guatemala City Mayor Manuel Colom Argueta as its presidential candidate, it was reported May 4. The FURD reportedly was being refused political party status by the government despite collecting more than the requisite 50,000 signatures.

Rene de Leon Schlotter was chosen the presidential candidate of the Christian Democratic party.

New opposition candidates named. The opposition Revolutionary party (PR) and the National Opposition Front (FON) dropped their civilian presidential candidates and chose military officers to oppose the government candidate, Gen. Kjell Laugerud.

The FON's new candidate, named in mid-September, was Gen. Efrain Rios Montt, a former army chief of staff and former director of the Inter-American Center of Military Studies in Washington, D.C. He replaced Christian Democratic leader Rene de Leon Schlotter. Rios' vice presidential candidate was ex-Finance Minister Alberto Fuentes Mohr.

The PR next changed its candidate, reportedly fearing it would be at a disadvantage in pitting a civilian against two officers. The new nominee was Col. Ernesto Paiz Novales, a former ambassador to Venezuela. He replaced Carlos Sagastume, who became his vice presidential candidate.

Murder of Communists reported. The Cuban press agency Prensa Latina said Guatemalan guerrillas had kidnapped a policeman, Abel Juarez Villatoro, and forced him to reveal the fate of the eight leaders of the Communist Guatemalan Labor party (PGT) who disappeared in September 1972, the newsletter Latin America reported March 2.

Juarez reportedly said the PGT leaders—six men and two women—had been arrested by police, tortured for 48 hours, and then thrown into shark-infested Pacific waters from an air force plane.

The government had denied any knowledge of the victims' disappearance.

The government's move against the PGT leaders baffled the victims' relatives and other politicians, who considered the PGT membership moderate, the Times of the Americas reported April 4. The party reportedly had survived the government's 1971 anti-leftist campaign by pledging not to practice or advocate violence against authorities.

Right-wing terror reported—Two peasants had been killed and an undisclosed number kidnapped recently, presumably by right-wing paramilitary organizations, the newsletter Latin America reported Feb. 9.

Deputy killed. Hector Solis Juarez, secretary of Congress, was shot to death by unidentified gunmen June 5.

Peasants, troops clash. At least eleven peasants and six soldiers were reported killed May 26 outside the eastern hamlet of Palo Verde, near Jalapa, when soldiers attempted to evict hundreds of peasants from land they had seized.

The peasants, possibly numbering up to 3,000, invaded land which they said belonged to them under documents dating back to the 18th century. Soldiers began making arrests soon after the occupation, and claimed they were fired upon by the squatters. A bloody battle ensued in which the 17 persons were killed and an undetermined number wounded.

Nearly 1,000 soldiers were flown into the area May 27 to prevent further bloodshed. However, peasants reportedly remained in possession of some of the seized land.

Teacher strike. A strike by about 10,000 state primary school teachers erupted into violence July 26–28. More than 300 persons were reported injured when striking teachers and university students clashed in downtown Guatemala City.

The striking teachers, supported by high school teachers, students and workers, demanded 50% wage increases. However, the Education Ministry offered only 10% hikes, and refused to negotiate until the teachers returned to work.

The government had dismissed 50 teachers in May in an effort to break the strike. President Carlos Arana called the stoppage "a cover for a Communist plan to overthrow the government."

Wage increases set. The government had agreed to raise wages for civil servants by 9.8%–32.9% and for teachers by 25%–27% from the beginning of fiscal year 1974, it was reported Nov. 9. The latter increases resulted from the massive teachers' strike in the spring and summer.

Unions denounce government. Labor union representatives in Guatemala City charged Oct. 20 that the government had increased poverty and repression throughout the country, according to the news agency LATIN Oct. 21.

Speaking after a parade to demonstrate "the active participation of the popular sectors" in celebrations commemorating the revolution of Oct. 20, 1944, the representatives asserted: "The government has killed the workers. It has given us only death. We want bread."

Foreign firms set oil venture. The U.S.-based Shenandoah Oil Corp. and Norway's Saga Petroleum A/S & Co. said they had agreed with a Luxembourg firm, Basic Resources International S.A., to explore and develop a 933,000 acre petroleum concession in Guatemala's Peten basin, to which Basic had beneficial rights, the Wall Street Journal reported March 27.

Shenandoah and Saga said a Basic subsidiary, Recursos del Norte Ltd., had discovered oil on the concession in northern Guatemala and had successfully completed a second well there. They said a third well was being drilled.

The companies said each would have a 25% interest in the venture, with the Basic unit holding the remaining 50%. Shenandoah would be the operator and the Basic unit would act as petroleum contractor in Guatemala.

Nine foreign oil companies would begin a $100 million prospecting program in December, mostly in the Peten region, it was reported Nov. 2.

Other economic developments. Among other economic developments:

The Guatemalan economy grew about by about 6% in 1972, it was reported Jan. 19. Exports as a whole earned more than $300 million during the year.

The Inter-American Development Bank Sept. 20 announced approval of a $17.5 million loan to help finance the second stage of a program to improve and build feeder roads in Guatemala.

The International Finance Corp., a member of the World Bank Group, was lending $15 million to Exploraciones y Explotaciones Mineras Izabal S.A. to help finance a nickel mining and processing project at Lake Izabal in eastern Guatemala, it was reported Aug. 8. The project was sponsored by the International Nickel Co. of Canada Ltd.

GUYANA

Oil exploration rights granted. The British firm Tricentral Guyana was granted offshore oil exploration rights over a 1,660 square mile area, the London newsletter Latin America reported Jan. 26. Three other companies—West German, U.S. and Guyanese—had been granted offshore prospecting rights during the past three months.

The discovery of oil in the Takutu basin, near the Brazilian border, was reported July 13.

Exploitation of interior begins. Some 700 young Guyanese, the first graduates of a two-year program called the Guyana Youth Corps, had settled on cooperative farms in the interior, the Miami Herald reported Jan. 24.

The program was designed to turn out young people with the skills and ambition to exploit the potential of the land, rivers and forests beyond the coastal plains, where 90% of the population lived.

Prime Minister Forbes Burnham backed the project in an effort to establish farms in the interior that could feed Guyana by 1975.

Food plants built. Small plants scattered around the country were part of Guyana's campaign to feed itself by 1975, the Miami Herald reported Jan. 31.

One of the larger units in greater Georgetown was already turning out barbecue sauce and cider and would soon produce ginger syrup, tomato paste and ketchup. Others planned would process fruits, coconut and chocolate.

Land turned over to government. A British firm, Bookers, Ltd. (Booker Brothers), turned over its surplus land to the Guyanese government, Prime Minister Forbes Burnham disclosed.

A few weeks earlier the government had announced it would confiscate all agricultural land not being used productively in the face of the occupation of unused Bookers property by hundreds of landless rural residents, the Miami Herald said March 4.

Riot police evicted the squatters after they ignored a government order to vacate the property so that orderly, government-controlled land redistribution could take place.

The occupation by the rural squatters followed a call by the American Society for Cultural Relations with Africa (ASCRIA), led by former Cabinet minister Eusi Kwayana, for a peasant uprising.

Government investment plan. The government presented to Parliament a development plan which provided for domestic investment totaling $1.15 billion in 1972–1976. More than half the total would be allocated to the public sector.

Reporting on the plan April 13, the newsletter Latin America said, "Although the plan is regarded as a step toward a Socialist system, with effort concentrated on the public and cooperative sectors, there will be private investment opportunities in about 40 projects."

New mine planned. The Guyana Bauxite Co. (GUYBAU), nationalized almost two years ago, announced plans to develop a new mine in East Montgomery.

Foreign relations. Guyana became the first English-speaking Caribbean nation to reach trade and technical assistance agreements with South Korea, the Miami Herald reported April 5.

According to the Herald March 16, Guyana and the Soviet Union had agreed to establish permanent embassies in their respective capitals to foster closer economic ties. The embassies were to open "as soon as feasible." A seven-man Russian trade mission had visited Guyana in February to discuss bilateral trade agreements.

East Germany, which recently established diplomatic relations with Guyana, would help build a $1 million glass factory in Georgetown, it was reported May 4.

2 defect to ruling party. The London newsletter Latin America reported Jan. 26 that two members of the People's Progressive party in parliament defected to the ruling People's National Congress.

New political party formed. Former Interior Minister Llewellyn John and an executive committee of eight members formed a new Guyanese political party, the People's Democratic Movement.

El Nacional of Caracas reported March 14 that, according to John, the party sought to maintain stable, efficient and democratic government at all levels and to eliminate corruption.

PNC wins elections. Prime Minister Forbes Burnham was assured a third five-year term of office when his People's National Congress (PNC) won a two-thirds majority in parliamentary elections July 16.

The PNC took 37 of the 53 seats in Parliament; the major opposition group, the People's Progressive party (PPP), won 14. The PPP and two other groups, the Guyana Liberator party and the People's Democratic Movement, issued a joint statement July 21 rejecting the results and accusing the government of fraud.

"What has been witnessed," the statement said, "was not a general election, but intervention by the army and police to enable Burnham to usurp power."

Two men were shot and killed July 16, reportedly when they tried to prevent authorities from taking ballot boxes from polling stations. The government had ordered the boxes from all 871 polling stations flown to the capital for counting. The order followed statements by the PPP leader, former Prime Minister Cheddi Jagan, urging his supporters to block entrances to polling stations to prevent tampering with ballot boxes before they reached local counting stations, according to a report July 17.

Burnham June 26 had denied reports that two soldiers had been killed June 23 during racial disturbances in an Atlantic coast village. He said the men accidentally had been run over by a truck.

Guyana's racial divisions were roughly reflected in its political alignments, with the slight East Indian majority supporting the PPP and the black minority backing the PNC. The PNC reportedly won and retained power by attracting voters from the East Indian middle classes.

The PPP had warned of government electoral fraud throughout the often bitter campaign. The opposition was particularly critical of the system under which Guyanese abroad were allowed to cast ballots virtually under government supervision. A survey of 1,000 voters listed in Great Britain for the 1968 Guyanese elections had found only 14% to be correctly registered.

Two PPP members sued to block postal and overseas voting for the current elections, but the High Court declined jurisdiction in the matter July 4.

The PPP earlier had blocked a proposed constitutional amendment lowering the voting age from 21 to 18, after accusing the government of registering young blacks while passing over much of the East Indian community.

Vote fraud charged—There was evidence that the government's massive victory in the July 16 parliamentary elections was due in part to widespread vote fraud, the London newsletter Latin America reported July 27.

Evidence provided by the opposition parties, independent foreign observers and some government supporters suggested that ballot boxes were broken open and packed by the government; thousands of unauthorized proxy votes were cast; opposition supporters were turned away from the polls; and nearly half the 33,000 persons listed as overseas voters did not exist. The government claimed it won 98% of the overseas vote, nearly 10% of the total electorate, worth four parliamentary seats under the proportional representation system.

Fifteen of the 16 opposition legislators boycotted the first session of Parliament.

Cabinet named—Burnham named a new Cabinet July 22 and took direct responsibility for national security, including the Guyana Defense Force and the police.

Twenty-three ministers were appointed, 12 of whom were "technocrats" or non-elected officials. New members included Oliver Harper as health minister, replacing David Singh, and Christopher Nascimento as minister of state in the prime minister's office. Six regional ministers were named for the areas into which Guyana would be divided under the government's development plan.

Air pact with Cuba. Guyana and Cuba signed a commercial air agreement July 28 that would permit Guyanese citizens to fly to Africa by way of Cuba instead of England.

The state-owned Guyana Timber Ltd. had contracted to sell Cuba $350,000 worth of timber, it was reported July 5. It was the first trade agreement between the two countries.

Cuba trip canceled—Burnham canceled a trip to Havana to attend celebrations of the 20th anniversary of the Cuban revolution, it was reported July 22. His recent recognition of Cuba had deprived PPP leader Jagan, a Marxist, of a major campaign issue.

HONDURAS

Farm plan. The government would spend $13.3 million on agriculture and livestock expansion and modernization, the London newsletter Latin America reported Jan. 12. Of the sum, $9.2 million would be provided by the Inter-American Development Bank.

El Salvador. President Oswaldo Lopez Arellano had met with El Salvador President Arturo A. Molina in Guatemala in what was viewed as a major step toward resumption of cordial relations between their two countries, it was reported Oct. 19.

JAMAICA

Programs to bridge poverty gap. In what was described as a "deliberate effort to break down class barriers," the Jamaican government began programs in five key areas—literacy, employment, housing, health care and nutrition, the Miami Herald reported Feb. 12.

The government was recruiting 20,000 volunteer teachers for its literacy program.

With an investment of about $4 million, it hoped to wipe out illiteracy in four years. (More than 20% of the population was illiterate.)

The Herald cited a $17-million short-term public works program, self-help projects, low-cost homes and plans for a network of community health aides. The programs were an attempt at ordered structural change.

The government was also trying to combat crime, the Herald noted. The administration had reinforced the island's police force to 3,300 men and made it more mobile.

Food plan announced. The government announced a new food plan called GROW (Growing and Reaping Our Wealth), aimed at encouraging greater agricultural production, the Miami Herald reported Feb. 6.

The program was divided into three parts:

■ Project Food Farms, owned and operated by the government, would undertake massive domestic food crop production.

■ Project Land Lease, providing small farmers with land they need to cultivate crops.

■ Project Self Help, under which financial assistance on favorable terms would be provided.

The government hoped that GROW would reduce Jamaica's $40 million annual bill for imported food.

The rest of the Jamaican economy remained sluggish, the Miami Herald reported Feb. 12.

The Inter-American Development Bank June 1 approved a $7.9 million loan to help launch the third stage of a Jamaican farm development program.

Dollar devalued. The government broke the Jamaican dollar's link with sterling and pegged it to the U.S. dollar at a devaluation of 6.5%, the newsletter Latin America reported Jan. 26.

According to the Miami Herald Jan. 19, one Jamaican dollar equaled 91 U.S. cents at the new value.

Tourist expansion planned. Tourism Minister P. J. Patterson said Jamaica planned to double its tourist accommodations in the next five years, the Miami Herald reported Feb. 6.

About 800 hotel rooms would be added in 1973, raising the total for the island to 9,800, Patterson said.

He said tourism revenues in 1972 totaled more than $100 million—an increase of 13.5% over 1971—but that greater efforts to increase accommodations could have put the increase at 20%.

A $50 million project was launched to renovate the waterfront of Montego Bay, the island's major tourist city, the Herald reported Jan. 7.

Construction planned. A 4,000-unit, prefabricated housing development was planned by Hutton's Worldwide Property at Innswood, near Kingston, the Times of the Americas said March 21.

A consortium of Japanese banks was to build the Caribbean's largest and most containerized port in Jamaica, Latin America reported March 2. A $15 million government loan would aid construction.

Campbell retires. Sir Clifford Campbell retired after 10 years as governor-general of Jamaica, the Miami Herald reported March 2. His last official act was to preside at the swearing in of Chief Justice Sir Herbert Duffus to act as the Queen's temporary representative.

Hoarding crackdown planned. The government said it would crack down on grocery suppliers in an effort to deal with shortages of certain food staples, the Miami Herald reported March 24.

An order published by the Ministry of Trade and Consumer Protection said importers, manufacturers, wholesale dealers and retailers would be prevented from storing these foods without making them available for sale.

Six convicted on drug charges. Six Americans were convicted of trying to export nine tons of marijuana out of Jamaica, the Miami Herald reported Feb. 8.

All were sentenced to six months at hard labor and fined $200 each.

Three of the men were also convicted of possessing marijuana and sentenced to a year in jail and fined $1,000.

Spanish to be taught. Latin America reported Feb. 16 that the teaching of Spanish was to be made compulsory in all Jamaican schools.

Venezuelan talks end. Prime Minister Michael Manley ended three days of talks with Venezuelan President Rafael Caldera in Caracas April 2. El Nacional quoted Manley as saying that he hoped the talks would strengthen relations between English-speaking Caribbean nations and their Latin American neighbors.

Refinery pact signed. The government said June 18 it had signed an agreement with the Moratti Group of Milan, Italy, for construction of a $350 million refinery capable of producing 250,000 barrels of oil a day. A new company, Arajam, would be formed in which Jamaica would have 10% participation with an option to raise its interest later to 20%.

PNP wins by-elections. The ruling People's National party (PNP) July 3 won by-elections to fill two seats in the House of Representatives vacated earlier by other PNP members. The party retained 37 House seats, the opposition Jamaica Labor party (JLP) 15, and an independent one seat.

U.S. envoy declared unwelcome. Prime Minister Michael Manley July 20 declared U.S. Ambassador Vincent W. de Roulet persona non grata and asked for his recall.

Manley said de Roulet's assignment had been prejudiced by unfounded allegations that the two countries made an agreement before the 1972 Jamaican elections precluding nationalization of the bauxite industry, in which U.S. concerns had invested heavily.

De Roulet told a U.S. Senate Foreign Relations subcommittee on multinational corporations in Washington July 19 that in 1971 he had assured Jamaican opposition leaders, including Manley, that the U.S. would not interfere in the 1972 elections. De Roulet said he was the "first outsider" to meet Manley after he won the elections, and Manley assured him he would not nationalize the bauxite industry.

Manley issued a statement later July 19 denying he had made any deal "of any character" with the ambassador. The U.S. State Department issued a similar denial July 20.

The Senate subcommittee was examining the purchase by U.S. firms of $508 million worth of U.S. government-backed insurance to protect their businesses in Jamaica from expropriation, it was reported July 20. Richard S. Reynolds Jr., president of Reynolds Metals Co., conceded under questioning that the insurance seemed excessive, but he claimed U.S. investments in Jamaica would have been much lower without it. The insurer was the Overseas Private Investment Corp.

MONTSERRAT

Elections, common mart. The Progressive Labor party of Chief Minister Austin

Bramble of the Caribbean island of Montserrat lost two of the seven elective seats comprising the legislative council, it was reported Sept. 28. His party had won all seven seats in the 1970 elections.

Bramble announced that Montserrat would join the Caribbean Common Market in May 1974, it was reported Oct. 26, leaving Antigua as the only small British Caribbean island refusing to join. However, the market's common external tariff would not apply to Montserrat before 1981. Montserrat had elected not to become part of the West Indies Associated States in January 1967.

PARAGUAY

Indian crisis. Pressure was mounting in Paraguay for an investigation of the settlement which housed a portion of the dwindling Guayaki Indian tribe, the Miami Herald reported Jan. 4.

The settlement in eastern Paraguay, near the site of the proposed joint hydroelectric power venture with Brazil, was founded 10 years ago by Paraguayan army officers. It was later adopted by some Asuncion businessmen.

A former army sergeant, Manuel Pereira, was charged in the media with mismanagement of 50 Guayakies under his charge, the Herald reported.

According to the reports, Pereira encouraged Guayakies from the settlement to recruit those who remained in the bush. Their survival rate at their new home was low because of disease and a new diet.

Assassination gangs had also attacked nomadic Guayaki villages. According to the Rev. Bartolomeu Melia, a Jesuit adviser to the Paraguayan bishops of Indian affairs, 12–20 nomadic Guayakies were killed near two villages in 1971. Five children who survived were either given away or sold, according to Melia. A 1972 survey indicated only 411 Guayakies had survived.

Elsewhere, the United Nations Human Rights Commission was urged March 29 to take "effective action" to prevent the extermination of Paraguay's Ache Indians, a peaceful nomadic jungle tribe of about 700. A representative of the Anti-Slavery Society of London told the Commission in Geneva that almost all Ache men had been murdered, and captured Ache young women were being sold into slavery.

Brazil grants credit. Brazil had granted Paraguay a $100 million credit at current international rates, gaining an advantage in Paraguay over Argentina, the London newsletter Latin America reported Jan. 12. The credit followed Argentine refusal to sell 15,000–20,000 tons of wheat to Paraguay to cover an acute shortage, the newsletter reported.

Itaipu pact with Brazil. Brazil and Paraguay signed a partnership agreement April 26 to build what was expected to be the world's largest hydroelectric project, at Itaipu on the Parana River between the two countries.

The pact was signed in Brasilia by Foreign Minister Mario Gibson Barboza and his Paraguayan counterpart, Raul Sapena Pastor. President Emilio G. Medici and Paraguayan President Alfredo Stroessner attended the ceremony.

Argentina, which had opposed the project for two years, recalled its ambassador from Brasilia to protest the agreement. Argentine officials had demanded prior assurance that projects such as Itaipu would not harm navigation downstream in Argentina, or jeopardize other Parana hydroelectric schemes planned at Yacyreta-Apipe and Corpus between Argentina and Paraguay.

The Itaipu project, with a planned capacity of 10 million kilowatts, reportedly would cost $2 billion. It was planned by the International Engineering Co. of the U.S. and Electroconsult SpA of Italy.

A dam 720 feet high and 4,600 feet long would create a 515-square-mile reservoir, half to cover Brazilian territory and half Paraguayan territory.

Brazil and Paraguay agreed to set up a joint company to build and run the project, and to divide the power production equally.

Stroessner had been reported under pressure by the Argentine government and his old friend Juan Peron, whose protege Hector Campora would become president of Argentina May 25, to delay the agreement.

Stroessner sent an emissary to Buenos Aires April 23 to deliver a personal letter to Campora. Stroessner said April 27 that Paraguay would continue its "optimal relations of friendship" with Argentina.

The Itaipu pact was approved by the Paraguayan Senate June 6.

The pact was approved 20-8, with the 18 senators from the ruling Colorado party and the two from the opposition Liberal party voting in favor and the eight senators of the opposition Liberal Radical party voting against.

The voting followed a week-long debate in which opposition senators criticized many of the pact's provisions, particularly the terms under which Paraguay would sell to Brazil its surplus energy from Itaipu. Critics said Paraguay should demand equal control of Itaipu with Brazil and a higher price for the surplus power, to be paid in U.S. dollars (not Brazilian cruzeiros, as the pact stipulated.)

Two independent newspapers, ABC Color and La Tribuna, published editorials attacking the pact for the 14th consecutive day June 6. ABC Color said the government had merely accepted the pact as written by Brazil.

The pact's ratification was reported July 20 to have been promulgated on completion of Congressional action, and the final agreement was signed Aug. 13.

The measure was rushed through the Chamber of Deputies as criticism of the pact continued in two Asuncion newspapers, ABC Color and La Tribuna. The criticism was considered ominous for President Alfredo Stroessner because it was approved by two of his top generals—the cavalry commander, Gen. Andres Rodriguez, and the artillery commander, Gen. German Martinez.

The newspapers accused Brazil of shaping the treaty and claimed Paraguay should receive much more than the $31 million in Brazilian cruzeiros allocated to it. Other opponents protested that a Brazilian would head the Itaipu board and that Paraguay had relinquished its right to amend the treaty.

Church, government talks. The government and the Roman Catholic Church had undertaken top-level negotiations to improve their relations, which had been strained for four years, it was reported June 1.

Stroessner, Banzer meet. President Stroessner and Bolivian President Hugo Banzer Suarez conferred July 4 in Nueva Asuncion, Paraguay, and the next day in Santa Cruz, Bolivia. The two generals agreed in a joint communique July 5 to improve transportation routes between their countries, beginning with the navigability of the Paraguay River, to promote "greater economic development." They also reaffirmed their countries' need for free access to the sea.

Release of political prisoners sought. Amnesty International, a London-based organization working for the release of political prisoners, urged Stroessner to release an estimated 150 Paraguayan political prisoners to celebrate his inaugural, it was reported Aug. 14. No government reply to the plea was reported.

Martin Ennals, Amnesty International's secretary general, noted Stroessner had freed some political prisoners in July but said there were still "in [police stations] of Asuncion and in different places of detention in the interior of the country ... persons detained who have not been formally charged with a crime, nor have they had access to appropriate legal counsel, nor have they been heard by a tribunal. Many of them have been detained for long years, some for as many as 15."

3rd party barred from election. The Democratic Liberal party was barred from taking part in the February presidential election, the newsletter Latin America reported Jan. 19. It was the third party barred from participating.

The Liberal Radical party announced that its candidate for the election would be Gustavo Riart, the newsletter had reported Jan. 12.

Stroessner, Colorados sweep elections. Gen. Alfredo Stroessner was elected to a fifth presidential term Feb. 11 over what was regarded as token opposition. His Colorado party simultaneously swept parliamentary elections, gaining two-thirds majorities in the 30-seat Senate and the 60-seat Chamber of Deputies.

An estimated 70%-74% of the million eligible voters participated in the elections, which took place without major incidents. An unofficial partial count in the presidential race gave 418,623 votes to Stroessner, 74,972 to Gustavo Riart of the Liberal Radical party, and 18,882 to Carlos Levi Rufinelli of the Liberal party. Three other parties were barred from the elections, and a fourth, the Febreristas, instructed its adherents to cast blank ballots.

The Liberal party charged that the Liberal Radical candidate lists violated certain provisions of the law, but the Electoral Council did not act on the charge before the elections.

Stroessner's reelection was made official by a resolution passed at a special session of Congress March 8. The official count: Stroessner's Colorado party 681,-306 votes, to 198,096 for the Liberal Radical party and 24,611 for the Liberal party.

Opposition party leaders had charged collusion after the 35% abstention and blank vote rate in the recent election was adjusted to 25%, the London newsletter Latin America reported March 2.

The small Liberal party accused the ruling Colorados and the main opposition group, the Liberal Radical party, of sharing the 10% difference between them. It was also rumored, Latin America reported, that the two parties had made a secret pact that would continue the country's "democratic" facade in the 1978 elections.

Stroessner inaugurated. Gen. Alfredo Stroessner, in power since 1954, was sworn in for another five-year presidential term Aug. 15.

Stroessner reappointed all Cabinet officials except the defense minister, Gen. Leodegar Cabello, and the industry minister, Jose Antonio Moreno Gonzalez, both in the Cabinet for 10 years. Cabello reportedly would serve in the Senate; Moreno was said to be ill. The Cabinet:

Interior—Sabino Augusto Montanaro; foreign affairs—Raúl Sapena Pastor; finance—Gen. Cesar Barrientos; education—Raúl Pena; public works & communications—Gen. Marcial Samaniego; justice and labor—Saul González; public health—Adan Godoy Jiménez; industry and commerce—Delfin Ugarte Centurion; agriculture—Hernando Bertoni; defense (acting)—Gen. Samaniego; minister without portfolio—Tomas Romero Pereira.

Stroessner's inauguration was preceded by the signing in Asuncion Aug. 13 of the Itaipu hydroelectric pact, the joint venture by Brazil and Paraguay to build a giant dam and power station on the Parana River, between the two countries. Stroessner witnessed the signing by Foreign Minister Sapena Pastor and Brazilian Foreign Minister Mario Gibson Barboza.

The coincidence of the signing and Stroessner's inauguration led Argentina, which opposed the Itaipu project, to cancel plans to send a high-level delegation to the inaugural. Instead, Argentina sent an anti-Brazilian historian, Jose Maria Rosa. In an apparent response to this gesture, Paraguay closed its border with Argentina Aug. 18-20, claiming "anti-government elements dedicated to terrorist action" were using Argentina as a base.

(An Anglo-Argentine businessman, Ian Martin, manager of a British meat plant in Asuncion, was kidnapped Aug. 27 and freed Sept. 6 when police discovered his abductors' hideout about 40 miles east of the capital. Police reported capturing several of the kidnappers, but did not reveal their identities. The police had charged Aug. 29 that the culprits were members of an Argentine Marxist guerrilla group, the People's Revolutionary Army [ERP], after allegedly finding a message with ERP symbols and slogans inside Martin's abandoned car. The kidnappers reportedly had demanded a ransom equivalent to $1 million.)

SURINAM

Strikes, riots, violence. Strikes and rioting swept Paramaribo, the capital of Surinam (the semi-autonomous colony known formerly as Dutch Guiana) in January and February. The unrest generally pitted black Creoles against the East Indian majority, the London newsletter Latin America reported Feb. 16. One of the protesters' main complaints was directed against what trade unionists called the exploitation of Surinam by foreign companies, particularly in bauxite production. Surinam's severe unemployment and inflation aggravated the tension, according to the newsletter.

The current unrest began Jan. 17 when striking customs officials defied a court order to return to work. The strike immediately spread to other sectors. Street demonstrations broke out and grew increasingly violent, with strikers occupying several ministries, newspaper offices, the radio station and other government buildings in Paramaribo Feb. 7. By Feb. 8 teachers, a third of the civil servants, sugar plantation employes and hospital nursing staffs were on strike, the London Times reported Feb. 9. A general strike called by the labor unions began at midnight Feb. 8, affecting the bauxite mines in addition to the other sectors of the economy.

Jules Sedney, Surinam's premier, Feb. 11 accused "Communists" of starting the current troubles. The following day several thousand persons, mainly Creoles, demonstrated in the capital, demanding the resignation of Sedney and his government.

Three persons were shot and wounded when police and shopkeepers opened fire during riots in Paramaribo Feb. 14–15. Stores were set on fire and plundered in the Chinese and East Indian quarters.

Some improvement in the strike situation was reported by the London Times Feb. 16. About half the customs officers and teachers and more civil servants had resumed work, according to the Times. Meanwhile, the Permanent Committee for the Dutch West Indies of the Netherlands' Lower House of parliament had barred any interference by Dutch troops in the unrest, the London Times continued.

The Surinam government announced Feb. 15 it would not participate in constitutional talks planned for the end of the month between the Netherlands, Surinam and the Netherlands Antilles to discuss their future relationship. The move was attributed to the current unrest.

After a brief lull, three persons were reported shot dead by police in renewed strike demonstrations the previous week in Paramaribo, the capital, the Miami Herald reported March 1. During two days of rioting, several commercial centers, stores, schools and government buildings, including the tax office, had been burned in Paramaribo.

Dutch draft autonomy statute. The Dutch government presented a new draft statute to replace the 1954 Realm of the Netherlands statute giving Surinam and the Antilles internal autonomy, the Times of the Americas reported March 15. The new proposals, seen as a stepping stone to full independence, called for elimination of Netherlands' involvement in all but the defense and foreign affairs of the two Dutch possessions, leaving responsibility for internal affairs completely in the hands of local authorities.

The present Realm of the Netherlands would become a Commonwealth and the present ministers plenipotentiary from the territories residing in The Hague would become high commissioners. A court of human rights with three judges from the Netherlands, Netherlands Antilles and Surinam would be established to handle disputes. The target date for implementation of the new statute was Jan. 1, 1975.

Sedney coalition defeated. Elections held Nov. 19 resulted in defeat for the primarily East Indian coalition government headed by Premier Jules Sedney. A predominantly black Creole coalition of five opposition parties, calling for Surinam's total independence from the Netherlands, won 22 of the 39 seats in Parliament.

The winning coalition, called the party of National Combination, was formed by a local banker, Henk Arron, leader of the National party of Surinam. Sedney's Progressive National party lost all its eight seats in Parliament, while its East Indian coalition partner, the Vatan Hitkarie party of Jaggernath Lachmon, retained its 17 seats. The extreme left National party for the Republic, part of the victorious coalition, increased its representation from one seat to four.

The victory for the opposition coalition was attributed to dissatisfaction over the Sedney government's handling of strikes,

TRINIDAD & TOBAGO

Cabinet shuffled. Prime Minister Eric Williams assumed the post of external affairs minister, the London newsletter Latin America reported Feb. 16. Kamaluddin Mohammed, who held the position four years, was named minister of local government and public utilities. Latin America noted that Williams had complained that the country was misrepresented at the 1972 conference of Caribbean foreign ministers on the use of seabed resources.

New governor general named. Ellis Clarke, former ambassador to the U.S., was named governor general, El Nacional of Caracas reported Feb. 4. The post, equivalent to chief of state and representative of the British Crown, was previously held by Solomon Hochoy, who resigned at the end of 1972.

Opposition party elects new head. Alloy Lequay was elected leader of the main opposition party—the East Indian-dominated Democratic Labor party (DLP), Latin America reported Jan. 12.

His election came at a special party election which ousted Vernon Jamadar, the party's head for three years.

Lequay, who had been the party's secretary general, said the Democratic Liberation party, a splinter group which broke away, three years ago, had rejoined the DLP.

Williams to retire. Prime Minister Eric Williams, in power 17 years, announced Sept. 29 that he planned to retire from politics but did not set a definite date. Leaders of his People's National Movement (PNM), at whose congress Williams made the announcement, asked him to remain in office until they selected a successor.

The PNM choice would automatically become prime minister, since the party held 34 of the 36 seats in the House of Representatives. The next general elections were due late in 1974.

The nine opposition groups, which boycotted the last elections, had threatened to also skip the next elections unless the government granted a number of demands to assure fair voting: abolition of voting machines, which the suspicious peasantry would not use; radio time for opposition candidates; the right to demonstrate; impartial supervision of polls and registration, and, possibly, proportional representation in the House.

In a related development reported Sept. 21, Attorney General Karl Phillips resigned after being publicly rebuked by Williams for seeking the ouster of the PNM chairman, Sen. Francis Prevatt, at the party's congress.

U.S. VIRGIN ISLANDS

St. Croix 5 convicted. Five St. Croix natives were sentenced to life imprisonment Aug. 13 for the murders of eight persons at the luxurious Virgin Island Fountain Valley golf course Sept. 6, 1972.

The courtroom erupted into uproar and confusion when U.S. District Court Judge Warren H. Young announced that each defendant had received eight consecutive life terms in prison. The handcuffed defendants shouted obscenities and struck out at the 23 U.S. marshalls guarding the tense courtroom, while defense lawyer William M. Kunstler shouted at Judge Young, "You can't do this!"

The trial was complicated Aug. 14 when two members of the jury, one of them the foreman, alleged in sworn statements that they were pressured into reaching guilty verdicts. Jury foreman Myron Alick, a black, asserted he was threatened by marshalls with a charge of perjury if he did not vote guilty.

Another juror, Lionel Rodgers, stated: "My verdict was not voluntary. It was the end product of pressure applied by . . . Young, who refused two verdicts and the majority of the jury who, to me, seemed to have had premeditated verdicts."

A third juror similarly stated Aug. 15 she was pressured into delivering a guilty verdict. She claimed to have been told that a charge against her brother, which had been dropped, would be revived.

Defense attorneys said they would appeal the verdicts and the sentences.

Meanwhile, Melvin H. Evans, governor of the Virgin Islands, announced Aug. 16 that he had summoned to St. Croix a force of about 40 federal marshals to shore up the local force of 100 policemen. He said they were being brought to maintain order in the wake of five murders in the previous three weeks.

Evans Oct. 15 accused the press of overplaying the racial overtones of the recent killings. Since September 1972, 21 murders had been reported; all but one of the victims were white.

Evans maintained that the killings had been isolated incidents, not a vendetta by native Crucians against whites. He said that if the press did not stop "exaggerating the situation," tourism in the Virgin Islands would not survive.

Evans' latter statement referred to the fact that many shops and restaurants were empty and hotels were closing because tourists were bypassing the island in the wake of news accounts of the murders. The Washington Post reported Oct. 15 that U.S. airlines were quietly diverting travelers to other islands in the Caribbean.

WEST INDIES ASSOCIATED STATES

Black Power violence in Antigua. A Black Power group, known as the Antigua Freedom Fighters, blew up the residence of Donald Halstead, the island's home affairs minister, the London Times reported June 24. Halstead was abroad at the time. The violence, the Times speculated, was intended to warn the minister against his apparent ambition to control the island. The Black Power movement in Antigua was said to be the strongest one in all the West Indies Associated States.

State of emergency in Dominica. A state of emergency was declared in the West Indies associated state of Dominica June 15 after a strike by civil servants, hospital staffs, dockers and shopkeepers paralyzed the island. The state of emergency was called by Premier Edward Leblanc to prevent "antidemocratic forces" from overthrowing his government.

The strikers were protesting a government decision to transfer a popular announcer, Daniel Caudeiron, from the government radio station to a politically less sensitive post in the civil service. The move was made because of Caudeiron's alleged sympathy with the Black Power movement, the London Times reported June 16.

A one-month extension of the state of emergency, to Aug. 15, was voted by the House of Assembly, the Miami Herald reported July 20. The extension, requested by Leblanc, had prompted the resignation of Deputy Premier and Finance Minister R.O.P. Armour, the Herald reported. The state of emergency had led to the closing of one newspaper, the Dominican Herald.

The ending of the state of emergency was reported Aug. 24.

Grenada independence approved. The British House of Commons approved an order Dec. 11 to grant full independence to the British West Indies associated state of Grenada, effective Feb. 7, 1974.

Agreement on the independence move had been announced July 30 after inconclusive talks held in March and May.

Grenada's opposition had refused to agree to a conference on a new constitution, the London Times reported May 31. Grenada had been a West Indies associated state in the Commonwealth since 1967, with full internal self-government but with Britain retaining responsibility for its foreign relations and defense. Talks on independence had also been held in March.

A number of teachers, bank employes, and gas, electric and communications workers struck in Grenada to protest against total independence for the island, the French newspaper Le Monde reported May 22.

Grenada to disband secret police—Premier Eric Gairy of Grenada was reported

Nov. 27 to have agreed to disband the island's secret police, appoint a special commission to probe charges of police brutality and increase the size of the regular police force with noncriminal recruits. Gairy had allegedly drafted criminals into the secret police force formed in 1970, initially to combat black power activists but used subsequently, according to critics of Gairy, to harass the opposition.

Gairy announced his decision following three days of protests and strikes over the alleged beating of three members of a radical opposition group called the New Jewel Movement by members of the special police. Authorities denied the charges.

Index

A

ABELARDO Ramos, Jorge—17
ABRAMS, Gen. Creighton W.—93
ABSHIANA Indians—147
ACHU Liendo, Rigoberto—130
ACOSTA Velasco, Jorge—165
ADERLEY, Paul—232
ADETT Zamora, Mario—52, 55-6
AEROLINEAS Argentinas—31
AERO-Peru (airline)—197
AGA KHAN, Prince Sadruddin—128
AGENCY for International Development (AID), U.S.—92
AGRICULTURE—54, 180, 182, 202, 236, 239, 240-1, 243. Argentina—36, 51. Brazil—70-2, 76-8. Chile—100, 122, 132. Colombia—134, 144, 146. Cuba—148-9, 153. Irrigation—162, 179, 181, 193-4, 236. Peru—193-4, 197
AGUERO, Fernando—183-4
AGUERO, Rafael—142
AIRCRAFT Hijackings—145, 149-51, 168, 225
ALARCON, Ricardo—112, 201
ALBAN Holguin, Carlos—141
ALCOREZA Melgarejo, Gen. Carlos—56
ALEJANDRO Gaitini, Luis—21
ALEMAN, Rear Adm. Francisco A.—26, 29, 33
ALEMAN, Miguel—176
ALENDE, Oscar—17, 24
ALESSANDRI Rodriguez, Jorge—87, 89
ALFA-Romeo—64
ALFONSIN, Raúl—42
ALGERIA—154
ALICK, Myron—247
ALL American Cables & Radio Co.—167
ALLENDE, Mrs. Hortensia Bussi de—112, 130-1
ALLENDE, Sen. Jose Antonio—29
ALLENDE Gossens, Salvador—9, 12, 32, 34, 79-80, 83-8, 93-4, 99-101, 103-13, 149
ALMASAN, Bujor—226
ALMEYDA, Clodomiro—85-6, 91, 105-6, 112, 117, 119
ALONSO, Jose—21
ALONSO Freiria, Consuelo—128
ALTAMIRANO, Sen. Carlos—83-4, 104, 120
ALTMANN, Klaus—195
ALVARADO, Luis—14
ALVAREZ, Col. Armando—60
ALVAREZ, Adm. Carlos—32, 51
ALVAREZ, Enrique—236
ALVAREZ Penaranda, Col. Raul—56-7
AMACO Oil Co.—49
AMARO Salup, Raul—154
AMERICAN Tunaboat Association (ATA)—8
AMERICAN Voting Machines Corp. (AVM)—230
AMIAMA Tio, Luis—155
AMODIO Perez, Hector—212
AMUNATEGUI, Felipe—92
ANACONDA Co.—81-2, 88-9, 91
ANAYA, Gen. Leandro—50
ANDA Aguirre, Gen. Vicente—165
ANDEAN Development Corp. (CAF)—7
ANDEAN Group—76-7, 222.
ANDEAN Times: Latin America Economic Report—15
ANDERSEN, Nyborg—50
ANDERSON, Jack—6-7, 73, 89
ANDERSON, Robert B.—187
ANDERSSON, Sven—128
ANDRADE Labarca, Nectario—230
ANDREOTTI, Giulio—24
ANDRES Perez, Carlos—230
ANILLO, Rene—151
ANOS de Soledad, Cien—143

ANTIGUA—9. Antigua Freedom Fighters—248
AQUEVEDO, Eduardo—86
ARAGONES Navarro, Emilio—153
ARAMBURU, Pedro—32
ARANCIBIA, Armando—83
ARAUJO Hidalgo, Manuel—166
ARAYA, Capt. Arturo—102
ARCE Carpio, Alfredo—55-7
ARCOS Perez, Mario—220-1
ARELLANO, Rear Adm. Daniel—83, 109
ARELLANO, Gen. Sergio—133
ARENA party—76, 119
ARGENTINA—1, 6, 54, 69, 153, 243. Arrests—39, 44. Assassinations—21, 26, 28-9, 44-5, 47-9. Economic & monetary developments—5, 20, 30-1, 35-6, 51. Fishing industry—8, 19-20, 67. Foreign relations—13, 19-20, 22, 28, 34, 42-3, 51, 82. Government & politics—29, 32; elections—17-9, 22-4, 39-42, 45-7. Military developments—17-9, 26, 32, 50-1. Social unrest—20-2, 25-30, 33-8, 43-5; strikes—25, 31, 40
ARGENTINE Association of Newspaper Publishers—43
ARIZA Gomez, Jesús—138
ARMED Forces—21, 26, 32, 60, 67-8, 80-1, 108, 110, 114, 153, 155-7, 204
ARMESTO, Ernesto—38
ARMOUR, R. O. P.—248
ARNAUD, Winston—158-9
AROSEMENA Gomez, Otto—164
ARPEL—15
ARRON, Henk—246
ARZABE, Ramiro—60
ASCANIO Peterson, Wellington—159
ASSASSINATIONS—21, 26, 28-9, 44-5, 47-9, 102, 200, 243
ASSOCIATED Press (AP)—3, 43, 120, 171
ATOMIC Energy—15, 30, 181
ATOMIC Energy of Canada Ltd.—30
AVIATION—7, 12-3, 31, 53, 76, 100, 108, 137, 197, 236, 240
AVILA Camacho, Manuel—176
AUGUSTO Martinez, Gen. Cesar—204
AUGUSTO Montanaro, Sabino—245
AULESTIA, Victor—164-5
AUSTRALIA—4
AUTHENTIC Party of the Mexican Revolution—176
AUTOMOBILE Industry—40-1, 50, 78, 64, 99-100, 180, 189. See also specific country
AYLWIN, Sen. Patricio—93, 105
AZCARRAGA Jimenez, German—56, 61
AZERO Sanzetenea, Col. Ramon—56, 61

B

BACA, Gov. Alberto Martinez—48
BACHELET, Gen. Alberto—80, 114
BAHAMAS—6, 9, 232-3
BAIRD, Capt. D. C.—113
BALAGUER, Joaquin—155, 158-61
BALBIN, Ricardo—17, 23-4, 37, 39-41, 45

BALBOA, Oscar—106
BALESTRA, Rene—17
BALPARDA Blengio, Luis—206
BANFI, Alberto—46
BANK America Corp.—88
BANKERS Trust Co.—131
BANK of Brazil—65
BANKS & Banking—5, 15, 31, 36, 51, 57-8, 64-5, 69, 78, 131, 134-5, 208
BANZER Suarez, Hugo—52, 55-7, 59-61, 126, 244
BAPTISTE, Fred—169
BAPTISTE, Reneld—169
BARATELLA, Mario—38
BARDELLI, Juan Bautista—198
BARNADAS, José—53
BARNES, John—118
BARREIRO Solorzano, Augusto—164
BARRIENTOS, Gen. Cesar—245
BARRIENTOS Ortuno, René—56
BARUJ de Da Rin, Moemi—30
BASCUNAN, Dewest—126
BATALLA, Hugo—217-8
BATISTA, José—75
BATLLE, Jorge—211
BAZAN, Raúl—112, 124
BEATLLE, Jorge—213
BEAULIEU, Daniel—171
BEDREGAL, Javier—60
BEDREGAL, Luis—56
BEILINSON, Aaron—33
BEJAMBRE, Cristobal—139
BELIZE (British Honduras)—233
BELMONTE, Maj. Elias—62
BENELLI, Msgr. Giovanni—24
BENITES, Leopoldo—14
BENITEZ, Antonio J.—32
BERGER, Maria Antonia—26
BERISSO, Rear Adm. Ruben—20, 199
BERNARDO, Rubens—63
BERRELLEZ, Robert—89
BERRIO, Puerto—139
BERTONI, Hernando—245
BETANCOURT, Carlos—224
BIDEGAIN, Gov. Oscar—41, 45
BIDEGAIN Creissing, Raul—218
BISON Petroleum & Minerals Ltd.—189
BITAR, Sergio—96-7, 119
BLANCHET, Paul—171
BLANCO, Armando—209
BLANCO, Juan Carlos—206, 218, 221
BLENGIO, Luis Balparda—211-2
BLUM, Muchel—121
BOENINGER, Edgardo—116
BOISSET, Yves—50
BOLENTINI, Nestor—208-10, 212-3, 219-20
BOLIVIA—52-62, 126, 244
BOLIVIAN Mine Workers Federation—62
BOLIVIAN Socialist Falange (FSB)—54-5, 57, 59
BONHOMME, Max—171
BONILLA, Gen. Oscar—119, 122, 133
BOOKERS, Ltd. (Booker Brothers)—239

INDEX

BORDABERRY, Juan Maria—204–6, 212–3, 216–21
BORNANCINI, Raúl—39
BOSCH, Juan—154–5, 158–61
BOTTINI, Federico—225
BOYD, Aquilino E.—3
BRACHO Campos, Jose—172
BRADY, Gen. Herman—103–4, 107
BRAMBLE, Austin—242–3
BRANDAO, Avelar Cardinal—69, 72, 74
BRANDT, Willy—129
BRANIFF International—45
BRASPETRO (Brazil state international oil monopoly)—65
BRAY 3d, Charles W.—151
BRAZIL—3, 5, 8, 12, 54, 57, 63–5, 69–78, 113, 195, 243
BRAZILIAN Democratic Movement (MDB)—63–4, 76
BRAZO, Leopoldo—17
BREA Pena, Jose Antonio—157
BREZHNEV, Leonid—178
BRIMICOMBE, Francis V.—26
BRIONES, Carlos—101, 111–2
BRITISH-American Tobacco Co.—45
BRITISH Honduras (Belize)—233
BROE, William V.—87–90
BROINES, Carlos—109
BROOKS, Edwin—66
BUCARAM, Asaad—166
BULGARIA—82, 100
BUNKER, Ellsworth—187
BURELLI Rivas, Miguel Angel—229
BURNHAM, Forbes—239–40
BUSACCA, Salvador—29
BUSH, George—3
BUSINESS Week (magazine)—166

C

CAAMANO, Claudio—157
CAAMANO, Gen. Fausto—157
CAAMANO, Francisco—155–6, 158, 160
CABALLERO Tamayo, Col. Jaime—56–7
CABELLO, Gen. Leodegar—245
CABRERA Giordano, Carmelo—209
CACERES, Ramon—218
CADEMARTORI, Jose—109, 119
CAICEDO, Alvaro—138
CALABRO, Gov. Victor—41
CALDERA, Rafael—11, 76, 222–3, 229–30, 242
CALDERON, Rolando—85, 129
CALVANI, Aristides—11, 223
CAMARA, Archbishop Helder—69, 72, 74
CAMBRONNE, Lt. Col. Luckner—169, 171
CAMPBELL, Sir Clifford—242
CAMPILLO, Luis Manuel—161
CAMPOBIANCO, Adalberto S. di—65
CAMPORA, Hector J.—12, 17–9, 23–4, 27–9, 31–7, 39–40, 58, 153, 243
CAMPOS, Maj. Humberto—60
CANADA—30, 100, 151, 177
CANADIAN Javelin, Ltd.—188
CANCEL Miranda, Rafael—200
CANO, Gen. Edwardo—116, 122
CAPRILES, Roberto—56, 61
CARCAGNO, Gen. Jorge Raul—32, 39, 43, 50
CARCIA Castro, Gregorio—160
CARDOZO, Jose—216
CARGILL Inc.—190
CARIDAD Jordan, Morcos—220
CARIBBEAN area—6, 144–5, 239, 241–2
CARPIO Becerra, Alfredo—194
CASADO, Manfredo—162
CASALDALIGA, Rev. Pedro—73–4
CASAROLI, Msgr. Agostino—24
CASE, Sen. Clifford P. (R., N.J.)—87
CASEY, William J.—11
CASIMIRO Castro, Pablo Rafael—161
CASTELLANOS, Jacinto—236
CASTELLO Branco, Antonio Borges Leal—74
CASTRILLON, Rev. Lucio—146
CASTRO, Jaime—141
CASTRO, Adm. Jose Toribio Merino—114
CASTRO, Walter—61
CASTRO Avedano, Col. Walter—55, 60
CASTRO Jimenez, Rear Adm. Hugo—116
CASTRO Rojas, German—119
CASTRO Ruz, Fidel—9, 100, 194, 123–4, 148–9, 151–2, 156
CASTRO Ruz, Raúl—149, 154
CATENA, Rev. Osvaldo—21
CATHOLICS, Roman—29, 52–3, 58, 68–9, 71–4, 93–4, 121, 146–7, 188, 244
CAUDEIRON, Daniel—248
CAVALIER, Jorge—145
CAYOJA Riart, Col. Humberto—52
CEAUSESCU, Nicolae—19, 149, 226
CELLA de Callegari, Pinuccia—26
CENSORSHIP—See PRESS & Censorship
CENTRAIS Electricas de Sao Paulo S.A.—69
CENTRAL American Association of Journalists—185
CENTRAL Intelligence Agency (CIA), U.S.—37, 86–92, 106, 113, 125, 197
CERDA, Eduardo—106
CERECEDA, Hernan—96
CERRO de Pasco Corp.—191–2
CERRUTO, Waldo—60
CERVI, Grazie Mary—123
CESIO, Juan Jaime—50
CHAMIZO, Julio—17
CHAMORRO, Pedro—184
CHARLES, Prince (Great Britain)—233
CHIAPPE Posse, Gen. Hugo—206, 210, 213
CHILE—3, 12, 57. Government & politics—93–7; cabinet changes—101–2, 105, 109, 114; elections—83–4, 86–92; military regime—110–32. Economy—82, 99–100, 116, 122, 132. Foreign relations—82, 131, 195. Uprisings—79, 100–1, 110–1. U.S. & ITT—86–92, 113
CHILE Hoy (newspaper)—79, 86
CHILES, Sen. Lawton (D., Fla.)—14
CHINA, People's Republic of—31, 51, 76, 82, 178
CHIYODA Chemical Engineering Co.—164

CHOQUE, Salustio—61
CHOU En-lai—31, 178
CHRISTENSEN, Ward L.—168
CHRYSLER Corp.—50, 181
CINEAS, Fritz—171
CIRNE Lima, Luis F.—71
CITICORP International Bank—189
CITIES Service Oil Co.—50
C. ITOH & Co.—78
CLARIN (Argentine newspaper)—45
CLARKE, Ellis—247
COAL—15, 51, 70
COBRE Panama (Japanese consortium)—189
COCA-Cola Co.—30, 180, 231
COCA-Cola Export Corp.—44-5
CODA, Rear Adm. Carlos—28
CODELCO (Chilean state copper company)—81-2, 99
COHEN, Moises—208, 210
COLBY, William E.—125
COLLAZO, Oscar—200
COLOM Argueta, Manuel—237
COLOMBIA—12, 144-5, 223. Economy 134-7. Guerrillas—137-40. Politics & government—136, 140-4. Social unrest—135-6, 146
COLOMBO, José Domingo—48
COLOMBO, Juan Carlos—50
COLON Martinez, Noel—199
COLORADO River—11, 179
COMIBOL (Bolivian state mining concern)—54, 57-8
COMMUNISTS—Check country involved
CONCHAN Chevron Co.—192
CONCHELLO, Jose Angel—176
CONNALLY Jr., John B.—167
CONTESTI, Ruben—26
CONTRERAS, Iriam—128
CORAL, Juan Carlos—17, 42, 45
CORDERO, Martin—130
CORVALAN, Sen. Luis—102, 118-20, 130
COSTA Rica—7, 151, 233-5
CREOLE Petroleum Corp.—226-7
CRIMMINS, John H.—10
CROWE, Sir Colin—4
CROWE, Judge Guthrie—127
CRUZ Brea, Gen. Jose Ernesto—160
CUBA—4-5, 8-10, 14, 34, 43, 51, 127, 148-54, 156, 191, 194, 225, 230, 240. Cuban Communist party—154
CURREA Cubides, Gen. Hernando—141
CZECHOSLOVAKIA—148-9

D

DaCRUZ, Anthony R.—26
DAGER, Jorge—228, 231
DANYAU, Gen. Cesar Ruiz—122
Da ROCHA Correa, Enrique—218
DARQUE Moreno, Francisco—165
DAVIS, Frederick D.—125
DAVIS, Nathaniel—106
De CARVALHO, Gen. Glauco—64
DeJESUS, Grancisco—203

De JESUS Checo, Gen. Rafael—158
De la FLOR, Gen. Miguel Angel—10
De la ROSA, Diogenes—187
De la RUA, Fernando—27
Del CANTO, Hernan—82, 85, 106
DELERONI, Antonio J.—48
DELERONI, Nelida Arana de—48
DELGADO Sanchez, Gen. Hernan—224
D'ELIA, Jose—215
De los SANTOS, Hugo Leonardo—220
De ROULET, Vincent W.—242
De SOUZA, Joao Francisco—72
DIAZ, Felix—218
DIAZ Bialet, Sen. Alejandro—29
DIMAS Alas, Tito—236
DIUGUID, Lewis H.—22
DOMINICAN Republic—9, 158-62
DOMINGUEZ Vargas, Sergio—174
DOMINIQUE, Marie-Denise Duvalier—171
DONALDSON, Tim B.—233
DORADO, Juan Carlos—60
DORTICOS, Osvaldo—12, 32, 34, 149, 152-4, 194
Dos REIS Veloso, Joao Paulo—69
DOW Chemical Co.—132
DUARTE, Hermes—144
DUFFUS, Chief Justice Sir Herbert—242
Du PONT de Nemours & Co., E.I.—113
DURET, Juan Carlos—50
DUVALIER, Francois—169
DUVALIER, Jean-Claude—169-71
DUVALIER, Simone—169

E

EARTHQUAKES—9, 11, 181-3
EAST Germany (German Democratic Republic)—34, 77, 147, 180, 226, 239
EASTMAN Kodak Co.—26
ECHANDI, Mario—234
ECHAVARRIA, Luis Fernando—141
ECHEGOYEN, Sen. Martin—212
ECHEVERRIA, Maria Teresa—137
ECHEVERRIA Alvarez, Luis—11, 100, 172, 176-9, 225
ECHEVERRY Mejia, Sen. Hernando—142-3
ECONOMIC Commission for Latin America (ECLA) (UN)—8-9, 70
ECONOMIC Developments: Cost of living—20, 31, 64, 82, 99, 135. Monetary developments—53-4, 64, 69-70, 78-80, 180-1, 208, 241. See also specific country
ECUADOR—3, 6-8, 163-7
ECUADOR Sun Oil Co.—164
EDELSTAM, Harald—128
EDUCATION—31, 34-5, 77, 93-4, 116, 122, 126, 147, 174, 207
EGYPTIAN General Petroleum Corp.—65
El COMERCIO (Peruvian newspaper)—195
El DESCAMISADO (Argentine magazine)—51
El DIARIO (Bolivian newspaper)—55

INDEX

ELECTRICITY—5, 40, 51, 54, 69, 77-8, 134, 148-9, 189, 193, 236, 243
ELECTROCONSULT SpA (Italy)—69
ELIZABETH, Queen (Great Britain)—177, 233
El MERCURIO (Chilean newspaper)—80
El MUNDO (Argentine newspaper)—48, 218
El MUNDO (Venezuelan newspaper)—155
El NACIONAL of Caracas (newspaper)—3, 6, 8, 13, 23, 53, 64
El NORTE (Argentine newspaper)—48
El PASO Natural Gas Co.—193
El POPULAR (Uruguayan Communist newspaper)—218, 221
El SALVADOR—235-6, 241
El SIGLO (Chilean newspaper)—133
EMPRESA Siderurgica Boliviana S.A. (SIDERSA)—54
ENERGY Resources development—15, 30, 51, 53-4, 57. See also ATOMIC Energy; ELECTRICITY; GAS, Natural; PETROLEUM Developments; see also specific country
ENGLER, Henry—209
ENNALS, Martin—244
ENRIQUEZ, Edgardo—109
ENRIQUEZ, Miguel—120
ENTel (Argentine state communications firm)—27
EPIAYA Indians—147
ERRO, Sen. Enrique—211-4, 216
ESCALONA, Julio—224
ESCOBAR, Gustavo—138
ESCOBAR, Maj. Mario—61
ESCOBAR Mendez, Miguel—144
ESCOBARI Guerra, Maj. Jaime—56
ESPINOLA, Cristobal—196
ESPINOZA Carrillo, Gerardo—85, 99, 102
ESPINOZA Villalobos, Luis—130
ESSO Oil Co.—50
ETCHEGOYEN, Julio Cesar—50
EUROPEAN Brazilian Bank (Eurobraz)—65
EUROPEAN Economic Community (EEC)—78, 177
EVANS, Melvin H.—248
EVARISTO Arns, Cardinal Paulo—68, 72-3
EXPLORACIONES y Explotaciones Mineras Izabal S.A.—238
EXPORT-Import Bank (Washington)—65, 77-8
EXXON Corp.—50, 89, 193

F

FABIANI, Angel—26
FADDA Cori, Claudio—95
FAENA, Alberto—26
FAGEN, Richard A.—125
FAIVOVICH, Jaime—94, 103, 105-7
FALKLAND (Malvinas) Islands—28, 43
FARIA Braga, Gen. Henrique—67
FARIA Lima, Adm. Floriano Peixoto—75
FAUTARIO, Brig. Hector Luis—32
FAVIO, Leonardo—38
FELIX Revas, Jose—224
FEOLA Casella, Amilcar—209
FERNANDES, Geraldo—71
FERNANDEZ, Alberto—82
FERNANDEZ, Lorenzo—229-31
FERNANDEZ, Marcelo—153
FERNANDEZ, Mirta Ercilia—128
FERNANDEZ de Soto, Anibal—135, 141
FERNANDEZ Maldonado, Gen. Jorge—15
FERRE, Gov. Luis A.—151, 202
FERREIRA, Antonio Carlos—66
FERREIRA Aldunate, Sen. Wilson—214
FERROSTAHL AG (West Germany)—65
FIAT Motor Co.—31, 51, 64
FIGUERES, Jose—151, 233-5
FIGUEROA, Luis—96-7
FIGUEROA Cordero, Andres—200
FINLAND—82, 100, 113
FIRESTONE Tire & Rubber Co.—38, 45, 64
FIRST National City Bank—131, 181
FISHING Industry—7-8, 19-20, 67, 153, 179-80, 189-91
FLEITAS, Carlos M.—211
FLEURY, Sergio—75
FLORES, Fernando—79-80, 105, 109, 119
FONSECA, Carlos—o185
FORD Motor Co.—30, 33, 49, 88, 113
FORTEZA, Francisco—210
FOSTER, William—127
FORTUN Suarez, Guillermo—56
FORTUNY, Ruben—48
FOURCAND, Serge—170
FRANCE—4, 65, 195
FRANCESE, Gen. Antonio—204-5
FRANCIS, Carlton E.—232
FRANCISQUE, Edouard—171
FRANCO, Generalissimo Francisco—22, 24
FREDES, Pablo M.—48
FREI Montalva, Eduardo—83-4, 87, 91, 115
FREIRE, Gen. Augusto—197
FREJULI—See JUSTICIALISTA Liberation Front
FRONDIZI, Arturo—17, 19, 29
FUENTEALBA, Sen. Renan—92-3, 105
FUENTES Mohr, Alberto—237
FULBRIGHT, Sen. J. William (D, Ark.)—125

G

GAETJENS, Joseph—170
GAIRY, Eric—248-9
GALIMBERTI, Rodolfo—29
GALLARDO, Mrs. Maria Eugenia Paz—126
GALLARDO Lozada, Jorge—126
GALLISA, Rep. Carlos (Independence, P.R.)—200
GAMOND, Eduardo—17, 24
GARCIA, Sen. Americo—17, 29
GARCIA, Manuel—173
GARCIA Marquez, Gabriel—142-3
GARCIA Ribera, Ambrosio—56, 61
GARCIA Valoy, Antonio—156
GARCIA Villasmil, Gen. Martin—221, 229
GARRETON, Oscar—104, 120, 129
GARRETON, Mrs. Oscar—129
GAS, Natural—51, 57

GEBHARDT, Hans K.—38
GEISEL, Gen. Ernesto—65, 75
GEISEL, Gen. Orlando—75
GELBARD, José—32, 42-3, 47, 51
GENEEN, Harold S.—87-90
GENERAL Mills, Inc.—190
GENERAL Motors Corp.—33-4, 51, 64, 88, 180
GEORGINO das Neves, Geraldo—74
GERBASI, Jose—117
GERMAN Democratic Republic (East Germany)—34, 77, 147, 180, 226, 239
GERMANY, Federal Republic of (West Germany)—65, 70, 129
GERRITY, Edward—88-9
GHIOLDI, Americo—17
GIBSON Barboza, Mario—11, 69, 76-7, 195, 243
GIOVANELLI, Luis—30, 38
GODOY, Jorge—97, 108
GODOY Jimenez, Adan—245
GOMES Christo, Col. Orlando—67
GOMES dos Santos, Archbishop Fernando—72
GOMEZ Hurtado, Alvaro—141-3
GOMEZ Morales, Alfredo—36
GONZALEZ, Pablo—173
GONZALEZ, Gen. Rolando—109, 122
GONZALEZ Heredia, Tito—226
GONZALEZ Marquez, Carlos—94
GONZALEZ Marten, Jorge—234
GORDILLO, Pedro—20
GOTUZZO, Rear Adm. Lorenzo—116
GRACE & Co., W.R.—193
GRANADA Mejia, Luis—145
GRANT, James D.—187
GREAT Britain—3, 28, 43, 232-3, 238-9
GRENADA—9
GREECE—65
GREENE, James—193
GRIMBERG, Enrique—44
GUATEMALA—31, 233, 236-8
GUAYAKI Indians—243
GUEDES, Edgar—209
GUERRILLAS & Terrorism—22, 25-30, 36-7, 44-5, 47-8, 63, 69, 82, 93-5, 114, 125-6, 136-40, 145, 155-61, 168-9, 171, 172-3, 185, 208-9, 212-3, 217-8, 220-2, 224-6, 236, 245. Arrests & sentencing—39, 52-3, 60-2, 64, 69. Coup attempts—52, 55-6, 59-62, 100. Hijackings—145, 149-51, 168, 225. Kidnapings—20-1, 26-7, 30, 34, 38-9, 44-5, 49-50
GUEVARA, Ernesto (Che)—61
GUICHARD, Olivier—170
GUILFOYLE, John W.—91
GUILLERMO Duran, Col. Luis—165-6
GUIMARAES, Ulysses—76
GUTIERREZ, Euclides—159
GUTIERREZ, Mario—55-6, 60
GUTIERREZ Ruiz, Hector—214, 217
GUTIERREZ Santos, Gen. Daniel—174
GUYANA—3, 180, 238-40
GUYANA Bouxite Co. (GUYBAU)—239

GUYANA Youth Corps—238
GUZMAN, Brig. Gen. Alberto—62
GUZMAN, Arturo—158
GUZMAN, Gen. Gustavo Leigh—115, 122

H

HAITI—3, 9, 117, 168-71
HALSTEAD, Donald—248
HANDEL, Hosch—197
HANNA, Arthur D.—232
HARDING, Mary Elizabeth—52-3
HARE, Paul J.—113
HAREWOOD, Guy Jackson—171
HARGROVE, James P.—184
HARRINGTON, Rep. Michael J. (D., Mass.)—124-5
HARVEY, William—58
HAYES, Charles—50
HEATH, Edward—177
HEINZ Co., H.J.—178
HEITMANN, Gen. Walter—122
HELMS, Richard—86-90
HENDRIX, Hal—87-8
HENNESSY, John M.—86
HENRIQUEZ Barra, Pablo—120
HERMAN Perez, Hamlet—157-8, 160
HERNANDEZ Colon, Gov. Rafael—151, 199-202
HERNANDEZ Foseca, Antonio—228
HERRAN, Tancredo—136
HERRERA Calderon, Gen. Alvaro—139-40
HEYWOOD, David—45
HIGHWAYS—54, 65, 135, 238
HIJACKINGS (Aircraft)—145, 149-51, 168, 225
HILTON Hotels Corp.—70
HOCHOY, Solomon—247
HOLGUIN, Alban—141
HOLGUIN Sardi, Carlos—141
HONDURAS—240-1
HORMAN, Charles E.—120
HORTON, Jack—179
HOUSING—189, 191-2, 241
HUERTA, Francisco—166
HUERTA, Rear Adm. Ismael—82-3, 85, 120, 123-4
HUMAN Rights Commission (UN)—243
HUMBOLDT, Ciro—56
HURTADO, Gomez—141
HURTADO, Gen. Jose Graham—192
HURTADO Diaz, Sen. Oscar—229
HUSAK, Gustav—149

I

IBANEZ, Sen. Pedro—95, 98
IBJAD, Ibrahim—43
IBM World Trade Corp.—50
ILLIA, Arturo—42
IMIAS (Cuban freighter)—127
INDIANS—65-6, 147, 243. See also specific group

INDUSTRIAL Developments—7, 15, 20, 53–5, 57, 64–5, 69–70, 77–8, 82, 100, 148–9, 189. Agriculture—See under 'A.' Fishing—See under 'F.' Manufacturing—20, 31, 70. Metals & mining—See under 'M.' Petroleum—See under 'P'
INIGUEZ, Miguel Antonio—48
INSUNZA, Sergio—109
INTER-American Committee of the Alliance for Progress (CIAP)—13
INTER-American Development Bank (IDB)—5, 15, 51, 54, 57, 61, 65, 77–8, 134, 164, 167, 170, 181, 185, 193, 208, 227, 236, 238, 241
INTER-American Juridical Committee (IJC) (OAS)—7
INTER-American Press Association (IAPA)—3, 9, 161, 185, 202–3
INTERNATIONAL Bank for Reconstruction & Development (World Bank)—64, 69, 134–5, 162, 181, 184–5, 189, 193
INTERNATIONAL Business Machines Corp. (IBM)—5, 236
INTERNATIONAL Development Foundation—92
INTERNATIONAL Engineering Co.—69, 243
INTERNATIONAL Monetary Fund—54
INTERNATIONAL Nickel Co. of Canada, Ltd.—238
INTERNATIONAL Petroleum Corp.—192-3
INTERNATIONAL Protein Corp.—190
INTERNATIONAL Telephone & Telegraph Corp. (ITT)—27–8, 86, 107, 113, 166–7, 202
IRIBARREN, Col. Hector A.—26, 29
IRRIGATION—See under AGRICULTURE
IRVING Trust Co.—131
ISAACS, Kendal—233
ISRAEL—236
ITALY—30

J

JABLONSKI, Henryk—149
JACQUES, Gen. Gracia—171
JAGAN, Cheddi—240
JAMADAR, Vernon—247
JAMAICA—6, 241–2
JANSEN, Adrian—117
JAPAN—5–6, 15, 65, 70, 78, 179, 181, 189, 193, 197, 200
JARRIN Ampudia, Gustavo—163
JEMIO Ergueta, Angel—61
JENTEL, Rev. Francois—72
JEWS—27
JIMENEZ Rodriguez, Manuel—156
JOHN, Llewellyn—239
JORNAL do Brasil (newspaper)—54
JOVA, Joseph John—13
JUAREZ Villatoro, Abel—237
JULIO, Julian—48
JUSTICE & Peace Commission—58
JUSTICIALISTA Liberation Front party (FREJULI)—17–9, 21–5, 27, 40–2, 45, 48
JUSTO, Victor—161

K

KALFON, Pierre—122
KENNECOTT Copper Corp.—81–2, 88, 91
KENNEDY, Sen. Edward M. (D., Mass.)—117, 129, 159, 212
KESTELBOIM, Mario—35
KIDNAPINGS—20–1, 26–7, 30–1, 33, 38–9, 44, 49–50, 63, 72, 137–9, 162, 168, 172–3, 175, 209, 225–6, 237, 245
KISSINGER, Henry A.—14–5, 86–7, 177, 187
KLACHKO, Mario Raul—30
KLEIN, Federico—81
KLOOSTERMAN, Dirk—30
KNOX, Clinton E.—168
KOGAN, Marcos—26
KOREA, People's Republic of (North Korea)—34
KOREA, Republic of (South Korea)—117
KORRY, Edward—90–1
KRANHACARORE Indians—66
KREBS, Max V.—42
KUBISCH, Jack B.—11, 113, 125
KULITZKA, Dieter—77
KUNSTLER, William M.—247
KWAYANA, Eusi—239

L

LABOR Unions (& Strikes)—20, 31, 35–6, 40–1, 44, 54, 61, 116, 135–6, 143, 166, 173, 180, 195–7, 216–7, 238
LABREVEUX, Philippe—123
LACHMON, Jaggernath—246
LAFONTANT, Roger—169
LAGOS, Mario—109
LAKAS, Demetrio—187
LALANE, Herberto—157
La MANANA (Uruguayan newspaper)—221
LAMARCA, Capt. Carlos—63
LAN (Chilian national airline)—108–9
La NACION (Argentine newspaper)—51
LANDIVAR, Capt. Ruddy—60
LANGUAGE—242
LANUSSE, Alejandro—17–8, 22–3, 26, 28–9, 32, 49
La OPINION (Argentine newspaper)—23
La PRENSA (Buenos Aires newspaper)—8, 195
LARA, Rodriguez—165–6
LARA Parada, Ricardo—137
La RAZON (Dominican Republic newspaper)—161
La SALVIA, Hugo Perez—226–7
La SEGUNDA (Chilean newspaper)—132
LASTIRI, Raul—29, 39, 41, 43–4
LATIN (Argentine news agency)—23, 76, 114
LATIN America (London newsletter)—8, 19, 22, 25, 27, 41, 43, 47, 50, 51, 52, 55, 68, 76, 82, 114, 154, 173, 220

LATIN American Energy Organization (OLADE)—15
LATORRE Sierra, Gen. Galo—165
LAUGERUD, Gen. Kjell—236-7
LEBERT, Jean-Pierre—170
LEBLANC, Edward—248
LEBRON, Lolita—200
LEBURTON, Edmond—177
LECHIN Oquendo, Juan—61-2
LEGROS, Hubert—169
LEIGH Guzman, Gen. Gustavo—107, 111, 119
LEIGUE Suarez, Luis—56, 60
LELLIS, Jorge—48
LEMA Patino, Raul—56-8
LEMMONS, Capt. M. B.—113
Le MONDE (French newspaper)—130, 220
LENIZ, Fernando—122, 131
LEONE, Giovanni—24
LEONHARDY, Terrance G.—172-3
LEQUAY, Alloy—247
LETELIER, Orlando—85, 101, 105, 109, 117
LEVINGSTON, Roberto—37
LEVI Rufinelli, Carlos—245
LIBYA—43
LICANDRO, Gen. Victor—216
LIENDO, Jose Gregoria ('Comandante Pepe')—119-20
LIMA Sobrinho, Barbosa—76
LIRA, Juan Enrique—111
LLAMBI, Benito—39, 48
LLERAS Restrepo, Carlos—141-2
LLORENTE, Rodrigo—134, 141
LOCKWOOD, Charles A.—33, 38, 44
LODGE, John Davis—22
LOMBANA, Gen. Carlos—140
LOPEZ Arellano, Oswaldo—241
LOPEZ Arias, Victor—62
LOPEZ Aufranc, Gen. Alcides—19, 22
LOPEZ Guevara, Carlos—187
LOPEZ Michelsen, Alfonso—141-3
LOPEZ Portillo, Jose—176
LOPEZ Rega, Jose—32, 39-41, 44, 46
LORIA, Juan José—53
LORSCHEIDER, Aloisio—69
LOSADA, Rigoberto—139
LUDWIG, Daniel K.—70
LUQUE, Capt. Horacio—207
LYLWIN, Patricio—108

M

MAGLIOCHETTI, Gen. Humberto—109
MALDONADO, Victor Alfonso—151
MALMIERCA, Isidoro—154
MANCHETE (Rio de Janeiro weekly)—76
MANCILLA, Marcelino—45
MANLEY, Michael—9, 12, 242
MANRIQUE, Francisco—17, 24, 37, 41, 45
MANUFACTURERS Hanover Trust Co.—131
MARI Bras, Juan—201
MARINASKY, Jose—30
MARISCOTT de Matos, Mariel—64

MARTI, Jose—149
MARTIN, Ian—245
MARTÍNEZ, Gen. Cesar—219
MARTÍNEZ, Brig. Ezequiel—17
MARTÍNEZ, Juan José—183
MARTÍNEZ Raymonda, José Rafael—17, 41
MARTNER, Gonzalo—106
MARTONES, Humberto—85
MARULANDA, Manuel ('Tirofijo')—139
MASHINOEXPORT (USSR)—54
MAS Mas, Antonio—209
MASSERA, Rear Adm. Emilio—51
MATTA, Eduardo—5
MATTE, Luis—119
MATTE Larrain, Arturo—89-90
MATUS, Carlos—119
MAYSER, Luis—58
MAZA Carvajal, Enrique—117
McCONE, John A.—86-90
McGEE, Sen. Gale (D., Wyo.)—187
MEDERO, Benito—208
MEDICI, Emilio G.—11-2, 66, 69-71, 75-6, 223, 243
MEDINA, Juan Abal—41
MELHADO Campos, Jose—68
MELIA, Rev. Bartolomeu—243
MENDIETA, Gen. Jaime F.—55, 61
MENDOZA, Gen. Cesar—111
MERCADO Jarrin, Gen. Edgardo—11, 43, 194
MERCEDES, Diomedes—159
MERCEDES-Benz—45, 70
MERINO Castro, Adm. Jose Toribio—111
MERRIAM, William R.—878
METALS & Mining—5, 10, 51, 53-4, 57-8, 65, 70, 78, 81-2, 95-9, 116, 131, 137, 146, 148, 181, 188-9, 191, 193, 227-8, 238-9. See also specific country
MEXICO—3, 11, 57, 129, 151, 168, 172-81, 192. Social unrest—172-6
MEYER Jr., Cord—91-2
MIAMI Herald (newspaper)—26, 66-7
MICHEL, Anibal—62
MICHELINI, Sen. Zelmar—212, 214
MIGUEL, Benjamin—62
MILLAS, Orlando—80-1, 83, 99
MINOPERU (Peruvian state mining company)—192
MINOSSIAN, Miguel—27
MIRANDA, Gen. Rogelio—54-5, 58
MITRIONE, Dan A.—209
MITSUBISHI Corp.—65, 78, 179
MOHAMMED, Kamaluddin—247
MOLINA, Arturo A.—178, 235-6, 241
MOLINA, Edgar R.—30
MONTAGNE Sanchez, Gen. Ernesto—194
MONTERO Cornejo, Rear Adm. Raul—105, 108-9
MONTONEROS (guerrilla group)—23, 33, 41, 46
MONTSERRAT—242-3
MOORER, Adm. Thomas H.—83
MOQUETE, Matos—162
MOR Roig, Arturo—19

INDEX

MORA Valverde, Manuel—233
MORALES Bermudez, Francisco—193-4
MORENO, Julian—21
MORENO Diaz, Sen. Maria Eugenia Rojad—143-4
MOSCOSO, Teodoro—200
MOURA Cavalcanti, Jose de—71
MOYA, Mario—225
MUJICA, Hector—224
MUNOZ, Col. Hugo—60
MUNOZ, Juan Jacobo—135
MURDOCH, Capt. Homar—211, 216-7
MURGAN, Jose Antonio—141
MURPHY, C. Gordon—191-2
MURPHY, Rep. John M. (D., N.Y.)—7, 186, 190
MURPHY, Rep. Morgan F. (D., Ill.)—144

N

NAGEL, Kurt—225-6
NARCOTICS—6, 11, 67-8, 144-5, 188, 202, 207, 242
NASCIMENTO, Christopher—240
NASIF, Lt. Col. Jacobo—27, 33
NATUSCH Busch, Col. Alberto—61
NAVARRO Tobar, Jose—116
NAZAIRE, Breton—169
NAZAR, Miguel—225
NEAL, Jack D.—89, 167
NETHERLANDS—70, 223, 246
NEWSPAPERS—See PRESS & Censorship, also specific publication
NEWSWEEK (magazine)—118
NEW York Times (newspaper)—4, 26, 42, 53, 67, 71, 108-9, 153, 188, 202
NICARAGUA—3, 9, 182-5
NIPPON Steel Corp.—78
NIVAR Seijas, Gen. Neit—160
NIXON, Richard M(ilhous)—10, 12, 151
NORBERTO D'Aquila, Hugo—20-1
NORDMANN, Joe—121
NORTH Korea (People's Republic of Korea)—34
NORTHROP Corp. (U.S.)—12
NORWAY—156
NUEVA Jornada (Bolivian newspaper)—61
NUMOZ Duque, Cardinal Anibal—146
NUNEZ, Ivan—94

O

OBREGON, Gov. Ricardo—44
OCCIDENTAL Petroleum Corp.—193
OCEANIC Exploration Corp.—193
ODENA, Isidro—29
ODUBER, Daniel—233
O ESTADO de Sao Paulo (Brazilian newspaper)—66-7
O'FARRILL, Gov. Gonzalo Bautista—174
OLAZABAL, Capt. Conrado—210
OLEAS Zambrano, Gonzalo—165
OLGUIN, Sen. Osvaldo—79
ONDARTS, Raul—17
OPINIAO (Brazilian weekly)—66, 68, 123

ORDOQUI Mesa, Joaquin—154
ORGANIZATION of American States (OAS) (Argentina, Barbados, Bolivia, Brazil, Chile, Colombia, Costa Rica, Dominican Republic, Ecuador, El Salvador, Guatemala, Haiti, Honduras, Jamaica, Mexico, Nicaragua, Panama, Paraguay, Peru, Trinidad & Tobago, U.S., Uruguay, Venezuela; nonparticipating member: Cuba)—5, 9-11, 13, 15-6, 86, 149, 152, 162, 170, 182
ORINOCO Mining Co.—228
ORNES, German—3
ORTIZ, Sen. Dardo—212
ORTIZ de Rosas, Carlos—43
OROZCO Romero, Alberto—172-3
ORTUZAR, Enrique—127
OSINDE, Lt. Col. Jorge—37
OSORIO, Ivan—182
OSPINA Perez, Mariano—141
OTERO, Ricardo—32
OTIS Elevator Co.—33-4
OVERSEAS Private Investment Corp. (OPIC)—87, 91, 242
OWENS-Illinois Inc.—202

P

PACHECO Areco, Jorge—209
PAEZ, Francisco Jose—42, 45
PAGUAGA Irias, Edmundo—184
PAIZ Novales, Col. Ernesto—237
PALAIS Debayle, Luis—185
PALMA, Anibal—93, 96, 101, 105, 112, 119
PANAMA—3, 6, 117, 152, 187, 189. Canal Zone—1, 3-5, 186-8
PAN American World Airways—45
PARAGUAY—3, 6, 69, 243-4
PASTRANA Borrero, Misael—135-8, 140, 144, 223
PATTERSON, P. J.—241
PAUL VI, Pope—24
PAZ Estenssoro, Victor—55-6, 59
PAZ Galarraga, Jesus—228
PAZ Soldan, Mario—61
PEDERSEN, Richard F.—11
PEGUERO de la Cruz, Col. Carlos—160
PELAEZ, Gomez—138
PEMEX (Mexican state oil company)—180
PENA Gomez, Jose Francisco—154-6, 158-60
PENA Jaquez, Toribio—157
PEOPLE'S Democratic Movement (Guyana)—239
PEOPLE'S National Congress (PNC) (Guyana)—239-40
PEOPLE'S National Movement (PNM)—247
PEOPLE'S Progressive Party (PPP) (Guyana)—239-40
PEOPLE'S Revolutionary Army (Zero Point)—225
PEPSI-Cola Co.—62, 231
PEREDA Asbun, Lt. Col. Juan—56, 61
PEREDO, Oswaldo ('Chato')—61
PEREIRA, Esteban—209
PEREIRA, Manuel—243
PEREYRA, Sen. Carlos Julio—214

PEREYRA Reverbel, Ulises—209
PEREZ Alfonso, Juan Pablo—227
PEREZ Caldas, Brig. Jose—204, 210
PEREZ Herrero, Maj. Antonio—154
PEREZ Jimenez, Marcos—228-31
PEREZ La Salvia, Hugo—76
PEREZ Vargas, Alfredo—157, 159
PEREZ y Perez, Enrique—158
PERKINS Motor Co.—181
PERON, Mrs. Eva Duarte—31
PERON, Juan Domingo—1, 17, 31, 33, 36-7, 43, 45-6, 49, 51, 100, 177, 221, 243. Elections—18-9, 22-4, 39-42, 45-7
PERON, Mrs. Maria Estela (Isabel) Martinez de—31, 40-2, 45-7, 51
PERU—3, 7-8, 13-5, 65, 190-8
PERU Copper Corp.—195
PETIT, Pierre—171
PETROBRAS (Brazilian state oil firm)—65
PETROCHEMIE (France)—54
PETROLEUM—11, 15, 49-50, 57, 61, 65, 78, 88, 90, 136-7, 146, 148, 163-4, 180, 189, 192-3, 201, 222-3, 226, 238, 242
PEUGEOT Automobile Co.—50
PFIZER, Inc.—88
PHILIPPI, Julio—131
PHILLIPS, Karl—247
PHOENIX Canada Oil Co.—163
PICASSO, Pablo—66
PICHARDO, Maj. Socrates—160
PICKERING, Guillermo—108
PICO Mantilla, Galo—164
PIERSON, Don—170
PIGNATARI, Francisco—65
PINDLING, Lynden O.—232-3
PINEL, Armando—60
PINOCHET Ugarte, Gen. Augusto—108, 115, 121-4
PLAZA, Galo—16, 149, 162, 182
POLAND—70, 149
POMAR, Gen. Manuel A.—26
POMPIDOU, Georges—177
PONCE Caballero, Jaime—59
PORTES Gil, Emilio—175
POVEDA, Rear Adm. Alfredo—165
PRADO, Maj. Gary—55
PRADO Salmon, Julio—56, 61-2
PRATS, Carlos—83-5, 93-4, 100-1, 105, 108, 110
PRESENCIA (Bolivian Catholic newspaper)—53, 62
PRESNO, Jorge—216
PRENSA Latina (Cuban press agency)—220, 237
PRESS & Censorship—3, 9, 43, 61, 66-8, 71-2, 74, 115, 123, 133, 143, 159, 161, 165, 183, 185, 195, 202-3, 214-5, 217, 219
PREVATT, Sen. Francis—247
PROGRESSIVE Liberal party (PLP)—233
PUEBLA University—173
PUERTAS, Gabriel—224
PUERTO Rico—151, 199-203
PUGA, Milton—98
PUIG, Juan Carlos—32, 39-40

PUIGGROS, Rodolfo—40, 46
PURO Chile (newspaper)—133
PURRIEL, Pablo—214

Q

QUESADA, Luis—94
QUIETO, Roberto—49
QUIJADA, Rear Adm. Hermes—28
QUIJANO, Raul—13
QUISQUEYAN Democratic Party (PQD)—160

R

RABASA, Emilio—11
RADDATZ, Ronald—88
RAFAEL Rodriguez, Carlos—9
RAILWAYS—65
RAIMUNDO Sojo, Jose—141
RALSTON Purina Co.—88
RAMALLO, Luis—120
RAMIREZ, Pedro Felipe—109, 126, 130
RANGEL, Jose Vincente—228, 230-1
RAVENNA, Walter—205-6, 209, 213, 219
RAYMOND, Adrien—169
RAZZETTI, Constantino—47
RED Cross—145
REFUGEES—128-9, 151, 171
REVOLUTIONARIES—See GUERRILLAS & Terrorism
REY, Brig. Carlos Alberto—28
REY de Castro, Luis—195
REYES, Francisco—94
REYES, Col. Jose Gil—56
REYES, Simon—62
REYNOLDS Jr., Richard S.—242
REYNOLDS Metals Co.—242
RIART, Gustavo—244
RICHARDSON, Elliot L.—202
RICHTER, Gen. Pedro—198
RIGHI, Esteban—32, 36, 39-40
RINCON Quinones, Gen. Ramon—139
RIOS Montt, Gen. Efrain—237
RISQUET, Jorge—154
RIVERO, Alejandro—226
RIVEROS Abello, Col. Alvaro—140
ROA Garcia, Raul—124, 150-1
ROBAINA, Jose Maria—214
ROBERTS, F. R. Anthony—232
ROBLEDO, Angel—32, 51
RODGERS, Lionel—247
RODRIGUEZ, Alberto—149
RODRIGUEZ, Gen. Andres—244
RODRIGUEZ, Pablo—100
RODRIGUEZ Iturbe, Jose—224
RODRIGUEZ Lara, Guillermo—164
ROGERS, William P.—10-2, 32, 150-1, 167-8, 224
ROJAS, Alejandro—97
ROJAS Carrea, Gustavo—143
ROJAS Pinilla, Gen. Gustavo—141-3, 146
ROMERO Pereira, Tomas—245
ROMIC, Radomiro—87
ROMO Escobar, Gen. Alejandro—165

INDEX

ROSENLEW (Swiss company)—54
RUA, Sen. Fernando de la—41, 45
RUCCI, Jose—36, 40-1, 44-5, 47
RUIZ Danyau, Gen. Cesar—105, 107
RUIZ Diez, Teodoro—7
RUIZ Velarde, Gen. Cesar—56-7, 62
RUMANIA—82, 197

S

SAENZ, Orlando—132
SAEZ, Rene—122
SAGA Petroleum A/S & Co.—238
St. JOSEPH'S Mining Co.—50
St. KITTS—3, 9
SALAS, Juan—113-4
SALAS Suarez, Miguel—226
SALLUSTRO, Oberdan—21, 30, 32
SAMANIEGO, Gen. Marcial—245
SAMUELSON, Victor—50
SANCHEZ, Gen. Eladio—56, 60
SANCHEZ, Gen. Juan Carlos—21, 32
SANCHEZ, Marcelo—67
SANCHEZ, Salvador—236
SANCHEZ de Bustamante, Gen. Tomas—25
SANCHEZ Sorondo, Marcelo—19, 27-8
SANDINISTA Liberation Front—185
SANDOVAL Alarcon, Mario—237
San JUAN Jr., Manuel—200
SANTANDER Industrial University—146
SANTILLAN, Carlos—44
SANTUCHO, Roberto—26, 33, 37-8
SANZ de Santamaria, Carlos—151
SAPELLI, Jorge—217, 220
SAPENA Pastor, Raul—69, 243, 245
SARAVIA, Capt. Rolando—60
SCALI, John—4-5, 112
SCALMAZZI, Gerardo—26
SCHLOTTER, Rene de Leon—237
SCHMID, Kurt—50
SCHMIDT, Giomar—30
SCIAPONE, Nora—17
SECURITIES & Exchange Commission (SEC), U.S.—235
SEDNEY, Jules—246
SEGNINI La Cruz, Pedro—228
SELICH, Andres—55-6, 59
SENDIC, Raul—218
SEPULVEDA, Gen. Claudio—85
SEPULVEDA, Gen. Jose Maria—105
SEPULVEDA, Gen. Mario—101
SEREGNI, Gen. Liber—206, 216-7, 219
SERRATE, Col. Mario—60
SERVETTI, Angel—216
SESSA, Miguel Juan—95
SEVILLA Sacasa, Guillermo—13
SHARP, Mitchell—151
SHENANDOAH Oil Corp.—238
SIBISA, Jorge—116
SIDDERS, Horacio—27
SIDERURGIA del Orinoco—227
SIEMENS AG—27-8
SIGNAL Oil & Gas Co.—193
SIHANOUK, Prince Norodom (Cambodia)—82

SILES Zuazo, Hernan—53, 59, 61-2
SILVA, Gerardo—141
SILVA Herzog, Jesus—176
SILVA Valderrama, Gerardo—136
SILVETTI, Jose—17
SINAMOS (Peruvian social mobilization agency)—194, 197
SINGH, David—240
SOBERON, Rector Guillermo—174-5
SOLANO Lima, Vincente—17, 23-4, 31, 38-40, 47, 49
SOLANO Lopez, Francisco—145
SOLANO Sepulveda, Luis Jose—137
SOLDATI, Santiago—27
SOLIS Juarez, Hector—237
SOMEX Oil Co.—178
SOMISA Steel Co. (Argentina)—20
SOMOZA Debayle, Gen. Anastasio—182-5
SORONDO, Sanchez—27
SOUPER, Col. Roberto—101
SOURANDER, Bo—121, 128
SOURANDER, Mrs. Margarethe—128
SOUTH Korea (Republic of Korea)—117
SOUTH Yemen—154
SPAIN—22, 100, 177
STANDARD Electric—27-8
STANDARD Oil Co. of California—192-3
STANDARD Oil Co. (Ind.)—49
STEEL, Rep. Robert H. (R., Conn.)—144
STENNIS, Sen. John (D., Miss.)—202
STROESSNER, Gen. Alfredo—69, 243-5
STUARDO, Julio—119
STUMPFF, Gustavo—60
SUCRE, Arturo—187
SUELDO, Horacio—17, 24
SULE, Anselmo—130
SUMBERD, Peter—123
SUMITOMO Shoji Kaisha—163-4
SUN Oil Co.—164
SURINAM—245-6
SUZANO—70
SWEDEN—113, 125
SWEET, Rear Adm. Jorge—122
SWINT, John A.—49
SWISSAIR—50
SZULC, Tad—125

T

TACK, Juan Antonio—4, 10, 187-8
TAGLE, Msgr. Emilio—94
TAIANA, Jorge—32, 34, 38, 46
TAMAGNINI, Hugo—44
TANTALEAN, Javier—7, 190-1
TAPIA, Jorge—82, 94, 195
TAPIA Alipaz, Jaime—56, 60
TEITELBOIM, Sen. Volodia—83-4
TEJERINA, Col. Raul—57
TELAM (Agentine news agency)—43
TERRA, Juan Pablo—213
TERUGGI Jr., Frank—117
TEXACO-Gulf consortium—163
THIEME, (Walter) Robert (or Roberto)—95, 102, 107, 109-10, 119
THIRD World Priests Movement—21

THOMAZ, Americo—76
THOMPSON, John—38
THREAD, Alix—171
TIMES (London newspaper)—104
TIMOSSI, Jorge—112, 114
TINOCO, Pedro—229
TITO (Josip Broz)—112
TOBAGO—247
TOHA, Jaime—117
TOHA, Jose—85, 94-5, 102, 119
TOLIMA, University of—146
TOMIC, Radomiro—110
TORRES, Juan Jose—58, 61-2, 126
TORRES Bodet, Jaime—176
TORRES Boursault, Leopoldo—121
TORRES de la Cruz, Gen. Manuel—104
TORRES Manzo, Carlos—179
TORRIJOS, Gen. Omar—4-5, 157, 187-8
TOSCO, Agustin—36, 40, 42, 49
TOURISM—241
TOYOTA Corp.—197
TRABAL, Col. Ramon—212
TRANSPORTATION—7, 30-1, 54, 64-5, 135, 238
TREJOS, Jose Joaquin—234
TREJOS Escalante, Fernando—234
TRELEW (Argentine naval prison)—28, 33, 43-4
TRICENTRAL Guyana (British firm)—238
TRINIDAD & Tobago—247
TRUDEAU, Pierre Elliott—130, 177
TRUJILLO, Rafael—158
TRUMAN, Harry S.—200
TURBAY Ayala, Julio Cesar—142

U

UGARTE Centurion, Delfin—245
ULATE, Otilio—234-5
ULTIMA Hora (Chilean newspaper)—133, 157, 208, 217
UNION of Soviet Socialist Republics (USSR)—8, 10, 54, 57, 76, 82, 113, 117, 148, 194, 226-7, 233-5, 239
UNIROYAL—180
UNITED Nations—3-5, 8-10, 123-4, 128, 182, 201
UNITED Press International (UPI)—43, 59, 86, 101, 131
UNITED States—4-5, 11, 22, 27-8, 58, 65, 113-5, 147, 167, 169, 179, 192, 200-2, 232. Chile—81-2, 86, 113, 117, 121, 124, 127, 131; ITT involvement—86-92, 113, 125. Congress—14, 149, 186. Drugs—6, 144-5. Foreign relations & trade—8-12, 15-6, 42-3, 53, 149-51, 190, 242; fishing rights dispute—7-8; kidnapings—5, 26-7, 30, 49-50. Panama Canal—3-5, 186-8. Vesco case—235
U.S. STEEL Corp.—228
URIANA Indians—147
URRUTIA Manzano, Enrique—119
URUGUAY—3, 5, 113, 215-6, 219-20. Government & military—204-7, 209-14, 217-21

USINAS de Minas Gerais (USIMINAS)—65
UZCATEGUI, Remberto—225-6

V

VALDEZ Angulo, Enrique—197
VALVERDE, Carlos—54-6, 59-60
VANDERLEY, Flavio—123
VANDOR, Augusto—21
VANUCCHI Leme, Alexandre—68-9
VARELA, Jose Antonio—221
VARGAS Caballero, Luis—196
VASCONCELLOS, Sen. Amilcar—204, 207, 209-10, 213-4
VASQUEZ, Jaime—128
VASQUEZ, Luis Lalo—212
VASQUEZ Carrizosa, Alfredo—11, 76, 147
VASQUEZ Castano, Fabio—137, 140
VASQUEZ Castano, Manuel—137, 140
VASQUEZ Rojas, Genaro—172
VEGA Moreno, Nestor—164
VELASCO Alvarado, Juan—11, 191-2, 194, 197, 222
VELASCO Ibarra, Jose Maria—163, 165, 167
VENEZUELA—15, 117, 222-31, 242
VENEZUELAN Guayana Corp.—227
VERGARA, Daniel—95, 101, 119, 130
VESCO, Robert L.—234-5
VIA Sur Co.—82
VIERA, Edwardo—221
VIGNES, Alberto—39, 222
VILARIN, Leon—114, 131
VILLA, Jose—152
VILLALBA, Jovito—228
VILLALOBOS, Gen. Jose—197
VILLALON, Hector—39
VILLANEUVA, Ernesto—46
VILLAR, Werber—130
VILLAS Boas, Orlando—65-6
VILLAZON de Armas, Crispin—141-2
VINA del Mar Refining Co.—127
VINCENT, Clement—171
VOLKSWAGEN—64
Von HOLLEBEN, Ehrenfried—63
VUSKOVIC, Pedro—110

W

WALDHEIM, Kurt—119, 233
WASHINGTON Post (newspaper)—8, 22-3, 27, 36, 53, 91-2, 222
WATKINS, Errington—233
WEHBE, Jorge—20
WELLS Fargo—65, 181, 193
WESSIN y Wessin, Gen. Elias—160
WEST Germany (Federal German Republic)—65, 70, 129
WEST Indies—248-9
WILKIE Jr., David B.—49
WILLIAMS, Eric—247
WOLF, Rodolfo—209
WORLD Bank (International Bank for Reconstruction & Development)—64, 69, 134-5, 162, 181, 184-5, 189, 193

INDEX

X
XAVANTE Indians—66

Y
YESSI, Julio—41
YUGOSLAVIA—112

Z
ZENTENO Anaya, Gen. Joaquin—55-7
ZERBINO, Ricardo—216
ZORRILLA, Rear Adm. Juan Jose—206
ZUFRIATEGUI, Col. Carlos—216